J. M. (John Mackinnon) Robertson

New Essays Towards a Critical Method

J. M. (John Mackinnon) Robertson

New Essays Towards a Critical Method

ISBN/EAN: 9783337010430

Printed in Europe, USA, Canada, Australia, Japan

Cover: Foto ©Thomas Meinert / pixelio.de

More available books at **www.hansebooks.com**

New Essays towards a Critical 🙵 🙵 🙵 Method

By

John Mackinnon Robertson

John Lane, *The Bodley Head*
London & New York   1897

Printed by BALLANTYNE, HANSON & CO.
At the Ballantyne Press

PREFACE

OF the following essays, those on Poe, Shelley, Clough, and the art of Keats and Burns, were written before the idea of a general "Critical Method" had been at all formally developed by the author. Each was a spontaneous attempt, made over ten years ago, to arrive by comparison and inference at a reasoned opinion on a critical issue over which there had been much dispute; and they are now revised and collected in the hope that, though in the past ten years our critical disputes have mostly turned on other topics, these discussions may still have an interest for readers who have not yet satisfied themselves that the old questions are disposed of. The principles involved are a permanent ground of discussion, and doubtless the poets of the past will yet be disputed over afresh.

It will readily be seen that no one of the studies named, except perhaps that on Poe, comes near applying all the tests mentioned in the preliminary essay on *The Theory and Practice of Criticism* as proper to a critical inquiry. They rather represent detached investigations in which a view of the nature of the necessary tests is arrived at. Thus the paper on *Shelley*

PREFACE

and Poetry is an attempt to discriminate argumentatively the values of Shelley's verse on its strict æsthetic merits, with little or no explanatory recourse to a study of his personality and its physical basis. And though that is a method more pleasing to critical youth (when it resists convention) than to maturer judgment, which seeks a more synthetic estimate, it is so far valid and useful that I let the essay stand with only the comment that were I now to set about judging Shelley I should describe his work in the light of a sympathetic study of his temperament and physique. In the essays on Keats and Burns, though they were written before that on Shelley, there is a measure of this duality of view; and the Shelley essay probably lacked it because in that case I was specially concerned to characterise a mass of technically bad work and resist extravagant over-estimate. The latest essay of all, that entitled *Stevenson on Burns*, is a final attempt, made on an interesting provocation, to reach a just verdict on Burns the man in terms of a revised ethic, relating the poet's life to his work with aforethought.

In the essay on Coleridge, again, the demonstration, such as it is, proceeds largely on a special study of the physiology and psychology of the subject, so that it is either more broadly wrong or more broadly right than that of the essay on Shelley, the question of æsthetic values being much more summarily disposed of, on the principles laid down in the earlier essay.

Lastly, in the study of Clough, which claims for him a status and a kind of recognition that have not latterly been given him, I have attempted to relate the criticism of the writing, as is fitting, to a view of the organism

PREFACE

and surroundings of the writer. I am aware that such inquiries, though often incidentally set up by past critics, are reprobated by some to-day when systematically dwelt upon. I wish the more emphatically to say that I hold them to be part of the business of serious criticism, and I count it a shortcoming in any of the following studies to have omitted them.

Another shortcoming, from their own point of view, is the incompleteness of the collation of critical opinions on the various points discussed. It is the more necessary to urge here that such comparison of critical judgments, with some reasoned explanation of their conflict, must be made if criticism is to be raised from the level of random self-expression to that of a scientific procedure. I have sought by annotations to make good to some extent the original deficiencies of the essays.

It is probable that some of them would not have been written had some later books and essays by other writers been earlier published. Thus the essay on Keats would hardly have been undertaken had Mr. Colvin's admirable monograph been in existence in 1884; and that on Poe,* as it avows, might not have been ventured on had I seen the essay of Hennequin sooner; though I think I should after all have been moved to attempt a critical plea for Poe as against many of the findings of Mr. E. C. Stedman, who, in the criticisms contributed by him to the recent complete edition of Poe's works, has passed from his older attitude of sympathy to that of a pseudo-judicial animus, still so common in the United States in regard to Poe.

* Published in three successive parts of the magazine *Our Corner*, in 1885.

PREFACE

In any case, each essay says in its own way something that had seemed to me to need saying, and to which I am disposed to stand; and therefore it is that they are here reprinted.

Finally I would anticipate the comment of critical readers that the essay on Poe, dealing with his morbid psychology as well as with his art, is in the main friendly, while that on Coleridge, with the same method, and dealing likewise with a pathological case, is in comparison at times hostile in tone. I trust that in the one case as in the other I have given due force to the physiological plea, though it fell to be made more strongly in the case of Poe, who clearly suffered from a progressive lesion of the brain. To any one who reflects on what this means, it must be grievous to see still going on in America the old process of malevolent insistence on the stumbles of the stricken man, with as little regard as may be to the abundant witness borne to his moral merit when free of active disease. Doubtless there is no final ethical line to be drawn between brain-malady and conformation of brain as sources of bad conduct; and for purposes of philosophy we ought no doubt to think of Griswold as uncensoriously as of Poe. But in a world in which moral judgment is only beginning to be scientific among even educated men, while it is vain to ask for a merely bad nature the compassion that many are ready to feel for a nature in part chronically mad, it is surely not too much to ask that in the latter case plain proofs should be treated as such, and not made ground for a kind of censure which in the case of a person of unquestioned insanity would be revolting to every one. It may be said that in the case

PREFACE

of Coleridge I have not been consistently compassionate, since I do at times speak with some asperity of intellectual vices which after all were rooted in flaws of physique, and in part contend rather against praise than against dispraise. Perhaps, indeed, such a difference of treatment is an illustration of that specific bent on the part of the critic which is described in the preliminary essay as a possible cause of deflection in his as in all men's judgment. The opening essay is expressly framed to point to the ideal tests for the rest of the volume, as for all criticism. As regards the cases in question I was of opinion that the doctrinal influence of Coleridge was in certain ways harmful, and needed to be gainsaid, while the general credit of Poe had not been justly maintained. The latter view is pretty fully defended in the essay on Poe; the former is partly justified in the essay on Coleridge, but partly depends for its acceptation on a variety of considerations which to state fully would heavily overload the essay as an estimate of one man and his work. They would lead us into a logical and a sociological estimate of religion for one thing. Such are some of the "artistic" difficulties in the way of scientific criticism. I can but desire that the reader will not think they have been overlooked or evaded.

CONTENTS

	PAGE
THE THEORY AND PRACTICE OF CRITICISM	1
POE	55
COLERIDGE	131
SHELLEY AND POETRY	191
THE ART OF KEATS	237
THE ART OF BURNS	259
STEVENSON ON BURNS	273
CLOUGH	301
APPENDIX: ACCENT, QUANTITY, AND FEET	333

THE THEORY AND PRACTICE OF CRITICISM

I

THE practice of criticism as a minor branch of fine letters, and the special connection of the name with that limited activity, have brought upon both name and function certain reproachful associations. Criticism and "the critical spirit" are jointly or severally impeached as if they were, or stood for, something out of the common way of life, something of which rightly constituted or normal people are not guilty. Seeing, however, that the censure is itself criticism, the protest must rank as one of the paralogisms set up by the random use of words. Criticism is obviously enough the expression of the most general and the most fundamental form of mental activity, indeed of the essence of all activity, the play of attraction and repulsion, liking and dislike. Even if the word be limited to the naming of a process of strife, it points to what the ancient thinker saw to be "the parent of things." The serenest and the dullest of us must needs criticise: there is no respite from the function while we live and think. That we are all critics is even more true than that we are all (necessarily) Socialists.

THEORY AND PRACTICE OF CRITICISM

But it is in the nature of things that words which properly stand for a general activity, come to stand in practice for a special form of that activity, so that as the maker of verse came of all makers to bear the name of maker or poet, and as among us in England the artist in colour came specially to bear the name of artist, in like manner the critic of fine letters has come specially to bear the name of critic. We do not speak of Mill and Mr. Samuel Butler and Mr. A. J. Balfour as "critics," though they have systematically played the part, one in philosophy, one in biology, and one in politics. The whole stress of the title falls on the gentlemen who argue or adjudicate on poetry and "style" and fiction. And, as must happen where any proclivity is specially cultivated, and so marked off from average conduct, the result is a considerable showing-up of infirmity, which is henceforth associated in average comment with the special pursuit. To judge from a good deal of modern talk, whereas writers in general are held to be irritable, and actors vain, and politicians untruthful, and priests intolerant, so it is held to be the characteristic of critics to be wrong. And in a sense it must needs be so, inasmuch as in the mass they express attractions and repulsions, and the mass of attractions and repulsions go far to cancel each other. But, at least, that implies that the critic of criticism runs his risks like the rest, and that, in short, the critic is only wrong as other men are wrong. Even the typical black sheep of the species, the trifling and snapping Zoilus of all ages, is plainly a man and a brother. He is unwise with the unwisdom which is the heritage of the species, and does but chance to find a printer for such levities and imbecilities of judgment as pass current at every picture gallery, and in every parlour in which two or three are assembled together to talk of the weather and the last "sex" novel. There is thus no reason, so far as mere bad criticism goes, for despair over the possibilities of critical science. It is the better criticism, the criticism of the intelligent, the witty, and the learned, that chronically sets up among cultured people, by force of its conflicts of judgment, discussions as to whether criticism can be in any true sense scientific, and even—the old paradox—whether it is worth doing.

The last question we must just dismiss, as we do that other, as to whether life is worth living. Whatever be the truth about the poet's singing, we do every one of us criticise because we must: the trouble is only too clearly that as a rule we pipe but as the linnets sing. The decisive proof of this is that those writers who expressly set out to veto judicial criticism, to restrict criticism to a mere process of descriptive cataloguing, always end by practising judicial criticism like other people. M. Taine, for instance, as has been noted by M. Brunetière, proposed at first to set up a criticism which should "neither proscribe nor pardon," which should merely describe and classify, "marking characters and tracing causes," as is done in botany. But from this attitude M. Taine entirely departed in practice, where he proscribed and pardoned like the rest of us, and that avowedly.* So Mr. Howells, after demanding on his own account that criticism should be merely descriptive, goes on criticising judicially—or otherwise.† Whether the literary practice of criticism is worth the while of any given writer is of course another question, the answer to which may be framed in view either of

* Brunetière, *L'Evolution de la Critique*, pp. 250, 273.
† See the point discussed in *Essays Towards a Critical Method*, First Series, pp. 122-128, 143; and in the Section (II.) on "Recent Nihilism."

the income he can make by the craft or of an opinion as to his capacity for it, and the possibilities of influence or fame it offers. And these latter issues finally turn on that as to the possibility of a criticism that shall be really scientific—that is, capable of persuading and convincing men by a consistent drawing of conclusions from premisses. To this issue, as I have said, critical people are always returning.

It is, however, the fact that those who have most systematically discussed canons and methods of criticism have almost never been eminent or industrious critics. The circumstance is singular, and not very encouraging. If we set aside the case of Lessing, and the later cases of Taine and Hennequin, we find that the leading practitioners in literary criticism have not concerned themselves greatly about a science of criticism, and that those who strove to attain a science of criticism have either not tried to pass much special criticism or have not succeeded in it.

I do not mean that we have not had principled and consistent criticism from eminent critics so-called. From Lamb to Lowell, from Hallam to Minto, from Lessing to Brandes, and from La Harpe to Lemaitre, we may count scores of able practical critics who reason their judgments, and who impress critical readers as fitted to judge of merit and demerit.* It is the getting behind spontaneous judgment, the ascertaining how and why we differ in our judgments, that the critics so-called have mostly left unattempted. And as this getting behind practice is strictly a philosophical process, they are indeed not to be blamed, as critics, for not attempting it; mental philosophy being one thing and literary and humanistic judgment another. But, for

* The phenomena of the historic evolution of criticism, and the conditions of these phenomena, I leave for separate treatment.

one thing, the attempt must be made by somebody, and one would fain see an experienced critic do it ; and for another, the study of criticism cannot be finally satisfactory to people of philosophic mind unless it be relatable to philosophy like other human activities. In philosophy, as we seek the "knowledge of knowledge," so we must aim at the criticism of criticism. And as we are all philosophers, in the sense in which we are all critics, we are all, by rights, concerned in the inquiry. A philosophy which does not contain a criticism of criticism is a faulty philosophy.

II

Still, in this as in other matters our philosophy need not be "harsh and crabbed," though it cannot be as the strains of Apollo's lute. After all, we simply want to understand thoroughly what we are about, in fine letters as in the useful arts. Our best critics, passing judgment on books, are found at times to clash with each other, as they at times clash with their readers' opinions ; and it need not be a more repellent business to analyse these discords than to listen to them. As it happens, the most considerable English treatise yet penned on the philosophy of criticism is entitled *The Gay Science*.* It was published over thirty years ago, and it may be that its very title, fantastic though ingeniously justified, has since served to conceal it from those most interested in its theme. Hennequin apparently knew nothing of it when he wrote *La Critique Scientifique*, though Mr. Dallas attempted, so far as he

---

* By E. S. Dallas (Chapman and Hall, 2 vols., 1866). This work re-states and expands some of the ideas of its author's earlier work entitled *Poetics* (Edinburgh, 1858).

went, to lay scientific bases for criticism, and went about the task with much skill, much knowledge, and much brilliancy. He called his theme "the gay science" because he thought that title, given of old by the troubadours to their pleasure-giving art, better fits the science which shall co-ordinate all the pleasure-giving arts; that is to say, the fine arts and fine letters. "Whatever we do," he remarks, in the course of an always lucid and often luminous argument, "has happiness for its last end; but with art it is the first as well as the last."* With the ancients and most moderns he decides "that science is for knowledge, and that art is for pleasure."† But whereas the Greeks, holding this, decided that the pleasure sought and given is that of "imitation," and that therefore all that criticism has to do is to study the ways of imitation; and whereas "the Germans," deciding that the pleasure given and sought is that of the beautiful, held that therefore all that criticism has to do is to comprehend the beautiful, Mr. Dallas protests that the business of criticism is clearly just "the science of pleasure."

It is a symmetrical and attractive argument. Soon, however, it strikes the wary reader that the scheme is enormously difficult; and in point of fact, Dallas's own treatment proves it to be so; for though he fills two volumes with the steps of his exposition (to wit, chapters on "Imagination," "The Hidden Soul," "The Play of Thought," "The Secrecy of Art," "Pleasure," "Mixed Pleasure," "Pure Pleasure," "Hidden Pleasure," "The Ethics of Art," "The Pursuit of Pleasure," "The World of Fiction," and "The Ethical Current"), he finally leaves his work unfinished. The two volumes were to have been followed by two more, but these never came.

* Vol. i. 89. † *Ibid.* p. 91.

And without seeking to check his reasoning through the too discursive chapters actually written, which certainly serve to prove him at several points an original and acute thinker, we may at once decide that not only is a complete "science of pleasure," even of intellectual pleasure, an extremely complicated and difficult undertaking, amounting to the main part of a system of psychology, but even an elaborate presentment of it will leave us facing the fundamental fact that "tastes differ," that different things give different degrees of pleasure, or give respectively pleasure and pain, to different people, or to the same people at different times. This fact it is that constitutes for many a fatal hindrance to the framing of any "science" of criticism.

If, however, we consider that the word at issue is allowed without question to be used of the systematic discussion of morals, and that "moral science" and "the science of ethics" are phrases in unchallenged use, it will appear that there is a sense in which processes of literary and æsthetic judgment may be put under a scientific treatment. The sense of right and wrong in conduct is clearly as relative, as variable, as the sense of good and bad in literature and art. It varies with periods, with countries, with persons, with times of life. Mr. Spencer's distinction between "absolute ethics" and "relative ethics" does not stand analysis: all that holds is the fact of degrees of peremptoriness in ethical judgment. It is the same with what we call "critical" judgment—the judgment of literary quality, of merit in literature and in literary men. But if in the field of ethical judgment there can be science, that is, ordered and concatenated reasoning, consistent inference, coherent explanation, the same is possible in the field of literary judgment. Or if we call moral science the science of expediency in conduct—an empirical and, to my thinking, fallacious way of speaking—we may equally call critical science the science of expediency in literary method or performance.

On this view, of course, our "science" is conceived in a different way from Mr. Dallas's. And it will be found, I think, that his formula will even have to be set aside if the province of criticism is not to be injuriously narrowed or imperfectly surveyed. The doctrine that the end of all fine art is to give pleasure is a sound one; and the doctrine that whereas art aims at pleasure science aims at knowledge is equally sound, taken as a general discrimination of the main activities of the artist and the scientist. But the two formulas, between them, miss mention of one of the main truths of the mental life, namely, that art and science, pleasure and knowledge, are always tending to overlap and combine. This may be seen (1) in an elementary way by merely noting that the man of science may aim at literary effect in his exposition, and that the artist, without being at all false to his function of giving pleasure, may, and does, convey knowledge—knowledge of persons, of places, of events, of costumes, of nature.* And the extensive study of art as art is clearly an acquiring of knowledge. But that is not all. There is (2) a process of science, of analysis, of study and measurement, behind the artist's art; and there is (3) a process of constructive art, as apart from mere detailed literary expression, in every completed scientific demonstration. "Ideal construction" is Mr. Lewes's name for the com-

---

* He may even be said to do more when he is a novelist, or a dramatist, or even a lyrist, inasmuch as in a sense he conveys knowledge of character. Mill's definition: "The truth of poetry is to paint the human soul truly: the truth of fiction is to give a true picture of life," is not strictly accurate, but it rightly points to kinds of knowledge which poetry and fiction may convey (*Dissertations and Discussions*, i. 67).

pleted process of knowledge of any kind; and his formula squares with the statement of some of the latest specialism.* Now, this "ideal construction," this attainment of a mental sequence which is held to symbolise a sequence of phenomena, is essentially an artistic process. If any one has a difficulty in admitting so much, let him think out for himself, first, the analogy between the work of a critical historian and that of a novelist. The work of the novelist is admittedly an artistic process. But it is only in non-essentials, in respect of data and limitations, that it is psychologically different from the historian's. The novelist, giving a voluntary definiteness to certain general conceptions of human nature, imagining certain types of person corresponding more or less to people he has seen, puts them in certain situations, and conducts them to a certain end. The historian, getting his data from the documents, is certainly tied down as to his end and his action; but that the task of arranging the narrative, of explaining connections, of making the facts group and flow and unify, is strictly a process of *imagination*, any one may satisfy himself who will try to compose a connected and interesting and *explanatory* narrative of any historic episode or series of events of which he has the bare facts separately set down for him. And if the explanatory historian is thus, in his own way, a constructive artist,† no less, or little less, is the economist

* See Professor Pearson's *Grammar of Science, passim*. Compare the contention of Professor Sylvester that there are many mathematical processes which "really belong to a sort of artistic and constructive faculty" (*The Laws of Verse*, p. 123 and *passim*.). Professor Sylvester seems to distinguish these processes from those of "demonstration." I venture to say that in demonstration itself there is an artistic process.

† When I wrote the above I did not know that the proposition had been in part laid down by such an eminent orthodox practitioner

or the sociologist, inasmuch as each has to go through a process of creative grouping of manifold data to the end of getting a reasoned whole out of a chaos of unexplained or irrelated facts. It is only a question of detail to carry the principle further, and show the artistic element in its degree in every science, down to mathematics. In fine, there is knowledge and knowledge ; and all knowledge that is complex, that consists of data connected by reasoning, is knowledge obviously resulting from an artistic or constructive mental process. But the great literary department of history, in particular, amounts in the end to a process of ideal arrangement, at once interpretative and representative of the given facts, which compares very plainly with the

in history as Bishop Stubbs. It is in his lectures on *Mediæval and Modern History* that the Bishop writes : "Whether there is or is not a science of history . . . there is, I am sure, an art of writing history. . . . It is necessary (for the historian) to look at his subject all round, to finish it off completely at every point and, while seeking for statuesque unity and perfection, to make truth and reality the first object. . . . The result will, if the writer has chosen his subject well, and with a due estimate of his own powers, be an artistic unity, a perfect image. . . . The second form of our art is analogous to painting, and its result to a picture . . . it requires a background and a foreground, scenery and perspective, as well as unity and symmetry" (pp. 97-98). Compare Professor Gardiner : "The statesman uses his imagination to predict the result of changes to be produced in the actually existing state of society, either by the natural forces which govern it, or by his own action. The historian uses his imagination in tracing out the causes which produced that existing state of society" (*History of England, 1603-1642*, ed. 1894, X., pref. p. vii.). It may be remarked that when Mr. Birrell (*Obiter Dicta*, p. 33) says of Bishop Stubbs that he and Freeman "are historical artisans : artists they are not," the criticism does not apply in the sense given above to the word artist. Mr. Birrell means that the Bishop and Freeman are inferior literary artists, which is at least true of Freeman. But that does not alter the fact that the writing of history is necessarily a process of imaginative construction.

processes of plastic and imitative art and so-called fiction.

Still, even this is not the whole of the rebuttal of Mr. Dallas's proposition that criticism is properly "the science of pleasure." It is quite impossible in practice to separate the criticism of mere literary effect, of poetry and style, of writing which specifically aims at "pleasing," from the criticism of testimony, of theory, of method, of moral tone, of conduct, of "criticism of life," of literary criticism itself. We only need to turn to the work of the greatest critics to see that they will not let themselves be restricted to mere discrimination of artistic "pleasure," in Mr. Dallas's sense of the term. They show, in fact, displeasure at errors of assertion, and pleasure over expressions of opinion as such. A great critic, a Sainte Beuve, or a Lessing, or a Taine, discusses conduct, theory, politics, institutions, points of history, characters, and other men's criticisms, as well as style and poetry, and "the beautiful." Now, although we are loosely agreed to restrict in practice the name of criticism to the criticism of the fine arts and fine letters (excluding the separate criticism of theory and practice in the sciences, philosophy, the useful arts, and the arts of conduct), we cannot hinder that a critic in the course of his work shall pass judgment on opinions, on conduct, on institutions, and on characters; and we cannot hinder that this passing of judgment shall rank as criticism, and affect readers substantially as the rest of his criticism does. So that we are finally led to describe and define criticism in general and in particular as simply a way of teaching, a means of propaganda, a method of trying to persuade other people to think as we do, whereof the science will consist, not in our literary estimates in themselves, but in our way of relating them to each other, and to other judgments in general. That is to say, criticism may or may not be scientifically done. We may be concerned only to have men share our view on poetry and fiction, or on this or that " school " of art; or we may seek also to have them look at life in general as we do, and share our religious convictions, our personal likes and dislikes, our standards of character and conduct, our anthropological theories. All expression of opinion on these matters by way of discussion of books and writers is criticism. And in the end, whether we speak only of poetry and style or take up all the subjects of a writer's art as well as his treatment of them, there is but one general way of justifying our view and logically persuading others to take it. That way is simply the proceeding from points agreed on to points in dispute, and showing that consistency involves one view as following on another. The "simply" here is indeed not to be taken as implying that it is as a rule a simple thing to establish a proposition of consistency in a matter of intellectual or moral dispute. Perhaps the bulk of all criticism, the mass of discussion in all grades, consists in our disputing over each other's inconsistencies of action, feeling, speech, or belief. But difficult as the business is, there is no evading it; and progress in criticism, science in criticism, consists in having a more intelligent regard to consistency, alike in the theory and in the practice of judgment. There is no other way. A man who refuses to accept the test of consistency as a criterion of truth is either confused by words or confused in the very faculty of judgment. In the former case he is a doubtful subject for enlightenment: in the latter, he is impossible. He may keep out of legal trouble; he may even be the most amiable of men; but he is not to be argued with.

THEORY AND PRACTICE OF CRITICISM

III

This much may be admitted by some who still argue that there can be no such test for literary effect as for propositions of fact, historical or scientific. Consistency, it may be argued, holds of actions or propositions of fact, not of appreciations or propositions of æsthetic judgment. This demurrer may be held to underlie the brilliant argumentation of Professor Edouard Droz, in his *brochure* on the subject,* *à propos* of the work of M. Brunetière on the evolution of criticism in France. Of this essay the ostensible thesis is that "literary criticism, in so far as it sets itself to judge the beauty of works, is not a science." A confusion here arises, I think, between the ideas of "science" and "a science," the ideas of accepted facts and the explanation of facts. "The beautiful," says M. Droz,† "is always under discussion; and the true always ends by imposing itself, when there are not too many interests involved." But what truth does this? M. Droz admits that interests affect the establishment of some truths. Then there are some alleged truths which are not true for all of us. The truths which finally impose themselves are, let us say, doctrines of physical science, of the movement of suns and stars, of the action of chemicals, and the laws of heat, light, sound, and so forth. When we come to other provinces of science, to geology and zoology, there is found to be dissidence over important propositions—by reason, let us say with M. Droz, of the interests involved. These interests are partly economic, as in the case of teachers

---
* *La Critique Littéraire et la Science*, 1893. Étude lue à la Séance de rentrée des Facultés de Besançon, Nov. 1891.
† *Ibid.* p. 8.

and priesthoods; partly personal or psychological, as where men simply recoil from an innovating doctrine, or from a disruption of their old theory of life. Now, we may fairly say that it is interests of the latter sort that check our acceptance of new literary forms, or our dismissal of old. We go by habit, and are loth to admit our past taste to have been bad, or the new taste to be better. Even where there is dispute over some works of an author as to whose other works the disputants agree, habits of feeling are at the bottom of the dispute. Is it to be said, then, that there is no science where there is such dispute? If so, there is no science where there is dispute in matters zoological and geological; and Darwinism is not science while pietists reject it. Surely M. Droz must modify his definition. Surely the argumentation of the *Origin of Species* was scientific, even when the majority derided it. If the proposition is merely to be this, that "science is universally accepted truth," or doctrine held true by all who make it their business to study the subject matter, we certainly close the discussion, summarily enough. But in doing this we merely set up a new and worse difficulty, for on that view the geocentric theory in astronomy, and the creational theory in zoology, were once "truth." It cannot be that M. Droz means this. Remarking on the classic exploit of Hegel, who just before the discovery of Ceres, said there was no use in looking for a planet between Mars and Jupiter, he admits that "men of science indeed are no more exempt from these aberrations than philosophers and critics."* Then, when he insists that "literary criticism, in so far as it sets itself to judge the beauty of works, is not *a* science," he merely means that an arbitrary literary

---

* As cited, p. 21.

estimate—such as, "*Eugénie Grandet* is Balzac's best work," or, "Hugo is a greater poet than Browning"— is not an established truth. But who ever thought anything of the sort? On the other hand, if the proposition be: "Flaubert is a greater artist than Feydeau," or, "Maupassant writes better than Malot," does not M. Droz admit that we are approaching a kind of proposition of which it may be scientifically said that its acceptance or rejection is to be explained in terms of greater or less psychological development or culture—this scientific view being, however, admitted to be acceptable as a rule only to those who accept the special propositions, just as a rationalistic view of Mohammed is acceptable only to non-Mohammedans? In fine, when instead of merely passing a judgment on a literary performance we reason that a given literary effect is reached by a certain process, or that a given literary appreciation is to be traced to certain limitations or developments in the appreciator, are we not bringing scientific method into the task of criticism?

In the end, as it seems to me, M. Droz makes this admission unreservedly; and his preliminary negation is rather an expression of his sense of the miscarriages of M. Taine and M. Brunetière in their particular attempts at the reduction of criticism to science, than a circumspect thesis as to the possibilities of the case. After a sharply effective attack on Taine's fashion of reaching a generalisation, he pronounces that "in this psychology of M. Taine, what obtrudes itself is the love of formula and the contempt of fact, which is also the contempt of science and of the scientific spirit—it is to that that I want to come."* Well, the concrete criticism was unanswerable; and we must agree with M. Droz that Taine often generalises recklessly and fallaciously. But

* As cited, p. 21.

again, surely M. Droz goes too far in charging him with a "*contempt (mépris)* of facts" amounting to a scorn of science? Was it not simply that Taine was too hasty in positing facts, too headlong in framing his formulas? It is quite true that "M. Taine has the taste for syntheses *(ensembles)*, but it is for those *he* has framed : as for those which nature and history present to him, he has scarcely glimpsed more than parts."* But is not this kind of prematureness and incompleteness just the usual fault of the pioneers of all science, or, let us say, of minds in the half-way stage between traditional apriorism and scientific positivism? Is it not really a way of seeking for science?

To that estimate, I think, we must come. It leaves us conceiving of a scientific criticism, while admitting that certain attempts at it are partly failures, and further that, as M. Droz contends, it is not framable by mere parody of the processes of the natural sciences—a kind of miscalculation to which we shall have to recur later. We must say with M. Droz that "the resort to the methods of the sciences, or, more exactly, the misunderstood outlines of the sciences, has in our time served the literary critics badly ;" but we also go on to say with him that, "in compensation, *that which is best in science*, the scientific spirit, has penetrated literary and moral studies ; whence it is that M. Taine"—even M. Taine—"despite his faults, has aided the advancement of his art." And this exercise of the scientific spirit, finally, consists in "*disciplining* our tastes, in teaching us to reason them out, to extend them, to increase their fineness and sensibility, and to augment also the pleasures they yield."†

In other words, we decide that there are canons or tests of consistency in criticism ; and that just as con-

---
* As cited, p. 23. † Pp. 30, 31.

sistency in propositions is the test of truth, just as relatedness or harmony in things or aspects is the source and criterion of visible beauty, so a twofold consistency, logical and æsthetic, is the test of rightness in criticism; the starting-point in the one case as in the other being, not any absolute theory of truth or beauty, but just a certain measure of common opinion. About this there is no difficulty; for when all is said about the arbitrariness of taste, there is as general an agreement on a few primordial points of literary judgment, among the members of any one civilisation or culture-sphere, as on the primordial propositions of natural science; the latter being, indeed, more apt to be obscured by a certain perverse metaphysic than the former.

To accept the test, of course, is one thing, and to conform to it, even when the application is clear, is another. To be human is to be inconsistent; and we can all peaceably assent to Voltaire's view of "the insane project of being perfectly wise." But that recognition, let us say once for all, is no more a stop to judgment in literature than to judgment in morals and in appetites. We must dree our weird.

IV

We might almost describe our critical science, then, as the science of consistency in appreciation, since the science of that would involve the systematic study of all the causes—in ourselves, in a book, and in an author—which go to determine our individual judgments. But seeing that the bare formula would seem in itself to exclude such systematic following up of the bases of appreciation, let us be content thus to indicate the scope of scientific criticism, without staking all on a formal definition. The business becomes quite formal enough as we go on.

Taken progressively, however, the steps are not in themselves abstruse. The first requisite, clearly, for a reduction of criticism to order, is a comparison of judgments. This, the preliminary to all progress in the influence of sciences commonly so-called, has been neglected in the practice of criticism to a surprising extent; and Mr. Dallas rightly stipulated for a reform on this head. It will be found that none of the "methods" yet put forward can dispense with it. A "science of pleasure," obviously, must set out with a recognition of the relativity of pleasure. Sainte-Beuve, who remains on the whole the typical critic in respect of versatility of appreciation, does actually resort the oftenest to the course of comparing judgments; and where his criticisms remain unsatisfactory they are so partly because he neglected this check on the personal equation. The method of Taine, again, after its complete application to any one case, leaves unmet the main question, since the critic's judgment may still seem arbitrary and wrong. Taine's method is, it will be remembered, to study every work as a product of three causal forces, the race, the social and physical environment, the "moment" or special influence of the time. It is, as a method, a valuable step to the right conception of a writer as being like every one else an organism in an environment, conditioned by that as well as affecting it. But it is plain that the estimating of every one of the factors specified is itself a process of judgment, open to fallacy and prejudice; and that the critic's view of every one of them is as much in need of scientific checking as the estimate which other critics may form of a writer or a book taken as *in vacuo*. Taine was taking for granted a number of sociological propositions which were themselves in the stage of tentative science, and which were thus a bad foundation for detailed judgments.

Let us put the case concretely. The old superficial French way of criticising Shakspere, say, and the not very old superficial English way of criticising Corneille, was to say that Shakspere had great passion and imagination but little judgment in the use of incident, and that Corneille is stiff and formal and declamatory. Taine's better way, as regards Shakspere, is to look to the characteristics of the robust audience for which Shakspere wrote, the methods in use on the stage, and the literary taste of the time; to describe all these vivaciously and, so far as may be, without animus, laying stress on the life and energy of the whole; and to make the gist of the criticism lie in the presentment of Shakspere as an extraordinary imagination or sensitive system, reacting or functioning in that stormy environment in virtue of his power of sensating and expressing it. Here we have clearly a deeper and more comprehensive process of thought, or at least of statement, than that of the old critic who merely "tried" Shakspere by "the rules." The old critic, indeed, was not wholly blind to all these considerations, but the ideas remained latent in him, so to speak. It was well done to bring them out; and equally the English critic will do well to think of Corneille as a dramatist with a given culture and literary tradition, writing specially for a courtly audience, in a literary form determined by its taste and culture and the genius of the language as thus far developed. In this way the real power at play can be sympathetically estimated. Taine's method is in fact a method of historical conception, involving judgments on a dozen points besides those of literary effect considered *in vacuo*, or the abstract merit of a tragedy as such; and the widening of the survey is almost sure to purge the student's mind of some of the prejudice which sets uncultured or narrow-minded people gibing against whatever in an alien product is specially strange to them. Yet not only does this widening of the survey still leave room for dispute on the original issue of the æsthetic merit of the given work, but it opens up new ground of dispute as regards the critic's view of the "race," his picture of the environment, and his account of the prevailing influence or "moment." On all of these heads he may be prejudiced, hasty, or arbitrary. He may falsely simplify his task by slumping the race in terms of a few of many characteristics, a few of many types; he may give a mere section of the environment as showing the whole, and he may be equally arbitrary as regards the "moment." Some of us think Taine has at times done all these things. Finally, on his own showing, we have to consider the author as a special psychological case, constituting, it may be, a notable variation in the race, reacting newly on the environment, and as much making as made by "the moment."* In such a case, much of the premises about the race and all the rest of it goes by the board: we have to deal with a problem in variation, to which these explanations are irrelevant as such.

The scientific criticism of Shakspere, then, even from the French point of view, would have to be carried yet further. On the point of the total æsthetic product, it would have to enter into those questions of text, of real authorship, of imitation and adaptation, which have been so little studied by our own essayists on Shakspere; while on the points of Shakspere's style and command of language it would listen carefully to all the leading

* Compare, however, Bagehot (*Physics and Politics*, pp. 32-30), who is more explicit than Taine.

THEORY AND PRACTICE OF CRITICISM

English critics, those who charge faults as well as those who insist most on Shakspere's supremacy. It would further go into the question of Shakspere's personality, his own physiology and psychology, as being more to the purpose than generalisations about the English race. It would further listen patiently to the German theories of Shakspere's didactic purpose, as well as the German anti-Shaksperean polemic; and on both heads it would rectify the German extravagance, or hold the balance between two German extremes, by the native good sense and practical logic which (without crediting it to "race") we have come to recognise as a common development of French literary life. It would thus supply an all-round estimate of Shakspere, to which all men might turn with profit, and from which Englishmen in particular, half hypnotised as they are by the mere prestige of Shakspere's name, might learn very much indeed.

Even thus, of course, we should have settled nothing once for all as, say, the law of gravitation is settled. We should only have carried out a process of circumspect persuasion, of reasoning from a common ground to a new ground, on a basis of fairly proved facts, and set up a basis for a certain amount of rational agreement among a certain number of educated people of different countries, interested in such a question of humanism; which agreement would in turn become, so far as it might avail, a force in fresh criticism and in fresh literary production. This is, broadly, the kind of influence scientific criticism can exercise. And it will perhaps not be disputed, even by outsiders, that it is as well worth exercising as the function of a lawyer or a soldier or a priest.

THEORY AND PRACTICE OF CRITICISM

V

This, however, is only a very general outline of the task of systematising or "scientising" criticism. Taine, after all, did but widen the critical outlook, or rather he methodised where the much-scrutinising Sainte-Beuve had freely gone before. He himself admitted * that while Sainte-Beuve "feared to crush the truth by enclosing it in formulas," it is yet possible to "extract a complete system from his writings," and this system is, on Taine's showing, the essence of Taine's.† But since a criticism proper, a judgment, is always at last an equation between the critic and his theme, the most methodic survey, we say, yields us not an objective fact but a subjective one, a phase of opinion, a teaching; and just in so far as that teaching or opinion strikes any one of us as arbitrary or fallacious, it fails of its purpose so far as we are concerned. There arises the old dispute, which can only be settled, if at all, by an appeal to consistency of fact, of reasoning, of decision. To guard against such disputes, to avoid giving ground for challenge, or, since there must be strife, to prepare the answer where a challenge is likely to come, is therefore the great strategic or systematic concern of the careful critic. His aim, if he be not a mere *frondeur*, and even then if he is a strong *frondeur*, is to persuade and convince, and to persuade and convince the judicious.

How then shall he best bear himself? His faculty, be it great or small, is to begin with a faculty of comparison; he must therefore, as we said, do much comparing—comparing of works, of men, of judgments on these. If he does but rise above being satisfied with

* *Derniers Essais*, p. 53.   † *Ibid.* pp. 58–59.

firing his squib or his arrow, with "having his say" in the general outcry, he must see that the ostensible chaos of opinion is open to some simple explanations which classify its forms. Writers and readers equally resolve into temperamental types, with specific prejudices or leanings of training, and certain kinds or degrees of culture. These lines of variation on both sides are the main conflicting forces in the struggle of literary action and opinion. The critic, then, must recognise that he can in general expect to appeal only to people largely or partially of his own cast of thought and feeling, people who have something of his kind of culture, something of his kind of "æsthopsychology," to use the cumbrous but useful term of M. Hennequin. The community of thought may be partial or extensive: it may extend only to matters of sociological or ethical judgment, or only to matters of technical literary appreciation, or only to matters of religion or philosophy; or it may reach over several or all of these departments. Whether, then, as regards any one or as regards all, his business is to aim at consistency, at carrying his readers with him from a common ground to a new agreement, to guard against inconsistency of appreciation alike on their part and on his own.

Disputes, however, are constantly arising which seem to turn not so much on inconsistency as on limitation; and the scientific side of criticism is as much concerned with these disputes as with any. A good critic, in our sense of a man with many forms of interest, with a manifold outlook on life, is by implication capable of appreciating many kinds of literary performance. He must be vowed to no artistic school, but open to the most diverse; and, if he have predilections he must not insist on them to the disregard of excellences which come less closely home to him. But all this, of course, is the counsel of perfection; and as a matter of fact the critic, in the degree of his fitness, is like the "author" and the reader a type with a temperament, with prejudices or leanings of education, with more or less of expert culture in the different matters with which he deals. He is thus sure sometimes to express a prejudice, or a limitation of sympathy, or an inexpert opinion; and like everybody else he is liable to variation of mood, which adds to the possibilities of inconsistency. Against these various snares he may guard with various degrees of success. Against the worst results of variation of mood he may guard by cultivating the habit of comparing himself with himself, of criticising his own work. But as regards his limitations and his antipathies he can only partially take precaution, and this only by a kind of discipline which few are ready to practise. In sum, it consists in carefully studying all the cases of wide appreciation in which he cannot feel with the many, and carefully estimating the calibre of the judgments with which he cannot agree. Suppose it be that he does not readily enjoy or admire Cervantes, or Calderon, or Schiller, or Hugo, or Browning, or Dickens, or Tolstoy, each of whom has won very high, and some very general praise, it is his business as a scrupulous and scientific critic to consider closely that praise, to ask himself narrowly whether he has missed the excellences on which it dwells, to consider the training, the bias, the cast of mind of those who bestow it, and then, if he thinks he fairly can, to explain it in terms of the prejudice, or limitation, or deficient culture of the admirers; or, if he cannot, to seek *objectively* for the merits which delight them, and to note these as forms of effect to which he is but slightly susceptible.

In fine, the perfect scientific critic, the critic of the

THEORY AND PRACTICE OF CRITICISM

future perhaps, might be conceived as prefacing his every judgment—or the body of his judgments—with a confession of faith, bias, temperament, and training. As thus :

"I have a leaning to what is called "exact" [*or* religious *or* mystical] thought, with [*or* without] a tenderness for certain forms of arbitrary [*or* spiritual] sentiment which prevail among many people I know and like. I value poetry as a stimulus to sympathy and moral zeal [*or,* as the beautiful expression of any species of feeling], caring little [*or* much] for cadence and phrase as such ; accordingly I value Browning and Dante and Hugo above Heine and Musset and Tennyson [or *vice versâ*]. Regarding literature and the arts as the crown of life, and fine letters as the flower of literature, I set the poets highest in the hierarchy of eminence [*or,* I seek to measure performers in the same line by their relative total intellectuality, so far as may be, and to compare performers in different lines by their relative reach and depth and energy in their own departments]. I am reverent [*or* irreverent] of august tradition and social propriety ; and I have little taste [*or* I care above all things], in imaginative literature, for those forms called realistic, as aiming at a close fidelity to everyday fact [*or* for those exercises of invention which carry me most completely out of my normal relation to my surroundings]. I am a Unitarian [*or* a Baptist, *or* a Catholic, *or* an Agnostic], having been brought up in that persuasion [*or* having come to that way of thinking in mature life]. In politics I am ——. My main physical diathesis is ——. Finally, I am —— years of age in this year ——. The dates of my essays will thus let the reader know how old I was when I wrote them." *

---

* Since this was penned I have found a very unexpected support for my suggestion in a passage of the exordium of the Duke of

THEORY AND PRACTICE OF CRITICISM

Happily, though no such confession has ever been categorically made, it is possible for the critical reader of criticism to draw up for himself a statement of every leading critic's idiosyncrasy, and thus to frame his own diagnosis and explanation of what he feels to be perversities or monstrosities of judgment, in respect of his own possibly fuller knowledge or expertness, or different education, or bias. Beyond that, I do not know that the errors of criticism can be rectified. That is to say, the critic, as likewise *his* critic, is finally on all fours with judges and doctors, in that he may make irretrievable mistakes. His one advantage is that they can hardly ever be homicidal. He may, given rope enough, hang himself; and he may bury himself. Other people he can at worst irritate or injure.

VI

If on this general presentment the task of criticism is still denied to be capable of being raised to a scientific status, I fear no further elaboration of the thesis will effect persuasion. But if it be now granted that the spirit of science may come into play in the work of

Argyll's *Unseen Foundations of Society*. It runs: "There is . . . even in the exact sciences an element known as 'the personal equation,' which has always to be taken into account; and this it is the business of every writer—even at the risk of some apparent egoism —to supply to those who read him. He can best do so by giving some indication of the direction from which he comes, and of the avenues of approach along which he has been led in dealing with his subject. Our reasoning may be the purest logic, and our opinions may be the plainest truth, and yet it may always be relevant to explain how we have come to hold them" (*The Unseen Foundations of Society*, preface). Of course the Duke does not offer just such a conspectus of his personal equation in political matters, as I have suggested in regard to criticism, or as others might propose to frame for him.

criticism as truly and as helpfully as in the studies of jurisprudence and medicine and ethics, it may be of interest to follow out a few of the lines of analysis and synthesis on which critical method has been carried, or proposed to be carried. I have said that the broadening of the outlook insisted on by Taine (and independently practised by some of our own best critics, as Arnold and Minto and Lowell) raises new possibilities of demur and dispute, since the critic has now more ways of going wrong. But on the other hand he has more ways of persuasion, and more ways of making his own artistic or constructive impression. For he too, like the novelist and the historian and the biologist, has his artistic side, his work of *Ideal Construction*, his task of making an intellectual whole to his own satisfaction out of his data, be they of character or performance or both. He may be only a bad artist in caricature, like the Tory reviewers who figured a "Johnny Keats" by way of damaging all who consorted with Radicals, or like a typical *Saturday* reviewer of the old sort, angry with his countrymen for admiring Ibsen; but an artist, good or bad, high or low, he remains, in so far as he rises above the primary function of scissors and paste. And if he be Lowell figuring for himself Lessing, he becomes an artist of much value to culture; and if he be Hennequin dissecting Flaubert, he ranks with the most penetrating of all the painters who have helped us to see in the flesh, in the harmonious unity of perception and presentment, remarkable human beings outside of our immediate ken.

It is hard to say whether Hennequin did any of his concrete studies deliberately on the lines laid down in his treatise *La Critique Scientifique*. A given critical study tends to be shaped by special artistic considerations. But Hennequin's method is easily applicable to any critical case; and in his skeleton or outline analysis of the work of Victor Hugo* he has suited the action to the thesis very exactly and instructively. The thesis is, in brief, that criticism to be scientific must proceed on three sorts of analysis, and arrive at three corresponding syntheses. The analyses are: (1) æsthetic, (2) psychologic, (3) sociologic. To put it in detail, an all-round survey of a work of literature or art must involve (1) a careful study of the book (or picture) to the end of noting the way in which the writer or artist makes his technical effect—that is to say (in the case of a writer) of his vocabulary, his cadences, his way of framing and tying sentences and paragraphs, his very punctuation, his tone or pitch of expression, his ways of picturing and describing, his choice of subjects, scenes, times, personages, characters, and abstract themes, and the nature of his effects, in terms of syntax, colour, metaphor, tone, use of association; (2) a similar analysis of the author's personality, by way of an explanatory hypothesis or statement of his characteristics, squaring these with their results as seen in his book; (3) a survey of the relation of public to author, noting the types of his admirers in the different classes (whether lettered or unlettered, old or young, expert or inexpert), with special reference to the different classes of his works. Each analysis ends in a synthesis; the author is shown to work with certain tools in certain ways; to have certain psychological peculiarities, which constitute his gifts and his weaknesses; and to have certain kinds of admirers for certain parts or all of his work, in virtue of

---

* He had previously produced a rounded and masterly essay on Hugo (reprinted in his *Quelques Écrivains Français*) which substantially conforms to the scheme of analysis in *La Critique Scientifique*, but not in all the details. The formal treatise therefore seems to have been thought out after the critic's concrete work was done.

THEORY AND PRACTICE OF CRITICISM

correspondences between him, as a product of faculty and training, and them, as a product of bias and previous literary culture.

In the special case of Victor Hugo, the analyses and syntheses work out somewhat thus:

1. Æsthetic Analysis.

I. Means.

a. *External Means*: (1) Great vocabulary, with predominance of indefinite terms; (2) Loose, abrupt, and elliptic syntax; (3) Repetitive composition, saying things over in different ways, use of equivalent sets of antitheses; (4) Prophetic and inflated tone; (5) Repetitive and antithetic description of places and persons; direct description of characters by explication; metaphorical way of setting forth abstract ideas.

b. *Internal Means*: (6) Choice of *epochs* (Middle Ages, oriental antiquity, picturesque or hideous modern phases); of *places* (sea and forest, large towns, cathedral, castle—the mysterious, the infinite, the coloured, the vague); of *times* (night, evening, shade, crises, trouble); of *personages* (beautiful or ugly, of sinister beauty or good ugliness, picturesque even if ragged costumes; simple minds doing one thing, minds doing antithetical things, such minds making right-about-face); of *abstract subjects* (meaningless talk, variousness of theme, use of commonplace, philanthropy, optimism, socialism, vague idealism and pantheism, use of the grandiose, the mysterious, of legend, of history, of universal life).

II. Effects (Synthesis of Means).

a. *General Effect*, "exalting," by (1) Richness and vividness of style; (2) Surprise of syntax; (3) Of metaphors, and their clearness; (4) Violent colouring of epochs and places; (5) Simplicity of personages; (6) Optimisic humanitarianism and deism; (7) Exaltation of tone; (8) Projection of objects by antithesis.

b. "*Amplifying Grandiosity*," by (1) Processes of repetition; (2) Absence of detail; (3) Distance of epochs; (4) Chiaroscuro of places; (5) Simplicity of personages; (6) Tone; (7) Subjects.

c. *Mystery*, by (1) Indefinite words; (2) Ellipses; (3) Immediate, total, and vague presentment; (4) Distance of epochs and

THEORY AND PRACTICE OF CRITICISM

subjects; (5) Vague metaphysic; (6) Obscurity of places; (7) Tone; (8) In general, leaning to the limitless, the poetic.

d. *Redundance, Emptiness, Unrealism,* by (1) Vocabulary; (2) Repetitions and verbal antitheses; (3) Simplicity of types; (4) Vagueness of epochs and places; (5) Frequent nullity of subjects; (6) General predominance of expression over purport.

e. *General emotion of suspense and surprise,* by (1) General antithetism; (2) Pursuit of strangeness.

f. *Accidental and negligible emotions of realism.*

2. Psychologic Analysis.

I. Causes.

Resumé of the æsthetic analysis and synthesis. Prevalence of the element of word over the element of idea.

Explanatory Hypothesis. Existence in Hugo of a superabundance of words, restraining the number of ideas, of percepts, and creating verbal ideas and conceptions. This would explain, (1) as regards the *superabundance* of the word,

    The vocabulary.
    Repetition of words and actions.
    Variations on empty subjects.
    Exalting effect—grandiosity, redundance.
    The *tone.*

(2) As regards the *absolute* character of words,
    The antithetism.
    The syntax, the *tone.*

(3) As regards the *limited* character of words,
    Immediate apperception of things without detail.
    Simplicity of personages.
    Humanitarianism and optimistic idealism.
    Epochs and places known only verbally.
    Verbal subjects and developments.
    Grandiosity.
    Inadequate unrealism.

(4) As regards character of words as *mere signs,*
    Abundance of indefinite words.
    Ellipses.
    Metaphors.
    Vague metaphysic.

(5) As regards the *exaggerating* character of words,
    The exalting effect.
    The tone.

THEORY AND PRACTICE OF CRITICISM

The grandiosity.
Simplicity of beings.
Beauty of places and things.
Ascendant developments.
General tension.
Indifference as to subject.
(6) As regards the fact that verbal quality is strongest where no experiential limitation exists,
The tone.
Gloom and distance of places, epochs, subjects.
Mystery.
Grandiosity.

PHYSIOLOGICAL INTERPRETATION.

Probable predominance, in the cerebral organisation of Hugo, of the elements of language, and of the third frontal convolution.*

3. SOCIOLOGICAL ANALYSIS.

I. FIXING OF CATEGORIES OF ADMIRERS.
(FRANCE, 1830-1888.)

For the Poems : men of letters, general readers.
Among the men of letters: all the "romantics," all the "Parnassians," some "Naturalists," few idealistic novelists, no notable critic, journalists.
Among the general readers: a large proportion of the instructed youth.
Sale : medium, relatively to the author's novels; considerable, for poems.
For the dramas : Men of letters, readers, men of the world.
Among the men of letters: the romantics, fewer Parnassians, no Naturalists, some idealistic novelists, no critics, most of the theatrical notice-writers and journalists.
Among the readers: a small proportion of the instructed youth. Among the men of the world; the less inapt to literary pleasures, Parisian theatre-goers.
Performances with declining success.
For the Novels : Men of letters; general readers.
Among the men of letters, the romantics, the Parnassians, some Naturalists, most of the idealistic novelists, all the newspaper novelists, some critics, the journalists.

* See *Quelques Écrivains Français*, p. 152, for a note on this point.

THEORY AND PRACTICE OF CRITICISM

Among readers : the generality ; chiefly the women ; the people. *Sale* enormous : persistent for *Les Misérables* among the people, for *L'Homme qui rit* among the educated public.

(ABROAD, 1830–1888.)

Insuccesses and general inappreciation, save in England, where one pupil, Swinburne; and in Italy. Success limited even in these two countries.

Then we have a categorical application, for each of the classes of Hugo's work, of the foregoing conclusions, with the effect of showing that in each case the admirers share those characteristics of Hugo which specially belong to the works in question—verbalism, exaggeration, simple-mindedness, lack of ideas, impracticality, humanitarian optimism and socialism, random realism. Thus we get a conception, through the case of Hugo and his public, of the intellectual peculiarities and defects of the French people in general, and of the literary classes in particular, from 1830 to 1886. "These psychological facts," says Hennequin, "are national. It would be easy to demonstrate as much by the social and historical facts of the present time : they are expressed notably by the political incapacity of the working people, by the intellectual abasement of the well-to-do classes; by the more or less pronounced romanticism of all the notable French literature of the present day." And in a threefold synthesis, artistic, biographic, and sociological, of all these analyses, he would sum up the scientific criticism of the case of Hugo.

It seems hardly possible to carry vigilance and exactness of method further;* and the whole scheme, in its

* It will be found instructive, however, to compare Hennequin's scheme with that of Mr. Arthur Lynch in his *Modern Authors*, a quite independent performance. Mr. Lynch's analytical plan divides into studies of each author's (1) Emotional Calibre; (2) Intellectual

way, seems to me a masterpiece of critical analysis. It improves in a measure on the method of Taine. It substitutes for a vague and largely arbitrary premiss of "race" characteristics an exact study of the characteristics of the author in hand, as gathered from his works themselves; it shows how special, how individual, was Hugo's literary bias; how he evoked applause in respect that many of those around him had his characteristics in a minor degree. On these heads Hennequin had previously shown the arbitrariness of Taine's implications as to race and environment, in that one race yields such divergent types, and one environment, one "moment," such differences of theme, predilection, and method. And yet Hennequin's own conclusions as to Hugo rather corroborate than confute Taine, for, as we see, he makes out Hugo's characteristics to be specially French; and if he were challenged as to the clear decline in Hugo's prestige, the triumph over his of methods alien to his, it is not easy to see how Hennequin could have denied that the "moment," though it did not make the artist, yet went far to make his success. For the characteristics of Zola and Daudet and Maupassant, for instance, are only in a small degree those of Hugo; and though a critic of scientific training in psychology, like Hennequin, might charge contemporary novelists with "romanticism," he could not well make out that any of those named, to say nothing of Huysmans, is lawless and fantastic and verbalist to the point of recalling Hugo. Can it be that, after rejecting as inexact and arbitrary Taine's

Grasp; (3) Knowledge of the Field; (4) Moral Power. The analysis is hardly complete, and the exposition is avowedly offered as a mere set of hints to a method; but it has so much merit that it only needed a more connected elaboration to make it an important critical treatise.

way of summarising the qualities of a race, Hennequin himself, in an access of pessimism, fell into Taine's error, and summed up the French nation without any attempt at discrimination as to what characteristics are specially French, and what common to most European nations? It would seem so. His own study of Dickens, who has had such popularity in England, sets forth justly enough that "with Dickens, ideas are rare and feeble,"* that the verbal faculty in him predominates over the reflective, that he idealises, that he misrepresented human nature, simplifying and twisting it, in his way, as much as did Hugo. It ought to follow, then, that Dickens had his English popularity in virtue of the commonness of his intellectual peculiarities and defects among the English nation; that his characteristics are "national." And seeing, further, that Dickens is to this day extremely popular in Germany, far more so than in France, it would follow that his peculiarities and defects, his vivacity and fantasy and humour and psychological superficiality, are in a high degree German characteristics. But Hennequin's essay, masterly so far as it goes, of course does not attempt to affirm these things, though in consistency it clearly ought. So that there would seem to be something wrong, something imperfect, in the sociological analysis and synthesis of the case of Hugo.

Yet again, we have only to turn to the able study of Victor Hugo's poetry by M. Charles Renouvier † to see that the æsthetic analysis of Hennequin may profitably be supplemented by a study of Hugo as an innovator in poetic technique, doing great things for French poetry in virtue of the elemental energy and egoism which

* *Quelques Écrivains Francisés*, p. 49. (All of Hennequin's volumes have been posthumously published. He died in 1889.)
† *Victor Hugo : le poète.* Collin ct Cie.

were perhaps the more puissant in him by reason of the very imperfectness of his culture. To Hennequin's psychological analysis, further, M. Renouvier adds * an important detail which Hennequin does not specify, namely, the extraordinary proclivity of Hugo to the *personalising* of everything inanimate and every abstract conception—a proclivity which is clearly to be explained in connection with Hennequin's view of his predominating verbal faculty. And though the treatise of M. Renouvier is not to be set above the scheme of Hennequin as a display of intellectual power, it may be that in respect of its more humanistic method, and of its avoidance of the snares of sociological generalisation, it gives finally the more satisfying because the more mellow presentment of Hugo's mind. It is not at all idolatrous: it freely exposes his faults: it has a chapter on his "Ignorance and Absurdity": the critic is content calmly to present the poet as he was, a mixture of great powers and astonishing weaknesses, without framing the picture in pessimism. Where Hennequin insists on getting his whole æsthetic and psychological knowledge of Hugo from Hugo's works,† M. Renouvier gets most valuable light from outside biographic testimony. It all goes to help him to convince us, to satisfy us, to shape our belief. And it all goes, further, to maintain the title of France to supremacy in literary criticism. When we read such works of penetrating judgment and just and original reasoning as those of M. Hennequin and M. Renouvier, how can we possibly accept the stern judgment of the former, prematurely

---

* His study appeared in sections in *La Critique Philosophique*, in 1889; Hennequin's book in 1888. But it is quite an independent inquiry.

† Cp. *La Critique Scientifique*, p. 65. Yet in his study of Poe he makes good use of biographical detail.

exhausted as he was with his unrelenting studies,* that his nation is in the mass given to verbalism, to rhetoric, to random and visionary ideas? No current literature can show two such studies of any of its leading writers as those we have just been considering.

And yet, after all, we find M. Renouvier, in a series of mostly wise and discriminating estimates of Hugo's generally extravagant criticisms, pronouncing him to have said "the last word" on *Hamlet* in his pyrotechnic pages on that drama. Here M. Renouvier applies none of the practical tests by which he makes such short work of the generalisations of Madame de Staël on romanticism and classicism, and of the hardly less rash generalisations of Sainte-Beuve on the technical developments of Chénier and Hugo. It would seem that M. Renouvier in his turn has his amateur or inexpert or uncritical side, his "blind spot": and it is in the direction of English literature,† of Shakspere and *Hamlet*. There he is merely adoring, not analytic.

From all which, let us draw not a pessimistic or a nihilistic conclusion as regards criticism, any more than we do so in view of the strifes and readjustments of other sciences, but simply this, that as art is long so is criticism; and that in its province are many mansions.

VII

If we come to such an attitude of compromise over powerful and vigilant and expert criticism, of course, we can have little to say in deprecation of hard words

* He died suddenly at 29, of a congestion, in the act of bathing in the open in spring weather.

† Cp. his pronounced praise (p. 31) of the "realism" of George Eliot, Thackeray, and Trollope, as compared with that of the French novelists.

THEORY AND PRACTICE OF CRITICISM

applied to the ordinary run of hand-to-mouth performers, at least among ourselves. There seems to be almost no such thing in England as the earning a steady income by the practice of pure criticism, as has been done in France by Sainte-Beuve, and by many lesser men. The function is, perhaps by consequence, little esteemed with us. And certainly the kind of work generally done in our journals, though it contains touches of wit and wisdom worthy of a more enduring framework, is not such as to win respect for the profession of critic. It mostly lacks not only intellectual weight but conscientiousness; and this almost inevitably, because the public appetite for good criticism is too small to induce the ordinary journals to pay fairly for it. Thus able and scrupulous men tend more and more to be repelled from the pursuit. As a matter of simple commerce, it is to be noted that a journalist is usually paid no more for a book review than for a leading article of equal length, though the careful reading of the book reviewed might be a week's work. So of course the work is scamped; much of it being done on time wages, like reporting and type-setting. Even where it is better paid for, and the critic is willing to take trouble, it is greatly hampered by the need of consulting popular prejudices, and even by the need of securing publishers' advertisements. "Critics," says a recent writer, "are the serfs of literature." Those who work for the journals are certainly at the mercy of the market. And over and above the evil economic and other conditions, whether by reason of them or by reason of our general backwardness in intellectual ethics, there seems to be a lack of the sense of responsibility among our average practitioners. Doubtless it is the old story of the serf developing a servile ethic, of the hack becoming callous. The function is surely responsible enough. The critic is free to deal out, as a rule anonymously, not only praise and blame but insult, misrepresentation, opprobrium, ridicule; and the extent to which he will pervert facts, words and principles, to gratify a prejudice or a resentment, is an ugly thing to see when it does not rather, as often happens, set up an impression of mere childishness. A judge on the bench is expected to put away, and generally does put away, the methods of his barrister days, and to set up for himself an ideal of decent impartiality. It is scarcely so with the average anonymous critic. It must be confessed that he does not even take much trouble to speak the truth, though false witness on his part may do incurable injustice. All that Mr. Howells has said of his unscrupulousness is broadly true. "The difficulty is," said one ingenuous author of some of the criticisms on his book, " to know whether you are dealing with blunderers or with cheats. It is often not a question of fairness or competence: it is a question of telling a flat falsehood." It is often apt to seem so to the scribe assailed. And it is finally true that few men are capable of using without abusing the power of mischief and offence, of insult and injustice, which the institution of anonymous journalism puts in the hands of thousands, enabling them as it does to say what they will, from the coward's castle of the "we," against men outside who cannot bring an injustice home to the doer, and who in general cannot even get a hearing for a rejoinder. Where there is not malice and perversity, mere carelessness may work untold iniquity.

In this matter, as in others, they do better in France. The great Sainte-Beuve is little open to blame in the matter of conscientiousness, save in certain cases where personal ill-will affected his spoken judgment. Here he is charged, even by admirers, with *canaillerie*; and on the other hand he was at times swayed by private friendship or social pressure. Still, the mass of his work is sound, and his general urbanity and painstaking with all manner of subjects and all manner of writers supply a model to all of his craft. When the young Taine came forward with his first books, Sainte-Beuve discussed them with a courteous and complimentary seriousness which, in England, no critic of his standing would have given to the work of an obscure youth. With us, Taine would have been satirised, sneered at, snubbed, being indeed very open to censure. And Sainte-Beuve, we can see, went through life constantly learning, constantly studying afresh for the express purpose of estimating rightly the new literature that challenged his judgment. He was "always opening new windows," as Mr. James testifies. And though a critic cannot add a cubit to his stature by such self-discipline, although he will not so make broad a mind which is cast in a narrow mould, or make generous a temper which is innately ungenerous, he may add range of vision and refinements of the sense of justice to a fair faculty. Indeed, without a deliberate and constant attempt to enlarge his own culture, no natural fairness of disposition can make him habitually discriminate well in one department of writing, much less deal proportionately with different departments. Even the bellettrist criticism of men of merely bellettrist culture tends to become insensitive on certain sides, since the crafts of poetry and fiction, to be duly progressive, must be coloured by the surrounding play of thought of all kinds; and apathy or ignorance on these other matters will leave the critic incompetent to appraise the work he deals with. Progress in criticism may be roughly said to arise in respect of the perception of new significances, new relations, new "connotations," as the philosophic term goes, in pieces of literature which have hitherto been read with a half-seeing eye, in the fashion in which people know classic phrases without any sense of their real purport or felicity. This is, indeed, the general law of all progress in civilisation or in intelligence: cross-fertilisation of cultures, contacts of diverse knowledges and methods, are the sources of new thought and mental effort in a society or in an individual; and we have seen that right criticism is but an orderly play of judgment, with a search for tests, to the end of consistency of opinion. Now it is obvious that, given a faculty for literary appreciation, every form of culture in addition to literary culture so-called, tends to throw a side-light or reveal a clue where the eye not so cultured would be apt to see nothing.

It is possible, indeed, to overrate the possible fructification of literary criticism by non-literary preparation. A critic of great original gifts, the Rev. Mr. Fleay, in his valuable *Shakspere Manual*, seems to imply that he owes the special results there set forth to his training in the physical sciences. Speaking of the metrical tests he so ably employs, he writes that "The great need for any critic who attempts to use these tests is to have had a thorough training in the natural sciences, especially in mineralogy, classificatory botany, and, above all, in chemical analysis."* He goes even further than this in his paper *On Troylus and Cressida:*

> "We must accept every scientific method from other sciences applicable to our ends. From the mineralogist we must learn by long study to recognise a chip of rock at once from its general appearance; from the chemist, to apply systematic tabulated tests to confirm our conclusions; from both, to use varied tests—tests as to form, as for crystals—tests as to materials, as for compounds;

* Work cited, ch. xii. p. 108.

THEORY AND PRACTICE OF CRITICISM

from the botanist we must learn to classify, not in an empirical way, but by essential characters arranged in due subordination; finally, from the biologist we must learn to take into account not only the state of any writer's mind at some one epoch, but to trace its organic growth from beginning to end of his period of work: remembering that we have often only fossils, and even fragments of fossils, to work from, when our object is to restore the whole living animal. When these things are done systematically and thoroughly, then, and then only, may we expect to have a criticism that shall be free from shallow notions taken up to please individual eccentricities: a criticism that shall differ from what now too often goes under that name, as much as the notions on the determining causes of the relations between wages and capital differ in the mind of a Stuart Mill and that of a Trades-Union delegate."*

I venture to say that this is a hasty and overstrained way of putting the case for the advantage to literary criticism from a hold on physical science. Mr. Fleay confounds the indirect effect of mental habit and expansion with a direct process of imitation; and his special parallels will not stand the two great scientific tests which he has so oddly omitted from his list—those of logic and psychology. For the capacity to recognise a given specimen of anything is not at all peculiar to the mineralogist. It is common not only to the chemist and the biologist but to the grocer, the butcher, the baker, the publican, the tailor, and the shoemaker, being simply a development of special knowledge. The method in each case is special. The grocer, for instance, tests his tea by taste and smell, and the tailor his fabric by a magnifying glass, as does the mineralogist with his rock; though all alike may in many cases judge of a substance at a single glance. And as every one of these can do his own work perfectly well without first learning the business of the others, so the literary critic may apply literary tests perfectly well without knowing gneiss from schist. Neither is biological

* Work cited, pp. 243–244.

preparation in itself any qualification for the apprehension of what is essentially a psychological process, the inference of a man's states of mind from his work, or the inference of his general capacity from a fragment of his writing. Hallam applied to Shakspere's case the principle of allowing for states of mind, though Hallam seems to have had no biological knowledge. What is perfectly true is that the practice of a physical science may suggest to a student a new analytical test in literature; but then the same test may occur to a student who has never meddled with that science at all. The new school of art experts, which claims to settle by exact tests the authorship of old pictures, as the users of the metrical test claim to clear up the authorship of old plays, was I believe founded by a man of scientific training; but his method is applied by men of a different training, perhaps more scientifically.* Mr. Fleay himself does not dispute that metrical tests were applied to the plays of Shakspere by other critics, for whom he does not claim any skill in mineralogy and palæontology, or even in meteorology—a science which might be supposed to offer points of analogy like another. The truth is, there is a right method, an exact and logical method, in reasoning *about* criticism, as there is in the application of metrical tests or the analysis of substances, and that exact method has not been here observed by Mr. Fleay; who, I do not hesitate to say, might very well have arrived at his metrical tests without any previous lessoning in physics and botany. On the other hand a man crammed with all the sciences might read Shakspere all his life without dreaming of metrical tests. The real gain to the literary critic from scientific knowledge, then, is not in

* See the recent work of Mr. Bernhard Berenson on *Lorenzo Lotto* (Putnams).

THEORY AND PRACTICE OF CRITICISM

the deliberate application or imitation of the investigatory process of any or all of the sciences. That would be a much vainer undertaking than Bacon's plan of arriving at natural laws by merely ledgering data. Indeed, there obviously can be no such imitation as is proposed, since neither microscope nor scalpel, neither re-agent nor hammer, can be applied to literary problems. Here we can understand the protest of M. Droz, above considered. The real gain in the matter, as we agreed with him, is likely to be, first, in the mere habit of exactitude, the avoidance of inconsistency, the sense of the importance of proofs; secondarily, in the probable stimulus to speculative or theorising thought; and ultimately in the probable widening of philosophic view in general, and of estimate of human capacity in particular. In the way of direct enlightenment bearing on his work as a critic, the literary man may really gain far more from human physiology and pathology than from any of the sciences Mr. Fleay specifies.

It is again fallacious, I think, to say as Mr Fleay does that

"Mathematical deductions from the doctrine of chances, and inferences from one set of numerical results to another, are mos valuable, and to be applied whenever possible. For instance, Dr. Abbott's deduction from Mr. Simpson's numerical statement, that 2700 words in Shakspere occur in two plays each and in no others —to the effect that four words only are to be expected as peculiar to any given pair of plays—is most valuable as well as ingenious." *

We need not discuss here whether in the particular case put any good results have been derived from the theorem, or whether Mr. Fleay has done any the better, as he supposes, in assigning the elements of *Henry VI.*, by reason of the formula of Dr. Abbott. What is safe to say is that such a theorem is not logically valid as a

* P. 243.

test, because the "doctrine of chances" in any form is a mere mode of hypothesis, and can establish no truth whatever; and because Dr. Abbott's deduction does not really follow on Mr. Simpson's statement. In another passage,* Mr. Fleay tells us that the "chances" are 20,030,010 to one against the selection by rhyme-test of the same ten out of Shakspere's 30 undoubted plays as are specified by Meres for a given period; and that therefore when it does make that selection the value of the rhyme test is conclusively proved "to a mind accustomed to the exact sciences." Now, the doctrine of chances is not a process proper to any of the exact sciences; it is emphatically a speculative and inexact process, which only seems exact because it is in terms of figures. The figures given represent no exact or other truth whatever, since it is not denied that even with "twenty million chances to one against" something happening, it *may* actually happen.

But even if all this were not so, it is obvious that the calculus of chances can only be applied, even on Mr. Fleay's lines, to a very few of the questions with which literary criticism has to deal; and his array of scientific methods which were to be applicable to criticism in general is in no better case than before. When the real authorship of the plays attributed to Shakspere is settled—a thing certainly well worth doing, and strangely neglected by many editors of what are lumped together for the public as "Shakspere's Works"—the main tasks of Shakspere-criticism are still to do. Mr. Fleay rightly declines to offer "æsthetic" criticism in his manual; but he will hardly dispute that such criticism is inevitable, or that it is desirable. Indeed, when he comes to the task of

* P. 134.

sifting out the non-Shaksperean matter from *Macbeth*, he necessarily resorts to æsthetic tests; and he does so without even an attempt at scientific methodism, since no physical science offers a plausible analogy to the psychological process involved. So with twenty other problems. The question of the fitness of Shakspere's work in any play or scene may at any time be raised; and here the calculus of chances and the methods of the mineralogist are of no avail. We must just fall back on general processes of reasoning, special to no science, with the special help, perhaps, of data from physiology and psychology, and the general help, it is to be hoped, of that ratiocinative cast of thought which all science tends to develop.

VIII

But even the help of physiology may be misused if it be not resorted to in a truly scientific spirit. Such misuse occurs in the remarkable work of Dr. Max Nordau on *Degeneration*, so much discussed of late in the literary world. Dr. Nordau claims to have produced in that treatise a work of critical science. "This book," he declares in his dedicatory preface to Professor Lombroso, "is an essay in a really scientific criticism, which does not judge a work by the emotions it arouses —emotions very contingent, capricious, and variable, according to the temperament and disposition of mind of each reader, but by the psycho-physiological elements which have produced it; and it seeks at the same time to fill a lacuna which still exists in your puissant system." Now, whether or not Dr. Nordau's book fills a blank in Professor Lombroso's system, it is obvious that on the one hand it does not abstain from "judging a work according to the emotions it arouses," and that, on the other hand, only in a lax and capricious way does it judge works by the psycho-physiological elements involved in their production. What Dr. Nordau does again and again is to deride and denounce literary performances on the score of the emotions they arouse in him in particular, and then to proceed to show that they have certain characteristics in common with the talk of imbeciles, lunatics, or maniacs. He does not get at the psycho-physiological symptoms of his authors by way of throwing light on their works; he usually infers the characteristics from the works; and his plentiful epithets show him to be as much under the sway of his primary literary impression or emotion as any one else. It is not to be disputed that he is right in some of his judgments. Rossetti, for instance, was certainly a neurotic; and his works are found to appeal to neurotics; but there is only a beginning of scientific criticism in noting these facts. They do not settle the question of the merit of the neurotic's work: they do but give one cue for the literary estimate. Dr. Nordau seems to suppose that he has settled the whole critical problem when he calls a writer a degenerate, with some contumelious adjectives thrown in. But we may agree that Swift, Byron, Kleist, Pascal, Leopardi, de Musset, Lamb, Heine, Poe, Coleridge, Dostoievsky, and Huysmans are all degenerates in the sense of having some form of neurosis, and yet reckon nearly every one of them a man of wonderful special gift or genius, much better worth studying than most writers of quite sound nervous structure. Nay, if we are to follow Dr. Nordau's master, Signor Lombroso, all men of genius without exception are to be labelled degenerates; and it is to be laid down that if they themselves live to a good old age the collapse occurs in their children—as in the case of Goethe and perhaps Shakspere. The

THEORY AND PRACTICE OF CRITICISM

sweeping theory of Professor Lombroso might be thought sufficient in itself to suggest to Dr. Nordau that the main business of psycho-physiological criticism is to ascertain the elements belonging *in common* to genius, normality, and neurosis, and to measure dispassionately the deviations from the norm, with a view to a theory of cerebral variation. But he falls into exactly the error committed by Signor Lombroso in his diagnosis of the criminal type. The Professor finds certain moral and physical phenomena among criminals, and straightway decides that these phenomena all connote criminality; whereas more circumspect observers can show that they abound among non-criminals. Dr. Nordau loads his dice in the same fashion, setting down as specifically degenerate certain tendencies which can be shown to exist in men whom he passes as perfectly sane. Discussing Mr. Swinburne, he writes that in that poet's verse "the world changes its aspect according to the character of the event which is occurring: it accompanies, like an orchestra, all the events which occur at a place. . . . . Here we have an idea purely delirious. It corresponds in art and poetry to hallucination and madness. It is a form of mysticism which we meet in all the degenerates."* And he goes on to diagnose this symptom in Ibsen and in Zola. Now, the slightest general knowledge of literature suffices to show that this "pathetic fallacy" (so described by Mr. Ruskin, another degenerate!) is an almost universal literary artifice or psychological proclivity. It would be difficult to find a poet who has not exemplified it. Milton does, in his account of the fall of Adam and Eve. Shakspere does, again and again, in his sonnets as well as in his plays. Schiller does, in *Wilhelm Tell.* Heine

* *Dégénérescence*, trad. Franç. i. 172–173.

carries the process further still, as in his lyric of the palm and the pine. Hugo does it continually. But Dr. Nordau's thesis may be disposed of once for all by collating his own verdicts. "If to-day English poetry all round is not unmitigatedly pre-Raphaelite," he declares, "it is solely due to the happy chance of having possessed, simultaneously with the pre-Raphaelites, a poet so healthy as Tennyson."* Now, not only was Tennyson unquestionably one of the pre-Raphaelites; not only did he freely resort to the use of the refrain, and to what Dr. Nordau calls "echolalia,"† but he supplies one of the most striking examples of the notion of sympathy in nature and mood in his early poem *The Sisters*, not to speak of *Claribel, The Lotos Eaters, The Last Tournament, Move Eastward Happy Earth*, and a number of the lyrics in *Maud*. What then are we to say of the science which marks off Tennyson as perfectly healthy and convicts Rossetti and Mr. Swinburne of degeneracy on the strength of symptoms which he abundantly exhibits? What has happened in this miscarriage is not a carrying of science too far, but a failure to carry it far enough. Science implies precision and consistency: Dr. Nordau has here missed both. A little comparison will show that what he takes for specifically morbid symptoms are phases of the primal instinct of song, recognisable as such in the

---

* *Dégénérescence*, i. p. 177.

† *E.g.*, the lyrics " Late, late, so late; " " Low my lute, breathe low my lute; " " Turn, fortune, turn thy wheel; " " Sweet and low, sweet and low," with the further line, " Low, low, breathe and blow; " " Break, break, break ; " " Sun, rain, and sun." Dr. Nordau points to Rossetti's " Forgot it not, nay, but got it not" (*Beauty*), as a sample of echolalia. But Tennyson has " Regret me not, forget me not " (song in first version of *The Miller's Daughter*). And Tennyson resorts as often as any poet to alliteration, which for Dr Nordau spells degeneration.

THEORY AND PRACTICE OF CRITICISM

songs of children and savages. He falls into the elementary fallacy of *cum hoc, ergo propter hoc;* and his ascription of normal literary expedients to malady when found with malady is on all fours with Signor Lombroso's assumption that, inasmuch as genius has been seen to run special risks of brain degeneration (even as gunners run special risks of deafness), therefore genius is a phase of degeneration. Many of the fashions and mannerisms to which Dr. Nordau points are affected by people with neither neurosis nor genius. And he is otherwise haphazard in his judgments. Mr. William Morris he describes as "much more sane intellectually than Rossetti and Swinburne," and as showing a "swing past equilibrium" only in his "lack of originality and the exaggerated instinct of imitation."* But Mr. Morris, as Dr. Nordau avows, commits echolalia; and he does it far oftener than Dr. Nordau seems to be aware of; while, on the other hand, the "instinct of imitation" and the "lack of originality" are the most marked intellectual symptoms of savages and children in general, and of stolid Christian citizens in mass. The whole theorem is astray. A degenerate must have some qualities in common with his normal or undegenerate neighbours. The business of psycho-physiological criticism is to ascertain whether special developments of any qualities are or are not necessarily phases of degeneration; and even when the point is ascertained we have not reduced the flawed poet, as Dr. Nordau apparently supposes, to the status of a madhouse patient.

I should be sorry to see Dr. Nordau meet these criticisms by applying the proposition he throws out in his preface—that literary men are sure to attack him because he has shown them up. That way of arguing,

---

* *Dégénérescence,* i. p. 175.

even if accurate, seems to be unprofitable, as it leaves it open to the literary men to say (what some of them do say) that Dr. Nordau himself has the symptoms of a neurotic, raging as he does at every eccentricity, and breaking out as he frequently does into vituperation of people whom on his own showing he should treat as invalids. Instead of meeting him in that fashion, I desire merely to express my regret that his unscientific use of his great powers of colligation and surmise, and his no less unscientific resort to the merest philistinism for sanction of his attacks on all manner of innovating thought, good, bad, and indifferent,* should tend to discredit scientific method among non-scientific people. I quite agree with Dr. Nordau that it is important to recognise the pathological element in such writers as Rossetti and Tolstoy; but the business of critical science in this direction seems to me to have only begun where in the hands of Dr. Nordau it ends. When we have settled, say, the bearing of Heine's spinal disease on his art and his ethics, we have but collated an effect with one of its casual conditions; we have so far neither discredited Heine nor disposed of his work, which remains incomparably more valuable than the work of the well-balanced Klopstock. Bare consistency dictates that, after finding moral and artistic perversity and intellectual fallacy in the work of degenerates, we proceed to recognise moral and artistic and logical imbecility in the work of the physically sane, and to philosophise accordingly. A writer whom Dr. Nordau

* For instance, he must needs maintain, as against all innovators, what he calls "an order of things which, during a long series of ages, has *satisfied logic*, subdued perversity, and ripened the beautiful in all the arts" (Trans. cited, i. 11). In such an endorsement of all use and wont, such an implicit faith that "whatever is, is right," science has no part. The attitude is indeed the very negation of the scientific spirit.

seems to accept as scientific, Dr. Maudsley, has affirmed that results of immeasurable value have accrued to the human race from diseased conditions of body and brain in certain cases. To denounce the disease is surely the method of the typical unscientific literary man rather than that of the scientific man turned critic. Once more, error comes of too little science, not of too much; but it takes a little scientific bent to see this; and many literary men will put the case quite otherwise.

IX

The danger, then, of Mr. Fleay's excessive way of putting things, and of Dr. Nordau's way, excessive with a difference, is that it may merely confirm some literary specialists in aversion to science of all sorts.* But of course Mr. Fleay is not to be charged with setting up a habit which flourishes in virtue of average egoism, ignorance, and arrogance. Those who fall into it pay the penalty in the restriction of their own powers. Thus we constantly hear petulant protests against the inevitable artistic effects of new ethical and scientific ideas, as well as against the modifications of language inevitably set up by the same forces. Men living in a close of mere literary technique and amateur reflection, however carefully it be gardened, and however choice be the flowers and fruits, are sure to pass some Chinese judgments on the world beyond, and to make provincial estimates of the relative stature of the

* The same may perhaps be said of Professor Sylvester's assumption of having formulated important "laws of verse" in what he calls "phonetic syzygy" or "symptosis" and "anastomosis." His idea that on these lines the technical criticism of lyric verse may be reduced to definiteness (*Laws of Verse*, p. 12), seems to me to be visionary—at least, as regards "Syzygy" and "Synectic."

men of their way of life and the men of other ways of life. And one of the sure signs of this atrophy and hypertrophy of the literary senses is the spontaneous anger which so many literary men show at the suggestion that literary judgment can be made subject to the method of science, even in the most general sense. There is here involved, indeed, one of the last problems of critical science, the problem of deciding when a specialty shall be held to have overbalanced an intellectual life. Even as the highest capacity runs the greater risk of collapsing into insanity, though it certainly *is* not insanity, the expert pursuit of any one art or activity runs the risk of subordinating many forms of mental activity to that one; so that the poet, going beyond the main region of his art, tends to see and express all his ideas in poetry, and the musician, equally, all in music; till the person of balanced and distributed culture is jarred and repelled by finding propositions which are properly of philosophy and casuistry and history and special psychology set down or swathed up in verse and music, which, by reason of the forcing of one method on disparate processes of thought, become for him bad as verse and music. The specialist may retort that the objector is but a dilettant; that music and poetry are fit to express all things for those sufficiently deep in music and poetry; and that only these higher developments are great or admirable. In strictness, such a dispute is insoluble, in the way in which deep temperamental oppositions of mind and bias are irreconcilable. But the critic may find a not unprofitable or thankless part of his work in framing a working ideal of culture and fitness as between diverging fanaticisms of taste, and so retaining for mankind the provinces that are in danger of being overrun and walled-in by the one-idea'd.

THEORY AND PRACTICE OF CRITICISM

With such tasks, such possibilities, and such duties, he has surely enough to do, as beside any brain-worker whatever. That there is for him no finality, no "last word," no objective fixity of result, such as men are wont loosely to connect with the idea of "science," will be made a reproach to him only by those who do not distinguish between the spirit and purpose of science and certain of its data. And that he is finally a propagandist, an artist in judgment, so to speak, will be held to mark him off from scientific function only by those who miss the very plain truth that all scientific teaching commonly so called is at bottom propaganda and the expression of an intellectual bias. At a time when it is zealously sought to turn this truth against all science, in the interest of Irrationalism, which is intellectual Anarchism, its use in the service of reason and science may perhaps be the more readily agreed to. And to the critic, finally, the certainty that, do what he may, he will leave inconsistency and oversight and fallacy in his work for the children of his tribe to detect, need be no more paralysing a thought than the general certainty of the mutation of all things. He plays his part like another. In the struggle of opinions for survival he takes his chance as all opinion-makers must.

POE
(1885)

I

SINCE all literary cases must be periodically rejudged, each generation's opinions on any phase of the past being part of its special relation to things, it is strictly as needless to justify the plea for a fresh trial in any one case as it is vain to deny it. Demurrers have been too often made to leave any difficulty about their rebuttal. Evolution is become a name potent to put down the most obstreperous conservative in criticism. It is involved in that law, however, that we shall all of us continue to have our particular leanings, and that some problems will peculiarly appeal to the general mind at given junctures. And while it is part of the here-ensuing argument that less than due hearing as well as less than justice has been granted in the case of Edgar Allan Poe, it is probably true that to-day even more than ever men feel the fascination of the general problem falling under his name.

Just because of its fascination, indeed, the Poe problem has been less methodically handled than most. Its aspects are so bizarre that critics have been more concerned to declare as much than to sum them up with scientific exactitude. First the ear of the world was won with a biography unparalleled in literature for its calculated calumny, a slander so comprehensive and so circumstantial that to this day perhaps most people who have heard of Poe regard him as what he himself called "that *monstrum horrendum*, an unprincipled man of genius," with almost no moral virtue and lacking almost no vice. It was an ex-clergyman, Griswold, who launched the legend; and another clergyman, Gilfillan, improved on it to the extent of suggesting that the poet broke his wife's heart so as to be able to write a poem about her. The average mind being, however, a little less ready than the clerical to believe and utter evil, there at length grew up a body of vindication which for instructed readers has displaced the sinister myth of the early records. Vindication, as it happened, began immediately on the publication of Griswold's memoir; only, the slander had the prestige of book form, and of the copyright edition of Poe's works, while the defence was at first confined to newspapers; hence an immense start for the former: but at length generous zeal triumphed to the extent of creating an almost stainless effigy of the poet—stainless save for the constitutional flaw which was confessed only to claim for it a human pity, and the faults of tone and temper which came of nervous malady and undue toil. Then there came a reaction, the facts were more closely studied and more unsympathetically pronounced upon; the unsleeping ill-will towards the poet's name in his own country still had the literary field and favour, and the last and most ambitious edition of his works is supervised by a none too friendly critic.* Good and temperate criticism has been forthcoming between

* This holds true, unfortunately, of the still later complete edition, by Messrs. Stedman and Woodberry.

whiles; but there is still room, one fancies, for an impartial re-statement of the facts.

"It would seem," writes Mrs. Sarah Helen Whitman, the American poetess, sometime the *fiancée* of Poe, and one of the vindicators of his memory, "it would seem that the true point of view from which his genius should be regarded has yet to be sought."* The full force of that observation, perhaps, cannot be felt unless it be read in context with some of the sentences in which Mrs. Whitman sets forth her own point of view :—

" Wanting in that supreme central force or faculty of the mind, whose function is a God-conscious and God-adoring faith, Edgar Poe sought earnestly and conscientiously for such solution of the great problems of thought as were alone attainable to an intellect hurled from its balance by the abnormal preponderance of the analytical and imaginative faculties."

" These far-wandering comets, not less than 'the regular, calm stars,' obey a law and follow a pathway that has been marked out for them by infinite Wisdom and essential Love." †

The theism exemplified in these passages appears to be the reigning religion in the United States, and is doubtless common enough everywhere else; and it certainly seems sufficiently clear that for people whose minds oscillate between conceptions of Poe's intellect as hurled from its balance and as wisely guided by a loving God who deprived it of the faculty of God-consciousness —for such people the "true point of view from which his genius should be regarded" must indeed be far to seek. That point of view can hardly be one from which you explain the infinite while perplexed by the finite; it is to be attained not *à priori* but *à posteriori*; that is to say, Poe's life and his works have to be studied with an eye, not to discovering a scheme of infinite wisdom, or even to finding a "point of view," but simply to the

* *Edgar Poe and his Critics*, p. 59.
† *Ibid.* pp. 33-4, 60.

noting of the facts and the arranging of them. The true point of view is surely that from which you see things.

Much, of course, depends on methods of observation. At the outset, we are confronted by the facts that Poe's father married imprudently at eighteen, and that the lady was an actress. That is either a mere romantic detail or a very important fact, according as Poe is regarded as an organism or as an immortal soul. Here indeed, the point of view means the seeing or the not seeing of certain facts; but as most people to-day have some little faith in the operation of heredity, it may be assumed that the significance of Poe's parentage is admitted when it is mentioned. Recent investigators have come to the conclusion that David Poe was not merely romantic and reckless, but given to the hard drinking which was so common in the Southern States in his time; and thus, coming of a father of intemperate habits and headlong impulses, and of a mother whose very profession meant excitement and shaken nerves, Poe had before him tremendous probabilities of an erratic career. As fate would have it, the man who adopted the little Edgar on the death of the young parents (they both died of consumption) did everything to aggravate and nothing to counteract the temperamental flaws of the life he took in charge. We know that Edgar's brother William Henry, who may or may not have been equally ill-managed by the friend who adopted him, turned out a clever scapegrace and died young; but certain it is that Mr. Allan was no wise guardian to Edgar. The habits of the house were Southern and convivial; the clever child was petted, flattered, and spoiled; and it seems that Poe might have been made a toper by his surroundings even if he had no bias that way. Again, Mr. Allan was rich, and Poe had no prospective necessities of labour, no sense of obligation to be methodical; which makes it the more natural that his later life should be a failure financially, and the more remarkable that he should exhibit unusual powers of close and orderly thought. Finally, the boy's shifting life; his four years' schooling in England (where in the opinion of his teacher, his guardian did him serious harm by giving him too much pocket-money), and later at Richmond; his brief military cadetship at West Point, his headlong trip to Europe, and his year's stay there, of which nothing seems to be now known, and his studentship at the Virginia University—all tended to deprive him of the benefits of habit, which might conceivably have been some safeguard against his hereditary instability; and at the same time his training tended to develop, though inadequately and at random, his purely intellectual powers, while supplying him with no moral guidance worth mentioning. Such a character required the very wisest management: it had either bad management or none. It was therefore only too natural that the youth should be self-willed and insubordinate at West Point, and much given to gambling at college.

The other side of the picture, however, must be kept in view. While apparently loosely related to life in respect of the normal affections (he seems to have had little communication with his brother, no very strong attachment to his sister, and no attachment to Mr. Allan), he was very far from being the unfeeling and loveless creature he was so long believed to be. He seems to have described himself accurately when he wrote of his uncommon and invariable tenderness to animals; and the intensity of his affections where they were really called out is revealed by the story of his passionate grief on the death of the lady, the mother of one of his comrades, who befriended him in schoolboyhood. Abnormal in his grief as in the play of all his faculties, and blindly bent even then on piercing the mystery of the sepulchre, the boy passed long night vigils on her grave, clinging, beyond death, to the first being he had learned utterly to love. And an important statement is made as to the manner of his marriage by a lady who knew him and his connections well.* The majority of respectable readers, probably, have regarded Poe's marriage to his beautiful and penniless young cousin as one of his acts of culpable recklessness; but according to the account in question, it was rather a deed of generous devotion. He had acted as a boy tutor to Virginia Clemm in her early childhood, and when, after his final rupture with Mr. Allan, he went to reside with his aunt,† the young girl acquired a worship for him. According to this story it was on Mrs. Clemm's impressing on him, when he contemplated leaving her house after being an inmate for two years, the absolute absorption of the girl in his existence, that he proposed the marriage. She was hardly fourteen, poor child, but she was of the precocious Southern blood, and her youth seems to have made her mother only the more fearful of the effect of separation from her adored cousin. Poe's marriage was on this view an act not of free choice but of prompt generosity. Whatever the truth may be, he was a very good husband. Devoted as she was up to her death, Virginia never gave him the full intellectual companionship he would have sought in a wife; but there is now no pre-

* Art. "Last Days of E. A. Poe," in *Scribner's Magazine*, March 1878.

† Mr. Ingram says (*Life*, i. 106–7) that Mrs. Clemm "never did know" where Poe went after the rupture (1831); and that "extant correspondence proves" that Poe did not live with her in 1831–2, "and, apparently, that he never lived with her until after his marriage."

tence that he ever showed her the shadow of unkindness, and it is admitted that in her last days he was tenderness itself. All which is a fair certificate of good domestic disposition, as men and poets go.

What then was there in Poe's life as a whole to justify detraction? When the testimony is fully sifted the discreditable charges are found to be: first and chiefly, that he repeatedly gave way to his hereditary vice of alcoholism; secondly, that he committed one lapse from literary integrity; thirdly, that he was often splenetic and sometimes unjust as a critic; fourthly, that he showed ingratitude and enmity to some who befriended him. Setting aside his youthful passionateness and prodigality, that is now the whole serious moral indictment against him. The insinuations and assertions of Griswold, to the effect that he committed more than one gross outrage, are found to be either proven false or wholly without proof; and many of the biographer's aspersions on his disposition have been indignantly repudiated by those who knew him well—as Mr. G. R. Graham and Mr. N. P. Willis, both of whom employed him. As for the alleged ingratitude to unnamed friends, it seems only fair to ask whether any such faults, if real, may not be attributed to the havoc ultimately wrought in Poe's delicately balanced temperment by fits of drinking.* Mr. R. H. Stoddard† has given an account of some very singular ill-treatment he received from Poe while the latter edited the *Broadway Journal*—treatment which at once suggests some degree of cerebral derangement on Poe's part; and a story

---

* In the memoir prefixed to the last edition of Poe's works, it is stated that he resorted at times to opium as well as to alcohol; and this seems likely enough. In that case there would be all the more risk of bad effects on character.

† In his memoir in Widdleton's ed. of Poe, 1880.

told of his resenting a home-thrust of criticism by a torrent of curses, goes to create the same impression. This was in his latter years, at a time when a thimbleful of sherry could excite him almost to frenzy, and when, according to one hostile writer, he had developed incurable cerebral disease. Setting aside the question of his fairness as a critic, which will be discussed further on, there remains to be considered his one alleged deflection from literary honesty. He did publish under his own name a manual of Conchology which apparently incorporated, without acknowledgment, passages from a work by Captain Brown published in Glasgow; and it is alleged by Griswold, and implied by Mr. Stoddard, that the American book is substantially based on Brown's. But there is really no proof of anything like important plagiarism, and the slightness of the evidence is very suggestive of a weak case. Mr. Stoddard, who exhibits a distinct and not altogether unnatural bias against his subject, prints parallel passages which do seemingly amount to "conveyance"; but he unjustifiably omits to answer the statement on the other side, that the *Manual of Conchology* was compiled under the supervision of Professor Wyatt; that Poe contributed largely to it; that the publishers accordingly wished to use his popular name on the title-page; and that, finally, the book, though corresponding in part to Brown's because avowedly based, like that, on the system of Lamarck, is essentially an independent compilation. Such is the statement of Professor Wyatt, and the matter ought to be easily settled.* What Mr. Stoddard does is to convey the impression that Poe copied whole-

* See, on this and all other matters concerning Poe, the *Life* by John H. Ingram, a work of painstaking vindication which earns the gratitude of every one interested in Poe. The American *Life*, by W. Gill, is mainly compiled from it.

POE

sale, though only a few appropriations are cited. Now, whereas naked appropriation of another man's ideas in his own wording, in a work of ostensibly original reasoning or imagination, must be pronounced a serious act of literary dishonesty, the incorporation of some one else's paragraphs or sentences is so common a practice among scientific and other compilers, that it may reasonably be classed as a conventionally innocent proceeding, not even to be likened to those innumerable acts of lax morality in commerce for which it is almost idle to denounce any offender singly. In any case, Poe never pretended to be doing anything more than a compilation, and he had a colleague in the work. For the rest, there is ample evidence as to his scrupulous honesty and fidelity in his relations with his literary employers; and it is not recorded that he ever inflicted loss on any man, any more than unkindness on those about him. We sum up, then, that Poe's mental and moral balance, delicate by inheritance, was injured by the drinking habits into which he repeatedly relapsed; but that his constitution was such that what was to others extremely moderate indulgence could be for him disastrous excess.

Now, it might be argued with almost irresistible force that such a case as this is one for pity and not for blame—that a man of Poe's heredity and obvious predisposition to brain disease is to be looked on in the same spirit as is one who suffers from downright hereditary insanity. But, seeing it may be replied that all vices are similarly the result of hereditary and brain conditions, and that we should either blame all offenders to whom we allow freedom of action, or none, I am inclined to rest the defence of Poe on a somewhat different basis; and to substitute for a deprecatory account of his moral disadvantages the assertion that morally he compares favourably with the majority of his fellow creatures. Whether that is either a vain paradox or a piece of cynicism let the reader judge.

It is, one sees, the habit of most people, in judging of any character in favour of which they are not prejudiced, to try it by the standard of an imaginary personage who is without any serious fault. The strength of this disposition can be seen at any performance of a melodrama in a theatre, the great body of the audience being obviously in strong sympathy with virtues of which there is reason to doubt their own general possession; and strongly hostile even to vices which they may fairly be presumed in many cases to share. In the phrase of Montesquieu, "mankind, although reprobates in detail, are always moralists in gross." As for the general disposition to condemn the vices we are not inclined to, that may be dismissed as a commonplace. And yet it is one of the rarest things to find these facts recognised in conduct. A rational moral code is hardly ever to be met with. Intemperance—to bring the question to the concrete—may be reduced in common with most other vices to an admitted lack of self-control; but it is clearly blamed for some other reason than that it evidences such a defect. If a man or woman falls hopelessly in love, however abject be the loss of self-command, the average outsider never thinks of calling the enamoured one vicious merely on account of the extremity of the passion. That, on the contrary, is regarded by many people as rather a fine thing. If, again, a man is either extremely selfish or extremely prodigal, while he may be censured for his fault, he is still held to be less blamable than the mere intemperate drinker. Sometimes the censure passed on the latter is justified on the score that his vice impoverishes others; but this is not always so; and in any case the selfish or ill-natured man and the spendthrift may do equal injury to the happiness of others. The truth is that the revulsion against the drunkard's vice arises from a keen sense of the physical degradation it works in its subject; and how strong and how instinctive this is can be told by many men who have contemplated in helpless fury the excesses of relatives or dear friends. In these cases severe blame may be justified by the feeling that the keenest reprobation is necessary to sting the drunkard into moral reaction; but it would be difficult to show that when a man is dead it is equitable or reasonable to apply the same degree of blame to him in reckoning his relation to his fellows. All criticism of dead celebrities should be regulated by two considerations : first, the risk or absence of risk that omission to censure for certain faults may encourage the living to repeat them; second, the need or otherwise for resisting any tendency to blame certain faults unduly. I confess I can see no other safe or rational principle on which to apply, in moral criticism of the dead, the general law that men's actions are the outcome of their antecedents and environment. If so much be conceded, it must be allowed that there is no more need to-day to denounce Poe for his unhappy vice than to asperse Charles Lamb—which Carlyle, however, has done with the self-righteousness of the chief of Pharisees. Nobody is likely to be encouraged in tippling by the fact that we speak with tender pity of Lamb's failing. The query—

> Who wouldn't take to drink if drink'll
> Make a man like Rip Van Winkle?

is not serious.

No one in these days, indeed, does think it necessary

to pass damnatory sentence on Lamb ; * and the difference between the ordinary judgments on Lamb and Poe is a striking sample of the capriciousness of average morality. Lamb's weakness for gin is regarded as morally on a level with his poor sister's chronic homicidal mania ; and of course, strictly speaking, his misfortune was as much a matter of cerebral constitution as hers. But surely if Mary Lamb is to be spoken of with pure pity for that during a fit of madness she caused the death of her beloved mother, and certainly if Charles is to be similarly pitied, we are committed to speaking gently of such a case as Poe's. Yet people whose feeling for Lamb is entirely affectionate speak of Poe with austere disapproval; and I cannot but think that the explanation of this and much other asperity towards Poe's memory is the singular quality of his literary work, especially of his tales. It has been remarked a hundred times that these are unique in literature in their almost complete destitution in the moral element, commonly so-called. They are one and all studies either of peculiar incident, intellectual processes, or strange idiosyncrasy ; and the ordinary reader, accustomed in fiction to a congenial atmosphere of moral feeling, and to judicial contrasts of character such as he sees and makes in actual life, becomes chilled and daunted in the eerie regions to which Poe carries him. The common result seems to be the conclusion that the story-teller was lacking in moral feeling; and though every one does not give effect to his conclusion as the Rev. Mr. Gilfillan did, such a conviction is of course not compatible with sympathy. How crudely and cruelly people can act on

---

* Mr. Birrell, in his essay on Charles Lamb (*Obiter Dicta*, 2nd series, p. 229), generously exclaims against some who do bestow on Lamb an odious pity. Save in the case of Carlyle, I had not before seen any trace of this.

POE

such semi-instinctive and unreasoned judgments is shown in the correspondence between Mrs. Whitman and Poe during the period of their engagement. "You do *not* love me," writes Poe passionately, "or you would have felt too thorough a sympathy with the sensitiveness of my nature to have so wounded me as you have done with this terrible passage of your letter—'How often I have heard it said of you, He has great intellectual power, but no principle—no moral sense'." One is disposed to echo the first clause; but the blow which Poe feels so acutely is only one of those moral stupidities of which naturally tender-hearted women are capable precisely because their moral and affectional sensibilities at times overbalance their common sense. Nothing could be more witlessly and inexcusably cruel, and at the same time nothing could be more absurd; for if Poe really were without principle any protests of his to the contrary could be worth nothing; and if the accusation were false he had been ruthlessly insulted to no purpose; but the cruelty was probably unconscious, or nearly so. Poor Mrs. Whitman wrote, as lovers will, to extract an assurance which could have no value in the eye of reason, but which emotion craved; for the moment half believing what she said, but wishing to be disabused of her suspicion by a passionate denial. That she obtained. The most fortunate thing for a man so impeached would be the possession of a strong sense of humour, though that might involve a coolness of head which would jeopardise the amour. But poor Poe, wounded as he was, took God to witness that "With the exception of some follies and excesses, which I bitterly lament, but to which I have been driven by intolerable sorrow, and which are hourly committed by others without attracting any notice whatever, I can call to mind no act of my life which would bring a blush to my cheek—or to yours." And after alluding to the malignant attacks that had been made on him, for one of which he brought a successful libel action, and the enmity he had set up by his uncompromising criticisms, he cries: "And you know all this—*you* ask *why* I have enemies. . . . Forgive me if there be bitterness in my tone." On which Mr. Ingram warmly comments that the man who wrote so must have been sincere. It is hardly necessary to urge it. Mrs. Whitman did but echo the idle verdict of conventional minds on an abnormal nature. With fuller knowledge she wrote after his death that, "so far from being selfish or heartless, his devotional fidelity to the memory of those he loved would by the world be regarded as fanatical;"* and all the evidence goes to show that, whatever were his faults of taste as a critic, his moral attitude to his fellow creatures was that of one who was, as he claims for himself, quixotically high-minded. The truth is, an extensive fallacy underlies the aversion which many people have for Poe—the fallacy, namely, of assuming that a large share of what is vaguely called moral or human sentiment, in an author or in any one else, implies a security for right feeling or conduct; and that the absence of such sentiment from an author's fiction, or from any one's talk, implies a tendency to wrongdoing. And the same fallacy, I think, lurks under the observation that Poe's mind, if not immoral, was non-moral. The assumption in question is a sentimentality that is discredited by accurate observation of life. We know, as a matter of fact, that Poe's attachments, once formed, were deep and intensely faithful; nothing, for instance, could be closer or

---

* *Edgar Poe and his Critics*, p. 48.

lovelier than the tie between him and Mrs. Clemm : and his sensitiveness was extreme where his affections were concerned, though his friendly employer Willis speaks of him as a man who in his business life "never smiled or spoke a propitiatory or deprecating word." In fact, if Poe's private life be compared with that of Hawthorne before the latter's marriage, Poe will seem the man of domestic and sociable tendencies, and the other a loveless egoist. His son-in-law tells us that Hawthorne had very little intercourse with his mother and sisters while living in the same house with them, and that he frequently had his meals left for him at his locked door.* Southey, too, saw little of his family. Yet no one shivers over Hawthorne and Southey as minds without hearts.

To return, in a perfectly dispassionate spirit, to Lamb, we see that his wealth of kindly sympathy did not save him from alcoholism ; and it could easily be shown that a great many moralists have been either gravely immoral characters or unamiable and variously objectionable. Many of us have never been able to regard Dante as a satisfactory personality, with his irrational and capriciously cruel code and his general inhumanity ; and a good many will agree that Carlyle, who was always moralising, was prone to gross injustice, and presents a rather mixed moral spectacle in his own life. The slight on Poe's moral nature was first published by the sentimental Griswold, who is proved to have been a peculiarly mean and malignant slanderer ; † and

* Mr. Henry James's *Hawthorne*, p. 38, citing Mr. Lathrop.

† Of Griswold Mr. Ingram writes (*Academy*, Oct. 13, 1883) that he "bore too unsavoury a character for public examination; but those interested in the subject may be referred to his own account (in the British Museum) why he repudiated his second wife. Thackeray, having proved him a liar, told him so publicly, and would not touch hi proffered hand ; while Dickens convicted him

the moral Mr. Gilfillan invented a gross calumny. Run down the list of men of genius of modern times who have discussed conduct and human nature, and you will find an extremely large proportion against whom could be charged blemishes of character and conduct from which Poe was free. The ferocity and fanaticism of Dante, the grossness of Chaucer, the hard marital selfishness of Milton, the brutality of Luther, the boorishness of Johnson, the ripe self-love of Wordsworth, the malice of Pope, the egoism of Goethe, the murky and selfish spleen of Carlyle, the bigotry of Southey—all these are repellent and anti-social qualities which cannot be charged against Edgar Poe. In short, the ideal man of lively moral feeling and entirely beneficent conduct, by contrast with whom Poe is seen to be an incomplete human being, has never existed in flesh and blood; and if we take the rational course of striking an average of poor humanity, we shall find, as before submitted, that our subject does not fall below it. We may even go further. In regard to the widespread and false notion that Poe was a libertine, we may endorse the assertion of Mr. Stedman "that professional men and artists, in spite of a vulgar belief to the contrary, are purity itself compared with men engaged in business, and idle men of the world."*
Let us in fairness confess that the average man or woman is likely to be one or other of these things—narrow, or bigoted, or cowardly, or fickle, or mean, or gross, or faithless, or coldly selfish, or disingenuous, or hard, or slanderous, or recklessly unjust; though one

---

of fraud, and made his employers pay for it." Poe's review of Griswold's *Poets and Poetry of America* shows (imprudently enough) the small esteem in which he held his future biographer, who seems to have made or kept up his acquaintance in order to retaliate for the critique in question.

* *Edgar Allan Poe*, p. 92.

or other of these qualities may co-exist with generosity, or philanthropy, or probity. If we recognise so much, we shall cease to sermonise on Poe's failings; and proceed rather to consider how rare and how fine his work was.

Yet another fallacy, however—to call it by no worse name—blocks for some the way to a sound appreciation. One American critic,* appealing to the prevailing dislike of Poe in the States, has grounded a sweeping depreciation of his work on the proposition that he was subject to brain epilepsy. On that head, clearly, there is no need for friendlier people to wish to make out a negative. To begin with, there is independent and unprejudiced testimony that Poe suffered from a brain trouble; and whether or not that trouble was cerebral epilepsy is a question of detail chiefly important to thoughtful specialists. During the serious illness which fell on Poe after his wife's death, Mrs. Clemm's nursing labours were shared by a true and valued friend of the little family, Mrs. Marie Louise Shew, who was a doctor's only daughter, and had received a medical education; and this lady has written as follows :—

" I made my diagnosis, and went to the great Dr. Mott with it. I told him that at best, when Mr. Poe was well, his pulse beat only ten regular beats, after which it suspended, or intermitted (as doctors say). I decided that in his best health he had lesion of one side of the brain, and as he could not bear stimulants or tonics, without producing insanity, I did not feel much hope that he could be raised up from brain fever brought on by extreme suffering of mind and body — actual want and hunger and cold having been borne by this heroic husband in order to supply food, medicine, and comforts to his dying wife—until exhaustion and lifelessness were so near at every reaction of the fever that even sedatives had to be administered with extreme caution." †

* Writing in *Scribner's Magazine*, vol. x. 1875.
† Ingram's *Life of Poe*, ii. 115.

POE

The latter details may be noted as telling us something of Poe's moral nature; the diagnosis as a fairly decisive deliverance on the brain question, especially when taken in connection with other medical evidence, and testimonies as to the startling effect of a mouthful of sherry or even a glass of beer on Poe at times. There is altogether good reason to hold that his brain was diseased. But what then? To say nothing of the well-worn saw that great wits have their place near the region of madness, biologists* have told us that cerebral and other disease may intelligibly be and has actually been a cause of exceptional intellectual capacity † What of Cuvier's hydrocephalus and Keats's precocious maturity? Even scrofula, and worse affections than that, have been maintained or surmised to promote cerebration: the formula being that certain conditions which are pathologically classed as morbid are psychologically important though impermanent variations. Cromwell's inner life has phenomena in some points analogous to Poe's; and if it comes to epilepsy, we have to reckon with a confident classification of Mahomet among that order of sufferers. Lamb was for a time in his youth actually insane. But why multiply cases? In what other instance has it been proposed to make light of a man's mental achievements because his brain is known to have been flawed? I am not aware that any deliberate attempt was ever made to belittle what merits Cowper has, because of his

* This was written before the thesis of "the insanity of genius" had become popular.

† The assailant knows as much, for he cites Dr. Maudsley as "very positive in his opinion that the world is indebted for a great part of its originality, and for certain special forms of intellect, to individuals who . . . . have sprung from families in which there is some predisposition to epileptic insanity." But the attack is as destitute of coherence as of justice and fitness of tone.

POE

affliction ; or that Comte's serious antagonists have ever given countenance to a condemnation of his philosophy as a whole on the strength of his fit of alienation, even though mad enough passages can easily be cited from his works. It has been left for an American, writing almost unchallenged by the literary class in Poe's native land, to proceed from an argument that Poe was an epileptic to a monstrous corollary of unmeasured detraction from almost every species of credit he has ever received.* Baudelaire, discussing Griswold's biography, asked whether in America they have no law against letting curs into the cemeteries : and it is hardly going too far to say that this latest attack on a great memory would never have had even a hearing in a well-ordered literary republic. To discuss it in detail would be to concede too much ; but I have

* To show how far malice may go astray in reasoning from misfortune to demerit, it may be worth while to point to the absolute failure of this writer's attempt to make Poe's brain trouble a means of discrediting his work. Poe, he tells us, passed through three psychological periods : the first, one in which he "seems to depend for artistic effect on minuteness of detail," as in the *Descent into the Maelström*, *The Gold Bug*, the *Case of Monsieur Valdemar*, and *Hans Pfaall* ("imitated," says the writer, with his usual culpable inaccuracy, "from the *Moon Hoax*") ; the second, a time of predilection for minute analysis, such as is shown in *The Mystery of Marie Roget;* and the third, a spell of morbid introspection, producing such tales as *The Fall of the House of Usher*. Now, what are the facts ? The last mentioned story was published in 1839 ; *Ligeia* —a story in the same "morbid" taste—in 1838 ; *Berenice*, *Morella*, and *Shadow*, all productions of the weird order, in 1835 ; *Silence* in 1838 ; and the eminently introspective tale of *William Wilson* in 1839 ; while *The Facts in the Case of M. Valdemar* appeared in 1845.; *The Murders in the Rue Morgue* in 1841, and *Marie Roget* in 1842. Thus we have the works of "morbid introspection" *before* the specifically cited studies in minute detail and minute analysis—the *Usher* story before the *Marie Roget* and the *Valdemar;* and such a production as *Morella* almost contemporary with *Hans Pfaall*. The theory of development breaks down at every point.

thought it well to cite the attack with the note that not only has no adequate recognition been given in America to Poe's intellectual eminence (I exclude the friendly memoirs and vindications), but this extravagantly wrong-headed denial of it secures the vogue due to a true estimate.

The ill-meant aspersion, let us hope, will after all make for a kindlier feeling, among those at least whose goodwill a man of letters need wish to have for his memory. In any case, it is incredible that any literary reputation should be for ever measured on such principles as those above glanced at. Whatever be the whole explanation of the treatment Poe has received in his own country, whether it be his small affinity to the national life or the abundance of the ill-will he aroused by pitiless criticism of small celebrities, criticism in the States must needs come in time to the temperate study of his work and his endowment on their merits. What follows is an attempt in that direction.

II

It is worthy of note that fully nine-tenths of the criticism passed on Poe, appreciative and otherwise, has been directed to his small body of poetry. The fact serves at once to prove the one-sidedness of the average literary man and the range of Poe's power. He had a working knowledge of astronomy, of navigation, of mechanics, and of physics; he certainly compiled a manual of conchology, and had at least dipped into entomology; he could work out cyphers in half a dozen languages; he delighted in progressions of close and sustained reasoning; he had a decided capacity for logic and philosophy; he eagerly followed and easily assimilated, or even in part anticipated, the modern physical theories of the universe; he was a keen and scientific literary critic; and in addition to all this he produced some of the most remarkable imaginative writing and some of the finest poetry of the century. But his critics have been, with very few exceptions, men of purely literary equipment; verse-writers and bellettrists and story-tellers, who judge only verse and prose and character. Sharing their deprivations, I have gone through most of their writings on the watch for an estimate of the scientific and constructive capacity shown in certain of the Tales, and have found an almost unanimous and doubtless judicious silence on the subject. An occasional non-committal phrase about the *Eureka*, and a few generalities on the scientific element in the Tales, represent the critical commentary on the ratiocinative side of Poe's intellect. Now, to treat his verse as his most significant product is to ignore half his remarkableness, and to miss those kinds of strength and eminence in his mind which most effectively outweigh the flaws of his character and the occasional exorbitances of his judgment. Save in his own country, indeed, the Tales have had popular recognition enough. Poe's countrymen never bought up Griswold's edition of his works, and have till quite recently been without a complete collection of them; but Mr. Gill has calculated that while the poems are five-fold more popular in England than in America, the stories are even more widely admired among us; and they have been thoroughly naturalised in France in a complete and admirable translation, chiefly by Baudelaire; besides being reproduced to a greater or less extent in nearly every other European language. Seeing that they were eagerly read on their first appearance in America, it must be assumed that, as Mr. Gill suggests, the public there were scared off by Griswold's slanders and the consequent myth. But if, with all this European vogue for the Tales, critics continue to descant chiefly on the poetry, the inference as to its impressive quality is irresistible.

Perhaps by reason of the sub-rational tendency to disparage specially an author of one's own country who is loudly praised by foreigners, some living American writers have spoken with absolute contempt of Poe's poetry. Mr. Henry James, for instance, has a strange phrase about his "very valueless verses;"* and Mr. Stoddart's strongest feeling in the matter appears to be an aversion to the refrains—perhaps not an unnatural attitude towards Poe on the part of a critic who believes a poet may have too much art. In these circumstances it may still be expedient to follow Mr. Stedman in bearing witness to the quality of Poe's poetry. It is perhaps true, as has been said by Oliver Wendell Holmes, that there is almost no poet between whose best and worst verse there is a wider disparity; but that is rather by reason of the fineness of the good than of the badness of the bad; and the latter, in any case, consists simply of the long poems of Poe's youth —*Al Aaraaf*, *Tamerlane*, and the *Scenes from Politian*. Mr. Lang, in editing the whole, has not scrupled to indicate his feeling that these are hardly worth reading; and while one feels that in that view perhaps the proper course were not to edit them, so much may be conceded.

---

* In the essay on Baudelaire in the volume *French Poets and Novelists*, ed. 1878, p. 76. Since this essay was first printed I find that in the Tauchnitz edition of his book Mr. James has altered "valueless" to "superficial." I let my criticism (*infra*) stand as it was written, only pointing out that the change of epithet is significant of weakness of ground, and that the second form is even worse than the first. When was verse so aspersed before?

In regard to some of the successful poems, again, there is to be reckoned with the disenchanting effect of extreme popularity; an influence of the most baffling sort, often blurring one's critical impression in a way for which there is hardly any remedy. The choicest air, as it had once seemed, may be made to acquire associations of the barrel organ; and it may ultimately become a fine question whether it was not a vice in it to be so associable. One may brazen out one's early attachment, as, I fancy, Mr. Arnold did when he lately insisted that *Lucy Gray* was a "beautiful success;" but when loyalty to an old opinion is justified merely by its survival, criticism is turned out of doors. So that, lest we are insidiously led into committing the unpardonable critical sin of certificating popular poetry by its popularity, it will be well to consider briefly in the concrete the merits of *The Raven*. Many of us, I suspect, have at one time developed a suspicion that that much-recited work is not poetry of the first order; and the suspicion is deepened when we reflect that the distinction of learning it by heart in our youth was conferred on it in common with other works as to which there can now be no critical dubiety. It is difficult to gainsay Mr. Lang when he impugns its right, and that of *Lenore*, to the highest poetical honours: both poems, like *The Bells*, have a certain smell of the lamp, an air of compilation, a suspicion of the inorganic. And yet a studious re-reading of *The Raven* may awaken some remorse for such detractions. Not only has it that impressiveness of central conception which is never lacking in Poe's serious work, but it is really a memorable piece of technique. It is hardly possible to say where inspiration lacks and mechanism intervenes: the poem is an effective unity. Some hold that the touches of plagiarism—the "uncertain" sound of the "purple curtain," and the collocation of "desolate" and "desert land," both echoes from Mrs. Browning's *Lady Geraldine*—* serve to discredit the whole; but that is surely false criticism. The problem is, whether the appropriations are assimilated; and they clearly are. Mrs. Browning herself expressed the commanding individuality of the work in the phrase "this power which is felt." The poem has that distinctive attribute of most of Poe's writing, the pregnancy of idea, the compulsive imagination which fascinates and dominates the reader. One feels behind it a creative and sustaining power, a power as of absolute intellect. To feel specifically the impact of this influence, let the reader compare the poem as a whole with *Lady Geraldine's Courtship*, and note how, ample as is the poetess's gift of speech, choice as are her harmonies, and fortunate as are many of her lines, there is yet a something spasmodic and convulsive pervading the whole, a tone of passionate weakness, in full keeping with the hysterical character of the girlish hero, which gives a quite fatal emphasis to the frequent lapses of expression, these seeming to belong to weakness and slovenliness; while in reading *The Raven* there is hardly for a moment room for a disrespectful sensation. The imperious brain of the "maker," as the old vernacular would straightforwardly name him, stamps its authority on every line; and the subtle sense of the artist's puissance remains unaffected by the despairing avowal of the conclusion. The speaker may sink prostrate, but the poem is never shaken in its

---

* One of the disputed points as to which there should never have been any dispute is the question of priority in these passages. One critic, who imputes plagiarisms to Poe, brusquely asserts that Mrs. Browning was the imitator. The plain facts are that her poem was published in 1844, and Poe's in 1845, and that Poe admired her poetry greatly.

serene movement and marble firmness of front. It has "cette extraordinaire élévation, cette exquise délicatesse, cet accent d'immortalité qu' Edgar Poe exige de la Muse," remarked on by Baudelaire; and nothing in the poem is more remarkable than the Apollonian impunity with which the poet is able to relax and colloquialise his phraseology. Mrs. Browning could not venture without disaster on such an infusion of realism into idealism as the "Sir, said I, or Madam," and "the fact is, I was napping:" her Pegasus, in view of his habitual weakness of knee, would be felt to have stumbled in such a line as

Though its answer little meaning, *little relevancy bore*"—

where Poe sweeps us over by his sheer unswerving intentness on his theme. The explanation seems to be that the writer himself is without apparent consciousness of artistic fallibility—that he is pure intellect addressing an abstract reader; and that, as he never seems to strain after words, he has a regal air of having said precisely what should be said; so that when we read of "a stately raven of the *saintly* days of yore," we hesitate to impugn the fitness of the term. What, then, is it in *The Raven* that takes it out of the first rank of poetry? Well then, first, the admixture of simple oddity, which is disallowed by Poe's own law that poetry is the "rhythmical creation of beauty"; and, second, the decomposability of the structure at two points, namely, the factitious rustling of the curtains, which have no business to rustle, and the falling of the shadow, which has no right to fall.* These

* Poe, in a letter given by Mr. Ingram (*Life*, i. 275), says his idea about the light was "the bracket candelabrum affixed against the wall, high up above the door and bust, as is often seen in the English palaces (!), and even in some of the better houses of New York." It will not do.

touches are "willed;" and, on reflection, have the effect of obtruding their art upon us; whereas the perfect poem must seem homogeneous and inevitably what it is. It is sometimes argued that the very continuity and clearness of the tale in themselves vitiate the work, as dispelling true glamour; and assuredly, though it is made apparently certain by Poe's own avowal that *The Genesis of the Raven* was a hoax,* there can be little doubt that the poem was most carefully put together. But to depreciate a work of art on such a ground as that is a quite illicit proceeding. Results must be judged on their merits. And, indeed, the mere flaws in the rationale of the piece, scarcely perceptible as they are, would not in themselves suffice to invalidate it, any more than the clear flaw in the logic of the second-last stanza of Keats's *Ode to the Nightingale* discredits that: they do but accentuate the force of the objection to the un-elevated though still dignified tone of the stanzas and the consequent narrative stamp on the whole. But even in making these admissions, the lover of verse must insist on the singular power of the composition; which remains more extraordinary than much other work that is more strictly successful. Poe's second-best verse has a distinction of its own.

If, then, *The Raven* is thus dismissed; and if, as must needs be, *Lenore* is pronounced a piece of brilliant mosaic, and *The Bells* is classed as a fine piece of literary architecture rather than a poetic creation, we shall have left but a small body of work from which to choose our specimens of Poe's fine poetry. But what remains will serve. Poe never professed to make poetry his main aim, or even an aim at all: it was his

* Professor Minto, however, declined to believe that it really was so.

"passion"; and what is here contended is that, many-sided as he was, he had a poetic faculty of the highest kind, among other powers which few or no other poets have possessed. The decisive credentials of perfect poetry are an organic oneness of substance, that substance being of a purer essence than ordinary speech; a quality of meaning which pierces to the sense without the methodic specification of prose; and a charm of rhythm and phrase which is a boon in itself, permanently recognisable as such apart from any truth enclosed. These, broadly speaking, are the "values" of poetry; and he who says Poe's verse is valueless must, I think, be adjudged to be without the poetic sense. Mr. James must presumably have meant one of two things: either that Poe's poetry conveys no moral teachings or descriptions of life and scenery—these constituting the "valuable" element in poetry for those to whom its special qualities do not appeal—or that its art is commonplace. The first objection need only be conceived to be dismissed; the second, supposing it to have been that intended, which I doubt, would need no answer beyond a few quotations. Among Poe's early poems is one *To Helen*, which he is said to have represented as being composed when he was fourteen, the *Helen*, on that view, being supposed to be the lady, mother of his school friend, who was kind to the boy, and whose death he so passionately mourned. In view at once of Poe's habit of mystification and of the nature of the poem, I cannot believe that is the true account of the matter. The verses are not those of a boy of fourteen. But they were undoubtedly written in Poe's teens, and I cite them as constituting one of the most ripely perfect and spiritually charming poems ever written at that or any age :—

POE

"Helen, thy beauty is to me
  Like those Nicæan barks of yore
Which gently, o'er a perfumed sea,
  The weary, way-worn wanderer bore
  To his own native shore.

"On desperate seas long wont to roam,
  Thy hyacinth hair, thy classic face,
Thy Naiad airs have brought me home,
  To the glory that was Greece,
  And* the grandeur that was Rome.

"Lo! in yon brilliant window niche,
  How statue-like I see thee stand,
Thy agate lamp within thy hand—
  Ah, Psyche! from the regions which
  Are Holy Land!"

Merely to credit these verses with "Horatian elegance," as some admiring critics have done, is to render them scant justice. They have not only Horace's fastidiousness of touch (with perhaps the single reservation of the unluckily hackneyed "classic face") but the transfiguring aërial charm of pure poetry, which is not in Horace's line. The two closing lines of the middle stanza have passed into the body of choice distillations of language reserved for immortality; and there is assuredly nothing more exquisite in its kind in English literature than the last stanza. To have written such verses is to have done a perfect thing. Turn next to *The Haunted Palace*, an experiment in the perilous field

---

* Some editions read "To the grandeur." I simply follow that reading which best pleases me. It is interesting to know, by the way, that these famous lines, in the edition of 1831, ran thus:

"To the beauty of fair Greece
  And the grandeur of old Rome."

What a transmutation!

POE

of poetic allegory. What poet had before essayed that with perfect success? I will not venture to say that no one has·; but I can call to mind no instance. According to Griswold, *The Haunted Palace* is a plagiarism from Longfellow's *Beleaguered City*,* a futile imputation, which only serves to help us to a fuller recognition of Poe's success. Personally, I have a certain tenderness for *The Beleaguered City* as being one of the first imaginative poems that impressed my boyhood; but no prejudice of that sort can hinder any one from seeing that the poem is vitiated by its nugatory didacticism— the fatal snare of the allegorist. Mr. James, in his *Hawthorne*, appears to think (though this is not clear) that he has caught Poe condemning himself in a critical declaration against allegory; but I suspect the inconsistency is more apparent than real. Poe almost never, so far as I can see, uses allegory for the purpose of sustaining a thesis, which is the thing he objects to. The generic difference between the allegory of *The Haunted Palace* and that of *The Beleagured City* is that the latter is a kind of confused sermon, while the other is a pure artistic creation—a changing vision projected for its own sake and yoked to no "moral." Didactic poetry there may be, in a happy imposition of poetic quality on a moral truth, which ordinarily gravitates towards prose; but to make allegory pointedly didactic is deliberately to impose prose on the poetic, and this Poe never does in his poetry proper. He simply limns his image and leaves it, a thing of uncontaminated art. *The Haunted Palace* is the allegory of a brain once of royal power, shrined in noble features, but at length become a haunt of madness—a half-conscious allusion,

* The *Palace* appeared first, April 1839; the *City* in November (Ingram's *Life*, i. 160). And Poe accused Longfellow of imitating him!

perhaps, to the poet's own dark destiny; but there is no precept, not even a hint of the ethical: the strange imagination is unrolled in its terrible beauty, and that is all. The singer is a "maker," not a commentator. And then the melody and surprise of the verse!

> " Banners yellow, glorious, golden,
>   On its roof did float and flow,
> (This—all this—was in the olden
>   Time, long ago);
> And every gentle air that dallied,
>   In that sweet day,
> Along the ramparts plumed and pallid,
>   A wingéd Odour went away."

Longfellow could do some things in rhyme and rhythm, but his genial talent did not accomplish such singing as this, and as little could he compass the serene height of strain which Poe maintains with such certainty.

Every charge of poetic plagiarism against Poe does but establish more clearly his utter originality of method.* Mrs. Browning and Longfellow, whom he is charged with imitating, are themselves facile imitators, who, somehow, do not contrive to improve on their originals; but Poe, in the one or two cases in which he really copied in his adult period, lent a new value to what he took. Where he seems to have adopted ideas from others the transmutation is still more striking. A writer already referred to, who is as far astray in

---

* There is a certain air of Nemesis in these charges against Poe, who was apt to be fanatical in imputing plagiarism to others. But it is remarkable that no one has ever pointed out that Poe's own excellent definition of poetry, "the rhythmical creation of beauty" (Essay on *The Poetic Principle*), is a condensation of a sentence by (of all men) Griswold. See Poe's notice of Griswold's *Poets and Poetry of America* (Ingram's ed. of *Works*, iv. 315). It may be noted that

laying as in denying charges of plagiarism against Poe, declares that his *Dreamland* "palpably paraphrases Lucian's *Island of Sleep*"—meaning, I suppose, the description of the Island of Dreams in the *True History*; and the statement is so far true that in Lucian there is a Temple of Night in the Island, and that the categories of the dreams include visions of old friends; but to call the poem a paraphrase is absurd. There is all the difference of seventeen hundred years of art between the Greek's semi-serious fantasy and the profound and magical note of Poe's poem:

> "By a route obscure and lonely,
> Haunted by ill angels only,
> Where an Eidòlon, naméd Night,
> On a black throne reigns upright,
> I have reached these lands but newly
> From an ultimate dim Thule—
> From a wild, weird clime that lieth sublime,
> Out of SPACE—out of TIME."

Genius, Mr. Arnold has well said, is mainly an affair of energy; and the definition would hold for all the work of Poe, whose creations, in the last analysis, are found to draw their power from the extraordinary intensity which belonged to his every mental operation —an intensity perfectly free of violence. Be his fancy ever so shadowy in its inception, he informs it with the impalpable force of intellect till it becomes a vision more enduring than brass. There is no poet who can so "give to aery nothing a local habitation and a name." It was perhaps not so wonderful after all that commonplace people should shun, as hardly belonging

Poe's treatment of Griswold in this notice is remarkably friendly; and whatever of offence he may have given his future biographer in his lecture on the same subject, the latter must have been a malignant soul indeed to seek for it, in the face of such amends, the vile revenge he subsequently took.

to human clay, the personality which brooded out such visions as these :*

> "Lo! Death has reared himself a throne
> In a strange city, lying alone
> Far down within the dim West . . .
>
> "No rays from the Holy Heaven come down
> On the long night-time of that town ;
> But light from out the lurid sea
> Streams up the turrets silently—
> Gleams up the pinnacles far and free—
> Up domes—up spires—up kingly halls—
> Up fanes—up Babylon-like walls—
> Up shadowy long-forgotten bowers
> Of sculptured ivy and stone flowers—
> Up many and many a marvellous shrine
> Whose wreathéd friezes intertwine
> *The viol, the violet, and the vine.*
>
> "Resignedly beneath the sky
> The melancholy waters lie.
> So blend the turrets and shadows there
> That all seems pendulous in air,
> *While, from a proud tower in the town,*
> *Death looks gigantically down* . . .
>
> "No swellings tell that winds may be
> Upon some far-off happier sea—
> No heavings hint that winds have been
> On seas less hideously serene."

With unwaning vividness the unearthly vision burns itself tremorless upon the void, till it is almost with a shudder of relief that the spell-bound reader cons the close :

> "And when, amid no earthly moans,
>   Down, down that town shall settle hence,
>   Hell, rising from a thousand thrones,
>   Shall do it reverence."

---

* In such poems, and in some of the tales, it may very well be that opium has had some part, as it so clearly had in the happiest inspirations of Coleridge.

POE

Perhaps such terrific imaginings can never be taken into common favour with healthy dwellers in the sunlit world; but it is hard to understand how any, having studied them, can find them forgettable. It cannot for a moment be pretended of these verses, even by the sciolists of criticism, that they lack "inspiration" and spontaneity of movement; detraction must seek other ground. We find, consequently, that the stress of the hostile attack is turned mainly on one poem, in which the poet's customary intension of idea appears to lose itself more or less in a dilettantist ringing of changes on sound. I have no desire to seem in the least degree to stake Poe's reputation on *Ulalume*, which trenches too far on pure mysticism for entire artistic success, and at the same time is marked by an undue subordination of meaning to music; but I cannot help thinking that the dead set made at that piece is unjustifiable. Mr. R. H. Stoddard is exceptionally acrid on the subject.

"I can perceive," he writes, in a memoir of Poe, "no touch of grief in *Ulalume*, no intellectual sincerity, but a diseased determination to create the strange, the remote, and the terrible, and to exhaust ingenuity in order to do so. No healthy mind was ever impressed by *Ulalume*, and no musical sense was ever gratified with its measure, which is little beyond a jingle; and with its repetitions, which add to its length without increasing its general effect, and which show more conclusively than anything else in the language the absurdity of the refrain when it is allowed to run riot, as it does here." *

Now, this censure is fatally overdone. Mr. Stoddard had on the very page before admitted that *Ulalume* was, "all things considered, the most singular poem that [Poe] ever produced, if not, indeed, the most singular poem that anybody ever produced, in commemoration of a dead woman." A critic should know his own mind before he begins to write out a judgment.

* Memoir in Widdleton's ed. of Poe, p. 130.

POE

Here we have an explicit admission of the extreme remarkableness of a given poem; then a denial that it ever "impressed a healthy mind;" then an unmeasured allegation that "no musical sense was ever gratified" with its musical elements. Let one stanza answer—the praise of the star Astarte :—

> "And I said: 'She is warmer than Dian :
> She rolls through an ether of sighs—
> She revels in a region of sighs :
> She has seen that the tears are not dry on
> Those cheeks, where the worm never dies,
> And has come past the stars of the Lion
> To point us the path to the skies—
> To the Lethean peace of the skies—
> Come up, in despite of the Lion,
> To shine on us with her bright eyes—
> *Come up through the lair of the Lion,*
> *With love in her luminous eyes.*"

Mr. Stoddard must be told that there are some of us who do not wish any of these repetitions away, and who think the culminating music is closely analogous to effects produced a hundred times by Mozart and Schubert and Beethoven, who had all some little gift of melody, and were considerably given to the "repetend," as Mr. Stedman happily re-christens the so-called refrain. The above-quoted stanza is the best, no doubt, and there *is* one flaw in it, namely, the "dry on," which is truly an exhaustion of ingenuity; but even here one is struck by the imperial way in which Poe buttresses his lapse with the whole serene muster of his stanza—so curiously different a procedure from the fashion in which Mr. Swinburne, for instance, or even Mr. Browning, scoops a rhyme-born figure into his verse and, consciously hurrying on, leaves it, in its glaring irrelevance, to put the whole out of countenance. Poe's few deflections from purity of style are dominated by his habitual severity of form. As for the charge of insincerity, it is enough to say that it has been brought against every poet who has artistically expressed a grief; it being impossible for some people to realise that art feeds on deep feelings, not at the moment of their first freshness, but when revived in memory. A more reasonable objection is brought against *Ulalume* on the score of its obscurity; but that too is exaggerated; and the announcement of one critic that it is a "vagary of mere words," of an "elaborate emptiness," is an avowal of defective intelligence. The meaning of the poem is this: the poet has fallen into a reverie in the darkness; and his brain—the critic says it was then a tottering brain—is carrying on a kind of dual consciousness, compounded of a perception of the blessed peace of the night and a vague, heavy sense of his abiding grief, which has for the moment drifted into the background. In this condition he does what probably most of us have done in connection with a minor trouble—dreamily asks himself, "What was the shadow that was brooding on my mind, just a little while ago?" and then muses, "If I have forgotten it, why should I wilfully revive my pain, instead of inhaling peace while I may?" This, I maintain, is a not uncommon experience in fatigued states of the brain; the specialty in Poe's case being that the temporarily suspended ache is the woe of a bereavement—a kind of woe which, after a certain time, however sincere, ceases to be constant, and begins to be intermittent. The Psyche is the obscure whisper of the tired heart, the suspended memory, that will not be wholly appeased with the beauty of the night and the stars; and the poet has but cast into a mystical dialogue the interplay of the waking and the half-sleeping sense, which goes on till some cypress, some symbol of the grave, flashes its deadly message on the shrinking soul, and grief leaps into full supremacy. Supposing Poe's brain to have been undergoing a worsening disease in his later days, this its last melody has even a more deeply pathetic interest than belongs to the theme.

Take finally, as still further test of Poe's poetic gift, the poems *El Dorado*, *Annabel Lee*, and *For Annie*. The first is a brief allegory, with something of a moral, but a moral too pessimistic to have any ethically utilitarian quality; the second a lovely ballad enshrining the memory of his married life; the third a strange song, impersonally addressed to one of the women to whom he transiently turned in his lonesome latter years —a wonderful lullaby in which a dead man is made placidly to exult in his release from life and pain, and in the single remaining thought of the presence of his beloved. In these poems we have the final proof of the inborn singing faculty of Poe. Some of his pieces, as has been already admitted, are works of constructive skill rather than outpourings of lyric fulness; and such a musical stanza as this—

> "And all my days are trances,
> And all my nightly dreams
> Are where thy dark eye glances,
> And where thy footstep gleams—
> In what ethereal dances!
> By what eternal streams!"—

has perhaps a certain stamp of compilation. But no unprejudiced reader, I think, will fail to discern in the three poems last named a quite unsurpassable limpidity of expression. They evolve as if of their own accord. In *El Dorado* the one central rhyme is reiterated with a perfect simplicity; *Annabel Lee* is almost careless in its childlike directness of phrase; and *For Annie* is almost bald in its beginning. But I know little in the way of easeful word music that will compare with this :

> " And oh! of all tortures
>   That torture the worst
> Has abated—the terrible
>   Torture of thirst,
> For the napthaline river
>   Of Passion accurst :
> I have drunk of a water
>   That quenches all thirst :
>
> " Of a water that flows,
>   With a lullaby sound,
> From a spring but a very few
>   Feet under ground—
> From a cavern not very far
>   Down under ground.
>
> " And ah! let it never
>   Be foolishly said
> That my room it is gloomy,
>   And narrow my bed ;
> For man never slept
>   In a different bed ;
> And to *sleep*, you must slumber
>   In just such a bed.
>
> " My tantalised spirit
>   Here blandly reposes
> Forgetting, or never
>   Regretting its roses—
> Its old agitations
>   Of myrtles and roses :
>
> " For now, while so quietly
>   Lying, it fancies
> A holier odour
>   About it, of pansies—
> A rosemary odour
>   Commingled with pansies—
> *With rue and the beautiful*
>   *Puritan pansies.*"

POE

Is there not here that crowning quality of emotional plenitude which, with perfection of form, makes great poetry as distinguished from fine verse : are there not here, in another guise, the urgent throb and brooding pregnancy which give to an andante of Beethoven its deep constraining power? We have all certain passional or sub-judicial preferences in our favourite poetry, setting one masterpiece above others for some subtle magnetism it works on us, we do not quite know how or why. "Huysmans," says a writer of ardently eclectic taste, "goes to my soul like a gold ornament of Byzantine workmanship."* Somewhat so might one express the mastering charm of those incomparably simple yet flawlessly rhythmical lines.

III

These few extracts are enough to show that as a poet Poe has a commanding distinction ; but if we find him remarkable in that regard, what shall we say of the range and calibre of the mind which produced the manifold achievement of his prose? The more one wanders through that, out of all comparison the more extensive part of his work, the more singular appear those estimates of the man which treat him merely as a poet of unhappy life and morbid imagination. Perhaps it is that in all seriousness the literary world inclines to Mr. Swinburne's conviction that poets as such are the guardian angels of mankind, and all other mind-workers their mere satellites ; perhaps that, despite Goethe's services to biology, it has a hereditary difficulty in conceiving a poet as an effective intelligence in any other walk than that of his art, and accordingly excludes in-

---

* Mr. George Moore, *Confessions of a Young Man*, p. 299.

stinctively from view whatever tends to raise the point. Or is it that the sense of the abnormality of feeling in Poe's verse, and in his best-known stories, gives rise to a vague notion that his performances in the line of normal thought can be of no serious account? It is difficult to decide; but certain it is that most of his critics have either by restrictedness of view or positive misjudgment done him serious wrong.

It is Mr. Henry James who, in a passage already quoted from, makes the remark: "With all due respect to the very original genius of the author of the *Tales of Mystery*, it seems to me that to take him with more than a certain degree of seriousness is to lack seriousness oneself. An enthusiasm for Poe is the mark of a decidedly primitive stage of reflection." One cannot guess with any confidence as to the precise "degree of seriousness" which Mr. James would concede; or how much seriousness he brings to bear on any of his own attachments; or what the stage of reflection was at which he cultivated an enthusiasm for, say, Théophile Gautier. One therefore hesitates to put oneself in competition with Mr. James in the matter of seriousness of character. But one may venture to suggest that the above passage throws some light on the rather puzzling habit of depreciation of Poe among American men of letters. Themselves given mainly to the study of modern fiction, they seem to measure Poe only as a fictionist; and, even then, instead of fairly weighing his work on its merits, they test it by the calibre of the people who prefer the *Tales of Mystery* to novels of character. Remembering that as boys they enjoyed Poe when they did not enjoy the novel of character, they decide that the writer who thus appeals to boyish minds can be of no great intellectual account. This is a very fallacious line of reasoning. It would make out Defoe to be an artist of the smallest account, though Mr. James has a way of connecting intellectual triviality with " very original genius," which somewhat confuses the process of inference. It would relegate Swift to a rather low standing, because boys notoriously enjoy *Gulliver's Travels*. That result would surely not do. It surely does not follow that Mr. Stevenson is intellectually inferior to Mr. Howells because the former wrote *Treasure Island*, beloved of boys, while Mr. Howells' books appeal only to people who know something of life. The fair, not to say the scientific method, surely, is to take an author's total performance, and estimate from that his total powers. This, Mr. James has not done, I think, as regards Poe, or he would not have written as he has done about "seriousness;" and, if one may say such a thing without impertinence, the kind of culture specially affected by Mr. James is too much in the ascendant among the very intelligent reading public of the States. These white-handed students of the modern novel are not exactly the people to estimate an endowment such as Poe's.*

If one critical impression can be said to be predominant for an attentive reader of Poe's prose, it is perhaps a wondering sense of the perfection which may belong to what Lamb called "the sanity of true genius," even where the genius borders on the formless clime we name insanity. This is no idle paradox. What I say is that while Poe's work again and again gives evidence of a mind tending to alienation, it yet includes a hundred

---

* Mr. Howells, it may be remembered, has followed Mr. James in speaking slightingly of Poe; and, indeed, the general current of American criticism is still in that direction. In face of these judgments, which dispose not only of performance but of calibre, one is driven to wonder how the writers estimate their own total powers, as against Poe's.

triumphs of impeccable reason; and that for the most part his intellectual faculty is sanity itself. It opens up a curious view of things to compare the opaque, lethargic, chaotic state of mind which in respectable society so securely passes for sanity, with the pure electric light, the cloudless clearness, of Poe's intelligence in its normal state; and to reflect that he has been called mad, and is sometimes described as a charlatan. How would his detractors, for instance, have compared with Poe in thinking power if they had had to deal with such a problem as that of the *prima facie* credibility of the "Moon Hoax," which Poe is falsely accused of imitating? The Moon Hoax was a celebrated narrative, the work of Mr. Richard Adams Locke, which appeared in the *New York Sun* some three weeks *after* Poe's *Hans Pfaall* had been published in the *Southern Literary Messenger*, and which made a great sensation at the time. The *Moon Story* gravely professed to describe the inhabitants, animals, vegetation, and scenery of the moon, as having been lately made out by Sir John Herschel with a new telescope; while Poe gave a minute narrative, touched at points with banter, of a balloon journey to the same orb; but there was little detailed resemblance in the narratives, and Poe accepted Mr. Locke's declaration that he had not seen the *Adventure* when he concocted his hoax. The point of interest for us here is that the hoax was very widely successful; and that Poe found it worth while afterwards to show in detail how obvious was the imposition, and how easily it should have been seen through by intelligent readers. "Not one person in ten," he records, "discredited it, and the doubters were chiefly those who doubted without being able to say why—the ignorant, those uninformed in astronomy —people who *would not* believe because the thing was so novel, so entirely 'out of the usual way.' A grave professor of mathematics in a Virginian college told me seriously that he had *no doubt* of the truth of the whole affair!" Accordingly, Poe appended to his *Hans Pfaall* story, on republishing it, an analysis of the other story, than which there could not be a more luminous exercise of psychological logic. His scientific and other knowledge, and his power of scrutiny, enabled him to detect a dozen blunders and clumsinesses; but perhaps the most characteristic touch is his remark on the entire absence from the narrative of any expression of surprise at a phenomenon which, on the assumptions made, must have been part of the discoverer's vision— namely, the curious appearance presented by the moon's alleged inhabitants, in that their heads would be towards the terrestrial gazer, and that they would appear to hang to the moon by their feet. The demand for an expression of astonishment at this was that of an intelligence which had carried the action of imagination to a high pitch of methodic perfection. The processes of sub-conscious inference which initiate conviction, the polarity of average thinking, the elements of evidence, all had been pondered and perceived by Poe with an acumen that is as singular as most forms of genius. And the result of the demonstration was no mere protraction of subtle introspection, but the masterly solution of an abstruse concrete problem. His facility in the explication of cypher-writing was astounding: witness his triumph over all challengers when he dealt with the subject in a Philadelphia journal and in *Graham's Magazine;* his unravelling of a cryptograph in which were employed seven alphabets, without intervals between the words or even between the lines; and his crowning conquest of a cypher so elaborate that no outsider succeeded in solving it *with the key*

POE

when Poe offered a reward as an inducement. Take, again, the essay on "Maelzel's Chess Player," in which he bends his mind on the question whether that was or was not an automaton; examines with an eye like a microscope the features of the object; passes in review previous attempts at explanation; and evolves with rigorous logic an irresistible demonstration that the machine was worked by a man, and of the manner of the working. The power to work such a demonstration is as rare, as remarkable, as almost any species of faculty that can be named. It is sanity raised to a higher power. Such performances, to say nothing of his prediction of the plot of *Barnaby Rudge* from the opening chapters, should give pause to those who incline to the view, endorsed by some respectable critics, that there was nothing extraordinary in Poe's feats of analytic fiction, seeing that he himself tied the knots he untied. But that criticism is invalid on the face of it. Why is Poe so unrivalled in his peculiar line if it is so easy to tie and untie complex knots of incident, and to forge chains of causation in narrative? Does any one ever dream of denying skill in plot-construction to Scribe and Sardou because they deliberately lead up to their *denoûments*? Is it the tyro who propounds deep problems in chess, or the schoolboy who imagines new theorems in geometry? The matter is hardly worth discussing. That the author of *The Murders in the Rue Morgue*, *The Adventure of Hans Pfaall*, and *The Mystery of Marie Roget* could be a mere intellectual charlatan, differing only from his fellows in power of make-believe, is what De Quincey would call a "fierce impossibility."

As a narrator and as a thinker Poe has half a dozen excellences any one of which would entitle him to fame. The general mind of Europe has been fascinated by his tales; but how far has it realised the quality of the work in them? It has for the most part read Poe as it has read Alexandre Dumas. Poe, indeed, wrote to interest the reading public, and he was far too capable an artist not to manage what he wanted; but it was not in his nature to produce work merely adequate to the popular demand. Hundreds of popular stories are produced and are forgotten, for the plain reason that while the writer has somehow succeeded in interesting a number of his contemporaries, his work lacks the intellectual salt necessary for its preservation to future times. Posterity reads it and finds nothing to respect; neither mastery of style nor subtlety nor closeness of thought. But Poe's best stories have a quality of pure mind, an intensity of intelligised imagination, that seems likely to impress men centuries hence as much as it did his more competent readers in his own day. Even at the present moment, when his *genre* is almost entirely uncultivated, such a hard-headed critic as Professor Minto sums up that "there are few English writers of this century whose fame is likely to be more enduring. The feelings to which he appeals are simple but universal, and he appeals to them with a force that has never been surpassed." To that generously just verdict I am disposed, however, to offer a partial demurrer, in the shape of a suggestion that it is not so much in the universality of the "feelings" to which he appeals as in the manifest and consummate faculty with which he is seen to frame his appeal, that Poe's security of renown really lies. Doubtless many readers will, as hitherto, see the narrative and that only; just as Poe himself points out that "not one person in ten—nay, not one person in five hundred—has, during the perusal of *Robinson Crusoe*, the most remote conception that any particle of genius, or even of common talent, has been employed in its creation. Men do not look upon it in the light of a literary performance." But one fancies that the age of critical reading is evolving, in which, notwithstanding a random saying of Poe's own to the contrary, men will combine delight in the artist's skill with due susceptibility to the result.

Even among those who perceive the immense importance of naturalism in fiction, there are, it is to be feared, some who are so narrow as to see no value in any work of which the naturalism is not that species of absolute realism that, selection apart, is substantially contended for by M. Zola, and is variously exemplified in his and other modern novels of different countries and correspondingly different flavours. Now, the effective vindication of Poe, to my mind, is that, weird and *bizarre* and abnormal as are the themes he affected, he is essentially a realist in his method. Granted that he turns away from experience, ordinary or otherwise, for his subjects, what could be more perfect than the circumspection with which he uses every device of arrangement and tone, of omission and suggestion, to give his fiction the air of actuality? Take his *Hans Pfaall*. Hardly any critic, save Dr. Landa in his preface to his Spanish translation of some of the Tales, has done justice to the exactitude and verisimilitude with which Poe has there touched in his astronomical, physical, and physiological details ; and employed them to the point of carrying illusion to its possible limit even while he has artistically guarded himself from the downright pretence by the fantastic fashion of his introduction. There is realism and realism. It was Poe's idiosyncrasy as a fictionist to examine, not the interplay of the primary human and social emotions either in the open or in half lights, not to be either a Thackeray or a

POE

Hawthorne, but to trace the sequences and action of the thinking faculty in its relation to the leading instincts and feelings of the individual; and this he does partly by studying himself and partly by comparing himself with others—precisely the method of ordinary humanist fiction. He is always an observer in this direction. His objection to the " Moon Hoax " was that it not merely showed ignorant blundering in its details but was wanting in proper calculation of the attitude of good observers ; so in his paper on " Maelzel's Chess Player " he unhesitatingly rejects one of Brewster's explanations as assuming too commonplace a stratagem ; so, in easily unravelling a friend's cypher, he laughs at the " shallow artifice " he sees in it ; and so in his Parisian stories he derides, in the police officer, the cunning which he finds so inferior to true sagacity.

Even the story of *The Black Cat* is realistic—realistic in the very wildness of its action. Any one in reading Poe can see how he consciously constructed tales by letting his creative faculty follow the line of one of those morbid fancies that probably in some degree occur at times to all of us, and of which, alas ! he must have had a tremendous share ; giving the recapitulation a gruesome lifelikeness by vigilant embodiment of the details he had noted in following the track of the sinister caprice. And so *The Tell-Tale Heart*, and *William Wilson*, and *The Cask of Amontillado* are realistic—realistic in the sense that they have had a psychologic basis in the perversities of a disturbed imagination : hence the uncanny fascination of these and other stories of his in a similar taste.* Whether that parti-

---

* See the *Saturday Review* of Nov. 28, 1885, for a well-expressed criticism to the same effect, published a few weeks after the foregoing, but doubtless by a writer who had never seen that. Cp. Hennequin, *Ecrivains Francisés*, pp. 120-130.

cular species of fiction will retain a hold on men is a matter on which it would be rash to prophesy; and indeed it may be that not only this but another class of Poe's productions—that which includes *The Fall of the House of Usher*, *Ligeia*, *The Masque of the Red Death*, *The Assignation*, and *Berenice*—may, as mankind progresses in rational culture, lose that peculiar impressiveness they have for so many readers to-day. These strange creations, whelmed in shade, seem to belong to some wild region, out of the main road of human evolution. To my own taste, I confess, they are less decisively and permanently impressive than such feats of daylight imagination, so to speak, as *Arthur Gordon Pym*, *Hans Pfaall*, *The Pit and the Pendulum*, or even *The Murders in the Rue Morgue*, and *The Purloined Letter;* but there is no overlooking the element of power, the intension of idea, which makes itself felt in the twilight studies as in the others. Like every man who has to live by steady pen-work, Poe produced some inferior stuff and some downright trash; but wherever his faculty comes at all fully into play it puts a unique stamp of intellect on its product, a stamp not consisting in mere force or beauty of style, though these are involved, but in a steady, unfaltering pressure of the writer's thought on the attention of his reader. And when we recognise this pregnancy and intensity, and take note that such a critic as Mr. Lowell was so impressed by the "serene and sombre beauty" of *The Fall of the House of Usher* as to pronounce it sufficient by itself to prove Poe a man of genius and the master of a classic style, we shall see cause to doubt whether any considerable portion of Poe's imaginative work belongs to the perishable order of literature.

As for the group of tales of the saner type, with their blazing vividness and tense compactness of substance—

beyond insisting on the importance of the capacity implied in these results, and the essential realism of the stories within the limits of their species, there can be little need to claim for them either attention or praise. Their fascination as narratives is felt by all: the only drawback is the tendency to argue that, because the non-realistic novel is potentially inferior to the realistic, this class of story is inferior to the realistic novel or story of ordinary life. To reason so is to confuse types. Lytton is a worse novelist than Thackeray because, professing both explicitly and implicitly to portray character and society, he is less true in every respect; and the idealistic element in George Eliot is of less value than her work of observation because it claims acceptance on the same footing while its title is, in the terms of the case, awanting. Here we are dealing with comparable things, with performances to be judged in relation to each other. But in Poe we deal with quite a different species of art. That familiar objection to his tales on the score of their lack of human or moral colour, expressed by Mr. Lowell, in his *Fable for Critics*, in the phrase "somehow the heart seems squeezed out by the mind," is the extension of the confusion into downright injustice. It lies on the face of his work that Poe never aims at reproducing every-day life and society, with its multitude of minute character-phenomena forming wholes for artistic contemplation, but—to put it formally—at working out certain applications and phases of the faculties of reflection and volition, as conditioning and conditioned by abnormal tendencies and incidents. He does not seek or profess to draw "character" in the sense in which Dickens or Balzac does; he has almost nothing to do with local colour or sub-divisions of type; his fisherman in *The Descent into the Maelström* is an unspecialised intelligent person;

POE

Arthur Gordon Pym similarly is simply an observing, reasoning, and energising individual who goes through and notes certain experiences: in short, these personages are abstractions of one aspect of Poe.* On the other hand Usher and the speakers in *The Black Cat* and *The Imp of the Perverse* merely represent a reversal of the formula; peculiar idiosyncrasy in their case being made the basis of incident, whereas in the others pure incident or mystery was made the motive. No matter which element predominates, normal character study is excluded; Poe's bias, as we said, being toward analysis or synthesis of processes of applied reason and psychal idiosyncrasy, not to reproduction of the light and shade of life pitched on the everyday plane. It was not that he was without eye for that. On the contrary, his criticisms show he had a sound taste in the novel proper; and we find him rather critically alert than otherwise in his social relation to the personalities about him. It was that his artistic bent lay in another direction.

As a tale-teller, then, he is to be summed up as having worked in his special line with the same extraordinary creative energy and intellectual mastery as distinguish his verse; giving us narratives "of imagination all compact," yet instinct with life in every detail and particle, no matter how strange, how aloof from common things, may be the theme. As Dr. Landa remarks, he has been the first story-writer to exploit the field of science in the department of the marvellous; and he has further been the first to exploit the marvellous in morbid psychology with scientific art. These are achieve-

* The unfinished *Journal of Julius Rodman* (published in Mr. Ingram's *édition de luxe* of the tales and poems) presents us with a somewhat more individualised type, but there too the interest centres in the incidents.

ments as commanding, as significant of genius, as the most distinguished success in any of the commoner walks of fiction; and a contrary view is reasonably to be described as a fanatical development of an artistic doctrine perfectly sound and of vital importance in its right application, but liable, like other cults, to incur reaction when carried to extremes. After *The Idiot Boy* and *The Prelude* came *The Lady of Shalott* and the *Idylls of the King*; after Trollope came King Romance again; and even if Poe were eclipsed for a time, posterity would still be to reckon with.

IV

There is still to be considered, if we would measure Poe completely, his work in the fields of abstract æsthetics, criticism, and philosophy; and to some of us that aspect of him is not less remarkable than his artistic expression of himself in verse and fiction. Even among his admirers, however, this is not the prevailing attitude. Thus Mr. Ingram, to whose untiring and devoted labour is mainly due the vindication of Poe's memory, considers that criticism was "hardly his forte;" and Dr. William Hand Browne, who, in his article in the Baltimore *New Eclectic Magazine* on "Poe's *Eureka* and Recent Scientific Speculations," has been the first bearer of testimony to the poet's capacity as a thinker—even this independent eulogist thinks it necessary to declare that in Poe's *Rationale of Verse*, "in connection with just and original remarks on English versification, of which he was a master, we find a tissue of the merest absurdity about the classical measures, of which he knew nothing." I cannot agree to the implications of Mr. Ingram's phrase, and I cannot but think that Dr. Browne has spoken recklessly as to Poe's knowledge and criticism of the so-called "classical measures," treating that question very much as other critics have treated the *Eureka*. That Poe in his schooldays was a good Latinist we know from one of his schoolfellows, who dwells especially on the delight with which he used to listen to Poe's conning of his favourite pieces in Horace.

The school in question was strong on the Latin side, and it is hardly possible that Poe, whatever he might do in Greek, could be otherwise than familiar with the orthodox scansions of the classic poets, ranking, as he did, as joint dux of the school.* In point of fact, he won distinctions in both Latin and French at the University of Virginia, which must surely count for something.

It requires, indeed, little scholarship to gather from the ordinary editions the received metres of Horace and the established scansions of the hexameter, which are what Poe puts in evidence in so far as he challenges the academic theory of classic verse. These are given with strict accuracy. The whole question raised is whether they stand by a scientific or by a merely traditional authority; and it is surely a device worthy of a mediæval

* That Poe's general culture was wide and effective it seems unnecessary to contend here, though some of his critics deny him such credit. His works must speak for themselves. It has indeed been pointed out by one critic that the nature of his reference to Gresset's *Ver-Vert*, in *The Fall of the House of Usher*, shows him to have used the title without knowing the poem; and Mrs. Whitman's merely forensic rejoinder only shows that she had not read it either. I fancy he may have dipped into the poem and noticed such a phrase as "le saint oiseau" or the concluding lines, and so entirely missed the nature of the narrative. His "stately raven of the saintly days of yore" suggests the same chance. But one such miscarriage, whatever be the explanation, cannot destroy the general testimony of his so various writings.

POE

schoolman to evade the inquiry by a sweeping charge of ignorance.*

In just this supercilious fashion have avowedly unfriendly critics disparaged Poe on other grounds, passing judgment without offering a jot of evidence. One is led to suspect that, while thinking for himself on science, Dr. Browne treated questions of classic metre with the unquestioning faith which other people give to the propositions of religion. Those who have looked with independent interest into the dogmas of classic prosody know that, whether right or wrong, Poe was dealing with a subject on which even reputedly "orthodox" opinion is hopelessly confused; and that the off-hand language of Dr. Browne pretends a certainty of expert authority which does not exist. Certain rules for scanning Greek and Latin verse pass current; but save in respect of nominal adherence to the arbitrary rules of a given text-book, there is no agreement among scholars; and it is safe to say that the traditional lore of the schools is a mass of uncomprehended shibboleths, framed without understanding and accepted on the same basis. Poe must have heard at school and university the ordinary directions for the scanning of classic verse. He was singular enough to think them out for his own

---

* The late Sidney Lanier wrote that "the trouble with Poe was, he did not *know* enough. He needed to know a good many more things in order to be a great poet." Alas, that is the trouble with all of us, small and great; and in more ways than one, in the subtler sense rather than in the simpler, it holds true of Lanier himself, to the point of the statement that he fell ever further short of being a great poet in the ratio of the growth of his conviction that he was one, and that his poetry was an expression of knowledge. Man of genius as he was, he did not finally succeed even in fulfilling his own law of severance between Art and Cleverness. Poe remains the greater poet because he *knew* better the function of poetry and its relation to truth.

satisfaction, and he thus found there was no satisfaction to be had from them.

What Poe urged on that head is, I venture to think, broadly just and well-timed. As he truly said, "there is something in 'scholarship' which seduces us into blind worship of Bacon's *Idol of the Theatre*—into irrational deference to antiquity;"* and as a matter of fact the prosody of the schools had never any better basis than one of Talmudic deduction from verse never scientifically studied. The *Iliad*, as Poe again says, "being taken as a starting-point, was made to stand instead of Nature and common sense. Upon this poem, in place of facts and deduction from fact, or from natural law, were built systems of feet, metres, rhythms, rules—rules that contradict each other every five minutes, and for nearly all of which there may be found nearly twice as many exceptions as examples." The notorious want of hearty enjoyment of ancient verse, *quâ* verse, among those who study it, and the naked and unashamed unnaturalness of our own enunciation of it, are sufficient to support Poe's protest against any mere dogmatic retort from the pedants; and I apprehend that no open-minded reader of his essay will have any difficulty in deciding whether the analytic poet or the ordinary scholastic is the better fitted to arrive at what the principles of rhythm really are. Poe seems to have had the eccentric taste to try to enjoy his Horace as he enjoyed his Tennyson. But to say this is to say that he undertook an almost hopelessly difficult task, and it would be going too far to say that he has succeeded as he thought he did. A full examination of the matter must be left to an appendix; but it may here be

* In this connection note the recent challenge to the traditionist grammarians by Mr. Gavin Hamilton in his treatise on the Subjunctive. Edinburgh: Oliver and Boyd, 1889.

POE

said that in the very act of coming to the conclusion that Poe's simplified system of feet in turn breaks down like the old and complex one as an anatomy of verse, we are led to acknowledge anew the singular originality and energy of his mind. It is no extravagance to say that in this matter it is better to err with Poe than to be "right" with Dr. Browne, for Poe's error is a brilliant effort to make a new system out of the wreck of one which he has rightly discarded, and he offers vivid argumentative exposition where academic orthodoxy offers inert and unreasoned rules. In every respect save the crowning point of scientific rightness it is a masterly critical performance.*

V

The close of the *Rationale* raises a question which has been generally decided against Poe—that as to whether he had any humour. Humour of the kind in which American literature is specially rich he clearly had not. Such attempts as his *X-ing a Paragrab* have none of the hilarious fun of those grotesque exaggerations which form one of the two main features of American humour;

* Mr. Stedman, in editing the recent complete edition of Poe's works, has seen fit to say that "the *Rationale of Verse* is a curious discussion of mechanics now well enough understood" (Introd. to vol. vi., p. xiv.). As very few of us are conscious of Mr. Stedman's sense of mastery, which he does not give us the means of sharing, I leave my Appendix on *Accent, Quantity and Feet* to exhibit other people's difficulties. And when Mr. Stedman further pronounces (p. xv.) that "one can rarely draw a better contrast between the faulty and the masterly treatment of a literary topic than by citing *The Rationale of Verse* and [Arnold's] three lectures *On Translating Homer*," I must take leave to say that he does but give us an uncritical endorsement of a prestige. Arnold's book is really a failure as a technical treatise.

and of its other constituent of subtle, kindly drollery, unembittered jesting at the incongruous in morals or in incidents, he can offer us almost as little. The explanation is that in respect of temperament he was too unhappily related to American society to have any cordial satisfaction in studying it; and that his sense of the comic had the warmthlessness and colourlessness of unmitigated reason. One sometimes finds him even pungently humorous, but it is always in a generalisation, or in derision of a fallacy or a fatuity; always in a flash of the reason, never in a twinkle of the temperament; and only those who are capable of what George Eliot once delightedly spoke of as the laughter which comes of a satisfaction of the understanding, will perceive that he possesses humour at all. His satire, indeed, is strictly in keeping with his criticism in general. The peculiar quality of that, which for some readers makes it unsuccessful, lies in this absolute supremacy of judgment. The apparent or rather the virtual ruthlessness of much of his critical writing is the outcome of the two facts that he had an extremely keen critical sense and that, in applying it, save when his emotional side was stimulated, as it generally was when he was criticising women,* he was sheer, implacable intellect. To him the discrimination of good and bad in literature was a matter of the intensest seriousness: of the faculty for doing mere "notices" of the mechanically inept and insincere sort turned out by so many of the criticasters who moralise about his lack of the moral sense—of that convenient aptitude he was quite destitute. To represent him, however, in the way Mr. Stoddard does, as a kind of literary Red Indian, delight-

* See Mr. Stoddard's memoir in Widdleton's edition of Poe, p. 165. "I cannot point an arrow against any woman," was one of Poe's private avowals. Still, he wrote contemptuously of Margaret Fuller,

ing in the use of the tomahawk for its own sake, is but to add to the darkening of critical counsel about Poe. The prejudiced critic in question speaks as follows :

> "Like Iago, he was nothing if not critical, and the motto of his self-sufficient spirit was *Nil admirari*. . . . It is a weakness incident to youth and ambition. . . . I do not think that Poe ever outgrew it, or sought to outgrow it. He believed that his readers loved havoc; Mr. Burton, on the contrary, believed that they loved justice. And he was right, as the criticisms of Poe have proved, for they have failed to commend themselves to the good sense of his countrymen. His narrow but acute mind enabled him to detect the verbal faults of those whom he criticised, but it disqualified him from perceiving their mental qualities. He mastered the letter, but the spirit escaped him. He advanced no critical principle which he established; he attacked no critical principle which he overthrew. He broke a few butterflies on his wheel; but he destroyed no reputation. He was a powerless iconoclast."*

I quote this as the most close-packed, comprehensive, and consistent piece of aggressively bad criticism by a not incompetent critic that I remember to have seen. From the malicious, not to say malignant, "Like Iago" to the overstrained depreciation of the "powerless iconoclast," all is unfair and untrue. The remark about "havoc" and Mr. Burton refers to a jesting answer made by Mr. Poe to one of his employers who deprecated his severity; an answer which to take as an expression of Poe's critical creed is discreditably unjust. He thought the severity complained of was deserved, and he merely made the light answer by way of soothing the uneasiness or silencing the objections of an employer for whose judgment he had no respect. To take seriously a phrase so uttered is to show either moral pedantry or prejudice. As to the view taken of Poe as

whom he disliked on both personal and literary grounds, as did Mr. Lowell.

* Memoir in Widdleton's ed., p. 89.

POE

a critic by the "good sense" of his countrymen, that must be left to the decision of the tribunal in question, if it can be got at; and the proposition that Poe's mind was narrow may profitably be left alone; while the other dicta may be best disposed of by laying down truer ones.

What may fairly be said against Poe's criticisms is that they have not the absolute artistic balance and completeness, the perfection of "form" which belongs to his tales and best poems. Criticism was not with him, as it has been said to be with Mr. Lowell and Mr. Arnold, a "fine art"; it was rather a science; and his critiques accordingly are processes of scientific analysis and summing-up, almost always restricted in a business-like manner to the subject in hand. What he might have done if he had had the opportunities of the two writers named, if he had had academic leisure and good media, is a matter for speculation; but what we do know is that he has left a body of widely various criticism which, as such, will better stand critical examination to-day than any similar work produced in England or America in his time. Mr. James, half-sharing the normal American hostility to Poe, thinks that his critical product "is probably the most complete specimen of *provincialism* ever prepared for the edification of men;" though he admits that there is mixed in it a great deal of sense and discrimination; and that "here and there, sometimes at frequent intervals (*sic*), we find a phrase of happy insight embedded in a patch of the most fatuous pedantry."* Well, provincialism is a very incalculable thing: so Protean and subtle that some people find some of the essence of it actually in the very full-blown cosmopolitanism of Mr. James,

* *Hawthorne*, p. 64.

whose delicate narrative art is so much occupied with the delineation of aspects of the life of idle Americans in Europe and idle Europeans in America, and so admirably detached from all grosser things. Putting that out of the question, and assuming that Mr. James is as qualified a critic of criticism in general as he has undoubtedly proved himself to be of the novel, we must in any case hold that he did not sufficiently consider the general conditions of criticism in Poe's day when he penned his aspersion. When we remember how matters stood in England, with Christopher North and the youthful Thackeray and Macaulay and the Quarterlies representing the critical spirit;* when we note how Carlyle, studying *Blackwood* and *Fraser* in those days, decides that "the grand requisite seems to be impudence, and a fearless committing of yourself to talk in your drink"; and when we try to reckon up what of insight and real breadth of view there was in all these, we shall find it difficult to accept Mr. James's standard. Provincialism is a matter of comparison. If it be decided that to deal as minutely as Poe did with the contemporary literature and writers of one's own country is unwise, the provincialism of the proceeding will still be to prove; and in the end a number of things in Poe's critical remains go some way to explode the detractions we have been considering. Particular judgments apart, there is a general pressure of reasoning power in his critical writing which is really not to be found in the works of later men, English and American, whose title is taken for granted by some of those who make light of Poe on this side. The reason-

---

* "Macaulay and Dilke and one or two others excepted," writes Poe (*Marginalia*, vii.), "there is not in Great Britain a critic who can fairly be considered worthy the name."

POE

ing of Mr. Lowell, outside of the field of pure literature or literary art, is always precarious and not seldom quite puerile : that of Mr. Arnold, even on points of literary effect, is too often trivially and cheaply fallacious ; but in Poe, though we may find critical caprice and extravagance, the standard of ratiocination, the ruling quality of the logic, is always high and masculine. And against a few extravagances of praise and dispraise, there are a hundred sure and true verdicts, given long in advance of general appreciation. When we look to see what line he takes as a critic, we find him delightedly extolling Tennyson as a great poet when men were still worshipping devoutly at the shrine of Wordsworth ; insisting from the first that the obscure Hawthorne was a genius of a far higher order than Longfellow ; welcoming Dickens as a great artist in the humours of character, but warning him that he had no gift of construction ; heartily eulogising Hood ; giving generous praise to Mr. Horne's *Orion ;* denying merit to the popular Lever ; pointing out that the still more popular *Valentine Vox* was not literature ; standing up for fair play to Moore ; keenly scrutinising Macaulay ; doing homage to Mrs. Browning ; paying the fullest admiring tribute to the memory of Lamb ; coolly and impartially analysing Cooper—always quick to give honour where honour was due, and to protest against critical injustice ; never once pandering to commercialism or tolerating the puffery of the undeserving ; never weighting his scales for the benefit of any, save perhaps when his idiosyncrasy made him exaggerate the merits of some women-poets. As for the pedantry, one may suggest that there are departments of criticism to which Mr. James, admirable critic as he is, may be a stranger ; and that it is yet not pedantry to be at home in these.

POE

Let us glose nothing : let us admit that in discussing the commonplace quality of Lever, Poe becomes so extravagant in his esteem of the kind of fiction to which his own faculty pointed as to say that "for one Fouqué there are fifty Molières," and to declare that "Mr. Dickens has no more business with the rabble than a seraph with a *chapeau de bras*"—here stultifying a previous utterance. There is nothing to be said for such deliration as that, of course: we can but set it down to the brain-flaw. Nor can it be denied that the temper of his writing is often faulty; that he shows "bad form" enough to justify M. Hennequin's use of the word "littlenesses." The note, in fact, is often sharply neurotic. But at the risk of being charged with neck-or-nothing partisanship, I venture hereanent to indorse the phrase of the friendly reviewer who pronounced Poe "potentially" one of the greatest of critics. It is a perfectly fair distinction. One finds that Poe's critical judgment was generally unerring; and that he invariably knew and told how and why he reached his verdict; and one finds in an utterly preposterous misjudgment on his part only a sign of momentary distraction. For the comparative bareness of the critical part of his work is no argument against his being a great critic. Indeed the very faults that are most flagrant in his critical work, the stress of temper over small matters and small writers, and the pedantic-looking persistence in theoretic analysis, clearly come of the spontaneous play of his critical faculty through the medium of a flawed nervous system, without check from the other faculties of character. Hence the air of "littleness," even of moral defect. It was not that, as the wiseacres said, he was without character; but that in him certain intellectual faculties were so developed as to go to work without control from the character, at least in his excited moods. And it was his hard fate that, as a hack journalist, he had to write in all moods, and on matters of journalistic attraction—a simple economic fact which is strangely disregarded by his gainsayers.* When he was not nervously excited, again, the very strength of his critical faculty tended to make him pronounce rigorously technical and unadorned decisions where other men would turn out polished and charming essays; but in the terms of the case his work is more truly critical than theirs. The truth is that in our literature pure criticism is very scarce. Some of our most popular and charming critics, so-called, are rather essayists than methodical judges of literature: they write *à propos* of books and authors, giving us in so doing a finished expression of their own sentiments and their own philosophy, often laying down sound literary opinions and displaying a fine taste; but leaving us rather to echo their conclusions out of esteem for their authority than guiding us to any science of discrimination on our own account. Writing as critics, they are adding to literature rather than effectively analysing it. With Poe it is altogether different. We read his criticisms not for their own literary quality but for their judicial value and their service to critical science; and though it follows that they can never be widely known, it is not unsafe to predict for them recognition and interest at a time when a great deal of the more

* We have his own anxious avowal in his masterly critique of *Barnaby Rudge*: "From what we have here said, and perhaps said without due deliberation (for, alas! the hurried duties of the journalist preclude it). . . ." The same explanation will account for the inconsistencies of phrase in the critique on Hawthorne. And some of the worst exhibitions in the *Broadway Journal* are to be set down to the fact, noted by Mr. Ingram, that Poe had at times to manufacture most of the matter for an issue, this when his physique was rapidly running down.

POE

"readable" products of modern critics are forgotten. Certainly Poe was in advance of his time in the rigour of his critical principles. The unrealised ambition of his literary life, the foundation of a critical journal which should be absolutely honest and be written by none but competent critics, giving the reasons for all their judgments, was utterly utopian. Neither the required critics nor fit readers then existed or yet exist in America, or for that matter in England. Now, as in Poe's day, it may be that the qualified craftsmen in the States have to waste their strength in miscellaneity; but however that may be it is certain that American criticism, like English, makes but a poor show beside the critical literature of France. For illustration, it must suffice here to suggest a comparison of the graceful and genial essay of Mr. Stedman, the best American estimate of Poe, with the article by M. Emile Hennequin in the *Revue Contemporaine*;[*] an analytical study which, reading it as I do when my own essay is as good as written, makes me feel as if my labour were mostly thrown away. M. Hennequin, perhaps, would not resent[†] the inference that he has learned some lessons of analysis from Poe; who, by the way, performed as remarkable a feat of analysis in his criticism of *Barnaby Rudge* as in any of his other productions. The decomposition of that story, the revelation of the writer's mental processes, and the deduction of the plot from the opening chapters, drawing as they did from Dickens an inquiry whether his critic had dealings with the devil, are things to be remembered in the history of literature. But if there were no such achievement to Poe's credit, and if he had not written his essay on the

[*] January 1885; reprinted in the volume *Écrivains Francisés*.
[†] M. Hennequin, alas! died suddenly in the summer of 1888, in his prime.

POE

American Drama, one of the ablest dramatic criticisms ever penned, that body of multifold criticism which stands in his works under the title *Marginalia* would alone suffice, to my thinking, to prove him a born critic. Barring some follies, some pretentiousness, some intended nonsense, and some inexplicable contradictions, which suggest either deliberate mystification or mixed authorship, that miscellany of paragraphs and essaylets is a perpetual sparkle of clear thought, into which one dives time after time, always finding stimulus, even if it be of provocation, always buoyantly upborne by the masterful mind.

But while we find Poe even in his college days making curious attempts to "divide his mind" by doing two things at once, and in later life musing intently on "the power of words," his thinking faculty was not limited to analysis and criticism. It so happens that he has given us, in addition to all his artistic and critical work, one of the most extraordinary productions of imaginative philosophic synthesis in literature. The *Eureka* has, indeed, no sociological bearing, save in so far as it incidentally throws out the suggestion that as "the importance of the development of the terrestrial vitality proceeds equally with the terrestrial condensation," we may surmise the stages of the evolution of life to be in terms of the variations of the solar influence on the earth, and that the discharge of a new planet, inferior to Mercury, might freshly modify the terrestrial surface so as to produce "a race both materially and spiritually superior to Man." The speculation is interesting, but remote from everyday interests. A remarkable detail in Poe's life and character is that he rarely touches on things political ; whence, perhaps, an impression that he had no sympathy with social movement and aspiration in general. On the strength, presumably, of the allusion to mob rule in *Some Words with a Mummy*, and of some sentences in the *Colloquy of Monos and Una*, Mr. Lang* confusedly decides that "If democratic ecstasies are a tissue of historical errors and self-complacent content with the commonplace, no one saw that more clearly than Poe." But the school of languid anti-democrats cannot rightfully claim Poe as being on their side. If they will read chap. vii. of the *Marginalia* they will find him expressing democratic sentiments in his own person; and in his *Fifty Suggestions* (not a very satisfactory compilation) they will find a remarkable prophetic judgment as to the revolutionary spirit in Europe. If further proof is wanted of Poe's essential democratism, I would cite the circumstance, not generally known, that in the *Broadway Journal* there appeared, while he was sole editor, an article entitled "Art Singing and Heart Singing," signed "Walter Whitman," in which are suggested for apparently the first time those doctrines as to democratic culture which have since become so familiar; and that there is the editorial note "It is scarcely necessary to add that we agree with our correspondent throughout." The fact remains, however, that Poe made no attempt at a sociological synthesis. Setting aside the constructive element in his tales, it is in his cosmogonic philosophy that we must look for the synthetic side of his mind.

VI

It resulted from the insistence of the "reasoning reason" in Poe that the train of thought which evolved the *Eureka* found expression also in his artistic work, while at the same time the growing insurgence of temperament gave an emotional cast to his philosophy.

* In the preface to the "Parchment" edition of Poe's poems.

POE

To say nothing of his psychological tales, we have the *Colloquy of Monos and Una* (as to the alleged plagiarising in which there is not a shadow of evidence) where two souls in heaven look back on the finished course of humanity; the *Conversation of Eiros and Charmian*, in which similarly one spirit tells another of how the race was destroyed; and *The Power of Words*, in which yet again two immortals talk of transcendental things. In this last dialogue there is a touch which for vastitude of imagination is perhaps unmatchable. "Come," says the spirit Agathos to Oinos, who is "new-fledged with immortality"—"Come! we will leave to the left the loud harmony of the Pleiades, and sweep outward from the throne into the starry meadows beyond Orion, where, for pansies and violets and heart's-ease, are the beds of the triplicate and triple-tinted suns." In the way of "brave translunary things" it will not be easy to beat that. This is indeed *poiesis;* and it was perhaps with a true instinct that Poe, flatly contradicting his own rule that a poem must be short to be truly poetic, recorded his desire that the *Eureka*, with all its logic and criticism, should be regarded as a poem. It is a great, impassioned, imaginative projection, beginning in just some such elemental swell of ideal emotion as gives birth to poetry. But there could be no greater mistake than to regard the *Eureka*, with its vast cosmogonic sweep, as a mere rhapsody. Dr. William Hand Browne, who has made it the subject of a sufficiently practical article, finds that its author possessed, "in remarkable excellence, the scientific mind."* Recognising this, Dr. Browne remarks that it

* It is one of the mistakes of Dr. Nordau to exclaim vociferously at M. Morice for naming Poe in the same group with Spencer and Claude Bernard (*Dégénérescence*, French trans. i. 242). Dr. Nordau evidently knows very little about Poe's performance.

POE

has been Poe's peculiarly hard fortune to be not only persistently maligned by his enemies but imperfectly estimated by his friends ; a truth which Dr. Browne goes on unconsciously to illustrate by denying Poe credit for *The Gold Bug* and *The Murders in the Rue Morgue*, and, as we have seen, by charging him with writing absurdly and ignorantly on the classical measures. These injustices, however, perhaps give only the more weight to Dr. Browne's eulogy when he attributes to Poe "the power of expressing his thoughts, however involved, subtle, or profound, with such precision, such lucidity, and withal with such simplicity of style, that we hardly know where to look for his equal : certainly nowhere among American writers." That seems to me quite true ; and there could be no better evidence in support than the *Eureka*, which only needs to be separately reprinted without its worrying dashes and without italics to rank as the most luminous and the most original theistic treatise in the language. This verdict may perhaps incur the more suspicion when I avow that I pass it in the conviction that Poe's reasoning breaks down, like all other theistic reasoning, when its conclusion is applied to the primary problem. It is the way in which he reasons up to a conclusion subversive of itself and of all other theisms, that makes this treatise unique in philosophy. It is plain, indeed, that Poe on his way reasoned himself out of his primary theism into an entirely new poly-pantheism ; and of course it is a plain proof of mental disturbance thus to wander on the path of an inquiry.* But let the mental

---

* It would seem indeed that only in his last years did he begin to pay much attention to religious problems. His previous attitude seems to have been conventionally, sometimes even vulgarly, orthodox—a surprising thing in the case of such a critical intelligence.

POE

overpoise be taken for granted, and the intellectual interest of the performance remains.

At the outset he decides with the most absolute arbitrariness that there is a finite "universe of stars," and an infinite "universe of space"—a proposition which certainly testifies to his failure to get behind the common illusion of space as the antithesis of existence. No less arbitrarily does he assume Deity, making none of the popular pretences to reach that hypothesis by way of elimination. "As our starting-point, then," he writes, "let us adopt the Godhead. Of this Godhead in itself, he alone is not imbecile, he alone is not impious, who propounds—nothing."* But, following the familiar, the fatal path of all theology, he will not admit that the inconceivable will be for ever unconceived, and, having to begin with affirmed its volition, he immediately after affirms that he has something else to propound concerning it:

> "An intuition altogether irresistible, although inexpressible, forces me to the conclusion that what God originally created—that that Matter, which, by dint of his Volition, he first made from his spirit, or from Nihility (!) *could* have been nothing but matter in its utmost conceivable state of—what?—of *Simplicity*. This will be found the sole absolute *assumption* of my Discourse." †

In other words, "*Oneness* is all that I predicate of the originally created Matter." But "the assumption of absolute Unity in the primordial Particle includes that of infinite divisibility," so that we yet further assume attraction and repulsion as primal characteristics of the universe, the first being its material and the second its spiritual principle.‡ "I feel, in a word, that here the God has interposed, and here only, because here and here only the knot

* *Works*, Ingram's ed., iii. 107.   † P. 108.   ‡ P. 114.

demanded the interposition of the God."* "Attraction and repulsion *are* matter." Then comes many pages of impassioned brooding on the conceptions thus set out with, and of quasi-mathematical extension of the premises, all leading up anew to the thing assumed at the outset—the finitude of the "universe of stars." "Gravity exists on account of Matter's having been irradiated, at its origin, atomically, into a *limited sphere of space*, from one, individual, unconditional, irrelative and absolute Particle Proper. . . ." † Thus we get rid of "the impossible conception of an infinite extension of Matter," and set up the other conception of an "illimitable Universe of Vacancy beyond." ‡

But here the poet flinches, as well he might, and we have this confession :

"Let me declare only that, as an individual, I myself feel impelled to *fancy*, without daring to call it more—that there *does* exist a *limitless* succession of Universes, more or less similar to that of which we have cognisance—to that of which *alone* we shall ever have cognisance—at the very least until the return of our own particular Universe into Unity. *If* such clusters of clusters exist, however—and *they do*—it is abundantly clear that having no part in our origin, they have no portion in our laws. They neither attract us, nor we them. Their material, their spirit is not ours, is not that which obtains in any part of our Universe. They could not impress our senses or our souls. . . . Each exists, apart and independently, *in the bosom of its proper and particular God."* §

And in the end the proposition is, on the one hand

"That each soul is, in part, its own God, its own Creator; in a word, that God—*now* exists solely in the diffused matter and Spirit of the Universe; and that the regathering of this diffused Matter and Spirit will be but the reconstitution of the *purely* Spiritual and Individual God ; "

while, on the other hand, this God is "one of an absolutely infinite number of similar Beings that people the

* *Works*, iii. 113. † P. 137. ‡ P. 163.
§ P. 164; italics Poe's.

POE

absolutely infinite domains of the absolutely infinite space."* And yet he had earlier insisted, in the spirit of modern Monism, on " the condensation of *laws* into law," and the conclusion that "each law of Nature is dependent at all points upon all other laws,"† a maxim which quashes his infinity of irrelated universes and Gods; and again he insisted : "That Nature and the God of Nature are distinct, no thinking being can doubt"‡—a doctrine which quashes his unitary Pantheism. Thus, on his own principle that "a perfect consistency can be nothing but an absolute truth,"§ he has definitely missed truth. It is the fate of all theosophies. And still his failure, in virtue of the mere energy and sustained imaginativeness of its reasoning, is a permanently notable philosophical document—this though his neurosis was visibly worsening at the time of the composition to the point of affecting its whole tone, and much of the reasoning. Capacity in this kind must be measured comparatively; and it needs neither dissent nor agreement, but simply acquaintance with the average run of theistic and cosmological reasoning, to come to the opinion that Poe is in these matters as abnormal, as intensely intellectual, as he is in everything else.‖ The

---

* *Works*, iii. 194.   † P. 147.   ‡ *Ibid.*   § P. 100.
‖ The very hostile critique of the *Eureka* by Professor Irving Stringham, reprinted in the notes to vol. ix. of Messrs. Stedman and Woodberry's edition, really concedes all that is above claimed for the treatise as an exhibition of intellectual power, though denying it all scientific originality and pronouncing the philosophical argument the "degrading self-delusion of an arrogant and fatuous mind." This is a sample of the language constantly used by American writers towards a man in whom brain disease can be diagnosed with moral certainty. Everything Poe wrote, in his final and swiftly failing years, is discussed by most of his detractors without a suggestion that it comes from a shaken reason. The note of malice is normal. Professor Stringham takes as absolutely certain the story that Poe once said : " My whole nature utterly revolts at the idea that there

book—for it is a book in itself—has, indeed, some bad passages, where he essays to be humorous; but as against this, it exhibits a competence in matters of abstract science, and a hold of scientific cosmic theory, that no English man of letters of that day possessed. Much subsequent scientific thinking is anticipated here; Mr. Spencer, in particular, might have drawn from it his fundamental principle of the correlation of progress and heterogeneity; and the poet is here found triumphantly

is any Being in the universe superior to myself." Now, that story (see it in Ingram's *Life*, ch. xviii.) has a most dubious aspect, coming as it does from a rather fanatical theist; and I confess I have always doubted its truth. If it *were* true, it would to a candid critic suggest incipient mania. On the other hand, it is essentially unjust so to discuss Poe's essay as to convey the idea that it ranks low among similar treatises. Professor Stringham calls it worthless, and a waste of time. If the same thing be said of the philosophies of Berkeley, Kant, and Hegel—as it might just as well be—the disparagement of Poe would be somewhat discounted. But the candour of the current American criticism of Poe may be gathered from a comparison of the language held towards his fallacies with that used in regard to the merely childish theism of Mr. Lowell and Mr. Lanier, and the random pantheism of Emerson. On this head it may be added that Professor Stringham's criticism of Poe breaks down even on some scientific issues. He affirms of Poe's doctrine that the universe is in a state of ever-swifter collapse: "than this, nothing could be more at variance with the great law of the conservation of energy." There is no such contradiction in the case; and if there were, it would be equally chargeable against Mr. Spencer's theory of rhythmal disintegration and reintegration. Again, Professor Stringham charges Poe with showing "fundamental ignorance of astronomy" in saying that "the planets rotate (on their own axes) in elliptical orbits," without noting the need for a source of attraction at the foci of the ellipse. Yet Poe had expressly said in his *Addenda* to the *Eureka* (printed before Professor Stringham's critique in the new edition) that the sun's axis of rotation was "not the centre of his figure," and in the main treatise he had cited Lagrange's doctrine as to a variation of the orbits of the spheroids from circle to ellipse, and back again, by reason of variation in their axes. I do not undertake to say that Poe's conception is sound; but I do say that Professor Stringham has misrepresented him.

and independently defending the Nebular Hypothesis at a time when former exponents of it had wavered and proposed to abandon it.

To Dr. Browne's important commentary it might be added that in the preliminary section Poe emphatically forestalls some of the strongest recent declarations against the absolute Baconian theory of discovery,* that with two sweeps of his blade he demolishes a position which Mr. Balfour has only been able to take by laborious assault in his *Defence of Philosophic Doubt;* that he estimates Laplace with the confident discrimination of an expert; and that he speaks with intelligence on questions of astronomy which all but experts shun. Such is his measure of success, of impressiveness, in an undertaking in which he finally fails.

VII

When, after thus discursively scanning the achievement of Poe, we return to the contemplation of him as a personality, there arises a feeling of absorbing wonderment at the strange paradox of his being; the extraordinary union of this regnant intellect with that ill-starred temperament; the weakness of the man foiling the strength of the mind. The facts are plain. While he was writing his most rigorous criticisms, and building up his cosmogony in the white light and dry air of the altitudes of his reasoning imagination, the man was not merely stumbling under the burden of his constitutional vice as if smitten by sorcery, but was living an emotional life of passionate yearnings and rending griefs. It was

---

* Compare Mill, *System of Logic,* B. vi., ch. 5, § 5; Jevons, *Principles of Science,* p. 576; Tyndall, *Scientific Use of the Imagination and Other Essays,* 3rd ed., pp. 4, 8-9, 42-3; and Bagehot, *Postulates of English Political Economy,* Student's ed., pp. 17-19.

a lamentable life. After his stormy youth, in the latter part of which we find him attacked by the most crushing hypochondria, there came the cruel train of pangs represented by the illness of his wife, who seems to have truly "died a hundred deaths" before the release came; and in this period it was, on his own account, that in a state of absolute frenzy between his woe and his bitter poverty,* which seemed to league itself with disease against the young victim, he first gave way to delirious alcoholism. His wife's death left him heart-shaken, the long agony of her decline having deepened his feeling for her into a passion of pitying worship. As years passed on, the unstrung emotionalism of the man made him turn first to one and then to another woman for sympathy and love—this while he maintained to the outside world, save in his lapses, his grave, lofty, high-bred calm of manner; and bated no jot of skill or thoroughness in his artistic work. While he makes distracted love to Mrs. Whitman, he never slackens in his keen derision of the transcendentalists, whose cloudy philosophy he could not abide. He writes his story of *Hop Frog* with his old impassable artistic aloofness, and

---

* In an article in *Harper's Magazine* for May 1887, entitled "The Recent Movement in Southern Literature," the writer, Mr. Charles W. Coleman, jun., says he has before him a series of letters written by Poe's employer on the Richmond *Literary Messenger*, in which it is complained that Poe "is continually after me for money. I am as sick of his writings as I am of him, and am rather more than half inclined to send him up another dozen dollars, and along with them all his unpublished MSS.," most of which are called "stuff." For his Pym story Poe asks three dollars a page. "In reality," says the employer, "it has cost me twenty dollars per page"—a statement which is not explained. At last comes this: "Highly as I really think of Mr. Poe's talents, I shall be forced to give him notice in a week or so at the furthest, that I can no longer recognise him as editor of the *Messenger*." One is not highly impressed by the tone of the writer; but Poe's neediness seems clear.

writes about it to "Annie" in a letter touched with hysteria. "Forced, unnatural, false," "strained, exaggerated, and unnatural," are the terms Mr. Stoddard applies to these love-letters and letters of ecstatic friendship; and we cannot gainsay him here, save in so far as he imputes falsity. The case is one which Mr. Stoddard's primitive scalpel cannot dissect: what seems to him bad acting is neurosis. On the side of the affections Poe's sensitiveness becomes absolute disease; till the man who was accused of having no heart is wrecked by his heart's vibrations. But the intellect is never really subjected: it is shaken and dethroned at times by the breaking temperament; but it is unconquered to the last. He becomes almost insane when his engagement with Mrs. Whitman is broken; but he again collects himself, and he goes his way in silence. It is eminently significant that, as Mr. Ingram notes, he shows no resentment at being charged with aspiring to be a "glorious devil," all mind and no heart,* as he

* Mr. Stedman in his latest criticism of Poe (Introd. to vol. vi. of new ed. of *Works*, p. 24) says of him, more in the manner of Griswold than in that of Mr. Stedman's earlier essay: "A speck of reservation spoiled for him the fullest cup of esteem, even when tendered by the most knightly and authoritative hands. Lowell's *A Fable for Critics*, declaring 'three-fifths of him genius,' gave him an award which ought to content even an unreasonable man. As it was, the good-natured thrusts of one whose scholarship was unassailable, at his metrical and other hobbies, drew from him a somewhat coarse and vindictive review of the whole satire." It is true that Poe's review is bad in tone; but that does not put Mr. Stedman in the right, or bear out his zealous panegyric of Mr. Lowell. He oddly omits to cite the "two-fifths sheer fudge," though he seems to think that Poe ought to have welcomed Mr. Lowell's kicks for the sake of his sixpences. As against this addition to the countless one-sided verdicts on Poe, I must point out, (1) that Poe in his critique exhibits anger only over Mr. Lowell's very coarse attack on Southern slaveholders in general; (2) that though Mr. Lowell's lines on Poe were sufficiently impertinent he makes no protest on that head; (3) that

was by some of the Brook Farm transcendentalists. The explanation, I think, clearly is that while he was conscious of his tendency to turn emotions into reasonings, he also knew his danger from his malady, and was eager to have it overlooked. "In the strange anomaly of my existence," says the narrator in *Berenice*—a story which offers abundant data for the "epilepsy" theory—"feelings with me had never been of the heart, and my passions always were of the mind;" and here there is a certain touch of self-study; but we must not be misled by the phrase. Passionately quick, on the one hand, to resent moral aspersions, and extravagant in his emotional outbursts, he had the pride of intellect in a sufficient degree to wish, in his normal condition, to be regarded as above emotional weakness. One who knew him in his latter days thought there was to be detected in him a constant effort for self-control.

Looking back on his hapless career, and contrasting his deserts with his lot, and with his reputation, one realises with new certainty the worthlessness of most contemporary judgments. There are stories of his scrupulous conscientiousness and of his social considerateness such as could be told of few of his detractors; and yet we find one of his women friends resorting to inaccurate phrenology to account for the defects she

Mr. Lowell's versification, on which Poe spends most of his blame, was really excessively bad, whatever his "scholarship" may have been, and cried aloud for a retort from the assailed metricist; and (4) that Poe's show of vindictiveness is as nothing compared with the passionate resentment exhibited in one of Mr. Lowell's letters, recently published (vol. i. p. 109), on the score of Poe's having charged him with a plagiarism. An obvious blunder in Poe's citation of the passage imitated, he actually declares to have been a wilful perversion, though the easy exposure of it would at once tend to discredit Poe's charge. For the rest, Mr. Lowell's critical treatment of Thoreau makes it difficult for some of us to see in him the "knightly and authoritative" critical paragon of Mr. Stedman's worship.

POE

inferred in his moral nature. Absolutely innocent in his relations with women, though his unworldly romanticism in their regard carried him into some miserable embroilments, he came to be reputed an extreme libertine; and his one fatal failing lost him some of the friendships he most needed; virtue and goodness being not always as merciful as might be—not to say a trifle stupid. One of the most intensely concentrative and painstaking of writers, he has been stigmatised as indolent and spendthrift. To quote once more from the judgment of Professor Minto in the *Encyclopædia Britannica*, a vindication which, it is to be hoped, will set the current* of a true appreciation of the man :—" Poe failed to make a living by literature, not because he was an irregular profligate in the vulgar sense, but because he did ten times as much work as he was paid to do—a species of profligacy perhaps, but not quite the same in kind as that with which he was charged by his biographer." Pity and praise, we repeat finally, are far more his due than blame. Morally he lives for us as the high-strung, birth-stricken, suffering man, "whom unmerciful disaster followed fast and followed faster," till, instead of the proud, noble countenance of the earlier days, we see in his latest portrait, as M. Hennequin describes it in his vivid French way, a "face as of an old woman, white and haggard, hollowed, relaxed, ploughed with all the lines of grief and of the shaken reason; where over the sunken eyes, dimmed and dolorous and far-gazing, there is throned the one feature unblemished still, the

---

* In the dearth of adequate estimates of Poe, it is much to be able to add to Mr. Minto's that of Lord Tennyson, published after this essay was first written. According to the newspaper report, the Laureate in conversation or correspondence ranked Poe highest among American men of letters, describing some more popular writers as " pygmies " beside him.

superb forehead, high and firm, behind which his soul is expiring." The pity of it all, and of the inexpressibly tragic conclusion, is too profound to be outweighed by the remembrance that the "delicate and splendid cerebral mechanism" remained, for its ratiocinative purposes, almost intact to the end. But it is by that magnificent endowment that the world is bound to remember him. Among the crowd of men of one or of a few capacities, winning distinction by giving their whole strength to this pursuit or that, and living with hardly any other intellectual interest, he stands forth as an intelligence of singularly various equipment and faculty. Science was not too dry for him; the analysis of style not too subtle or frivolous: he could frame exquisite verse and stringent logic with equal mastery and equal zeal. As a boy he had a turn for swimming such as would have led many men into a career of sheer athletics; in a paper on *The Philosophy of Furniture* he embodies a passion for minor æsthetics such as can serve some men for a life's mission. For him there were no parochial boundaries in the world of the intellect: he was free of all provinces; over proud of his range, perhaps, but with an unusual title to be proud. And thus it is that we are fain to think of him as more than a poet, more than a critic, more than an æsthete, more than a tale-teller, more than a scientific thinker; a strange combination not seen in every age, and lastingly remarkable as such. He was a great brain.

COLERIDGE

(1893)

I

IN the best known passage of his Life of Sterling, Carlyle describes Coleridge as fascinating the younger spirits of his latter day by reason, above all things, of his philosophic orthodoxy.

"He was thought to hold—he alone in England—the key of German and other transcendentalisms; knew the sublime secret of believing by the 'reason' what the 'understanding' had been obliged to fling out as incredible; and could still, after Hume and Voltaire had done their best and worst with him, profess himself an orthodox Christian. . . . To the rising spirits of the young generation he had this dusky sublime character. . . ."

Of the character of this whilom pillar of the faith, Carlyle's own famous portrait has served most Englishmen as an estimate, marked as it is by all his mastery of light and shade. And inasmuch as portrait-drawing was really the work in which Carlyle excelled, his picture of Coleridge, whom he had seen and listened to, remains one of the documents for a future estimate of the man. But all of Carlyle's portraits are at once dramatic and didactic; and he is as far from explaining Coleridge as he is from explaining the French Revotution. He is above all things a preacher, even in portrait-painting; and the end of his performance here is to hold up his subject to the pitying censure of the reader, as being so sadly lacking in those qualities of decision and industry which the critic so highly esteemed in others, though for his own part he was never equal to packing his own portmanteau, and was in his way only less dilatory a worker than Coleridge. The passion for moralising on character, however, is not quite so strong to-day as it was in Carlyle's time, being in part superseded by the desire to understand it; and now that Coleridge's weakness has been sufficiently preached upon, it may be possible to get a little fresh profit from a simple study of his organism, in itself and in relation to its environment.

II

The study is now much facilitated by three books— the able critical biography of Mr. H. D. Traill (1884); the copious Life by Professor Brandl (1886), which although faulty and at times pedantically ill-judging, is helpful; and the very full and careful memoir prefixed by Mr. Dykes Campbell to his recent (1893) admirable edition of the poetical works.* In these Coleridge becomes fully perceptible as an organism and not merely as a moral warning, or an erring soul *in vacuo*. He begins to be at once intelligible in his heredity, son as he was of "a perfect Parson Adams," a cleric and pedagogue of an extreme absent-mindedness and unambitiousness, that is to say, a brain and body lacking in certain of the nervous correlations

* Another Life, by the poet's grandson (Macmillan and Co.), is mentioned by Mr. Campbell as being in preparation.

COLERIDGE

which make for efficiency in life and conduct.* On the side of judgment, the Rev. John Coleridge was capable of quoting Hebrew, as being "the immediate language of the Holy Ghost," to his rustic congregation at Ottery St. Mary; on the side of physique, he suffered from gout; and of his thirteen children, by two marriages, five died before Samuel, the youngest, reached manhood, while only four of the nine sons outlived the eighteenth century.† The little Samuel (born 1772), on his own telling, grew up "fretful, timorous, and a tell-tale," characteristics which he attributes to domestic mismanagement, but which no management could have wholly prevented. His early traits, his sensitive dreaming, his fretfulness, fitfulness, apprehensiveness, ill-health, and alternate woes and ecstasies, clearly mark a specific temperament, and carry in them the promise of all he is to be. Certainly he was as ill-managed as such a child could be, with a commonplace and uneducated mother, a wool-gathering father, a jealous nurse, an average infant-schooling, and a free run in all sorts of imaginative juvenile literature; all this being followed later by months of strangely precocious tavern-haunting with an injudicious uncle, and then by the years of often unhappy schoolboyhood at Christ's Hospital, which were on the whole no better and no worse for him than the rest of his preparation. At no stage were his weaknesses corrected by kindly discipline. Always he was precociously intellectual, never sturdy or prudent; always excessive in sentiment, lacking anchorage, judgment, and organic tenacity. Yet all along, from the schoolboy days to the last years

* Coleridge's friend, physician, and biographer, Dr. Gillman, insists on the close resemblance between his temperament and his father's (*Life of Coleridge*, 1838, p. 3).

† The father was fifty-five at Samuel's birth, and the boy was his mother's tenth child.

of grievous rest, when the battle of life was lost, he had for his associates a subtle and singular charm, a charm at once physical and intellectual, leaving men in doubt whether they were fascinated by the ever musical monologuing voice or by the strange stream of thought it translated. We might not ill picture his intellectual life to ourselves as a long fragile tissue of musical speech, attaining here and there to a wondrous iridescence, and always touched with an obscure pathos of frustration. To this speech boys and men listened with wonder, with pity, with derision, with perplexity; but they listened always.

His leading intellectual traits from the first were this abnormal facility of discourse and an equally abnormal fluidity of mind. At school he swam in medicine, metaphysics, theology, and the *Philosophical Dictionary;* "sported infidel," according to his own later account—that is to say, rejected with Voltaire the Biblical narratives and dogmas; and at the same time read in the Neo-Platonists—in Taylor's English translation, his most trustworthy biographer thinks. At the same time, the physical ill-luck of his early years continued, and a physique which was low on the vascular side to begin with, and had acquired ague in infancy, now caught rheumatic fever, a sufficiently bad preparation for the struggle of existence.

On his artistic side, again, his plasticity kept him in the imitative stage as long as most beginners; and his most notable early record is his lavish enthusiasm for the sonnets of Bowles, then winning a success of mood and mode. It would be hard to try a man's constancy by the test of his persistence in his boyish loves; but there is something instructive in the nature of Coleridge's first literary devotion, and the fact of his later ridicule of its fruits and his still later justification of it.

COLERIDGE

At seventeen he was making countless copies of Bowles for his friends; at twenty-five he was writing the three "Nehemiah Higginbottom" sonnets, burlesquing the Bowles manner, as copied by himself and his friends Lamb and Lloyd. Writing his "literary biography," so-called, he apparently comes back to a sympathetic view of Bowles, and as to his own practice confusedly suggests that out of diffidence of his powers he had written in a style which he at the time felt to be inferior; this without making it clear whether he thinks this style was that of Bowles or another. The changes and the pretence of harmonising them are alike Coleridgean. The explanation offered by himself, as Mr. Campbell says, is "what he was then willing to believe were his reasons for writing the parodies." What is of importance to notice is that in his youth Coleridge shows neither much verbal felicity in his own verse (with perhaps the exception of the boyish *Genevieve* lines),* nor much sense of verbal felicity in others; for Bowles never attains to more than a feeble tunefulness; and there lay to the boy's hand in English literature many more delightful performances, which might have been expected to appeal to such an artist as he was one day to show himself. All that is at all novel or individual in Bowles is the pensive mood; he in a manner revives the sonnet; but the technique is quite unoriginal, save for a leaning to new adjectives ending in "y." Coleridge's *Sonnet to the Autumnal Moon*, dated in his sixteenth year, has indeed some strength and melody of flow; † but these qualities are little developed in his

---

* That is, those so entitled, not the poem *Love*, which Christopher North seems to have had in mind in extolling *Genevieve*.

† The *Advent of Love* stanza, ascribed by himself to his fifteenth year, seems to have been written much later. See Mr. Campbell's note in his edition, p. 641.

COLERIDGE

later verses up to the brief great period, of which the suddenness, the unconnectedness, is as remarkable as the beauty of its fruits.

In part, no doubt, the lateness of the development of Coleridge's sense of poetic beauty is to be attributed to the general lack of any such sense in his pastors and masters. It was still the day of mechanical scansion and didactic appreciation. So uncritically had he been taught English that at twenty we find him writing the phrase "beneath the studious cloisters pale," thus showing that he read Milton's "cloister's pale" as = "pale cloisters." Headmaster Boyer certainly took special pains to introduce English literature into the studies of the School, beginning in 1784 with English grammar, till then untaught, and later introducing the accepted poetic classics ; but these did not then include Spenser ;* and not from Boyer would a pupil learn the magic of Milton's† and Shakspere's rhythms.‡ All the same, the cases of many young poets—Milton, Pope, Keats, Shelley, Poe, Browning, Tennyson—lead us to expect that a great faculty for verse of any kind will

---

* Brandl's *Life of Coleridge*, Eng. trans., p. 17. Cp. the *Biographia Literaria*, ch. i.

† "The solemn lordliness of Milton" is all Coleridge recognises at twenty-four. (Letter cited in Mr. Campbell's *Memoir*, p. xxx.) Brandl (*Life of Coleridge*, Eng. trans., p. 33) speaks of him as imitating *Lycidas* in the early *Monody on the Death of Chatterton* ; but the passage on frost and canker-worm to which Brandl refers is only in the later version of the poem, not in the earlier. See both in Mr. Campbell's edition, pp. 8, 61. The echoes of *Il Penseroso* and *Comus*, which Brandl (p. 46) believes he detects in the *Autumnal Moon* sonnet, will not bear examination. Only the word "fleecy" is used by both poets.

‡ Though Boyer, according to Coleridge's note on *Dura Navis* (Campbell's ed., p. 2) and his account in the *Biographia Literaria*, insisted on the value of simplicity of style, and derided the "O thou's" to which Coleridge was always resorting.

COLERIDGE

show itself early, at least to some extent; and it becomes a puzzling question how Coleridge could go on composing *Religious Musings* and other *Sibylline Leaves* up till his twenty-fourth year, attaining at most a rhetorical impressiveness and an odic emphasis,* and should then suddenly irradiate in the musical splendours of *Kubla Khan* and *The Rime of the Ancient Mariner*, and the ethereal harpings of the first part of *Christabel*. These three masterpieces were begun or done in 1797, his twenty-fifth year. Just after that again there are some successes, such as *Love* (1798-99) and *The Ballad of the Dark Ladie* (1798); but thenceforth, with very few exceptions,† we have the merely respectable performances of the earlier academic manner; and to the last Coleridge figures for us as a poet with some magical moments, never quite regained. The why of this is a problem that has not even been recognised, much less solved,‡ and it must surely be worth solving.

* *Lewti, or the Circassian Love Chant*, which, in Mr. Campbell's edition, is dated 1794, is certainly a lyrical success; but its real date seems to be 1798. See Brandl, p. 190, and Mr. Campbell's note, p. 567. The poem was first published in the *Morning Post*, in 1798, and it has much of the quality of the great poems of 1797-98.

† Among these should be noted the fine poem *Dejection*, belonging to 1802, and *The Snowdrop*, a fragment printed for the first time in Mr. Campbell's edition, which has some exquisite lines. *The Pains of Sleep* (1803) marks clearly the now malefic results of the opium habit, but has much of the drug's inspiration. From this time onward the best of Coleridge's pieces are those which express his penitence and despair, as *The Blossoming of the Solitary Date Tree* (1805), the blank verse lines (1807) *To a Gentleman* (Wordsworth), and *The Pang More Sharp than All*. The musical *Day-Dream* (? 1807) has bad lapses of technique.

‡ Mr. Traill (ch. iii.) fully recognises the isolated character of Coleridge's best poetry, in time and character, but does not attempt to explain the singularity; and even fixes 1800-4 as the period of a "fatal change of constitution, temperament, and habit," as if Coleridge had been a success at the outset. Mr. Traill speaks as

COLERIDGE

III

It may seem an extravagant thing to say, but I cannot doubt that the special quality of this felicitous work is to be attributed to its being all conceived and composed under the influence of opium in the first stages of the indulgence—the stages, that is, in which he himself felt as if new-born, before the new appetite itself proved to be a disease.* There is a difficulty about the dating of *Kubla Khan*, which Coleridge himself attributed to 1797, but which Mr. Campbell thinks may belong to 1798. In any case, the particular opium-eating which produced *Kubla Khan*, declared by Coleridge to have been his first indulgence, is known not to have been the very first;† and the psychological peculiarity of the shorter

if Coleridge had caused no distress to friends and kinsmen before 1800, whereas he had accumulated a great burden of despair as early as 1796. See the letter to Poole in Mrs. Sandford's *Thomas Poole and his Friends*, i. 184-193.

* Since this essay was first published, I find that though practically everybody else had regarded opium as the ruin and not the inspiration of Coleridge as a poet, the shrewd Whately long ago said that the great poems impressed him as the opium dreams of a man of genius. See his *Life* (abridged ed.), p. 416.

† He may before have taken it only for physical trouble; now he took it for mental. (See Mr. Campbell's Memoir, p. xliv., *note*. Cp. Brandl, p. 182.) Mr. Traill, after citing at length (p. 61) Coleridge's own well-known statement, prefixed to the poem, that he had the *Kubla Khan* dream after taking an "anodyne," strangely allows (p. 96, *note*) another of Coleridge's statements to cancel the surmise that the poem was an opium product. He finally decides (p. 100) that the opium-eating "may conceivably have begun" about 1801. But Coleridge himself, in a letter of 17th May, 1801, speaks of having taken laudanum in an illness, and he does not speak of it as a new thing. (See the passage in Mr. Campbell's Memoir, p. lvii.) It is practically certain that he had taken opium years before. See Mr. W. A. Wright's letter of February 20, 1894, in the *Academy*, which carries the date to 1796, on the testimony of an unpublished letter of Coleridge.

poem is essentially that of the longer. They are both abnormal to his whole previous technique, which ran to rhetoric and involution, turning thought and feeling to abstraction,* whereas the uniqueness of the new work consists in the extreme concrete simplicity given to visions far aloof from experience. Though both methods are essentially subjective, there has been a psychological inversion; and though at the time Coleridge had been intellectually much influenced by the society of Wordsworth, and perhaps even more, as Mr. Campbell thinks, by that of Dora Wordsworth, it is clear that something more than these influences came into play. The *Rime* was projected by Coleridge, on the basis of a dream by his friend Cruikshank; and Wordsworth did almost nothing to it beyond, as he stated later, suggesting part of the machinery; his own account being that he withdrew from his preliminary co-operation on it because, as he said, "our respective manners proved so widely different that it would have been quite presumptuous in me to do anything but withdraw from an undertaking upon which I could only have been a clog." It was quite in Coleridge's nature thus to be inspired first by his friend's dream and further by Wordsworth's data; but the artistic evolution is his own, the development being quite un-Wordsworthian: and we know from Wordsworth's characteristically patronising note on the poem in the second edition of the *Lyrical Ballads* that he disapproved of its scheme, and thought the Mariner too unsubstantial. We can

---

* Mr. Lowell, without suggesting any explanation, pointed out that the "felicity of speech in Coleridge's best verse is the more remarkable because *it was an acquisition*. His earlier poems are apt to be turgid, and in his prose there is too often a languor of profuseness . . ." (Address on the unveiling of Coleridge's bust at Westminster Abbey, May 7th, 1885.)

guess, with Lamb, how Wordsworth would have given him a local habitation and a name, a means of livelihood, and a theological system. Coleridge, on the other hand, met the criticism of the didactic Mrs. Barbauld by saying that the poem had too much instead of too little moral—what moral there was having no doubt been suggested by Wordsworth. But Coleridge's poetic bent hitherto had been almost wholly didactic or reflective; and though his early fancifulness or "shaping spirit of imagination" implied the gift on which the drug worked, it is only as a result of abnormal brain-states that the new and great performance becomes intelligible. So that what men regard as his mere bane, the drug to which he resorted as a relief from suffering, and which De Quincey declared to have "killed Coleridge as a poet," is rather, by reason of its first magical effects, the special source of his literary immortality.

What Coleridge would tend to under the mere influence of Wordsworth is to be seen in *The Three Graves: a Fragment of a Sexton's Tale*, a doggerel narrative of which the management is almost as inept as the versification. Seldom has a striking theme been so lamely handled; and seldom did Wordsworth himself reach worse depths of bathos than Coleridge here flounders-in through scores of stanzas. Such imbecilities as this:

> "It happened then ('twas in the bower
>   A furlong up the wood;
>   Perhaps you know the place, and yet
>   I scarce know how you should)"

and this:

> "Well! it passed off! the gentle Ellen
>   Did well nigh dote on Mary;
>   And she went oftener than before,
>   And Mary loved her more and more:
>   She managed all the dairy,"

represent the serious application of the professed Wordsworthian principles of style to narrative verse by the author of *Kubla Khan*. And years after the fourth part of this lamentable ballad had been mercifully closed, we find him penning the penitent note :— "*Carmen reliquum in futurum tempus relegatum.* To-morrow ! and to-morrow ! and to-morrow ! " If none of his repentances had been better motived, his case had been happier. That he could produce such work after accomplishing the *Ancient Mariner** is only to be explained on the view that his opium at times transfigured and enskied him, and that in his intervals, as far as art went, he was only an imitative performer of unstable judgment, at times sinking to an artistic abjection on a par with his temperamental collapse.

Of course, seeing that he took opium more or less to the end, it will not do to say that even for him, with his special gift and constitution, the drug could at any time make all the difference between inspiration and failure. It was the early effects only that seem to have availed for poetry. The anodyne soon wrought him more of mental as well as bodily harm than it could do of good; and on the other hand it is clear that he set out in life with extraordinary gifts. Lamb's account of his remarkableness at school and in youth is supported by many other testimonies, including that of Hazlitt, who later in life became his political and personal assailant ; and he made a deep impression on Wordsworth and others by his talk long before he could be charged with regular opium-eating. But it remains true, for one thing, that his poetry exhibits the immense differences

---

* Such is the dating of Mr. Campbell. One suspects that it represents an earlier imitation of Wordsworth, made before the physiological experience which carried him past at once the theory and the practice of Wordsworth.

above set forth; and for another thing there is something in his whole life and cast of character that squares with the view of him as a strangely compounded creature, capable, under special conditions, of performances quite incommensurable with his average work. He was emphatically a man moved by others, leaning on friends, drifting rudderless before winds of sympathy or necessity, taking shape and colour from anything rather than a central purpose. Opium was for him one more determinant; and in the first stage, before his fibre was sodden or degenerate with it, it might well be the most marvellous of all the influences he underwent. And it ought surely to be rather a comfort than otherwise thus to find a soul of goodness in the evil thing, to see a compensation in his weakness rather than merely to deplore and denounce it.

IV

However that may be, it is clear that if he had never tasted opium, Coleridge's life would have been no less a failure. Whether or not he might have been cured of his craving or his complaint in a fortnight, as Dr. Brandl thinks, by means of coffee and cognac, he was constitutionally lame in the will; and the will, considered as a faculty for steady action, is a bodily function to be studied like another. The case may now be past confident diagnosis in detail, but it is broadly clear. Cardiac disease, of which he died, is indeed early implied in Hazlitt's description of the "purple tinge" of his complexion; and whatever were his diathesis there can be no question of the frailty of his temperament. Carlyle's idealistic formula in its unexplaining way covers the fact: Coleridge was a combination of great

COLERIDGE

faculties with a feeble personality. Hence, to begin with, the dazzling impression which his talk so generally made; for he had so little of personal poise and self-sufficing character that all his powers and ideas played freely for any society in which he found himself, just as they did in his pencillings on the margin of any book he read. His mind was as a great lamp in the hands of a child: there was no temperamental sense of dignity, no ordered and conscious and purposive relation to life, such as should make a man discriminate in his activities and confidences; his way of getting in touch with the people he met was of a piece with his way of taking shape from his chance circumstances. Southey put it on record that in Coleridge's talk in youth he "heard the same things repeated to every fresh company, seven times in the week if it were in seven parties," and a clerk at Malta* noted the same habit, which comes out also in the prose writings. He was reminiscent and repetitive without being stable or self-poised—nay, because he was not stable or self-poised. It belongs to such a nature to be at once capricious and plastic; its rare acts of spontaneous volition relate to no general aim, and so have the momentary air of coming of self-will; while in its normal action it is helplessly servile to its surroundings.

And this radical unfittedness, while it brings the natural fineness of the ill-shrined faculties into high relief, must needs affect the play of the faculties themselves. A greatly efficient mind is one in which great powers are bent by a strong character to great purposes; and a fine mind whose temperamental spine, so to speak, is feeble, must needs sink into a hundred intellectual frailties. A man from the first sees life and the

* Campbell's Memoir, p. xxv.

problems of life through his temperament, his character, as well as through his arguing or talking powers; and if the temperament be viscous and pliable to others,* his views will tend to be transient, one effacing another till by sheer drifting he has found some final and fixed environment. Thus it is that Coleridge goes on changing and changing in opinion: an "infidel" at school; a Unitarian and a Radical in youth; a Hartleyan before his standing is discredited; an anti-Pittite while his near friends are so; a Tory reactionist with the majority; a Kantian, a Fichtean, and a Schellingite in turn; an orthodox pietist and Church-of-England man when he is unalterably dependent on protection and sustenance, and is no longer capable of fronting the world on his own feet. Of course the opinions so drifted into are all scientifically worthless; the final pietism is really more uncritical than the first boyish scepticism can have been. The reasoning and verbalising faculty functions for all views in turn, as it is swayed this way and that, on the flaccid stem of temperament, by this and that wind of contemporary doctrine. In the last refuge, where the winds are mostly tempered to the failing organism, the closing droop is that determined by the inherent weakness—the need to rest on a tradition with a prestige, the reflex clutch at the most august and unconditional doctrine of salvation. The aging intelligence pays its tearful tribute of faith at the behest of the tottering staff on which it leans.

Coleridge's main change of opinions, then, is a result of his mere sense of moral helplessness, his sense of openness to harsh criticism, his need of a stay on some

* He confessed to "the lamentable difficulty I always experienced in . . . abstaining from what the people about me were doing" (*Biographia Literaria*, ch. x., Bohn ed. p. 83).

COLERIDGE

broad basis of established opinion, after so many speculative changes. His later clinging to faith is very much of the nature of his pathetic clinging to the helpful friendship of Poole. There was no "stalk of carl hemp" in him to keep him up to his theoretic standards. He could criticise unanswerably Wordsworth's canons of poetry, the sudden lift in his own practice having involved the critical perception of Wordsworth's errors of reasoning and of art; but while he had been with Wordsworth he had been swayed to adopt them; and at all times he was a kind of intellectual ivy, needing some kind and stable housemate to cling to. He left his wife because she needed that he should support her, temperamentally as well as financially—in the former sense when he failed in the latter. Dorothy Wordsworth, who as it was gave up her life to her brother, and to whom Coleridge seems to have been at one time attached, might conceivably have made his life very different had she been his wife, though she would have had a sore handful. It is instructive to see how much more steadily he worked when he was cared for by wise friends, as the Clarksons, the Morgans, and the Gillmans, who checked his laudanum, the once magical servant which had grown to be so dreadful a master. Thus weak, and needing inward as well as outward support, he could at times seek to win social credit by commonplace abuse of opinions with which at other times he admittedly sympathised. He speaks of being "disgusted" with the "infidelity" of men more steadfast and single-minded than himself; and in his later years he invariably speaks of Frenchmen with the silliness of an ignorant Cockney.* It is instructive to contrast two of his utterances on Atheism, one in his

* See the *Biog. Lit.*, ch. x. (Bohn ed., p. 85); Ashe's ed. of *Miscellanies*, pp. 21, 56; and *Table Talk*, Ashe's ed., per index.

COLERIDGE

operose hostile critique on the trivial tragedy *Bertram*, a critique later included in the *Biographia Literaria;* the other in intercourse with his friend and disciple Allsop. The written passage declares that it cannot

"be denied without wilful blindness that the so-called system of nature (*i.e.*, materialism, with the utter rejection of moral responsibility, of a present Providence, and of both present and future retribution) may influence the characters and actions of individuals, and even of communities, to a degree that almost does away the distinction between men and devils, and will make the page of the future historian resemble the narration of a madman's dream."

The reference is to the *Système de la Nature* of d'Holbach; and the pretence is that its doctrine caused the Terror in the Revolution. The man who could thus rant for vulgar orthodoxy had held by the Revolution till after the Terror was over; had denounced the English Christians who urged an exterminating war with France in the name of Christianity:* and was wont to confess in abject remorse that his own life, with all its religion, had been ruined and shamed by self-indulgence. And he was later to say to his friend:

" The law of God and the great principles of the Christian religion would have been the same had Christ never assumed humanity. It is for [saying] these things and such as these, for telling unwelcome truths, that I have been called an Atheist. It is for these opinions that William Smith assured the Archbishop of Canterbury that I was (what half the clergy are in their lives) an Atheist. Little do these men know what Atheism is. Not one man in a thousand has either strength of mind or goodness of heart [enough] to be an Atheist. I repeat it. Not one man in ten thousand has goodness of heart or strength of mind to be an Atheist. And were I not a Christian, and that only in the sense in which I am a Christian, I would be an Atheist with Spinoza." †

* See the note to *Religious Musings* in Mr. Campbell's ed., p. 56.
† *Letters, Conversations, and Recollections of S. T. Coleridge*, edited by Thos. Allsop, 3rd ed., p. 47.

COLERIDGE

But yet again the opium drunkard would speak of the sturdy and wholesome Richard Carlile as "that wretched man," and compare his mind to a hell; this perhaps within a day or two of adjuring the same interlocutor:

" Pray for me, my dear friend, that I may not pass such another night as the last. While I am awake and retain my reasoning powers, the pang is gnawing; but I am, except for a fitful moment or two, tranquil: it is the howling wilderness of sleep that I dread."*

To use one of his own phrases, he is the vassal of vicissitude, such vicissitude as makes the idea of a continuous personality behind it seem more fantastic than a dream of the changing of souls.

V

How far this discontinuity of thought is to be set down to the opium habit, which would as it were double the swing of the pendulum, and how much to constitutional irrelation, is a matter for mere guess and suggestion. It stands to reason that a physiological process which yielded such artistic fruits as the *Rime* and *Kubla Khan* would affect to some extent the more abstract states of the intelligence, and certainly the state of the more intellectual emotions, thus developing his critical perceptions, which ran less risk than the poetic afflatus of being soon worn out. But he is discontinuous by nature. His intellectual life from first to last is that of an ineffectually gifted man, with inspired moments and much vain fluency. The outstanding characteristics of his style at all times are its uncommon copiousness and its frequent kindlings into either luminous theory or

* *Ibid.* pp. 42, 49. See also the letter to Wade (cited by Mr. Campbell, p. x. c. ii.), in which Coleridge compares himself to a "spirit in hell."

COLERIDGE

vital freshness of phrase and argument. To educated or uneducated readers and hearers, we can see, he must always have been a remarkable performer in speech : even a hostile reader must admit the general security and masterliness of his hold of language, in comparison, for instance, with the performance of Hazlitt, whose command of right expression, at times noticeable, is on the whole so unoriginal. Coleridge's prose utterance, wisdom apart, has the dignity which his character lacked. There is no better expression either of the effect his talk generally produced on new hearers, or of the impression often set up by his writing, than his own striking paragraph on the wonderfulness of prose, itself one of the best illustrations of his style :

> "It has just struck my feelings that, the Pherecydean origin of prose being granted, prose must have struck men with greater admiration than poetry. In the latter, it was the language of passion and emotion; it was what they themselves spoke and heard in moments of exultation, indignation, etc. But to hear an evolving roll, or a succession of leaves, talk continually the language of deliberate reason in a form of continued preconception, of a Z already possessed when A was being uttered—this must have appeared godlike. I feel myself in the same state when, in the perusal of a sober yet elevated and harmonious succession of sentences and periods, I abstract my mind from the particular passage, and sympathise with the wonder of the common poople, who say of an eloquent man— He talks like a book!"*

But save for the points of light and solidity his prose is unedifying and unconvincing. "Glorious islets in the haze" is Carlyle's most favourable hint of his philosophic monologuing ; and the description holds pretty well of all his prose works. His dilatoriness and discursiveness are not to be matched in serious literature of good standing; and his most formal and concise reasoning, as in the theses and scholia of the twelfth

---

* Given in the *Remains* and in Ashe's vol. of *Miscellanies*, p. 183.

COLERIDGE

chapter of the *Biographia Literaria*, can be absolutely incoherent in logic, putting the vaguest analogies for steps in sequence.* If this can happen when he is bent on precision, it is small wonder that his talk should, as Hazlitt put it, "start from no premises and come to no conclusion;" that his books should be assortments of fragments; and that his treatise on Method should be a perfect illustration of methodlessness.† It is vain to claim, as De Quincey did, that there was a cosmic sweep in his logic: he may at times continue an argument after a digression, but even then the digression is likely to be "gross as a mountain, open, palpable;" and often there is no solution, no return. There are hopeless disjunctions in his mental processes; it is a pathological case; and when he explains that he suspends his essay on imagination in the *Biographia* on the advice of a friend, he is only giving himself an excuse for a stoppage which would have occurred anyhow.‡ His mind was incapable of the steadfast persistence needed to round a system of philosophy. And so it is with his life: its solutions of continuity are fatally chronic. He would have left Christ's Hospital to be a cobbler's apprentice, which his father, clergyman and pedagogue, would placidly have made of him to begin with; he was eager again to be a surgeon; he fled

---

* Ferrier pointed out (*Blackwood's Magazine*. March 1840, p. 295) that several of the theses are copied in whole or in part from Schelling, and worsened in adaptation. This point is discussed below.

† He complained that the editors of the *Encyclopædia Metropolitana*, for which it was written, "bedeviled, interpolated, and topsy-turvied" his original performance. Campbell's Memoir, p. ciii.; Brandl, p. 357. It is difficult to believe that they lessened its fitness for its purpose.

‡ As to this, however, see section vi., hereinafter, for a still more damaging explanation.

from college and enlisted in the dragoons for reasons still only to be guessed at, and went back as inconsequently; on a hint from a friend he planned the emigration to the Susquehannah with Southey and the rest; then he dallied with the idea, dropped it, and resumed it as chance swayed, and finally was bitterly reproachful when the saner Southey, seeing the madness of it, definitely threw it over. He married a girl whom chance threw in his society, and soon found he had been all along in love with another. He made friends, good and bad, by good luck or bad, and at one time or other he had a rupture with nearly every one of them—with Lloyd, Lamb, Southey, Stuart, Poole, Wordsworth, the Wedgwoods. He longed to be back with his wife when he was away from her in Germany, and could not live with her when he returned. Yet again, when he had gone fortuitously to Malta, and had got a remunerative and easy post there, he grew sick for home, and threw up the situation. Throughout his life we find him drifting all over England, from place to place, from home to home, restless, rootless, impotent. As with his life, so with his opinions. Owing no doubt to the moral support of friends like Poole, who saw how the Terror had been wrought by the machinations of Burke and the *noblesse* and the Anglo-Prussian coalition against the Republic, he maintained his enthusiasm for the French Revolution when the common run of Englishmen were recoiling at its excesses; denouncing Pitt and Burke and acclaiming Tooke as late as 1796: away from his "beloved Poole," in Germany (whither he went in 1798) and elsewhere, he turned commonplace patriot and Tory when the Directory and the First Consul proceeded on the path of conquest that had been fatally marked out for the Republic by its enemies. And at every stage of his progress he was enthusiastically convinced : he read Burke in 1795 with "horror," and assailed Pitt with fury; and in later years he was just as horror-stricken and enraged with everything of the nature of Jacobinism. So in his philosophical opinions he was generally the convert of the last philosopher he had read, naming one child after Hartley and another after Berkeley, and later successively taking on the colour of one German transcendentalist after another, always more or less unable to say whether a given opinion was theirs or his. It was not mere unscrupulousness : he would avow his general debt freely : it was often sheer breach of recollection. Lessing, Herder, Kant, Schiller, Schlegel, furnished him with æsthetic and critical ideas which he far more often appropriated than he acknowledged them ; it is impossible to be sure when his thoughts are his own. On the side of his finances, such a man must needs be in a parlous state, however systematically he was helped by friends and admirers. At the height of his fame (1821) he was driven to write MS. sermons "for lazy clergymen, who stipulate that the composition must not be more than respectable for fear they should be desired to publish the visitation sermon."* Always embarrassed, he went on spending hugely on his then costly opium, perpetually failing in his literary promises, planning books which he neither wrote nor could write, announcing series of lectures and beginning a week late or missing a night, unless he was with friends who kept him wound up. For the worst of these things, as for his relapses into opium drinking, he had fits of abject remorse ; but the worst things were only the acute phases of a congenital diathesis, an obscure discontinuity of nerve structure.

* Letter to Allsop, vol. cited, p. 85.

COLERIDGE

About his perpetual changes of opinion, on the other hand, though he directly and indirectly sought to palliate or justify some of them, he had no shame: no instinct of gravity or self-respect could ever make him look round a new position circumspectly enough to make sure whether he could stand to it. He derided his old opinions as jauntily as he embraced new, exclaiming against his "squeaking penny-trumpet of sedition"* when he began to turn Tory, and contemning all scepticism when he began to turn orthodox. Some of his changes are hardly credible. In Allsop's volume we are told how he sympathetically cited the "beautiful tale of Tieck" which sets forth that beggars are social blessings inasmuch as they move us to charity; and we have the note of his own writing in which he praises the "true and touching words" of the lady who in the story laid down that view, and says he "cannot refrain from praying inwardly that the time may be far distant when such sentiment shall be scouted by our women."† Yet in his own notes on Sir Thomas Browne, made in 1802, on a passage laying down the very same doctrine:

"Statists that labour to contrive a commonwealth without any poverty, take away the object of our charity, not only not understanding the commonwealth of a Christian, but forgetting the prophecies of Christ,"

he made the comment:

"O, for shame! for shame! Is there no fit object of charity but abject poverty? And what sort of a charity must that be which wishes misery in order that it may have the credit of relieving a

---

* Letter cited by Mr. Campbell (under date 1798), p. xlii.
† *Letters*, etc., as cited, pp. 35-38. This was late in Coleridge's life.

small part of it—pulling down the comfortable cottages of independent industry to build almshouses out of the ruins!"*

This earlier and incomparably saner utterance Coleridge would in his last years, no doubt, have dismissed as a superficial and shallow view,† proper to the preparatory period of Spinozism and heterodoxy, in which he held by Unitarianism because he recoiled from the ethics of the doctrine of the Atonement, later felt by him to be metaphysically sound, inasmuch as it alone could give him comfort on his own account. Allsop, whose sympathy with Coleridge is not very intelligible, insists that "Coleridge ever retained the convictions of his early earnest youth;"‡ and we have seen his remarkable declaration to this friend on the subject of Atheism. But Allsop concedes that "in later years, when his health failed, when his bodily sufferings were great and constant, he leant to a system, a scheme rather, which should, if it might be, reconcile [orthodox] religion with philosophy;" and his later writings abound in asseverations of utter Christian orthodoxy.§ Then his freethinking protests to Allsop were only one more illustration of his profound temperamental and mental inconstancy, which could permit of vacillation almost to the last. That such a mind should ever

* Ashe's ed. of *Miscellanies*, p. 304.
† Cp. the note cited in Mr. Campbell's Notes, p. 586.
‡ Pref. to work cited, 2nd ed. Compare the equally confident conviction of Dr. Gillman (*Life*, p. 225, &c.), another intimate, to the contrary. It is plain that Coleridge was always vacillating.
§ Compare the conclusion of the *Biographia Literaria*, and the *Statesman's Manual* and its appendices. From protestations of piety he was capable of passing into a peculiarly rabid fanaticism. Thus we have him declaring: "If men .... acknowledge no national unity, nor believe with me in Christ, I have no more personal sympathy with them than with the dust beneath my feet" (*Table Talk*, May 3, 1832). To this complexion came the creed of professed love and brotherhood.

COLERIDGE

have acquired for itself a general authority with critical men, as apart from any estimate of its particular doctrines, is a proof of the ease with which men can be impressed where there is a genius for expression : that such a lifelong turncoat and victim of his own moral impotence should be to the last ready to hector and lecture on the faults of others, real or imagined, is a striking proof of the tenacity of the instinct of self-esteem even in a foundering soul, periodically sunk in despair.

VI

Not less remarkable, perhaps, is the fact that Coleridge won and for a time kept his philosophic prestige despite of his being convicted of plagiarisms unparalleled in literary history. I have said that his sins in this kind often came of sheer breach of recollection ; and they are so gross that they rather help us to understand his other lapses of memory than become intelligible from these. They make it clear, indeed, that his own accounts of the growth of his opinions can never be trusted. When he assures us that where he agrees with Schelling and Schlegel he is often only using their words for thoughts he had himself attained to,* we remember how he could announce as ready for the press a book of which nothing was ever written,† and we are forced to conclude that such coincidences as he alleges are hallucinations. The worthlessness of his testimony on disputable points may be sufficiently seen from his explicit allegation :‡—"No one has

---

* *Biog. Lit.*, ch. ix. (Bohn ed. p. 72).
† Cp. Allsop as cited, pp. 81-3 ; *Miscellanies*, as cited, p. 18 ; and Campbell's Memoir, p. cxxii.
‡ *Biog. Lit.*, ch. x. p. 106.

charged me with tricking out in other words the thoughts of others," when he has in the previous chapter* admitted that he has been charged with plagiarism. Mr. Traill's statement † that Coleridge knew nothing of Schlegel when he coincided with his views of Shakspere, is disproved by documentary evidence. Coleridge himself only claimed that he had anticipated Schlegel in early talk and in his first lectures at the Royal Institution, which (as usual) he misdated when making the claim. They were delivered in 1808, the year of Schlegel's lectures at Vienna.‡ But Mr. Traill's denial refers to the preserved reports of the lectures of 1811–12 and the notes of 1818. Now Coleridge himself admits in his ninth lecture of the course of 1811–12 that he had seen Schlegel's book; and in a letter to Crabb Robinson § he accorded Schlegel unmeasured praise as a commentator. What seems true is that Coleridge as early as 1798 propounded to Hazlitt a view of Hamlet which anticipated Schlegel's. But the view in question was no very recondite reflection, being indeed only a pathetic interpretation of Hamlet in terms of Coleridge's own fatal tendency to talk rather than act; ‖ and the influence of Schlegel is clear on many other points. Robinson noted at the outset of the lecturing (1808) that the discourses "adopted in all respects the German doc-

---

* *Biog. Lit.* p. 72.
† *Coleridge*, p. 165.
‡ See Campbell's Memoir, p. lxxvi. and Ashe's ed. of the Lecture Notes (Bohn), pp. 30, 127, 342–3.
§ See it cited by Brandl, p. 322.
‖ The essence of this conception, as it happens, was long before expressed by Henry Mackenzie in his essay on Hamlet in *The Mirror* (Nos. 99 and 100, under dates April 18 and 22, 1780). This very sane and intelligent criticism anticipates, among other things, Lamb's explanation of Hamlet's violence towards Ophelia.

trines, clothed with original illustrations and adapted to an English audience."* Again, Dr. Brandl notes how he argued on primeval culture "in such close connection with Herder's *Kalligone* that Crabb Robinson's notes of the lecture read almost like the index to the first chapter of that work," and that in other lectures of the course he clearly follows Kant's *Kritik der Urtheilskraft* and *Metaphysik der Sitten*, as well as Lessing's *Hamburgische Dramaturgie*, No. 69.

There can be no doubt that Coleridge owed much to the *Dramaturgie* in general; but seeing that number 69 is itself mainly a transcription from Wieland, who made a defence of Shakspere which must have occurred to many readers, the particular parallel cannot be pressed, and we are reminded that it is easy to press parallels too far. We may even say with Mr. Lowell: "He owed much to Lessing, something to Schiller, and more to the younger Schlegel; but he owed most to his own sympathetic and penetrative imagination."† In such matters the very plasticity shown by the receptive faculty is itself a kind of originality; and it is easy to point to luminous criticisms in Coleridge's notes which are all his own. On the other hand, however, Coleridge has made a number of appropriations in philosophy which cannot be so creditably accounted for; and we should miss some all-important items in the diagnosis of his mind if we overlooked them.

We have seen that the charge of borrowing from Schelling and Schlegel had been urged against him during his lifetime; and it was renewed by De Quincey in 1834;‡ but it was in Professor Ferrier's paper of

* Brandl, p. 296.
† Address on the unveiling of the bust at Westminster Abbey.
‡ *Tait's Magazine*, Sept. 1834.

1840 * that his practices were most damagingly exposed. It undertakes to show, with regard to the *Biographia Literaria*, that

"One of the most distinguished English authors of the nineteenth century, at the mature age of forty-five, succeeded in founding by far the greater part of his metaphysical reputation—which was very considerable—upon *verbatim* plagiarisms from works written and published by a German youth when little more than twenty-five years of age."

It cannot judicially be questioned that Ferrier made out his case: the answers made by Hare to De Quincey † and by Sara Coleridge to Ferrier break down as vindications. The worst of the case is that Coleridge's half admissions of indebtedness, and claims to original attainment of the same ideas, cover many pages of deliberate translation and adaptation; and that, as Ferrier from his metaphysical standpoint put it,

"In every instance in which we meet with remarks more than usually profound, bearing upon the higher mataphysics, it is Schelling and not Coleridge that we are reading."

Coleridge, indeed, is at times flatly disingenuous, parading the acknowledgment of a trifle when he is borrowing the whole gist of a passage, and professing to translate "in part" a paragraph of forty-nine lines in which his own contribution is only six. It becomes difficult to resist Ferrier's destructive suggestion that his alleged reason for stopping short in the chapter on the Imagination is a feint; and that the chapter really stopped because the scattered suggestions of Schelling on which Coleridge had begun to work (he re-adopted from Schelling's Germanised-Greek the term "esem-

* "The Plagiarisms of S. T. Coleridge," *Blackwood's Magazine*, March 1840.
† *British Magazine*, Jan. 1835.

plastic" which he professed to have coined) were not carried to any clear exposition—that the English writer, in short, had to stop because his original did not help him out. Yet further, Ferrier, proceeding on a cue from Hamilton, shows in detail that all the learning on philosophical history paraded in the fifth chapter of the *Biographia* is silently stolen from the German writer Maass; and yet again that Coleridge's lecture (xiii) *On Poesy and Art* is "closely copied, and many parts of it translated, from Schelling's *Discourse upon the Relation in which the Poetic Arts stand to Nature.*"

But even this is not all. Hamilton (forgetting that Ferrier had given the details as to Maass on his own prompting, and making the general charge as one to be added to Ferrier's list) followed up the charge of plagiarism on this head with one of blundering, declaring that the chapter in the *Biographia Literaria* on the history of the doctrine of Association, "in so far as it is of any value, is a plagiarism, and a blundering plagiarism, from Maass." Pointing out some of the blunders, Hamilton goes on to characterise Coleridge as a "literary reaver, whose ignorance of French alone freed France from contribution."

"Coleridge's systematic plagiarism," he adds, "is perhaps the most remarkable on record—taking all the circumstances into account, the foremost of which, certainly, is the natural ability of the culprit. But sooth to say, Coleridge had in him more of the ivy than of the oak—was better able to clothe than to create. The publication of his literary Table-Talk, etc., shows that he was in the habit of speaking—as his Biographia, etc., show that he was in the habit of writing—the opinions of others as his own." *

All this is unhappily true. One other decisive illustration may serve, regarding at once the Table-Talk

* Hamilton's ed. of Reid's Works, 1846, p. 893.

COLERIDGE

and the writing. In the former, under date June 15, 1827, we have this remark:—

"Perhaps the attribution or analogy may seem fanciful at first sight, but I am in the habit of realising to myself Magnetism as length; Electricity as breadth or surface; and Galvanism as depth."

Now, this theory, whatever it be worth, is a plain adaptation from Schelling; and it is further embodied at length in Coleridge's so-called *Theory of Life*—that is, in the essay so entitled, published by Dr. Seth Watson in 1848, and described by him as a joint production of Coleridge and Dr. Gillman, but, in view of the style, probably rightly claimed by Mr. Ashe* as substantially Coleridge's. Gillman may have contributed some of the natural-history data; but it is incredible that anybody but Coleridge can have put together without acknowledgment such an undisguised compilation of the published views of another philosopher. Its main thesis is the ancient and familiar one, maintained by Goethe as well as Schelling, and adopted indifferently for their contrary purposes by some Theosophists and some Atheists—that "life" is not to be defined in terms of any merely biological data, but is to be regarded as embracing the whole field of things, and is to be defined as "the principle of Individuation." This "individuation" is a characteristic existing in a low degree in a metal, in a higher degree in insects, fishes, and inferior animals, and in the highest degree in man. Then the principle of individuation is sought to be brought in line with physics by the generalisation that "a power acting exclusively in length is (wherever it be found) *magnetism;* that a power which acts *both* in length and breadth is (wherever it be found) *electricity;* and finally, that a

* In the prefatory note to the essay in his volume of the *Miscellanies*.

power which, together with length and breadth, includes depth likewise, is (wherever it be found) *constructive* agency." This last is first identified with chemical agency, but further affirmed to be at work in organic reproduction; and the primary magnetism is declared to be, "to the same kind of power, working as reproductive, what the root is to the cube of that root." For the rest, the "depth" of inorganic bodies is pronounced to be constituted by their gravity. It is hardly necessary to discuss the scientific value of this theorem, further than to say that it is a most instructive example of what can be done in the way of sham-definition and make-believe science by an elastic intelligence with great command of utterance and forms of dialectic, great confidence in its own guesses, and no concern whatever for scientific evidence. But whatever be its value, it is necessary to put distinctly on record, what Dr. Brandl only hints, that it is in every detail a simple restatement, albeit with oversights, of views advanced by Schelling in his *Ideen zur Philosophie der Natur* (1797), his *Von der Weltseele* (1798), his *Einleitung zu seinem Entwurf eines Systems der Natur-philosophie* (1799) and his *Darstellung des Systems der Philosophie* (1801) and later works.* Coleridge certainly does not

* An excerpt from the impartially made summary of the last-mentioned work in Noack's *Philosophie-Geschichtliches Lexikon* will suffice to show some of the correspondences: " Die Cohäsion, als Function der Länge, activ gedacht, ist Magnetismus, und die Materie in Bezug auf sich selbst als Ganzes gedacht, ist ein unendlicher Magnet.... Cohäsions-verminderung, absolut betrachtet, ist Erwärmung; die Wärme wird auf dieselbe Weise geleihet und mitgetheilt, wie die Elektricität..... Im Licht ist die absolute Identität selbst, d. h. das Licht ist dieselbe als Thätigkeit, nicht als Kraft. Die Wärme ist eine blosse Existenzweise des Lichts.... Weder durch Magnetismus, noch durch Elektricität wird die Totalität des dynamischen Processes dargestellt, sondern durch den chemischen Process, welcher jene beiden in sich aufnimmt,

fully expound Schelling's system : he entirely overlooks the phenomena of Light and Heat, which Schelling included in his formulas; but it was clearly from Schelling that he took his scheme, such as he made it. The nakedness of the plagiarism is somewhat covered by the early avowal in the *Biographia:*

" For readers in general, let whatever shall be found in this or any future work of mine that resembles, or coincides with, the doctrines of my German predecessor, though contemporary, be wholly attributed to him ; provided that the absence of distinct references to his books, which I could not at all times make with truth as designating citations or thoughts actually derived from him, and which I trust would after this general acknowledgment be superfluous, be not charged on me, as ungenerous concealment or intentional plagiarism." *

But the avowal, which Ferrier showed to be extremely misleading, is on the face of it equivocal ; and when we remember Coleridge's readiness to impute plagiarism to others,† his singular laxity of practice, which extended to his verse translations,‡ becomes an important datum in our conception of his character, and

durch beide vermittelt wird und mit dem Galvanismus identisch ist. Alle so genannten Qualitäten der Materie sind blosse Potenzen der Cohäsion," etc. A theorem of Length, Breadth, and Depth is further wrought out in Schelling's work on *Bruno* (1802), to the end of rising from the conception of space, the " absolute equality of the three dimensions," to that of a " quadrate " formed in union with the "infinite idea of things." Coleridge's final doctrine of the Trinity, again, may be clearly traced to Schelling's further theorem that the Infinite, the Finite, and the Eternal, form a trinity in unity ; the Finite in itself being equal to the Infinite, though emerging as a suffering and temporarily defeated God, the Infinite being the Spirit, which is the unity of all things, and so on.

* Ch. ix. p. 74.
† For instance, Erasmus Darwin and Scott. See Allsop, as cited, pp. 27, 29, and 186 ; and compare the references to Hume in ch. v. of the *Biographia, end.*
‡ See Mr. Campbell's Notes, pp. 614–621, and Ferrier's article.

COLERIDGE

in our estimate of the value of the esteem accorded to him as a thinker. So is the drift of the *Theory of Life* in itself. In Schelling's formulas there is an elusive germ of scientific suggestiveness. Of Coleridge's essay, albeit a work of great imaginative grasp, capable of inspiring other minds to more durable work, the main effect is to reduce the word "life" to utter insignificance by making it stand for the entire universe, as if it were his destiny to turn language positively or negatively to the frustration of real knowledge.

VII

Yet the fact of Coleridge's influence over young and other minds in his latter days is one of the salient facts of English intellectual life in the second quarter of the century, and it calls for recognition and explanation. It is to be understood through parallel cases, and through a study of the historic circumstances. He brought to the task of vindicating the orthodoxies much on the one hand of the verbal or talking gift of Dryden, who, similarly pliable and unmasculine, gave such fascination to his many changes of faith; and on the other hand much of the full-toned ratiocinative manner of Burke, who clothed common reactionary prejudice with such lavish trappings of apparently reasoning rhetoric.* All three alike made great play with bad cases; all three were either admittedly or demonstrably

* It is instructive to compare the portraits of Dryden and Coleridge in particular. Both are of lax tissue: and there can be no more complete misconception of Dryden than Mr. Swinburne's likening of him to Browning's great-jawed "crown-grasper" (*Miscellanies*, p. 26). Vascular degeneration is part of the medical diagnosis for both poets, and is apparent in the last illness of Burke also.

COLERIDGE

swayed by influences incompatible with just judgment; and all three found willing hearers—Dryden latterly in the least degree, but only because his last cause was least luckily chosen, as regards popularity. If Dryden could win adherents for Rome, and Burke could delight the Conservatism of his age by his praise of privileged prescription, Coleridge might well captivate the day of Canning and Wellington, and its immediate posterity, with his copious and cloudy asseveration that the highest philosophic truth coincided with the Athanasian creed—especially seeing that he had proved his genius by his poetry and his gift of criticism by his lectures. A generation seeking port after stormy seas was glad to accept any philosophy that went with church-going. He met the need of belated orthodoxy for a respectable account of itself; and just as Burke, in Coleridge's words, "until he could associate his general principles with some sordid interest, panic of property, Jacobinism, etc., was a mere dinner bell,"* so Coleridge himself only became revered when his philosophemes were felt to be necessary to the credit of creed. His literary prestige at once helped and was helped by his vogue as a Christian philosopher, even as it happened at the same period with Chateaubriand in France. To this day, the satisfaction he gives by many of his literary analyses is a lead to sympathetic interest in his sham analyses of knowledge; and the occasional vivid rightness of his concrete judgments lends a reflected light to his vain dogmatisings. No writer of any penetration equals him in plausibility and the air of secure demonstration. But neither does any writer of good calibre fall below him in defect of foundation and cohesion. His fluency was his philosophic snare, as happens with

* *Table Talk*, April 8, 1833.

a writer of our own day whose gift of copious poignant and original expression is even greater—Dr. James Martineau; and his philosophic work, like that of Martineau and Pfleiderer, is simply a protracted circling on the affirmation that men have a decisive and self-authenticating intuition of deity. It is the solution of Tennyson: "The heart answers, I have *felt*." All the theses and scholia of Coleridge are but embellishments of this assumption :

> " I became convinced that religion, as both the corner-stone and the key-stone of morality, must have a moral origin; so far, at least, that the evidence of its doctrines could not, like the truths of abstract science, be wholly independent of the will. It were therefore to be expected that its fundamental truth were such as might be denied; though only by the fool, and even by the fool from the madness of heart alone ! . . . . The belief of a God and a future state . . . . does not indeed always beget a good heart, but a good heart so naturally begets the belief, that the very few exceptions must be regarded as strange anomalies from strange and unfortunate circumstances. From these premises I proceeded to draw the following conclusions. First, that having once fully admitted the existence of an infinite yet self-conscious Creator, we are not allowed to ground the irrationality of any other article of faith on arguments which would equally prove that to be irrational which we had allowed to be real. . . ." *

And so on. This, which he represents as the philosophy of his Unitarian period, and as yet enabling him to attain to " final reconversion to the whole truth in Christ," is the gist of his latest doctrine; and it exhibits Coleridge as holding his religion just as a Mohammedan holds his. The very function of philosophy is here abdicated in the act of parading it; and what is offered as a theorem, an explanation of theism in relation with atheism, collapses into an admission that from the theistic standpoint (as is indeed the case)

* *Biog. Lit.*, ch. x. pp. 96–97.

atheism is inexplicable, and only arbitrarily to be got rid of by epithets, ranging from "fool" and "bad heart" to "anomaly." As if it were not the business of a theistic philosophy of conduct and character to account theistically for follies and resolve anomalies.

His attitude on subsidiary dogmas is in keeping with his method on the cardinal points. Faced by the beginnings of Egyptology, he flabbily blusters about "French infidels," and predicts that Genesis, as conveying "the rapid progress in civilisation and splendour from Abraham and Abimelech to Joseph and Pharaoh," will be found "worth a whole library" of inferences from the monuments.* He contrives to deny in advance the doctrine of evolution, already adumbrated; † and holds to the mediæval dogmas that "the earliest Greeks took up the religious and lyrical poetry of the Hebrews," ‡ and that "the sacerdotal religion of Egypt had, during the interval from Abimelech to Moses, degenerated from the patriarchal monotheism." § Wherever his orthodoxy came into play, in his later years, his judgment was worthless; and when he discusses such an issue as that of the genuineness of the Mosaic books,‖ his reasoning is more disingenuous than that of an average divine. He actually declined to try to translate *Faust* because he held much of the language to be "vulgar, licentious, and blasphemous." ¶ On politics he is more profitable, speaking at times with a wisdom and humanity in advance of his age, as when he protests against the prevailing offensiveness of the tone of English books on America,** perhaps forgetting, but more probably ignoring wisely, the fact that that tone

* Essay on the *Prometheus*. Ashe's ed. of *Miscellanies*, p. 56.
† *Ibid.* p. 65. ‡ *Ibid.* p. 62.
§ *Ibid.* p. 57. ‖ See *Table Talk*, May 20, 1830.
¶ *Ibid.* Feb. 16, 1833. ** *Ibid.* April 10, 1833.

was a good deal the result of American provocation;*
or when he denounces the English misgovernment of
Ireland.† He was sound, too, on the land principle,
and sometimes notably acute and original on economics;‡
but just as often he finds a form of justification for a
prejudice or a privilege or a prescription; and he had
no foresight of the healthy development of democracy,
any more than he had a biological conception of the life
and the correlation of States. His formula of Permanence and Progression, which Mill extols, is but an
adaptation from Burke;§ and it is quite misleading to
credit him, as Mill does, with a really scientific grasp of
his doctrine; though the reminiscence of what he had
seen and held in opposition to Burke made his Conservatism less nakedly irrational than Burke's; as the
memory of his youthful Nonconformity set him on
giving a worthier theory of the Church Establishment
than that held by his fellow Tories. His well-known
and often quoted defence of Burke, as having proceeded
on the same principles in advocating the American and
denouncing the French Revolution—a piece of sophistry
which has found singularly unanimous acceptance with

* The prediction of a great strain on the Union, for which Carlyle sometimes gets much credit, was also made by Coleridge (*Table Talk*, Jan. 4, 1833.) But it was also made by Macaulay, *Misc. Writings*, ed. 1868, p. 145 (Essay on James Mill, 1829).

† *Table Talk*, Feb. 5, 1833.

‡ E.g., *Table Talk*, March 31, 1833, where he approves of a graduated property-tax, but also wants "a large loan," going on to insist rightly enough that much harm was being done by over-accumulation of "capitals." (Cp. May 4, 1833.) Mill's verdict that in political economy he "writes like an arrant driveller," is sufficiently violent, and contrasts significantly with the fashion in which on other matters Mill tries to find disinterested wisdom in Coleridge's personal equation.

§ "The two principles of conservation and correction" (*Reflections on the French Revolution*, ed. 1790, p. 29).

COLERIDGE

Burke's admirers—was simply an indirect plea for himself. By making out the consistency of Burke, he could give a colour of consistency to his own change of front from hot vituperation to effusive eulogy of that writer. The personal equation always counts for much. Malthus he abused with all the anger of a blind begetter of children:* and when he is partly right in his economics it is rather by reason of sheer antipathy to the new commercialism than by any scientific comprehension of it, such as Malthus might have helped him to.

The summary of all his positions is that he follows the channel of the emotion of the time being, never checking one by another. He has been justly praised by Mr. Traill for his passage on the emotionalism of mobs:

"The passions, like a fused metal, fill up the wide interstices of thought and supply the defective links; and thus incompatible assertions are harmonised by the sensation, without the sense of connection." †

But this holds strictly true of his own philosophy and ethic, in mass and detail. Of principles he could never keep hold; and in the end his doctrine was nine-tenths the expression of what was left in him in the way of "the passions," to wit, abjection, animosity, and the need for emotional support. Now, there is a truth behind his one-sided advice that "the best way to bring a clever young man, who has become sceptical and unsettled, to reason, is to make him *feel* something in any way"‡—the truth that just reasoning or judg-

* *Table Talk*, August 12, 1832.
† First *Lay Sermon*. Compare the passage in *The Friend* (Sect. ii. Essay iv.) on the Method of Shakspere—which again is in part reproduced in the Essay on Method.
‡ *Table Talk*, May 17, 1830.

ment proceeds from strong impressions or intuitions. But the truth is turned into pure psychological falsehood, to begin with, by the implication that only faith has the basis of feeling, and that doubt or disbelief has no such root; and, further, the acceptance of feeling as at once motive and criterion, advocate and judge, transforms the psychological truth into logical fraud. He who has no strong temperamental basis for his beliefs will be no very powerful thinker; but he who is not moved to bring his every temperamental impulse to the test of consistency has only half the thinker's outfit. And such a one was Coleridge. In direct antithesis to the glorification of prejudice above cited, we find him formally declaring, in a "confession of belief" dated 1817:

> "I reject as erroneous, and deprecate as *most* dangerous, the motion that our *feelings* are to be the ground and guide of our actions. I believe the feelings themselves to be among the things that are to be grounded and guided." *

Again we have the note in the *Aids to Reflection* condemning the glorification of prejudice by other people:

> "The indisposition, nay, the angry aversion to *think*, even in persons who are most willing to *attend*, and on the subjects to which they are giving studious attention—such as Political Economy, Biblical Theology, Classical Antiquities, and the like—is the phenomenon that forces itself on my notice afresh, every time I enter into the society of persons in the higher ranks. To assign a *feeling* and a determination of their *will*, as a satisfactory reason for embracing or rejecting this or that opinion or belief, is of ordinary occurrence, and sure to obtain the sympathy and the suffrages of the company. And yet to *me*, this seems little less irrational than to apply the nose to a picture, and to decide on its genuineness by the sense of smell." †

---

* Gillman's *Life*, p. 359.
† Note on Aphorism vii. Cp. Aphorism lxiii.

COLERIDGE

And yet again in the same book* we are told that Religion flourishes in a country

"where the Mysteries of Faith are brought within the *hold* of the people at large, not by being explained away in the vain hope of accommodating them to the average of their understanding, but by being made the objects of Love by their combination with events and epochs of History . . . . and above all by early and habitual association with Acts of the Will."

Thus does the broken intelligence sway helplessly from side to side, as it is stirred to reason by the unreason which provokes it, or terrified into unreason by the reason which outgoes its own. To take either the one mood or the other as typical is to miss the central fact of the case. It is the perpetual oscillation that specially constitutes Coleridge; and those friends and vindicators who, like Mill and Coleridge's own relatives, make up a personality from one set of his utterances, are only adding to the world's stock of misconceptions. The relatives, of course, could not be expected to give a picture which by its contradictions would recall the character of the man; and Mill, even in the heat of his zeal for the science of Ethology—which he never grasped save empirically, and never developed as he proposed—discoursed *à propos* of Coleridge on national character as conditioning ideas, without once seeing how character conditioned the ideas of Coleridge. Yet never did vacillation of character connect more obviously with vacillation of thought than in the author of *Aids to Reflection*.

VIII

All this consists obviously with what we have seen of his physical susceptibility and disconnectedness, his weakness of fibre and lack of stable relation to things

* Aphorism cx.

concrete. His cues are his cravings, his impulses, his impressions, his temperamental attractions and repulsions. But it follows that his excellences, his successes, also correlate with his temperament and mould: so much has appeared in the study of the sources of his best poetry, and it must hold good of his other felicities. His outstanding quality of character being impressibility, and his outstanding mental quality a genius for expression, he is at his best or strongest didactically where he expresses his sense of literary effect—the gift of perception and expression in others. Thus it is that he makes such an impression by his sifting* of the matter of the controversy, raised by Wordsworth, on the use of the language of ordinary life in poetry—a problem not indeed so difficult of solution as some eulogies would make out, but certainly well solved by him in an age when good analytical reasoning on æsthetics was far to seek. Here his instinct and his reasoning were happily conjoined. He rightly claimed† that his mind was always "energic," by which he did not mean "energetic," but that it played reflectively on all things which touched it, seeking spontaneously to relate all impressions to general truths. We have seen that too often the effort was wholly astray, from fault of method and vice of presupposition; and at times it was astray from æsthetic defect, whether of constitution or culture, as in his judgments on painting. He declared that his three months' stay at Rome gave him more insight into the principles of the fine arts than he could have gained in twenty years in England;‡ and it may well have been so; but his taste in pictures must have been poor, to judge from his laudation of Sir George Beaumont's;§ and though "he could

* In the *Biographia Literaria*. † Campbell's Memoir, p. lxiv.
‡ *Table Talk*, March 1, 1834. § *Table Talk*, July 24, 1831.

scarcely contain himself" in listening to Beethoven, his likening of Rossini to "nonsense verses"* does not strengthen the claim to musical appreciation which he coupled with the admission that he had no "ear for music." Where he is easily ahead of nearly all his contemporaries, is in his intelligised perception of the qualities of literary masterpieces hitherto only vaguely enjoyed. When his environment and his faculty co-operate, the fruits are delightful. Let the limp stem but be upborne by some steady breeze, or by some companion stalk, and it energises at once, so that even though the initiative be from the outside, the gifted intellect will of its own virtue work wonderful things. On the stimulus of Wordsworth, coinciding with a new physiological stimulant, Coleridge produces rarer and subtler poetry than Wordsworth's; on the stimulus of Schlegel, he produces a criticism of Shakspere more suggestive, more intimate, more finely-fingered than Schlegel's; on the stimulus of Schelling, he yields ideas for which Schelling is grateful.† Coleridge on æsthetics, on poetry, on style, is always fascinating, always suggestive even when wrong; it is the perpetual play of mind, on questions where mind is for the time unvitiated or untrammelled by temperament and subservience to dogma, or where the good and not the bad in the temperament comes into effect, that seizes and impresses the young reader of the lectures on Shakspere and Milton and literature generally, the Table Talk, the *Biographia Literaria;*

---

* *Table Talk*, Oct. 5, 1830.

† Sara Coleridge's introd. to the *Biographia*, 1847, p. xxxviii. See also Clough's *Prose Remains* (ed. 1888, p. 105), as to Schelling having praised Coleridge to Jowett and Stanley, protesting that it was "an utter shame to talk of his having plagiarised from him, Schelling." It is not clear that Schelling knew all the facts.

and it is the natural surmise from such a display of intellectuality that makes the young reader fain to hold to the religion by which Coleridge held. It is easy to see how the mere distinction of phrase and text and tone, the pervasive suggestion of insight, could capture and convince high-minded young men of that time like Maurice and Sterling, unprepared by solider thinking to appraise the manifold Coleridgean doctrine; and how it could even set up an unfeigned respect in the young Stuart Mill, more sensitive than his hardier elders to the æsthetic charm of Coleridgean exposition, less quick than they to cut through the surface tissues to the feeble substructure, and above all comparatively untouched by the contemptuous personal revulsion from Coleridge's weaknesses of life and character which the elder Radicals had felt in standing near him.

And while we note the unstrung and unerect susceptibility to chance and to other minds which makes Coleridge's life and work at times seem like a mere series of pulls and pushes from the outside, let us not overlook the *per contra*, as regards either his associates or his immediate successors. Mr. Dykes Campbell, noting the reciprocal influence of Wordsworth and Coleridge, has well said:

"Although Dorothy Wordsworth produced nothing directly, her influence on both men was of the highest importance. . . . . Nor was the influence, in action and reaction, of the men on one another less potent. Coleridge's was by far the more active, as well as the finer and more penetrating, and the immense receptiveness of Wordsworth must have acted as a strong incentive to its exercise. And this is true, I believe, notwithstanding that there are more distinct traces of Wordsworth's poetry on Coleridge than the converse: for Coleridge, by virtue of his quicker sense, was the more imitative, while in Wordsworth's case influences from without never reacted directly, but permeated his whole being, and were so completely assimilated as to have become part of himself before any of their results came to the surface." *

And Charles Lamb, who by his prose so strongly sets up the impression that may be made in painting by an Old Master—the sense of a lost and irrecoverable way of doing things, of a remote and inimitable beauty—even he, in his greatest critical work, not seldom sets us wondering how much of that bent to and skill in æsthetic analysis which make him so great and so new a critic, and of that splendid coloration and energy of style which make him so great a writer, was developed in him by the talk of the ever-observing, ever-discussing, ever-reading, and ever-criticising Coleridge. The young Charles Lamb shows small promise of the author of the essays *On the Tragedies of Shakspere*,† *On the Genius and Character of Hogarth*, and *On the Barrenness of the Imaginative Faculty in the Productions of Modern Art;* and it is impossible not to surmise that but for some special nourishment and stimulation, in that age of raw sensation and wooden prejudice, those rare gifts could not have come to such maturity. Lamb's striking misjudgments, besides, in the case of some of the Elizabethans, suggest that he was helped to his best views.

* Memoir, p. xxxvii. It is worth noting that the maxim that every great and original author must create the taste by which he is to be enjoyed—a maxim usually credited to Wordsworth—is by him acknowledged to be Coleridge's (*Essay, Supplementary to Preface*, to 2nd ed. of *Lyrical Ballads*. *Works*, Morley's ed., p. 874). Much of this Preface and Essay suggests Coleridge. The saying that the true antithesis to Poetry is not Prose but Science (*Preface* as cited, p. 853) seems to be echoed from Coleridge, who often makes it. (*Biog. Lit.*, ch. xiv. p. 148; *Lectures*, p. 183, etc.)

† Lamb's thesis that Shakspere is to be read, not acted, seems to have been adopted from Coleridge. See Crabb Robinson's *Diary*, 3rd ed. i. 184. Cp. the passage in Gillman's *Life*, p. 280, cited on p. 239 of the Bohn ed. of the *Lectures*.

IX

The service done by Coleridge can hardly be stated more highly than this; and alongside of the service must be placed the dis-service. Always desultory,* he never followed any of his deeper studies with the patience which alone can yield solid results; his way of life made continuity impossible for him till he was too frail for steady toil; and his facility of phrase often led him into mere mock solutions. He gave a superfluous encouragement to verbalism in philosophy all round. Even on his ground of æsthetics he is capable of making a mere arrangement of formulas pass muster for an analysis. His faculty being one of verbal expression, he tends to make verbal exercise take the place of investigation, especially, of course, in theology, where he was wholly in the air. His reasoning there becomes what Selden declared the doctrine of transubstantiation to be, "nothing but rhetoric turned into logic;" and it becomes so at times on ground where he might have done better, the habit of verbal solutions seducing him. Thus in the second essay *On the Principles of Sound Criticism* † he makes the discrimination that "the venison is agreeable because it pleases; while the Apollo Belvedere is not beautiful because it pleases, but it pleases us because it is beautiful." This is plainly a spurious distinction. The venison is not agreeable *because* it gives pleasure: "giving pleasure"

---

* His own early admission: "I seldom read except to amuse myself, and I am almost always reading" (Letter to Thelwall, cited by Mr. Campbell, p. xxix.) may be set against the claim in the *Biographia*: "Seldom have I written that in a day, the acquisition or investigation of which has not cost me the previous labour of a month" (Bohn ed., p. 106).

† Ashe's ed. of *Miscellanies*, p. 11.

COLERIDGE

= "agreeable:" it gives most of us pleasure of a kind that we agree to put under some such term as "agreeableness;" just as the statue gives most of us a pleasure which we agree to put under the term "beauty." But the venison and the statue may alike fail to give pleasure to some persons; and to say that the statue *is* beautiful, as if its beauty were non-relative while the agreeableness of the venison is a term of relation, is sheer fallacy, and just the kind of fallacy into which Coleridge was always being led by his transcendentalism, which is essentially an evasion of analysis under the pretext of making it. That the error was inveterate, and not a matter of one loose expression, appears from his further citation* of some traveller's statement that the people of Dahomey have no word for beauty or the beautiful, but merely say of things that they are "nice" or "good"—an egregious case of *a priori* fallacy. It would be possible to show that the Dahomeyans did not call any one thing beautiful, only by showing that they applied the word to some other thing. The pretence that a word in any language *can* mean only nice and good without its being distinguishable from a word of greater force, is as bad a paralogism as can readily be produced. The traveller, according to Coleridge (who does not remember his name or his precise words), explains that in Dahomey the sense of beauty "is as yet dormant, and the idea of beauty as little developed in their minds as in that of an infant;" which is a mere evasion of the difficulty of difference of standards. The Dahomeyans admittedly admire certain types of women for their looks, more than others, and thus have a sense of beauty just as truly as they have a sense of what we call the "nice" or the "good," in

* *Ibid.* p. 13.

both of which categories their judgments are quite as little "developed," practically speaking, as in the others. All this blundering, so far as Coleridge is concerned, comes of his determination to establish *a priori* knowledge by way of supporting his religious faith—or else of his sloth.

The same tendencies lead him on the other hand into the most gratuitous literary blunders. Of the latter, Macaulay gibbeted (albeit by mistake, and therefore with the wrong evidence) a distressing example, which his biography has given to all the world—a piece of random assertion only to be explained as a case of the fortuitous wish begetting the thought without any resort to facts. Coleridge, recklessly following up a warning against "converting mere persons into abstractions" in the writing of prose, made the strange assertion: "I believe you will very rarely find in any great writer before the Revolution the possessive case of an inanimate noun used in prose instead of the dependent case, as 'the watch's hand' for 'the hand of the watch.' The possessive or Saxon genitive was confined to persons, or at least to animated subjects."* Macaulay comments in his journal: "About twenty lines of Shakspere occurred to me in five minutes;" and he gives: "In dreadful trial of our kingdom's king" (*King John*); "Nor let my kingdom's rivers take their course" (*ibid.*); "The law's delay" (*Hamlet*); "My bosom's lord sits lightly on his throne" (*Romeo and Juliet*); "Why then All Souls' day is my body's doomsday" (*Richard III.*).† He might have added, from Milton, "their bellies' sake" (*Lycidas*); "cloister's pale" (*Il Penseroso*); "the heaven's wide pathless way"

---

* Notes of Lectures on *Style*, of 1818, printed in the *Remains;* also in Ashe's ed. of *Miscellanies*, p. 183.

† Trevelyan's *Life*, ch. xii.

COLERIDGE

(*ibid.*); "the chimney's length" (*L'Allegro*); "life's lease" (*Epitaph on the Marchioness of Westminster*); "tapers' holy shrine" and "cymbals' ring" (*Ode on the Nativity*)—all cases "before the Revolution." But Coleridge's first sentence speaks of "prose;" and these instances—all save one—are in verse.* It is difficult to see, indeed, what force could be attached to the fact that the old prose-writers seldom gave the Saxon genitive to the name of an inanimate body. The writers of to-day, and of intermediate generations, do it still seldomer. In the nature of the case, such genitives cannot often occur. But so far from their being vetoed by the old writers, we find them in unnecessarily frequent use. I open Bacon at random and find the line "more by *an hour's* discourse than by *a day's* meditation." In the Bible we repeatedly have "a day's journey;" and the titles "A Winter's Tale," "A Midsummer Night's Dream," &c., cannot be set aside as poetry. Such phrases as "river's bed," "bed's head," "staff's length," "shilling's worth," are all good pre-Revolution English. The statement breaks down as to prose and verse alike. And equally idle is the protest in the *Table Talk*† against the "vile and barbarous vocable *talented*. . . . Why not *shillinged, farthinged, tenpenced,* &c.?" The analogy here is frivolous. As well denounce "gifted," or "moneyed," which is used by Coleridge himself;‡ or "landed interest," or "horsed," or "housed," or "cabined," or "kennelled," or "dowered," or "terraced," or "hundred-gated Thebes," or "helmeted," not to speak of

---

* I must confess to having overlooked the qualification myself in the first issue of this essay. The oversight was brought to my notice by my friend, Mr. T. D. Robb. Macaulay probably noted only the second sentence, which is unqualified.

† July 8, 1832.   ‡ *Table Talk*, July 4, 1830.

COLERIDGE

Milton's "sworded" cherubim. It happens—as was noted by Macaulay, though he too objected unreasonably to the word *—that "talented" came into use first in theology, having reference to the parable of the talents. Had Coleridge known this he would hardly have made his protest, which came ill in any case from a maker of many new words, some of them needless and bad. He had simply carped at random.

This irresponsible turn of mind affects even the best critical work of Coleridge. His Shaksperean criticism, compared with most of what went before, is so good that we can scarcely grudge him the praise bestowed by Mr. Traill; but, even setting aside the question of the borrowings from Schlegel, it has plenty of weak places. Mr. Traill's imperishable dictum that he was "loyally recognitive of the opacity of milestones" will not hold in fact any more than in style. It praises him for exactly what he was not. His criticism at times becomes vicious, as does Schlegel's, from the determination to make out that whatever Shakspere did must be right, as where he refuses to see that Hamlet's "To be" soliloquy is inconsistent with his having just before seen his father's ghost. A rational criticism must recognise that the soliloquy is a literary addition inconsistent with the action; and this recognition leads up to the knowledge of the play as a series of accretions, pre-Shaksperean and Shaksperean, on the nucleus of the primitive tale. That there was a primitive tale Coleridge knew,† but he never once takes the fact into critical account. At another time he extols Shakspere for never depicting a miser, on the ground

* See Trevelyan's *Life*, ed. 1881, pp. 150, 416.
† *Biog. Lit.*; *Satyrane's Letters*, ii.; and *Lectures*, p. 240.

that avarice was not a permanent species of passion.* He will always have Shakspere the Uncaused Cause in drama, doing all things well; † and the same arbitrariness enters into his eulogy of Milton, as when he defends the presentment of God the Father against Pope's criticism, after having once admitted its force.‡ Not even the verdict of Mr. Lowell can put his status as a philosophical critic beyond question; for it is precisely in philosophical generalisation that Mr. Lowell himself is least satisfying.§ He had too much predilection to Coleridge's own intellectual sins of developing his philosophy uncritically from his sentiments, and of finding in a play of words an account of the constitution of things.

* *Lecture Notes*, Bohn ed., p. 99. He actually alleges that "as a passion, avarice has disappeared." See also p. 102. On this ground he pronounced the miser of Plautus and Molière obsolete. The reader of *Eugénie Grandet* can supply the comment.

† "There is not one of the plays of Shakspere that is built upon anything but the best and surest foundations." *Lecture Notes*, p. 99.

‡ Cp. Lecture Notes on Milton (Bohn ed., p. 520) with *Table Talk*, Sept. 4, 1833.

§ In the address on the unveiling of Coleridge's bust, Mr. Lowell made the observation: "Many of his hints and suggestions are more pregnant than whole treatises, as where he says that the wit of *Hudibras* is the wit of thought." This unfortunate example only serves to confound Coleridge. His dicta are: (1) that wit "consists in presenting thoughts or images in an unusual connection;" (2) that *this connection* may be by *thoughts*, or by *words*, or by *images*;" and (3) that "the first is our Butler's especial eminence; the second, Voltaire's," and the third predominantly Shakspere's. This criticism is really a bad confusion of a not very complex psychological problem. And it is followed up by the further vain generalisation that " the wit of thoughts belongs eminently to the Italians, that of words to the French, and that of images to the English " (Ashe's ed. of *Miscellanies*, p. 122). It would be much truer to say that the wit of words (= puns) belongs eminently to the English, that of thoughts to the French, and that of images to the Italians. But the terms are hopelessly confused and confusing. They are probably misadapted from some German.

COLERIDGE

A less serious fault, arising from his verbal endowment and his defective hold on actuality, is Coleridge's way of repeating or dwelling at serious length on verbal distinctions even where they are in themselves justifiable, as when he recurs again and again to the different force of the terms sublime and beautiful, or works out repeatedly his explanation that pedantry consists in an incongruous employment of language, and not in the resort to technical terms for the purpose of precision of statement. In his very argument he falls into that De Quinceyan pedantry which parades its manipulation of terms like a juggler walking round before his performance. And here we come back to that lack of personal dignity and considerate reticence which is part of Coleridge's heredity from his father, who likewise exhibited that very habit of expatiating superfluously on the significance of words. The kind of distinction attaching to the work of Coleridge, in common with that of De Quincey, has in it an element of concession to the strain of childishness in them. They are never great as even the homely Wordsworth was great, by force of massiveness and determination. Wordsworth we can hardly help respecting; Lamb we cannot help loving; Coleridge and De Quincey we are always somewhat moved to pity, even when we are able to take a reverent view of their performance.

But the period of reverence for either is now probably over. Their prestige stood at its highest in the generation between theirs and ours, when the discredit of their personal weakness had in large measure passed away with their presence, and the literary and religious appreciation of their writings played freely, and not very critically. In both cases, orthodoxy has covered a multitude of sins. The three middle decades of the period from 1800 to 1890 have in England been those

COLERIDGE

of maximum orthodoxy, the struggle between all the innovating ideas of the revolutionary period and the general reaction having resulted for the time in the ascendency of the latter; and at that time the fact that a writer combined Christian faith with literary genius counted for more in his favour than all his vices did against him. The vices of Coleridge have been commiserated by pietists who would have held them up to disgust had they been those of a "materialist." And yet nothing could be more dubious, more nebulous, than the support given to orthodoxy by the reasonings of Coleridge, as distinguished from his mere declamations. His so-called *Aids to Reflection*, which became the most popular of his prose works in virtue of its comforting pretence of giving piety the support of reason in the person of a re-converted Unitarian, only rises above Christian platitude to plunge into mists of logomachy, or to undulate on a switchback voyage of inconclusive criticism. There is no more characteristic section in it than the comment on Aphorism CIX (Taylor's) as to Original Sin. The oscillating analysis ends in a citation and endorsement of an incisive note penned twenty years before, choice in style and valid in statement:

"This most eloquent treatise [Taylor's *Deus Justificatus*] may be compared to a Statue of Janus, with the one face, which we must suppose fronting the Calvinistic Tenet, entire and fresh, as from the Master's hand; beaming with life and force, witty scorn on the Lip, and a Brow at once bright and weighty with satisfying reason!—the other, looking towards the '*something to be put in its place*,' maimed, featureless, weather-beaten into an almost visionary confusion and indistinctness."

No better account could be given of Coleridge's own commentary, which, proceeding from a scholastically unphilosophical theorem as to the mysteriousness of Evil, ends in a helpless protest that everybody admits

COLERIDGE

it to be a Fact, and evades the theistic dilemma with the warning, in capital letters: "BEWARE OF ARGUMENTS AGAINST CHRISTIANITY WHICH CANNOT STOP THERE, AND CONSEQUENTLY OUGHT NOT TO HAVE COMMENCED THERE." The absurd second clause exhibits the tactic of the orthodoxy of the time. It was known that, as in the previous century, many people would listen to reason up to the point of impeaching Trinitarianism and Bibliolatry who would recoil from any exposure of the fallacies of Theism. The cue was, therefore, to warn such minds that the criticism of any part of the creed led up to the dissolution of the whole. Of course it was not a deliberate and dissembling calculation of means to ends, but rather the half-conscious grasp of weakness at any weapon that seemed likely to avail. Coleridge latterly seems to have held in his heart that arguments against Christianity ought never to be begun at all. In any case, he was too irretrievably broken in his latter years, save in wistful moments of forlorn lucidity, to follow such arguments out to a scientific end, which would have meant the final negation of all theism; though, could the worn organism but have seen it, the sanity of creedless science, explaining his own sad journey in terms of his congenitally flawed structure, might have given him the serenest of all resting-places. As it is, the sinking wanderer pipes feebly in the market-place for the sympathetic applause which he needs so much—pipes ditties of strange tone to those whom ever and anon he feels to be incapable of comprehending him, but whose bewildered assent is the complement of his own despairing self-delusion. His theoretic vindication of the doctrine of the Trinity consists in making out that Deity is Trinity only in a metaphysical sense in which every man may be made out a Trinity, and lends no

COLERIDGE

help whatever to the belief in the Incarnation, with which doctrine as a statement of historic fact the Coleridgean formula of the Trinity has no compatibility whatever. The final effect of his teaching on these matters is simply to prove how much respect can be secured for solemn verbiage by a master in verbalism.

And as a master in verbalism, rather than a philosopher, Coleridge finally ranks for students of philosophy. He is perhaps the subtlest of non-German obscurantists, but an obscurantist his merely theological purpose always makes of him; and he could not escape the fate of all such performers, which is self-stultification. He ends in flat contradiction in philosophy as in everything else.* The central statement of the elaborate

---

* One may, of course, push a charge of inconsistency too far. Mr. Lang has well pointed out (in *Letters on Literature*) that while laying down the maxim that poetry means " the best words in the best order," Coleridge explicitly disparages Virgil on the score that if you "take away his diction and metre" there is nothing left. But diction and metre are just the words and their order. (Cp. *Table Talk*, July 12, 1827; July 3, 1833; with May 8, 1824, and August 11, 1832.) Coleridge, however, meant to show that Virgil was a great master of verse, but poor in ideas; and after all it may be worth while to suggest that a poet can be a poor intelligence apart from his verbal art. In other passages Coleridge has given definitions (whether or not original) of poetry which supplement the technical formula of " the best words in the best order," and apply to the artistic product tests which grade the poets in terms of the order of thought in which they work. *E.g.*, " As poetry is the identity of all other knowledges, so a poet cannot be a great poet but as being likewise inclusively an historian and naturalist, in the light, as well as the life, of philosophy: all other men's worlds are his chaos" (Note on Barry Cornwall, in Ashe's ed. of *Miscellanies*, p. 347). In the *Biographia* (ch. xv., Bohn ed., p. 155) he writes: " No man was ever yet a great poet, without being at the same time a profound philosopher. For poetry is the blossom and the fragrancy of all human knowledge, human thoughts, human passions, emotion, language." (Cp. Wordsworth's " The breath and finer spirit of all knowledge." Pref. to *Lyrical Ballads*.) Again he

system belatedly set forth as his by Mr. Joseph Green is that the human will, distinguished from the Reason or Speculative Intellect or Mind, is the "ultimate fact of consciousness" and the "immovable ground of a philosophy of Realism." But the gist of Coleridge's own attempted rebuttal of what he regarded as Materialism is the insistence that the faculty of knowing facts and principles as such must be antecedent to or concurrent with their recognition,* and obviously the recognition of Will *as* Will implies the simultaneity of the percipient intelligence or judgment, so that Mr. Green's "only tenable base" is a chimera—one term of a duality verbally separated from the other, without which it cannot be thought.

X

As to the better influence of Coleridge on English thought and literature, it may to a certain extent be compared with that of the so-called pre-Raphaelite school in painting in more recent times. It was the disintegrating and perturbing influence of an appeal to standards at once new and old as against standards

---

attempts a definition in terms of the psychological effect of poetry : "The excitement of emotion for the purpose of immediate pleasure, through the medium of beauty" (*Essay on the Principles of Criticism ; Miscel.* p. 10), This, which is elaborated in one of the lectures of 1811 (Ashe's ed. of *Lectures*, &c., p. 47), is on the whole less happy than the definition given by Poe; "The rhythmical creation of beauty." It should be noted, by the way, that the formulas of "words in the best order" and "the best words in the best order," as definitions of good prose and poetry, constitute one more Coleridgean plagiarism. He always gave them as "my" rule; but the first is only a variation of Swift's "proper words in proper places" (cited at end of Johnson's *Life of Swift*), and the second is an obvious extension of the first.

* See *Table Talk*, Sept. 21, 1830.

COLERIDGE

merely contemporary and conventional. His own manifold intellectual experience, ranging from one extreme to the other of the fields of opinion, made him a kind of palimpsest, of which the final record was something much more complex and qualified than the dogmas it sought to vindicate, and of which the very confusion was suggestive. Thus he counted negatively or indirectly for much. The bigoted and unconscientious critics, the unoriginal versifiers, the Paleyan theologians, the brutal or platitudinous politicians of that age are discredited in comparison with him by their rudeness and dulness, their triteness, their shallow barbarity. He brings back the breath of greater times, and brings forward the promise of better times to come. We may say of him what Emerson less truly said of himself, that his fame is the measure of the narrowness of his age. But when we speak thus of his age it must be with regard not to all its forces, but only to those which were predominant; for around him there were men of very different types—Keats, Shelley, Byron, Wordsworth, Hallam, Bentham, James Mill, Herschel, Young, Dalton—all of whom were working to make the new age, and most of whom produced a larger body of sound work than he. His most ambitious treatises have ceased to occupy the modern intelligence; his philosophy is lost in mist; his social gospel, despite its superiority at many points to that of the society to which he appealed, is too inadequate even to be discussed; his final orthodoxy is too abject, his mysticism too thin, even for the Church. ·It is significant that, while his works are separately reprinted and accessible, there is no complete edition of them; and that the recent decisive edition of the poems is mainly made up of plays and translations which are no longer of any standard repute. Of the thick volume so perfectly edited by Mr. Campbell, only some twenty pages, by general agreement, are deathless. The translations which bulk so largely were hardly worth reprinting, and will certainly cease to be read by Englishmen before the originals, despite Professor Brandl's strange endorsement of the English claim, ascribed first to Scott,* that Coleridge has improved on Schiller. Such versification as this:

> " She seems to have
> Foreboded some misfortune. The report
> Of an engagement, in the which had fallen
> A colonel of the Imperial army, frightened her," †

is surely worse than anything in Schiller, bad as his versification sometimes is.

That Coleridge equally failed as a dramatist and writer of dramatic verse on his own account there can no longer be any question. His remark to Allsop‡ that his own *Remorse* was a great favourite of his, and that the translation of the *Wallenstein* § was a specimen of his happiest work during the prime manhood of his

---

* Hazlitt praised the *Wallenstein* version highly, as does Mr. Gladstone (*Essay on Leopardi*); and Mr. Lowell pronounced it "What I may call the most original translation in our language, unless some of the late Mr. Fitzgerald's be reckoned such." (*Speech on unveiling of the bust.*) The collocation was distinctly unlucky.

† Act iv. scene 3, in Coleridge's translation, which does not at all correspond with the final text of Schiller. Not only, however, did Schiller alter greatly on the version translated, but Coleridge took endless liberties with it (Cp. Gillman, *Life*, p. 146). Brandl makes the extraordinary statement (p. 260) that Coleridge translated so faithfully that the original text could be reconstructed from his version; and then avows that Coleridge made many alterations and additions (pp. 261-2). One surmises some blunder by the translator of Brandl's own book.

‡ Letters, &c., as cited, p. 51.

§ Compare this with his expressions to Wedgwood concerning "the accursed *Wallenstein*" (cited by Mr. Campbell in his notes, p. 602).

COLERIDGE

intellect, before he was "crossed by fatality," is the proof that his critical appreciation of dramatic excellence and energy in Shakspere was not founded on any capacity for similar things in himself. Of all his personages, not one breathes the breath of life: they are almost as purely personifications of qualities as any in the plays of Jonson. That he should be thus insensitive, with all his fineness of literary palate, is puzzling; and the only explanation which suggests itself is that he had on the one hand no such new impulsion from the outside to right activity in dramatic writing as he had in verse and in æsthetics from Wordsworth and the Germans; while on the other hand his opium did not lend itself to the creation of dramatic character as it certainly did to the visualising of fantasy, and perhaps did later to the analysis of literary effect. There have been other critical writers with a keen taste for inspiration in poetry and an incapacity to write verse comparable with their prose, e.g., Lamb and Lowell; but both of these seem to have realised their failure, whereas Coleridge seems not to have done so, save at odd moments, as when he remarked that he had supposed himself to be imitating Shakspere's versification in the *Remorse*, and only afterwards found that he had but been tracking Massinger and Beaumont and Fletcher.*

XI

What then does the name of Coleridge finally represent for us in literature? Principally, we must say, a handful of poetry with a singular charm; an abnormal product of an abnormal nature under abnormal conditions. The *Ancient Mariner* is a triumph of sheer

* *Table Talk*, Feb. 17, 1833.

COLERIDGE

poetic style; or more strictly, a triumphant application of a rare method to a strange theme; and its mere technique and treatment keep it perpetually fascinating. In the handling of a moral fantasy we have enshrined for us a harmony and variety of colours, a wealth of rightly felt and phrased impressions of the real inner and outer world, such as no other poetic work can surpass. The quality which in Coleridge had to serve for strength of character, namely intellectual zeal, here attains to a success of sincerity which is perhaps only possible in virtue of a weak relation to actuality. The mariner's visionary tale is told with a conviction that would be notable in fiction of the most natural kind; and it is the sincere and simple expression of the unreal tale in terms of the most vivid of real perceptions that gives it its irresistible impressiveness. The psychological method is much the same as that of Poe, that other abnormal neurotic type, ill-compounded with a difference, who, though allowing little praise to Coleridge,* was evidently influenced by him, and exhibits the traces in many echoes of phrase and coincidences of opinion as well as in the main movement of his mind.

What made the artistic success of *The Ancient Mariner* makes the success of such very different themes as *Christabel* and *Kubla Khan*. It is as beautiful verbal realisations of fantasy, of dream, that they keep their secure dominion over the literary sense. To follow the story of *Christabel* (in the first part: the second flags) is like following the fortunes of a cloud in a clear and windy sky; the action, the idea, the aim, is

---

* In the *Letter to B——*, which constituted a preface to an early volume of his poems, Poe called Coleridge "a giant in intellect and learning" (*Works*, iii. 315, 317), but went on to criticise him. Later he speaks of him disrespectfully enough. Cp. vol. iii. 241, 365.

naught; the witchery of the form and the movement is continuous. It is not easy to be patient with those who, like Mr. Traill,* adopting Coleridge's own words of depreciation, dismiss *Kubla Khan* as "hardly more than a psychological curiosity." That Lamb should at first have felt somewhat thus † is intelligible in respect at once of the essential humanness of his own sympathies and of the utter newness of Coleridge's effect, so immeasurably removed from all the forms of literature in which Lamb's genius was steeped, so essentially different from such effects of his own dream-fancy as *The Child Angel*, where human pathos penetrates and perfumes all. Coleridge's poem is the visualising of an opium-dream, a rarity of sensation at least as well worth literary immortality as any other experience whatever; and the feat is accomplished with a magic of sound and thought wholly incomparable. The radiant vision hangs in his words transparent and complete as a rainbow, and permanent as marble. And he who can escape the thrill which comes of the images, and the spell born of the creative art; he who can miss the mastery of such lines as

> " A savage spot, as holy and enchanted
> As *e'er* beneath a waning moon was haunted
> By woman wailing for her demon lover,"

—where the convinced assumption of the customariness of the unearthly instantly lends conviction to the picture in hand—such a one must be lacking in some literary nerves, so to say. Those who pronounce the poem incoherent must just have failed to follow the very simple transition between its stanzas.

These indestructible artistic values, the fortuitous

* *Coleridge*, p. 60. See also Brandl, p. 186.
† Letter to Wordsworth, Ainger's ed. of the Letters, i. 305.

fruit of what so many still regard as a merely ruinous vice, remain for us after the analysis alike of the artistic and the philosophical work of the artist. It is indeed not wholly a comforting reflection that a life of manifold aspiration and much serious though desultory effort is at last a human utility in virtue mainly of the chance brain-blooms of a season of physiological ecstasy, the large plans of its succeeding years being traced in sand. But the ill-starred Coleridge in the end comes off not ill beside his friend the well-governed Wordsworth, whom we have learned * to see as the foiled devotee of a vain purpose, "laying great bases for eternity" with a vast scheme of a poetico-philosophic system, and attaining felicity only in some of the unforeseen by-ways of the task. Nay, a world which at best does but carry from age to age certain saved handfuls of beauty and wisdom to show for an infinity of striving lives, cannot pronounce the case of Coleridge to be very much out of the common way.

* See the essay of the late Professor Minto in the *Nineteenth Century*, 1889.

SHELLEY AND POETRY

(1884)

I

THE singular strife of critical opinion as to the value of Shelley's poetry—strife hotter to-day, perhaps, than ever before—might almost be said to justify those who define all criticism as a more or less pretentious expression of individual likes and dislikes, among which no canon can ever authoritatively decide. Every famous writer, of course, is to some extent disputed over; but such extremities of contradiction as are to be found among the comments by leading critics on Shelley it would be difficult to match in connection with any other name. "When," says Emerson in his essay on *Poetry and Imagination*, "people tell me they do not relish poetry, and bring me Shelley, or Aikin's Poets, or I know not what volumes of rhymed English, to show that it has no charm, I am quite of their mind." Mr. Arnold has spoken no less emphatically to similar effect, pronouncing the selections from Shelley in Mr. Palgrave's *Golden Treasury* a "gallery of failures." But Mr. Swinburne, on the other hand, meets all such judgments with a body of indignant rejoinder and counter-eulogy which, so far as force of language goes,

SHELLEY AND POETRY

entirely balances the dispraise; and critics of we earned reputation are found to take his side. Who to judge between such disputants? Are the anarchi of criticism to be left free to proclaim that it has first principles? That can hardly be; but it is v evident that to lay down an efficient and generally c vincing law in the matter will be extremely difficu and that he would be worse than presumptuous w should now affect to dismiss the dispute with a m verdict on one side or the other. If the controvers to be anything more than a collision of dogmatic traction and hyperbolical praise, it must be conduc with more regard to scientific method than has yet b shown in it. It becomes plainer day by day, inde that our criticism will have to be systematised in directions to meet the needs of a generation with 1 notions on old themes and but a scanty respect authority; and the most humble inquiries will hav be conducted with some sense of the changed cor tions if they are to justify themselves. The natur the subject is such, however, that even a restri study, such as our investigation of the truth al Shelley's poetry, involves the raising of wide issues important principles; which makes the undertakin the would-be systematising critic, confronted by methods and established creeds, a hazardous one ind

It is probable that much of the inflexibility of position among critics on literary questions is du their judgments on dead celebrities having begun 1 formed at a time of life when the sympathies are r stronger than the critical faculty. Liking for a p character and way of thinking determines the at ment of young readers rather than deliberate stu his way of writing; and these early sympathetic at ments are very apt to preclude the fuller and

SHELLEY AND POETRY

impartial study when the capacity for it comes. On all hands are to be met men who were attracted in their young days to Byron or to Shelley or to Wordsworth by something congenial in the character and teaching of one or other of these poets, and who at maturity are positively unable to read the favourite old poetry in cold blood, so deeply is it associated with early enthusiasm or passion. And perhaps in no poet's case is this sympathetic tradition so potent as in that of Shelley. To those who were inspired in youth by his passion for liberty and human brotherhood it is apt to seem almost heartless to test the old pæans by unimpassioned critical standards, and analyse the language which had once been too dazzling for unmoved contemplation. But just such appraisement and analysis must be made if the problem about Shelley's poetry is to be seen in any better light than that of prejudice. We must forget our partialities, and grant it to be quite an open question whether a poet whose thought and life we admire is admirable *as* poet. And by way of helping towards this assumption of the judicial position it may be well to remind the Shelleyite that when Shelley drew up a letter of protest to the editor of the *Quarterly Review* after its attack on Keats, he indicated that he took up a distinctly critical attitude as to his brother poet's works while calling for fair-play.

"There was no danger," he said, after claiming considerable merit and promise of future excellence for *Endymion*, "that it should become a model to the age of that false taste with which, I confess, it is replenished;" and after urging that the greater part of *Hyperion* is "surely in the very highest style of poetry," he goes on: "I speak impartially, for the canons of taste to which Keats has conformed in his other compositions are the very reverse of my own."

SHELLEY AND POETRY

Keats, who, says Lord Houghton, "singularly enough, never seems to have had much personal sympathy" with Shelley, and who criticised so acutely, might have had something to say as to the faults of his champion's work; and it is one of the many regrettable things in their lives that these two poets, both fated to die young, and linked in remembrance as they are, should not have known each other and influenced each other's art as they so well might. Shelley, in all probability, would have profited the more. If there is one quality that the mass of his verse lacks it is the element of flesh and blood, of the "simple, passionate, sensuous," to use Milton's unforgettable definition. Nothing will more clearly bring out the special character of Shelley's poetic thought than a comparison of his longest poem, *The Revolt of Islam*, with *Endymion*, and of *Prometheus Unbound* with *Hyperion*. There is cause to suspect that by no means all readers of Keats have gone enthusiastically through *Endymion;* but how much more reason is there for doubting whether one reader in twenty has scanned every line of *The Revolt of Islam*. Both poems are away from human life, but how differently does one poet idealise from the other! From the first lines the contrast is complete. Keats's foot is firm on the earth, however far his fancy may fly: he half turns old dreams into life, with his ardent sense of earthly beauty: his pulse throbs through all his singing: it is the poesy of warm-blooded youth, dreaming itself alive in the world's spring-time. With Shelley, the case is almost precisely the reverse. Brooding on the present, and inspired by an intellectual idea, he turns life into a dream, spiritualising his youth and maiden into phantoms who move in a world of abstractions and visions, "where the wild bee never flew."

Take, again, the poems of *Hyperion* and *Prometheus*

SHELLEY AND POETRY

Unbound, and see how the two singers deal with the stricken Titans. *Hyperion* misses final success because it lacks action and has only a pictorial interest where the form promises something more, and because the appeal to our sympathies is faint; *Prometheus Unbound* has action; and the preliminary appeal to human sympathy is strong; and yet the figures and the pictures in *Hyperion* have much the larger measure of definiteness. They are sculpturesque in their stillness: while the moving throng in the lyrical drama are of a shadowy consistency, abstractions mingling with spirits, and all uttering unearthly speech. The vital idea of the poem is embroidered with fantasy till it hardly counts with us: if we read on it is because we care more for fantasy than for human significance in song. Nothing, of course, is thus far decided as to which kind of poetry is the more to be commended: we have drawn distinctions, but have not considered precedence. It may be, however, that a Shelleyite interposes to urge that the poet who at once embodies intellectual ideas in his verse and weaves them on the most imaginative backgrounds, is superior to him who but partially idealises primary passion and finds his inspiration in sense rather than in abstract thought. Shelley, it may be claimed, is great, just in virtue of these qualities of etherealness and devotion to ideas. Here we face one side of our critical problem.

I have assumed that Keats, in proportion to his popularity, has more readers for his *Endymion* than Shelley has for *The Revolt of Islam*, and so much will probably be granted; but in any case the question to be considered is as to which poem a cultured reader ought to find the better worth reading—Keats being thus contrasted with Shelley, it is understood, not with the idea of deciding which is on the whole the greater poet, but merely for purposes of elucidation. The first point to be examined is that of the comparative attractiveness of the verse-forms; and there will presumably be no dispute as to the movement by couplets being much the freer mode of expression. As the question is not which is the finer poet, we will not ask whether Keats in his poems in stanza writes better or worse than Shelley, but simply note that a poem in the less artificial form seems to be more readable than the complex. Shelley tells us in his preface that for one thing he has adopted the Spenserian stanza, not because he thinks it a "finer model of poetical harmony" than blank verse, "but because in the latter there is no shelter for mediocrity; you must either succeed or fail." Beyond this, however, he was "enticed also by the brilliancy and magnificence of sound which a mind that has just been nourished upon musical thoughts can produce by a just and harmonious arrangement of the pauses" of the stanza. All that is clear here is that Shelley felt the elaborateness of the stanza gave it a certain prestige apart from the quality of the language; that he saw the freer form demanded better work to make it popularly impressive; and that he laid great stress on effects of sound. We infer, on the one hand, that he has great wealth of diction; but, on the other, seeing that he took little more than six months to a poem of 526 Spenserian and several other stanzas, we suspect that he was not very keenly alive to the necessity for finish and concision. And in the very first stanza of the poem proper we find that in point of fact he attains neither the one nor the other. Here it is:

> "When the last hope of trampled France had failed,
> Like a brief dream of unremaining glory,
> From visions of despair I rose, and scaled
> The peak of an aërial promontory,

SHELLEY AND POETRY

    Whose caverned base with the vexed surge was hoary,
    And saw the golden dawn break forth and waken
    Each cloud, and every wave—but transitory
    The calm, for sudden the firm earth was shaken
    As if by the last wreck its frame was overtaken."

That is a fair sample of Shelley's stanza verse, and it will hardly be denied that, spasmodic as is the movement, it is diffuse in expression and false in its rhymes. "Like a brief *dream of unremaining* glory" is a weak line, and "Whose caverned base with the vexed surge was hoary" is an unmistakable instance of the process by which a poet gets his idea from the need of a rhyme. Then we must read "promon*tory*" and "transi*tory*" to rhyme with "glory;" and we note again that the poet is constrained to announce the occurrence of an earthquake by the irrational phrase "transitory the calm," through the sheer necessity of making an effect in sound. Now, by way of clearing the ground, it is right that we should ask ourselves for what reason we read a poem of this quality—why we should submit to the perusal of thousands of demonstrably irrelevant or supererogatory lines, and to a thousand shocks of mispronunciation or false assonance. It is easy to say why we read the poems we feel to be finished in workmanship. We get from them the combined pleasures of perfectly choice expression and exquisite cadence, and, in the case of their being rhymed, harmony of sound. They may express joy or sorrow, or they may describe objects or action; in any case our delight is essentially one of perfect satisfaction in the manner in which the thought is expressed, our special sympathy with the thought being an additional factor in our impression. Take any of the familiar felicities of English poetry: take Shakspere's

SHELLEY AND POETRY

" Full fathom five thy father lies;
Of his bones are coral made;
Those are pearls that were his eyes;
Nothing of him that doth fade
But doth suffer a sea change
Into something rich and strange "—

who does not feel here the thrill of recognition of the inexpressible fitness of the phrase "a sea change," with its electric suggestion of an infinite range of idea, and the perfect development of the thought into the "something rich and strange," the poignant note blending into the round and perfect chord?

It is from masterpieces that we deduce canons of art, and that lovely snatch of song will carry us a long way. Two laws are illustrated by it: one, that the finest poetic touches are so by reason of a quintessential quality of meaning—a peculiar concentration or centrality of significance. "Poetry," says Emerson, in the essay before cited, "is the perpetual endeavour to express the spirit of the thing, to pass the brute body, and search the life and reason which causes it to exist." That is one way of putting the law that the singer must go to the heart of his theme and give us, not catalogue, but typical detail; not facts, but the intensest generalisation—a law which is always in danger of being misconceived when incidentally formulated, and which we shall have to elaborate later on. Our second law is the simple and obvious one that the poet shall have the art to conceal his art—that when he uses the form of rhyme his collocation of ideas shall never suggest his exigencies. Too much stress cannot be laid on this. If the versifier cannot subdue his medium he should leave it alone. We have seen that Shelley felt superior poetic quality was necessary to success in blank verse; but while that is true, it is also the fact that to write fine verse in stanza demands greater effort than is needed for fine blank verse. The explanation of the apparent contradiction is that "success" is a relative term, depending for its value on the taste of readers; and that a poet may "succeed" with an inferior poem in stanza by reason of the prevailing inherited taste for rhyme, who would not have obtained general attention for a poem without that attraction. To many people mere rhyme gives so much satisfaction that they will overlook any number of false notes for the sake of the true, and pardon any irrelevancies by which the desired effect is reached. Such readers make the "success" of second-rate rhymed verse; but the critic knows that as much preparation and skill as go to produce tolerable rhyming poetry would bring forth blank verse of a higher quality, though people might not consent to read the latter. The final trouble is, however, that not one poet in ten will take half the pains to blank verse that he bestows on rhyme, the comparative easiness of the form almost invariably seducing them into commonness. A poet chooses blank verse for a long poem because it is easier than rhyme, and, inspired as he is by a desire to minimise his labour, he probably does not even produce good blank verse. The whole matter has a curiously paradoxical aspect. Rhyme and stanza mean multiplication of difficulty; and yet, the habit of all versifiers being to attempt rhyme, on the one hand the art of doing the difficult work is positively more frequently acquired than that of doing the easier, and on the other the ordinary reader will, other things being equal, rather tolerate bad work in the rhyming form than insist on purity in combination with simplicity. After all, however, it is an unsettled question whether the precision and subtlety of meaning, in conjunction with ever-varying cadence, which is attained in some forms of blank verse—for instance, in some poems of Mr. Arnold and Mr. Henley—does not constitute as valuable an artistic result as even the choicest work in rhyme.

Applying all this to Shelley, we decide that, seeing he is so far content to find his account in the primitive love of rhyme for rhyme's sake as to pad out his longest poem with innumerable far-fetched chimes and spurious echoes, and seeing he is thus diffuse throughout even in excess of his natural tendency to diffuseness, the work is technically bad. It is difficult to see how any other critical judgment can be maintained. It may perhaps be urged that every poet makes numbers of bad rhymes, and that constant accuracy is impossible ; and it may be contended that the poem contains much concise phrasing. To the first plea the answer is that Shelley's rhyming in his longer poems is far below the average work of distinguished poets. Spenser, his model, makes far fewer bad shots than he ; indeed, if Shelley is not so reckless as Mrs. Browning, whose rhyming is outrageously and deliberately vicious, he must be ranked next to her in degree of offending among the poets for whom a high rank is claimed. Mrs. Browning held that the merest resemblances in sound were as legitimate as perfect rhymes—a doctrine concerning which it may here be said that it is repugnant to almost all students of poetry ; but Shelley formulated no such principle, and there is no need to discuss it in his connection. As for his occasional tersenesses, these are for the most part as purely fortuitous as any of his rhymes, and moreover are rarely noteworthy. He hits on such a phrase as " transitory the calm," bad as it is, by sheer stress of verse-form ; but triumphs of pregnant expression are scarce indeed in *The Revolt of Islam*. The one claim which can be made for the poem as a piece of poetic workmanship is that it at times

SHELLEY AND POETRY

attains a sonorous and impressive rhetorical quality—some of that "magnificence of sound" at which the poet aimed. It is but fair to quote some of these passages—they are really few. Here is one :

> "The Queen of Slaves,
> The hood-winked angel of the blind and dead,
> Custom, with iron mace points to the graves
> Where her own standard desolately waves
> Over the dust of prophets and of kings.
> Many yet stand in her array—' she paves
> Her path with human hearts,' and o'er it flings
> The wildering gloom of her immeasurable wings."
> *Canto IV., Stanza* 24.

Here, be it noticed, force is attained by real intensity of phrase, sound rhyme, and fairly natural sequence of ideas—factors the lack of which wrecks almost every alternate stanza—along with that steady verbal flow which is so often effected in the poem by dispensing with these. Another passage might be cited from the fifth stanza of Canto XI. :

> " Her lips were parted, and the measured breath
> Was now heard there ;—her dark and intricate eyes,
> Orb within orb, deeper than sleep or death,
> Absorbed the glories of the burning skies : "

but here the effect is less satisfactory, though it arrests attention. Now, if such passages were thrice as numerous as they are, they would surely be an inadequate return for all the hours that a faithful perusal of the poem occupies, an insufficient offset to the long irritation of the wire-drawn phraseology, the vaporous thinking, and the intolerable rhymes. Shelley considered the stanza of Spenser "a measure inexpressibly beautiful"—an overpitched claim in any case ; but how shall a mere set of recurrent cadences support to infinity a train of incoherent and intangible

SHELLEY AND POETRY

ideas? Many people approach all celebrated poetry with a certain unquestioning reverence, much as pious people listen to a sermon; holding that utterance of this kind has a peculiar sanction and must be profitable just because it takes this form. Whatever be the origin of the feeling as regards the poets, it is emphatically to be cast out in the interest of healthy intellectual life. We must come to a poem as to any other form of human utterance, demanding worthy reward. It is simply foolish to spend our reading hours in absorbing rhythms and rhymes, unless we are all the while obtaining the intellectal food and nerve stimulus of finely worded thought or delightful fancy. That it so ministers to us is the only excuse poetry can offer for its existence. Why should a writer choose the metrical form for what he has to say? That he sings because he must, is a plea which will only avail him when he clearly does well to sing. If he would stand well in the eyes of thoughtful men, he must be able to say that his thought has lost nothing of its weight and force in the process of metricising, but has gained the charm, the incisiveness, and the memorableness which verse can give. What are rhyme and rhythm without these attributes? To prize them for their own sake is playing with toys; the occupation is little more respectable on the part of adults than the systematic collection of postage stamps. Around us lie all the garnered knowledge of the ages, all the sciences, all the philosophies, all the captured beauty of the arts: and "yonder all before us lie deserts of vast eternity:" how shall we answer to ourselves and our children for priceless days spent, far from these treasures of our race, listening to fantastic jingle, sterile of all sane significance? We can but say that we have read all the conventionally accepted poetry

SHELLEY AND POETRY

because we heard it was fine; and that our resulting knowledge of its true quality is mainly useful as enabling us to preserve from waste of time and labour others who have no ambition to be specialists. We are able to certify that so much verse merely cumbers library shelves, and is no more worth the attention of the general reader, desirous of an all-round culture, than it is worth his while, as a student of science, to repeat for his own edification all the futile experiments of which he finds record in his books. It is the function of the critic thus to counsel readers; and if men of letters do not so order their department with good will, it will be invaded and the work taken out of their hands barbarously enough by workers in other branches of study, justly wroth over the disproportionate space still allotted to mere *belles-lettres* in the culture-time of the majority.

II

But we have still to meet the challenge as to the quality of Shelley's thought, apart from any of the defects of his utterance. I have spoken of the "vaporous thinking" in *The Revolt of Islam;* and I can conceive a protest being made against the expression, as being a begging of the question if nothing worse. Shelley's "imagination" is held by many to be important enough to outweigh all his technical shortcomings; and it is the character of the ideas in his larger poems that is understood to be founded on by those critics who assert him to have "outsung" all but a few of his tribe. It is necessary to treat such an issue with special vigilance, there being an equal danger of seeming to say too much and of seeming to say too little in setting forth the

SHELLEY AND POETRY

"laws of poetic truth and poetic beauty" in this connection.

Mr. Arnold has laid it down in his essay on Byron that "all the personal charm of Shelley cannot hinder us from at last discovering in his poetry the incurable want, in general, of a sound subject matter, and the incurable fault, in consequence, of unsubstantiality." Now, this judgment, while in a sense right, seems to me to open the way for any amount of misconception and unsound criticism, and I cite it as bringing us face to face with the central crux of our subject. The sense in which it is right, I suspect, is not that intended by Mr. Arnold. He has in his essay on Wordsworth depreciated that poet's most famous Ode as lacking the character of poetic truth of the best kind; the central thought has, he says, no real solidity. I make bold to dispute the principle which is implied in that judgment, and which, I take it, is reasserted in the passage before quoted, as well as in another sentence in the Byron essay in which Byron is praised because "his topics were not Queen Mab, and the Witch of Atlas, and the Sensitive Plant," but "the upholders of the old order" which he detested—"George the Third and Lord Castlereagh and the Duke of Wellington and Southey." Praise of this kind means, if it means anything, that there is a presumption in favour of the poet who chooses the latter rather than the former set of subjects, those by implication being stigmatised as "unsound." I have no fear of not having abundant acquiescence in my dissent from a judgment which works such confusion in our notions of poetry as this does. We may set aside the question—sufficiently dealt with by Mr. Swinburne —as to the fairness of placing Shelley's most fanciful poetry against Byron's political verse, saying nothing of Shelley's bold dealings with political problems and

SHELLEY AND POETRY

ignoring Byron's *Hours of Idleness* and oriental tales. The turn for these unfair contrasts is Mr. Arnold's main critical vice. What most concerns us is the theory he has laid down; and there can be little doubt that the great majority of lovers of poetry will instantly recoil from it. What, they will be disposed to ask, is the distinction between poetical and prosaic ideas if the satirising of George the Third and Southey is fitter occupation for a poet than singing about Queen Mab and the Sensitive Plant? Is politics better poetic matter than fairies and flowers, with or without the introduction of human problems into the fairy world? Is Shakspere's finest poetry to be found in his historical plays? Are we to put *Henry VI.*—be it Shakspere's or not—above the *Midsummer Night's Dream?* The chances are that most people who care for poetry would, if consulted off-hand, flatly reverse Mr. Arnold's ruling, and declare that the Witch of Atlas and Queen Mab and the Sensitive Plant *are* themes for the poet, and that Wellingtons and Castlereaghs, regarded as political obscurantists, are not. Which side would be right? My modest verdict would be—Neither!

Let us avoid all heat and carry on our inquiry judicially: let us go back to our law that poetry is a concentrated, melodious, incisive, and delightful expression of ideas, and see how far that sanctions a classification of themes into good and bad—sheep and goats, as it were. Evidently it supplies, on the surface, no such sanction whatever, and it will not be an easy matter to extract one by a process of sound inference. All that it entitles us to say is that a theme which cannot be treated at once melodiously and with penetrating expression is unfit for the poet. Observe, we say "theme," not "idea." And where shall we find such a theme? I confess I cannot confidently undertake to name one, and till I can I, for one, will not venture to pronounce any "subject" unfit for a poem. This is a very different thing from saying that a given proposition may or may not be poetical. You may take the most advantageous theme in the world—love, death, memory, beauty, or hope—and fail to say anything poetic about it: I fear the chances are a hundred to one against any one of us writing verse on one of these themes which shall not contain what we call "prosaic" touches, that is, expressions which are neither subtle nor musical, neither weighty nor charming. But that does not affect the fitness of the theme. On the other hand you may, if you are a poet—an exceptionally fine poet—perhaps say something poetic about a button or Sir Richard Cross. Of course the chances are about a million to one against anybody succeeding in such attempts as these. Having regard to the range of human capacity we may say that, in view of the enormous weight of the presumption against anybody writing good poetry on the subject of the multiplication table, a wise man will not make the experiment, or at least will not publish the result; but within the ordinary range of poetic attempt we should be slow indeed to taboo subjects. One limitary canon we may lay down: that it is inconceivable that comic verse can ever charm so profoundly as the best serious poetry; and that to treat a comic theme, however cleverly, is to work deliberately on an inferior plane. But further than that canon—which, be it observed, covers a good deal of ground—we should hesitate to go. Let me fortify these observations by quoting from what an original critic, Mr. Henry James, has recently said concerning the art of fiction in an essay* which, despite lapses in other fields, proves him one of the

* *Longman's Magazine*, September 1884.

SHELLEY AND POETRY

acutest critics in this regard as well as one of the most accomplished writers of his time :

" We must grant the artist his subject, his idea, what the French call his *donnée;* our criticism is applied only to what he makes of it. . . . We may believe that of a certain idea even the most sincere novelist can make nothing at all, and the event may perfectly justify our belief; but the failure will have been a failure to execute, and it is in the execution that the fatal weakness is recorded. . . . Art derives a considerable part of its beneficial exercise from flying in the face of presumptions; and some of the most interesting experiments of which it is capable are hidden in the bosom of common things. Gustave Flaubert has written a story about the devotion of a servant-girl to a parrot, and the production, highly finished as it is, cannot on the whole be called a success. . . . Ivan Turgénieff has written a tale about a deaf aud dumb serf and a lap-dog, and the thing is touching, loving, a little masterpiece. He struck the note of life where Gustave Flaubert missed it—he flew in the face of a presumption and achieved a victory."

It is at once a sad necessity and an instructive one to have to say that Mr. James, while here laying down an eminently just principle, tacks on to it an unjust judgment. Flaubert's *Cœur Simple* is a masterpiece ; and I am driven to explain Mr. James's failure to feel this as I have elsewhere ventured to explain his criticism of Flaubert's *Education Sentimentale,* by imputing to him a certain languor of perception, a certain slowness to read himself into a sympathy that he does not quite spontaneously fall into. With this necessarily brief and quasi-dogmatic denial of his particular verdict, let me proceed nevertheless to say that the general proposition is strictly scientific, and that it may be applied fundamentally to the art of poetry, merely noting that Mr. James uses the word "idea" in its inexact sense of "subject" or *motif,* and that the term "execution" has its special import for workers in each art.

To show how Mr. Arnold's principle would confuse our judgments, it is sufficient to apply it to his own poetry; and we may do this without any thought of how he regards his own work. If we adopted his attitude we should say that *The Future* is a much less "sound" theme than *Haworth Churchyard* or *Rugby Chapel*; that *The Scholar Gipsy* and *Balder Dead* are inferior subjects; and that *The Forsaken Merman* is desperately unsubstantial. The central ideas of the first and the three last poems are assuredly wanting in "solidity." No instructed man will admit it to be sound anthropology to say that primitive life on this earth was more blessed, more elevated, more peaceful, or more leisurely than the life of to-day, as Mr. Arnold teaches in *The Future*. Yet which of us will not prefer that poem emphatically to the solidly motived *Haworth Churchyard* and *Rugby Chapel?* Which of us does not find in the one the charm of fine music, and in the others failure to attain complete charm and music save for a few lines at a time? How, again, from Mr. Arnold's point of view, shall we tolerate *The Forsaken Merman*—a poem which we actually find much more admirable than *Haworth Churchyard?* Evidently we conform to another canon, the canon which demands, not total or final conformity to reason as the criterion of poetic fitness, but continuity of feeling or thought on the granted assumptions of the poet. It is not scientific or logical justice of doctrine or thesis that secures success: it is faculty for artistic treatment, the faculty of at once interesting and delighting us. I do think, I confess, that *The Scholar Gipsy* is overrated, in its entirety, by university men; that its web of ideas is in part neither happily planned nor deftly woven; and I do not think the fifty pages of *Balder Dead* satisfactory reading; but will any one say that either subject—provided it be treated at considerably less length—is not a promising one for a poem? No more than he

SHELLEY AND POETRY

would reject *Philomela* because it sings a myth. We do not go to poetry for arguments and facts: to do so would be to imitate the legendary personage who asked what was proved by *Paradise Lost*. We certainly ask that the poet's thoughts shall *cohere*—that they shall be the result of his careful thinking; or that when he resorts to myth and fantasy he shall use his utmost skill to make these melodious and exquisite; but it no more spoils his poetry for us to know that his serious thought is after all mistaken than to know that the myth is myth. Edgar Allan Poe, in his boyhood, takes up the legend of "the angel Israfel, whose heart-strings are a lute, and who has the sweetest voice of all God's creatures;" and, juvenile as some of his touches are, he turns the fantasy into one of the choicest of melodies—a thing we remember like an air of Schubert's. The same poet's long juvenile poem, *Al Aaraaf*, is not more fanciful in motive, but it turns out a failure, simply because of its inferior workmanship. *Israfel* is rounded off thus:

> If I could dwell
> Where Israfel
> Hath dwelt, and he where I,
> He might not sing so wildly well
> A mortal melody,
> While a bolder note than this might swell
> From my lyre within the sky.

It is only a young poet's dream; but just because he has taken the pains and had the genius to turn his dream into quaintly sweet word-music, it endures for us. Certainly we decide that the poet who deals only in fantasy has less cumulative value for us than one who is not only fanciful but thoughtful, and who sings his thoughts as finely as his fancies. When we look about for our greatest poet we pitch on Shakspere because of his all-round grasp and mastery; but in doing so we are sufficiently far from saying that any themes are unworthy because not "sound," or any poetry faulty as such because "unsubstantial." Keats's *Hyperion* is impermanent, not because it deals with myths, but because it does not put them in the right artistic atmosphere or give them the right artistic balance, because the great poetic power spent on the theme thus misses the final felicity of being "inevitable," to use Wordsworth's word. Milton's mythology, equally "unsound," has the decisive advantage in treatment. Assuredly, as Mr. James remarks, there will never be an end of the old fashion of "liking" certain kinds of subject and certain methods; and it is inevitable that, given two poets of about equal technical talent, he who seems to us to think soundly will stand higher in our estimation than he whose reasoning we believe to be faulty; but if the mistaken thought be choicely sung it remains good poetry, *qua* poetry. It would be a hard saying indeed that whenever a particular way of thinking is seen to be practically astray, all artistic expression of it becomes valueless. One of the strongest attractions the literature of the past has for us is the light it casts on the inner life of vanished generations; and if prose can thus attract us by simply letting us see into effete habits of thinking, it is very certain that good poetry will continue to charm, no matter what may be its subject-matter. The subject-matter of Dante is tolerably "unsound;" but he remains an immensely greater and more readable poet than many subsequent rhymers with much more knowledge and far fewer illusions. And in any one generation there is no security that the right-thinking man will always have the superior power of expression. It might happen in any case that—

SHELLEY AND POETRY

> while
>
> Mr. Leech made a speech
> Angry, neat, and wrong;
>
> Mr. Hart, on the other part
> Was right, but dull and long.

Filmer's *Patriarcha* is a much better written book than Locke's refutation of it. The reason may be that while Locke could see the other man's thesis was unsound he could not at once attain the vividness and precision which his antagonist developed by reason of confidence; but it might easily be that the mistaken reasoner had by nature the faculty of effective expression to a much greater degree than the other, there being as certainly a varying faculty of expression as a varying height, complexion, and weight among men. It is to be hoped we can all relish a clever speech by Lord Salisbury or Sir William Harcourt without being disturbed by its fallacies : nay, may we not relish the literary cleverness the more because we feel the assault on our opinions is innocuous? One's own party's opinions, sound as we feel them to be, are unhappily not always expressed with literary cleverness. The love of literary " form " is an inestimable safeguard to the polemist against narrowness, whether in regard to the thought of the past or to that of his own day.

Returning then to Shelley, and continuing our methodical exploration, let us consider the nature of the ideas—the "imagination"—of *The Revolt of Islam*. We have seen reason to abstain from passing judgment against any subject as being unsound or unfit : what we have to do is to examine in what manner the subject is treated, how the poet's "imagination" works. But it will be useful to ascertain from Shelley's preface what it was he aimed at doing. We know from his preface to *Prometheus Unbound* that he believed he disliked didactic poetry. "Didactic poetry," he there said, "is my abhorrence;" adding, with much truth but doubtful consecutiveness: "nothing can be equally well expressed in prose that is not tedious and supererogatory in verse." And of *The Revolt of Islam* he gives us the following account:

> "The poem (with the exception of the first Canto, which is purely introductory) is narrative, not didactic. It is a succession of pictures illustrating the growth and progress of individual mind aspiring after excellence and devoted to the love of mankind; its influence in refining and making pure the most daring and uncommon impulses of the imagination, the understanding, and the senses; its impatience at 'all the oppressions which are done under the sun;' its tendency to awaken public hope and to enlighten and improve mankind; *the rapid effects of the application of that tendency;* the awakening of an immense nation from their slavery and degradation to a true sense of moral dignity and freedom; the bloodless dethronement of their oppressors, and the unveiling of the religious frauds by which they had been deluded into submission; the tranquillity of successful patriotism, and the universal toleration and benevolence of true philanthropy;"

and so on for a dozen lines more, the list concluding with "the transient nature of ignorance and error, and the eternity of genius and virtue." And this, forsooth, is the scheme of a non-didactic poem! It is all "narrative!" It is to be feared Mrs. Shelley was too partial when she attributed to the poet a "logical exactness of reason;" and that he was no less mistaken when he imagined he had a faculty for metaphysics. The fallacy of his distinction between didactic and narrative is transparent to the verge of absurdity; it recalls that other "fallacy" confessed to by Pepys—the diarist's expedient of paying another man to pay for him at the theatre, by way of circumventing a vow to spend no more money on plays. Impressed, no doubt, by the dulness of the didactic poetry of Wordsworth and Cowper, Shelley hastily concluded that to be didactic

SHELLEY AND POETRY

was to be dull; and that the true poetic walk was that of fantasy—moral lessons becoming poetical in that environment and there only. The former dogma has survived Shelley, and is perhaps to-day one of the commonest of superstitions in connection with literature; yet it is falsified by a hundred of the fine passages in English poetry. Turn to *Measure for Measure*, and read:

> "Spirits are not finely touched
> But to fine issues; nor nature never lends
> The smallest scruple of her excellence
> But, like a thrifty goddess, she determines
> Herself the glory of a creditor,
> Both thanks and use."

Turn to *The Winter's Tale*, and read:

> "Nature is made better by no mean
> But nature makes that mean; so, over [even?] that art
> Which you say adds to nature, is an art
> That nature makes."

Take from *Troilus and Cressida* one of Ulysses' speeches:

> "Time hath, my lord, a wallet at his back
> Wherein he puts alms for oblivion. . . .
> Take the instant way
> For honour travels in a strait so narrow,
> Where one but goes abreast; keep, then, the path;
> For emulation hath a thousand sons. . . .
> One touch of nature makes the whole world kin,
> That all, with one consent, praise new-born gauds,
> Though they are made and moulded of things past,
> And give to dust that is a little gilt
> More laud than gilt [gold?] o'er-dusted.

Take the motto from Chapman which Shelley puts at the head of the dedication of his poem, after his preface:

SHELLEY AND POETRY

> " There is no danger to a man that knows
> What life and death is: there's not any law
> Exceeds his knowledge: neither is it lawful
> That he should stoop to any other law."

What is all this but didactic poetry? As it happens, the didactic intention of *The Revolt of Islam* is "gross as a mountain, open, palpable," apart from the *naïf* disclosures in the preface, though the narrative form is kept up throughout; but didactic intention and narrative form alike fail to make the work successful poetry for us, simply because the poet does not attain to that clarified expression which *is* fine poetry. The thinking is, as I have said "vaporous" in terms of its own standards : the fault is not that the poem is fanciful but that the fancy is ill-managed. In point of fact there is no reason why narrative verse should be better poetry than didactic verse, save this, that in the nature of things it is less difficult to maintain vividness and retain attention in a long narrative than in a long reflective poem. But in literature in general there is wofully little room to choose between the mass of bad narrative poetry and the bad didactic poetry; and when we examine the outline of Shelley's poem we are far enough from being stimulated to eager attention by the nature of his story. This narrative of spectral tenuity, with its phantasmagoria of dreams and visions, boats and voyages, caves and palaces, is not the kind of thing to repel tedium through five hundred stanzas. Not that we condemn the narrative as such : we simply decide that in default of clear and coherent conception and fine execution the narrative will not maintain our interest. When, however, the execution—that is, the concatenation of ideas, the phraseology, and the rhyming, together —is found to be crude, headlong, slipshod, the poem is condemned past all appeal.

SHELLEY AND POETRY

III

It may well be that, without some further exposition, this judgment will remain unconvincing to those who feel in all Shelley's verse the presence of a stress of feeling, an intellectual exaltation, which is absent alike from the polished didactic verse of Pope, the narrative of such moralists as Crabbe, and the descriptive verse of writers like Thomson. This sibylline ecstasy, they insist, is something abnormal; it proceeds from and induces an emotional condition differing in kind from that which belongs to the poetry of the second-rate men; it means inspiration, genius. And there is undoubtedly something even in Shelley's unsuccessful poetry which gives colour to these convictions—something which still requires to be analysed and explained.

It is undoubtedly of the first importance that the poet in the act of writing shall be in a certain state of cerebral excitement: only in that condition is he "inspired"; and the stress, the intensity of his thinking is of necessity apparent in his poetry. Yet none the less must his emotion be under control of his art, and deliberately directed to the task of stimulating his faculty of expression. This is the law of poetic creation, the paradoxical law of all art, that the once spontaneous feeling or state shall be consciously reproduced to the extent of suggesting the fittest form of utterance; the emotional and the intellectual functions, or let us say the passive and the active conditions, the perceiving and the creative faculties, combining to produce the most effective expression. And if the two functions are not duly efficient, if one operates to the complete or partial exclusion of the other, we have

SHELLEY AND POETRY

either verse which lacks intensity or verse which lacks form. As a rule we find both defects, in varying proportions, in unsuccessful work, because it is the tendency of each to induce the other. At all events, if inadequacy of artistic faculty does not involve descent in quality of thought, it has the equally disastrous effect of making the poet blind to such descent on his part, which may occur in the most ecstatic states of feeling; while on the other hand, incapacity to feel or imagine intensely limits of necessity a writer's power to attain concentrated expression. In Shelley's long poems we generally find the thought as impassioned—not to say excited—as we could wish, but the controlling intellectual function all too weak; though the majority of readers, being more emotional than reflective, respond to the poet's excitement with little regard to his coherence or intelligibility; somewhat as the penitents in a revival meeting are carried away by exhibitions of hysteria around them. It is to be feared the more facile emotionalists will always dislike the critic and his method, but he must persist all the same.

Shelley, then, fails in *The Revolt of Islam* because he never masters his thought; his seeming inspiration being simply cerebral excitement inadequately controlled. His hurrying fervour, which, thus unchecked, would have led him to express himself imperfectly even in prose, leads him headlong into all the traps and temptations of verse, which confuse his thought in detail tenfold, and warp his words to his constant artistic discomfiture. He tells us, in his unhappy preface, that he has "exercised a watchful and earnest criticism" on his work as it grew; but he goes on to say—and the confusion of statement is noteworthy—"I would willingly have sent it forth to the world with that perfection which long labour and revision is said to bestow. But I found that if I should gain something in exactness by this method, I might lose much of the newness and energy of imagery and language as it flowed fresh from my mind." We may infer what the "watchful and earnest criticism" was worth. Alas for the rarity of patient thinking as of patient work among the gifted! As if the "newness" of haste were better than the originality attained by pondering; as if "energy of imagery and language" were best reached by taking whatever imagery and language came first to hand! Not thus are great poems produced by young brains; though young poets and superficial critics will doubtless go on for many a day talking about "spontaneity" and "inartificiality" as if the qualities pointed to by these terms were the children of carelessness. We find such a critic as Mr. R. H. Stoddard deciding that his countryman, Bayard Taylor, possessed "too much rather than too little" art, and missed "spontaneity" because he "premeditated" too much. And yet it is many centuries since a critic of poetry struck out the conception of "ars celare artem." A poet may miss spontaneity for want of imagination; but if his work shows traces of labour it is because he has not art enough, not because he has too much; because he had nothing particular to premeditate, or because he premeditated too little; never the reverse. The art which goes on niggling to bad purpose is weak art: it is the artistic intention gone astray through timidity or shortsightedness.

In a letter* written after the publication of the *Revolt* to a friend who criticised it, Shelley reaches a truer view of his art. After expressing himself as full of confidence about his poem when he compares it with

---

* See Mrs. Shelley's note on the poem.

SHELLEY AND POETRY

"contemporary productions of the same apparent pretensions," he goes on to make this confession: "Yet, after all, I cannot but be conscious, in much of what I write, of an absence of *that tranquillity which is the attribute and accompaniment of power.*" Here was a true perception. Tranquillity is the condition of the mind which has attained clearness of thought, is sure of its opinions, and has finally conquered the means of expression; none of which achievements can be claimed for Shelley in respect of *The Revolt of Islam.* It is a quality present in all masterly work—in Shelley's fine work as in that of other poets—in the shape not of lack of animation, but of perfect self-possession, whether in serene or emotional writing. You see it in *Israfel;* the steady light of the poet's lucid brain shining through his changing fantasy. Shelley, as we shall see, attained such lucidity at times; but he certainly did not in *The Revolt;* and the highest praise we can give him in the matter is that he at length became convinced of his shortcoming, passing from his first opinion about revision to the directly contrary declaration: "I could materially improve that poem on revision."* Unhappily the "many corrections" he proposed to make in it were never effected, and it remains a portentous failure, the monument of a poet's fatal facility, a warning to all cultivators of spontaneity so long as it shall remain known in literature. It is hardly worth while to meet the claim of some of Shelley's admirers, that after all he *did* carefully correct, because his manuscripts are found full of alterations. That fact could prove nothing whatever as to his taking pains in composition, even if there were no specific declarations to set against it. It is simply impossible to write verse, especially in an

* See Mr. Garnett's *Shelley Memorials*, pp. 153 and 159.

SHELLEY AND POETRY

elaborate stanza, without a great deal of balancing between words and experimenting in rhymes; and the most headlong versifier may easily have a much more blotted manuscript than the most fastidious, just because he makes his inevitable experiments on his paper instead of in his head. One speculates as to whether Shakspere's having "blotted scarce a line" is not a proof of great deliberation in writing—relatively to his presumptively unparalleled rate of cerebration—rather than of carelessness. However that may be, the fact is palpable that whatever correction Shelley bestowed on his work in his longest poem was superficial, and inadequate even at that, seeing that, apart from metrical flaws, the poem is but a weary mass of uncastigated expression, there being hardly a page that has not half-a-dozen forms of bad writing. Bad rhyme, bad grammar, *banal* phrase, preposterous figure, fustian rhetoric, confused logic, meaningless collocations of words, extravagant comparisons, ideas thin-spun to puerility—all these are there in the most fatal abundance, unredeemed by countervailing beauties or by subtle or striking thought.

IV

I have dwelt thus long on *The Revolt of Islam*, not in the belief that Shelleyites found on it in particular, but in the conviction that when a decisive critical judgment is come to on that poem the relative rank of the others is the more easily settled. If we decide that the poet is free in his choice of a subject, but that he stands or falls by his treatment of it; that good poetic treatment consists in concentrated and charming expression; and that the work of *The Revolt of Islam* is on the whole neither effective nor charming, we should be far on the way to

SHELLEY AND POETRY

settling whether *Prometheus Unbound, Alastor, The Cenci, Hellas, Epipsychidion, Adonais, The Witch of Atlas,* and the longer of Shelley's remaining poems, are substantially fine poetry or otherwise. But we shall perhaps decide the more quickly if, instead of continuing uninterruptedly the process of exclusion of bad work, we now turn to certain shorter poems in which we find a marked degree of those qualities of finish, beauty, and condensation for which we have thus far looked in vain. In regard to the more popular of Shelley's short poems there is still much necessity for discrimination. We are probably all agreed, say, that *The Cloud*, even though a trifle too clever to reach the final charm of simplicity, is a masterpiece of controlled fancy and delicate yet reposeful art, presenting a combination of beautiful phrase, wealth of imagery, and music, such as had not appeared before in the language. There are one or two doubtful passages—see the eighth line of the third stanza and the last two of the fifth—but the poem is as a whole a marvel of technique and of beauty, equal in technique to Poe's *Raven*, and more transparent, more free from suspicion of the mechanical. It is a poem which must have cost intense, and probably involved long, artistic meditation; and its dazzling finish is the more remarkable in view of the poet's general tendency to helter-skelter. Through all its difficult structure the rhyming is practically flawless and unforced, and the line of thought perfectly straightforward. So long as men continue to love rhyme and rhythm and loveliness of phrase and fancy that poem will give them delight. It is not uncommon, however, to hear *The Skylark* coupled with *The Cloud* in respect of its finish, while set above it on the score of its intellectual scope; and *The Skylark* is distinctly and seriously faulty in the former regard. Whether it is really on a higher intellectual plane need

SHELLEY AND POETRY

not be discussed when it is asserted, as now, that it is ruinously defective in point of technique. Of its twenty-one short stanzas, I venture to say, not more than four are fairly sound. Let the reader go over the poem line by line, and see for himself. The second line, "Bird thou never wert," is an entirely infelicitous extension of the "blithe spirit;" the "from heaven *or near it*" is 'prentice-work in idea as in rhyme; and the fifth line will not scan. In the second stanza we have: "Higher .... and higher from the earth thou *springest*," and "Like a *cloud* of *fire* the deep blue thou *wingest*." What, next, is to be said of the lines: "Thou dost *float* and *run*—Like an *unbodied* [embodied?] *joy** whose *race* is *just* begun?" How reconcile such terms? In the next three stanzas we have the rhymes "even" and "heaven," and "clear" and "there," and "cloud" and "overflowed." Then we stumble on the hopeless passage:

"From rainbow clouds there flow not
Drops so bright to see
As from thy presence showers a rain of melody."

In stanza ninth comes the very forced figure of the maiden's music which "overflows her bower;" and in the next is the curious "bull" of the glowworm

"Scattering *unbeholden*
Its aerial *hue*
Among the flowers and grass which screen it from the view."

Stanza twelfth, despite a bad rhyme, is really fine:

---

* I was much derided by one critic for this suggested emendation, on the first publication of this essay. I have since found, first, that it had before been confidently made by such an ardent Shelleyite as James Thomson ("B. V."), and, secondly, that the point had long before been disputed over, till it was found that Shelley actually wrote "unbodied." I am still fain to say that the other word would have been better.

SHELLEY AND POETRY

> "Sound of vernal showers
> On the twinkling grass,
> Rain-awakened flowers,
> All that ever was
> Joyous and clear and fresh, thy music doth surpass."

But if we praise that, we can hardly tolerate the fourteenth:

> "Chorus hymeneal,
> Or triumphal chaunt,
> Matched with thine would *be all*
> But an empty vaunt
> *A thing wherein we feel there is some hidden want.*"

Set aside the twelfth, sixteenth, eighteenth, and twentieth stanzas, and none is left that will stand careful reading. The phrase "What *objects* are the *fountains* of thy happy strain;" the line "waking or asleep;" the whole of stanza nineteenth; and the three last lines of the twenty-first, are the remaining blemishes. ✓ Now, most of these details are capable of being weighed and discussed with as much precision as almost any question in grammar or logic; and if they are candidly faced there can hardly be any difference of opinion about them. They constitute a series of jarring faults of execution, and effectively take the poem out of the class of masterpieces, despite the quality of the thought, which is attractive if not new or profound.

Take now one or two of the poet's best lyrics, and see what it is in them that is admirable. I will not quote any of the more familiar, such as *Love's Philosophy*, *The Hymn of Pan*, the lines beginning "One word is too often profaned," the *Lines to an Indian Air*, "Music, when soft voices die," or any of the Laments. I will rather cite one brief *Dirge*, and a stanza *To the Moon*, of which the first is rarely noticed and the second even

SHELLEY AND POETRY

more rarely, Mr. W. M. Rossetti having excluded it *
from his unannotated edition. Here is the *Dirge:*

> "Rough wind, that moanest loud
> Grief too sad for song;
> Wild wind, when sullen cloud
> Knells all the night long;
> Sad storm, whose tears are vain,
> Bare woods, whose branches stain,
> Deep caves and dreary main,
> Wail for the world's wrong!"

The discerning reader has doubtless halted over that "when" in the third line, and the "stain" in the sixth. These are certainly stumbling-blocks; and, despite the invectives of Mr. Buxton Forman against the emendators of his beloved poet, I venture to say that "stain," though retained in all editions, is clearly a misprint for "strain;" while "when" might very plausibly be altered to "who in," and "knells" to "knellst." These changes made, the poem is practically perfect. Read now the lines *To the Moon:*

> "Art thou pale for weariness
> Of climbing heaven, and gazing on the earth,
> Wandering companionless
> Among the stars that have a different birth,
> And ever changing, like a joyless eye
> That finds no object worth its constancy?"

There are two more lines, suppressed in some editions, which constitute this a fragment; but they only mar the perfection of the stanza given, which I take to be one of Shelley's finest things. In these two poemlets, as in a number of the better-known short poems, we

---

* Mr. Rossetti has a rather puzzling editorial method. I find that the admirable sonnet, "Keen fitful gusts are whispering here and there," is dropped from his *Keats.* It was bad enough that it should not appear in Mr. Arnold's selection in the *English Poets:* Mr. Rossetti's omission is unpardonable.

have choice illustrations of his best poetic qualities, which may be summed up as delicacy and opulence of fancy, and tender, musical, piercing expression of what Mr. Ruskin calls the "pathetic fallacy"—the reading of human feeling into the things of nature.* Here (printers' errors apart) we have these attributes without any marring carelessness or racking of language : we are reading subtle, "inevitable," pregnant, memorable poetry.

Apply, then, the standards here adopted to, say *Prometheus Unbound*, and see how far they authorise praise of that work as a whole, or any definite portion of it. Raising no question whatever as to the substantiality of the theme, let us consider how far it has been impressively or subtly handled—how far the result is vivid, clarified, vital, and delightful for us. Is it not the case that, despite great passages, for the most part the subject is wrapt in a kind of "luminous fog;" that instead of condensing the emotions set in action by the theme the poet wanders off into every kind of diffuse and fantastic digression, creating for us an endless range of "rich windows that exclude the light, and passages that lead to nothing"? What pathos, what charm, is there in the "pathetic fallacy" as expressed here? We grant the poet his Spirits, his Echoes, his Spirits of the Hours, his Oceanides, his Jupiter and Phantasm of Jupiter, his Earth and Spirit of the Earth, and all the rest of it ; but he who handles such machinery has laid on himself a heavy burden of

* Cp. Nordau, as cited above, p. 47. Before Ruskin, Professor Spalding wrote of " those analogies between the mind and the things it looks on, which are the fountains of genuine poetic feeling." But he gave the highest credit for feeling these analogies to—Thomson of the "Seasons"! (*Hist. Eng. Lit.*, ed. 1853, p. 338.) Perhaps it would be fair to say that Thomson's failure is one of affected execution.

SHELLEY AND POETRY

being at every turn at once intense and fascinating, musical and meaningful. Now there are passages of beautiful if somewhat soprano blank verse in *Prometheus Unbound*, and some exceedingly melodious lyrics ; but the unhappy fact remains that they are embedded in a large body of falsetto declamation and rhyming verbiage. What are we to make of such singing as this :

SECOND VOICE (*from the springs*).

"Thunderbolts had parched our water,
   We had been stained with bitter blood,
And had run mute, 'mid shrieks of slaughter,
   Through a city and a solitude."

*   *   *   *   *   *

FOURTH VOICE (*from the whirlwinds*).

"We had soared beneath these mountains
   Unresting ages; nor had thunder,
Nor yon volcano's flaming fountains,
   Nor any power above or under
Ever made us mute with wonder."

FIRST VOICE [*i.e.*, that of the mountains].

"But never bowed our snowy crest
As at the voice of thine unrest."

SECOND VOICE.

"Never such a sound before
To the Indian waves we bore.
A pilot asleep on the howling sea
Leaped up from the deck in agony,
And heard and cried, 'Ah, woe is me !'
And died as mad as the wild waves be."

And this :

"Once the hungry Hours were hounds
   Which chased the day like a bleeding deer,
And it limped and stumbled with many wounds
   Though the nightly dells of the desert year."

SHELLEY AND POETRY

And this :

> "O gentle moon, thy crystal accents pierce
> The caverns of my pride's deep universe,
> Charming the tiger joy, whose tramplings fierce
> Made wounds which need thy balm——?

There is really no need to quote samples. All the Songs and Choruses of Spirits, and the utterances of Demogorgon generally, may be averaged as sound and fury, signifying nothing. A question has even been raised as to whether the favourite stanza in Asia's song, beginning :

> "My soul is an enchanted boat,
> Which like a sleeping swan doth float
> Upon the silver waves of thy sweet singing"

has any particular meaning. I should not be disposed to push that inquiry, seeing that the passage is verbally pellucid, extremely musical, and charming in its fancy though a little confused in its imagery ; and in the same way I should gratefully accept the semichorus beginning:

> "There the voluptuous nightingales
> Are awake through all the broad noon-day ; "

and one or two other lyrical felicities. But a few such tuneful passages cannot make *Promethetus Unbound* rank as a great work. It is to be noted, indeed, that the favourite portions have no real connection with the central theme, the "enchanted boat" passage, for instance, being worked up from a fragment originally entitled by the poet *To One Singing*, just as Byron introduced into *Manfred* a song he had addressed to or written for his sister. Thus do the poets get their inspirations. We do not grudge them their expedients ; but we are entitled to demand that their hoarded gems shall be adequately set ; and the more relevant work in

SHELLEY AND POETRY

Prometheus Unbound, though less crude in execution than *The Revolt of Islam*, is for the most part unsatisfying. It is a far cry from the thunder and lightning of Æschylus to the Shelleyan aurora borealis. In the blank verse, as in the rhymed, we have a few starry points, as this:

> "As thought by thought is piled, till some great truth
> Is loosened, and the nations echo round";

And this:

> " Praxitelean shapes, whose marble smiles
> Fill the hushed air with everlasting love."

And there is splendid power in the opening apostrophe. But the true Shelleyite adores *Prometheus Unbound* in its nebulous entirety; and when people of culture are found thus fascinated by a coruscating haze we are forced to raise the question whether their own intellectual furniture is of a very substantial kind. Who are the people who find mental nourishment and abiding charm in the soft or strained falsettos of Shelley's nymphs and spirits, and the vapourings of his phantoms? Do they combine with a critical literary taste a clear vision of the great issues of life? Are they close students of men and things; and do they affect any harder thinking than that of belles-lettres? It would be unwarrantable to say that there are not out-and-out Shelleyites whose intellectual outfit is of the completest kind; but it may be suspected that a large proportion are to be classified as lovers of the sentimental in philosophy and the mythical in history; and that the competent minds which delight in Shelley generally set aside as valueless two-thirds of his work. This at all events may be said with confidence, that a reader who finds poetry of the highest kind in Shakspere's tragedies; who finds a charm in Wordsworth's best distillation of reflection and feeling; who appreciates both the incomparable art and the deeper emotion of Tennyson; who is moved by the best verse of Arnold; who follows and enjoys the psychologising of Browning; who has assimilated the best European fiction of these generations; and who, withal, follows with interest the thought of his time and adopts its conceptions of man and nature—that such a reader cannot conceivably find enduring satisfaction in the larger part of Shelley's product. If one feels the fine qualities of the short pieces in which the singer really reaches our heart-strings, the moving naturalness of the thought and the " simple, passionate, sensuous " quality of the language, one simply cannot accept as successful poetry the spasmodic rhapsodies of the long compositions.

V

We shall not, however, rightly understand the case until we fully recognise the remarkable faculty which underlies Shelley's worst as well as his best work—the freedom in the use of words, in which, judgment apart, he excels all previous English poets save Shakspere. It is no doubt this extraordinary capacity for mere verbal movement which overpowers most Shelleyites; it seems so wonderful, so superhuman, so independent of the ordinary trammels of thought and speech, that men in their surprise cease to be critical, and simply bow down and worship. And it must be acknowledged that his faculty of ecstatic speech is at times exhibited by Shelley in sustained flights which do not get lost in cloudland. If I were asked to say in which of the poems over a few hundred lines he is most successful, I should name *Epipsychidion* and the *Lines written among*

SHELLEY AND POETRY

the Euganean Hills. In these pieces, though they have not, as it were, gone through the process of gestation which made possible the ripest of his short poems, he is working in the stuff of human feeling; not versifying delirious aspirations, but pouring out his own heart; and though we have agreed that to the poet no subject is tabu, it stands to reason that he has a much better chance of attaining excellence of song when he uses the material of his deepest experience than when spinning the cloud-webs of his wandering fantasy. And so the poem *written among the Euganean Hills*, though done in haste and not free from weaknesses, has a touching quality for all lovers of poetry, the throb of the poet's heart running through all its swift transitions. It really attains the indispensable quality of intension, the poet in the stress of his emotion becoming one, as it were, with all he sees, and attaining in his commentary a white heat of thought. So too in *Epipsychidion* he achieves a transfiguration of passion, moving in the process, it is true, towards his favourite cloudland, but never letting the note of his eager passion die away, never getting quite lost sight of. It is a unique poetic faculty which has produced these two poems, with their eager rush of ideas, that "pard-like, beautiful and swift" motion which charms so many readers into measureless applause; and we shall do well to take pains to appreciate their fine qualities, for they stand alone among Shelley's poems of more than two hundred lines in respect of combined intensity and finish. With the *Ode to the West Wind*, they represent his highest achievement in the most ambitious forms of lyrical poetry, and give us the measure of his mentality. Wild, passionate yearning, undefined aspiration, expressed with an eagerness always tending towards incoherence and unintelligibility—this is what Shelley has to give us in the most strenuous of his prosperous flights; and it may be left to readers to say for themselves finally whether at his highest such a poet is one of the greatest poets.

It is sometimes contended—it is contended by Mr. Myers in his admirably written essay in *The English Poets*, after he has condensed into a cogent argument the "floating criticism" of those whom Shelley does not satisfy—that the poet was developing, and would have done stronger work had he lived; but this is going beyond the data. Shelley was indeed becoming a little more self-critical, and he rejected some very bad passages which he had written for *Epipsychidion;* but that poem as it stands, and *Adonaïs* and *Hellas*, give no indication of any real progress on his part towards a firmer grasp of life and thought than he exhibited four years earlier. It is unwarrantable to take Shelley's poetry as the work of a youth whose intellectual powers were only half developed: at twenty-eight as at twenty his thinking is spasmodic, ill-digested, unsubstantial; and, looking to his precocity, we have some reason to believe that had he lived he would have given the world no solider work than he has done. If people would study the facts of his life dispassionately they would see that though in his moral nature the beauties far outgo the faults, he had not the mental constitution of a sane and profound poet. Hallucinations such as are recorded of him are not credentials of intellectual greatness: we have only to place his pathetic life, with its crazes, its flurries, and its miseries, beside that of Goethe, without raising any question of morals, to see the difference between abnormality of function such as his and balanced poetic strength. And even in respect of his art, of his technique, it cannot be claimed for Shelley that his progress was promisingly steady. *The Skylark*, according to Mrs.

SHELLEY AND POETRY

Shelley, was written in the same year as *The Cloud*—
1821 ; and side by side with the metrical perfection of
the latter poem and the lilt of the *Hymn of Pan* we have
also the slipshod work of *The Sensitive Plant*, an essentially unsuccessful production, were it only in respect of
the impossibility of scanning it regularly for any three
stanzas together. And in *Hellas*, also written in 1821,
as an offset to the clarion song with which it concludes,
we have not only rhyming passages of the most extravagantly meaningless description, but quantities of the
most prosaic blank verse Shelley ever turned out—much
of it mere lumbering transcripts of the gazettes, and
much more little better than noisy melodrama. We have
Mahmud telling Ahasuerus :

"Thou art an adept in the difficult lore
Of Greek and Frank philosophy ; "

and bits of chorus such as this :

" I saw her [Wrong] ghastly as a tyrant's dream,
Perch on the trembling pyramid of night,
Beneath which earth and all her realms pavilioned lay
In visions of the dawning undelight."

When we read such propositions as : "wolfish change,
like winter, howls to strip the foliage in which Fame,
the eagle, built her aërie ; " and such figures as "the
cold, pale Hour, rich in reversion of impending death,"
it is idle to ask us to believe that the poet was developing into a close thinker and truly artistic singer. And,
to come to perhaps the most delicate point in our
summing up, even *Adonaïs*, one of the poems of 1821,
partakes of the nature of a brilliant failure. It has
certainly a comparatively small percentage of quite bad
or absurd lines ; but none the more does it exhibit ripe
art or pregnant utterance. The show of passion, the
"wild and whirling words" in which the poet pours his

SHELLEY AND POETRY

plaint for his dead fellow singer, have the effect of impressing many readers; and indeed it is impossible to be quite cold to such a storm of eloquent wailing; but I doubt whether any one of a fairly judicial habit of mind can go through the poem thoughtfully and, mindful of the actual facts of Shelley's relation to the dead man, yet laying no stress on his blunder as to the cause of Keats's death, pronounce it the moving expression of a sincere human grief. It has neither the symptoms nor the contagious pathos of heartfelt mourning. Milton's *Lycidas*, with all its noble beauty, had partly set a precedent for rhetorical requiems; but where Milton's rhetoric is august and golden, Shelley's is shrill, hysterical, almost bombastic. It is not by declamatory lamentation of this sort that we are moved to mourn for poets or any one else. Take against the whole profuse outcry of *Adonais* a few sad stanzas of *In Memoriam*, with their controlled but potent feeling; or even a few such simple lines as these from *In the Garden at Swainston:*

> "Two dead men have I known
> In courtesy like to thee;
> Two dead men have I loved
> With a love that ever will be;
> Three dead men have I loved,
> And thou are last of the three";

or four mellow, melancholy lines of Arnold's on Clough:

> "Hear it from thy broad lucent Arno vale
> (For there thine earth-forgetting eyelids keep
> The morningless and unawakening sleep
> Under the flowery oleanders pale)"—

and Shelley's dirge beside them sounds windy and theatrical.

They positively will not bear cool criticism from readers of this generation, these lengthy performances

SHELLEY AND POETRY

of his, be they late or early. *The Witch of Atlas* may be read with satisfaction by votaries of belles-lettres on the strength of its thin trickle of rhyme and dilettantist fancy-spinning, regardless of such an unspeakable line as that ending in " dairy " in the sixteenth stanza ; but the weakest of the *Idylls of the King* is strong and interesting in comparison. *Julian and Maddalo* sometimes has a word said for it by critics who find it impossible to say any good of *Rosalind and Helen*, but no one has yet shown where the general merit of the former poem lies. It has one noteworthy and often-quoted passage ; but what are we to make of such lines as these :

" I recall
The sense of what he said, although I mar
The force of his expressions " :

" His child had now become
A woman, such as it has been my doom
To meet with few "— ?

And what excuse can be made for the final collapse of the story in the absurd declaration :

" She told me how
All happened—but the cold world shall not know "— ?

One after one, on examination, the long poems for which so much has been claimed are found to be faulty, diffuse, charmless, ill-considered, wearisome—so much "rhymed English," as Emerson bluntly put it. *The Cenci* best bears study, and it must be allowed that Shelley has handled his ill-chosen subject with no small energy and pains. It is sometimes claimed for him that his tragedy places him next to Shakspere among modern English poets ; but to pronounce such a judgment on the datum that no tragedy of importance had been produced between Shakspere and Shelley is to use misleading language. *The Cenci* has indeed a quality of emotion and stress not to be found in the intermediate work; but all the same it fails to take rank as an original and successful drama. Half a dozen times over we find direct imitations of Shakspere, but of Shaksperean concision and lifelikeness there is little. It has the literary faults of the "poetic drama" without that terse intensity of style which in Shakspere seems to fuse the most extravagant imagery into living speech. The plagiarisms might be taken as results of failure of memory, like the repeated use of the word "wilderness" in *Prometheus*, and of "islanded" elsewhere; but these are all symptoms of intellectual defect; and, for the rest, the shortcomings of the work are of a vital kind. The poet tells us in his preface that he has "avoided with great care in writing this play the introduction of what is commonly called mere poetry;" but in point of fact the declamation is constantly in Shelley's own poetic style; and he introduces the merest of "mere poetry" just where it is most inadmissible, as when[*] Camillo is made to say of Marzio:

> "He shrinks from her regard like autumn's leaf
> From the keen breath of the serenest north."

Most fatal defect of all, Beatrice is quite imperfectly individualised, being here a personage of all too Shelleyan fecundity of phrase, who in her supreme moments, with one exception, substitutes verbose violence for the terrible simplicity of genuine feeling in extremity. The exception is the last speech of all, which is entirely and astonishingly excellent. These lines and some others, including those introducing Beatrice's song, do recall Shakspere; and suggest questions as to Shelley's cerebral variability; but our

[*] Act v. scene 2.

final judgment must be that while *The Cenci*, despite its impracticable subject, is in respect of literary quality more readable than any other of Shelley's longer works, it is not fated to become a classic. In its kind it is superseded by Browning.

There is little need to review in detail the rest of our poet's large body of work. Those who set him high do not as a rule found to any extent on his political and satirical verse, recognising presumably that while his achievement in those directions is considerable, it is of no particular account in regard to the question of his rank among the higher poets. Much of it, however, has the high merit of directness and naturalness—praise which, it should be said, cannot be given to such pieces as the Odes to Liberty and to Naples —and this measure of practical success in the poet's less poetic work ought to be kept in view in our final estimate of him. Mr. Arnold has strikingly described Shelley, in one of his choice phrases, as an "ineffectual angel, beating in the void his luminous wings in vain;" but when we remember what his political influence has been since his death, the characterisation is felt to be astray. Its true aspect is, from the point of view of the present criticism, in regard to Shelley's attempts at concentrated poetic criticism of life. But let it be reiterated in conclusion that mere failure to criticise life soundly is not the condemnation of a poet. What has been contended in this inadequate inquiry is that not the rightness of a poet's thinking but the charm of his expression of it is his title to praise; and what is rightly to be decided against Shelley is that in his longer works his thought, such as it was, is quite inadequately meditated for purposes of beautiful expression. With counter arguments to the effect that Shelley's personality glorifies his poetry for us we have here nothing to do.

THE ART OF KEATS
(1884)

WHEN Mr. Irving, some ten years ago, made a sensation in London by his remarkable creation of a melodramatic Hamlet, it was said that strange questions were known to be put with bated breath in the boxes about the fourth act or so. "What is the end?" and "What becomes of Hamlet?" were among the problems alleged to have been thus propounded by persons who discovered on trial that the social make-believe of knowing Shakspere as a matter of course, somehow did not procure one a thorough familiarity with his works. The story was doubtless in large measure an embellishment; at least it is difficult to believe that any of the numerous patriots who know Shakspere by faith alone would thus break down convention; but it is an effective way of setting forth the tendency of poor humanity to lose hold of literature which everybody is presumed to know; and it would bear telling in regard to more things than "Hamlet." In the perusal of some of the many criticisms which have lately appeared on Keats, there is apt to arise a suspicion which can most concisely be expressed in the bold generalisation that it is not the popularity of a poet which produces new editions, but new editions which maintain a poet's popularity. One

THE ART OF KEATS

speculates as to whether Mr. Forman's recent magnificent edition of Keats supplied a felt want, or whether the want came to be felt after the date of publication; and whether it was then experienced by many who were unable to satisfy it. And one can hardly resist the conclusion that there is a close relation between the amount of cerebration going on in the critical world, and the size and cost of the new editions with which that world is confronted.

Whatever be the demerits and motives of the critics singly and in the mass, they have assuredly the merit of stimulating the public to read. It is pretty certain that the production of Mr. Forman's edition has indirectly promoted the sale of others, and also led to much dipping into *Endymion*. The result must in many cases have been a certain degree of perplexity; and though Mr. Forman's edition has drawn forth much pertinent and educative criticism, there is perhaps still room for an attempt at a reasoned estimate of the value of Keats's work. The body of criticism on Keats, indeed, is about as difficult to assay conclusively as the poet's performance. There is first to be dealt with the phenomenon of the laborious and costly production of all Keats wrote; then the explicit and implicit homage paid him by a patient critic like Mr. Forman, and many able writers in the general press; and against this is to be set the considerable mass of detraction got by adding admissions of admirers to charges of censors. The difficulty presents itself in a peculiarly precise and puzzling form in the critique by Mr. Arnold prefaced to the selections from Keats in Mr. Ward's *English Poets*. One sentence in that paper begins with : " We who believe Keats to have been by his promise, at any rate, if not fully by his performance, one of the very greatest of English poets;" and a page or two further on comes

THE ART OF KEATS

this final judgment: "His *Endymion*, as he himself well saw, is a failure; and his *Hyperion*, fine things as it contains, is not a success." How is a guileless reader to reconcile such utterances? Keats's longest poem, which may practically be reckoned his most important, is pronounced a failure; the next longest is put in the same category, leaving but a small quantity uncondemned; and this by a critic who thinks he was by his promise, and in large measure by his performance, one of the very greatest of English poets. No reasoning can well acquit Mr. Arnold of having left a hiatus in his work; but it is perhaps possible to reach a position from which at least the rationale of both the eulogy and the detraction may be perceived; and at which the admiration of one school may be partly sympathised with at the same time as the impatience of their extreme opponents.

One dispute about Keats may be settled by approaching it straightforwardly and simply. There is a common impression, indicated in Byron's reflection on the erroneous story of Keats's sufferings from adverse criticism, and in Carlyle's contemptuous reference to him, that the author of *Endymion* was a feeble creature, seriously lacking in self-control. That view of him is strongly supported by some of the letters to Fanny Brawne, one of which, written before his illness, is singled out by Mr. Arnold with much severity, if not altogether without justice, as having "in its relaxed self-abandonment something underbred and ignoble." Mr. Arnold, however, goes too far when he says it is "the sort of love-letter of a surgeon's apprentice which one might hear read out in a breach of promise case or in the Divorce Court." Foolish surgeons' apprentices do not say such things as this: "I have been astonished that men could die martyrs for religion—I have shuddered at it. I shudder no more—I could be martyred for my religion—Love is my religion—I could die for that." The matter can best be seen round by contrasting these passionate outbursts with Keats's protestations at other times of his disposition to regard women as he did roses and sweetmeats, as "children to whom I would rather give a sugar-plum than my time." Now, the passion and the puppyism are alike natural consequences of British social arrangements, which at once discountenance the sexual instincts, and tend—then greatly and still much—to develop in women only the sexual attractions. It is the result of our asceticism that we both find passion ignoble and are capable of being ignobly passionate. The chances are that Keats did not do more "underbred" things than the average "well brought-up" young man whom Mr. Arnold would cite as a model.

Here, then, there need be no confusion. Keats, let us agree, could be both masculinely superior to the sexual instinct and masculinely slave to it; and it consists with either fact that he should before his illness show so much "flint and iron," as Mr. Arnold puts it, such a haughty and secure superiority to popular opinion. Nor is it astonishing that he should at one time speak slightingly about poetry and the popular appetite for it; and at another proclaim his thirst for glory and his devotion to poetry, or proudly declare the public his debtors for his verses: such changeableness being as well ascertained a quality of young manhood as any species of fickleness is of the other sex. If any insist on being rigorous, let them remember that Keats was probably a diseased organism long before he began to spit blood; that phthisis goes with both erotic and intellectual precocity; and that precocity is in itself disease.

THE ART OF KEATS

If it be settled that apparently conflicting views of Keats's character are simply contemplations of him in different aspects, it may be possible to come to a satisfactory decision about the value of his poetry without pronouncing any school of criticism to be out of court—to harmonise the judgment that *Endymion* and *Hyperion* are failures, with the verdict of an *Athenæum* critic that "not in English literature, nor perhaps in any literature, is rapidity combined with steadiness of growth so astonishingly as in Keats's case." After much theorising it is beginning to be generally understood that a poet is really, as old maxims had it, a specialist; that he starts with a peculiar gift of expression, and that he cultivates that gift. Carlyle, who of all critics possessing genuine insight is about the least patient, the least careful to check himself, is responsible for some amount of misconception on the subject. The passage in the essay on Burns, in which he contemns Keats and dogmatises on the nature of poetry, is worth remembering in this connection:

"Poetry, except in such cases as that of Keats, where the whole consists in a weak-eyed maudlin sensibility, and a certain vague random tunefulness of nature, is no separate faculty, no organ which can be superadded to the rest or disjoined from them, but rather the result of their general harmony and completion. The feelings, the gifts that exist in the Poet are those that exist, with more or less development, in every human soul: the imagination which shudders at the Hell of Dante is the same faculty, weaker in degree, which called that picture into being."

There is just enough truth here to carry the error. If poetry is no separate faculty, how is it that such a strong imagination as Carlyle's own, even when united with a keen sense of literary art and a considerable mastery of language, could not produce good verse? He has everything but the final felicity of being at home in metre—a case scarcely to be paralleled save in that of

Charles Lamb. Two such cases, however, are amply sufficient to prove that besides understanding and imagination the poet must possess three special aptitudes, full command of words, a subtle feeling for cadence, and an equally subtle sensibility, by force of which last he is for ever attracted to the uncommon, whether beneath the common or beyond it. Having these, he may, by reason of other endowments or limitations, be either a great poet or only a charming one; but, great or limited, his function as poet is to see and say things in the finest way rather than to teach; and in point of fact, instead of having all his faculties in harmony, he must cultivate his gift partly at the expense of his other faculties, and best succeeds when most possessed by that one. Now, Carlyle spoke ignorantly when he allowed Keats nothing but a "weak-eyed maudlin sensibility." Keats's critical judgment at times shows itself as robust as that of Burns, and considerably more subtle. There is not in English literature anything closer, firmer, or more clear-headed in the way of terse self-criticism than the preface to *Endymion*. To call the writer of that merely maudlin is absurd. The remarkable thing is that a young poet should combine such a power of rigorous judgment with such a capacity and passion for painting cloudland. What we must believe is that Keats had the intellectual endowment to make a great poet in time, though so much of his work is of the kind we should expect from one less than great.

But the first thing to be set forth is the measure in which he possessed the poetic faculty proper. That instead of possessing a mere "random tunefulness of nature" he had a singular aptitude for cadence and a marvellous capacity of exquisite phrase, is now pretty universally felt. Mr. Arnold goes so far as to say that

THE ART OF KEATS

"no one else in English poetry, save Shakspere, has in expression quite the fascinating felicity of Keats, his perfection of loveliness." Carlyle's "random" may be defended by some on the score that Keats's good things are found among so many bad, but that does not seem to be what Carlyle meant; and if he really could appreciate the goodness of the good things it was his business to confess distinctly their existence. A conclusive illustration of Keats's power of melody and choice phrase is the *Ode to a Nightingale*, certainly one of the most beautiful poems in any language; and one stanza is about as decisive as the entire poem :

> " Thou wast not born for death, immortal Bird !
> No hungry generations tread thee down ;
> The voice I hear this passing night was heard
> In ancient days by emperor and clown :
> Perhaps the self-same song that found a path
> Through the sad heart of Ruth, when, sick for home,
> She stood in tears amid the alien corn ;
> The same that oft-times hath
> Charmed magic casements opening on the foam
> Of perilous seas, in faery lands forlorn."

It must be confessed indeed—even Mr. Forman allows it—that the logic of the stanza is wrong ; and it will scarcely do to argue, as Mr. Forman does in regard to the faulty first stanza, that the obscurity is appropriate; but, setting aside the fourth line above quoted, which has a rhyme-making ring, there can be no debate whatever as to the bewitching beauty of the lines and the strange charm of their "cloudy companionship." Nor can there be found in our language more "melodious pain" than this :

> . . . That I might drink, and leave the world unseen,
> And with thee fade away into the forest dim :

THE ART OF KEATS

>   Fade far away, dissolve and quite forget
>   What thou amongst the leaves hast never known,
>   The weariness, the fever, and the fret
>   Here, where men sit and hear each other groan;
>   Where palsy shakes a few, sad, last grey hairs,
>   Where youth grows pale, and spectre thin, and dies;
>   Where but to think is to be full of sorrow
>   And leaden-eyed despairs;
>   *Where Beauty cannot keep her lustrous eyes,*
>   *Or new Love pine at them beyond to-morrow.*

Nothing more musically melancholy has been done before or since; and here no touch could be wished different. Had Keats always or often written thus his position to-day would be triumphantly secure; but unhappily only a very small proportion of his work can be put beside the *Ode to a Nightingale*. That he has nevertheless ranked since his death as a generally successful poet is the result of two causes, one the scarcity of perfect work, the other the inability of most readers to discriminate clearly between good work and bad. It may seem presumptuous to say it, but it must be said that the most prominent critics still distinguish ill between Keats's fine and inferior workmanship. There is a very general recognition of the admirable character of the sonnet *On First Looking into Chapman's Homer;* but very little reference to a finer sonnet of his still, which I will here quote :

>   Keen, fitful gusts are whispering here and there
>   Among the bushes, half leafless and dry;
>   The stars are very cold about the sky,
>   And I have many miles on foot to fare.
>   Yet feel I little of the cool bleak air,
>   Or of the dead leaves rustling drearily,
>   Or of those silver lamps that burn on high,
>   Or of the distance from home's pleasant lair;
>   For I am brimful of the friendliness
>   That in a little cottage I have found;

THE ART OF KEATS

> Of fair-haired Milton's eloquent distress,
> And all his love for gentle Lycid drowned;
> Of lovely Laura in her light green dress,
> And faithful Petrarch, gloriously crowned.

That, I make bold to think, is the best sonnet Keats wrote, though, strange to say, Mr. Arnold has not had it inserted among the pieces given in the *English Poets*, which include eight sonnets.* The Homer sonnet, though distinctly done in the grand style, and terminating, as Mr. Forman observes, "with the noblest Greek simplicity," is of a less rare kind of execution. With the exception, perhaps, of the last two lines, it could quite conceivably have been written by, say, Leigh Hunt,† who was capable of the orotund roll of the earlier part, and who might have avoided the two weak lines in the sonnet—

> Round many western islands *have I been*

and

> Till I heard Chapman speak out loud and bold.

The first eight lines, in short, show no incomparable inspiration; whereas the whole of the sonnet quoted is poetical in the highest degree. It has the crowning

---

* And though Mr. Swinburne declares, with evident reference to that on Chapman's Homer, that Keats "has certainly left us one perfect sonnet of the first rank, and as certainly he has left us but one" (*Miscellanies*, p. 216).

† Lest any hastily scoff, let me point out that when Leigh Hunt, Shelley, and Keats agreed each to write a sonnet on the Nile, Leigh Hunt's production was decidedly the best of the three. The two opening lines:

> It flows through old, hush'd Ægypt and its sands
> Like some grave, mighty thought, threading a dream—

and the line on Cleopatra:

> The laughing queen that caught the world's great hands—

would have done credit to any English poet. Yet this sonnet, too, is excluded from the *English Poets*.

THE ART OF KEATS

grace of an entire, a divine simplicity, beside which the Chapman sonnet savours of artificiality; and its tiptoe finish is as unmatchable in its way as that of the other, whether you call it Greek or not. A poet, besides being genius and artist, has his special inspirations, his lucky moments; and one of these gave birth to the most perfect poem of Keats, in which the one shadow of a spot, the irregularity of the second line, is hardly more of a blemish than a dimple.

Among Keats's Odes, next to that *To a Nightingale* I should place that *On Melancholy*. It perhaps never attains to the perfect music of the other, but it is just as distinctly an emanation of genius, the work not of a clever versifier but of a man whose imagination lives naturally in another medium than that of prose common sense. It has the incommunicable distinction which comes of the laying on of the poet's hands. The middle stanza is perhaps a little "precious," a little suggestive of the weaker developments of a modern æsthetic cultus which makes much of Keats; yet even in this stanza the workmanship is delicately charming, and the last is both beautiful and massive : *

> She dwells with Beauty—Beauty that must die;
>   And Joy, whose hand is ever at his lips,
> Bidding adieu; and aching Pleasure nigh,
>   Turning to poison while the bee-mouth sips;
> Ay, in the very temple of Delight
>   Veil'd Melancholy has her sovran shrine,
>   Though seen of none save him whose strenuous tongue
>   Can burst Joy's grape against his palate fine:
> His soul shall taste the sadness of her might,
> And be among her cloudy trophies hung.

* Since this was written I find that Professor Dowden has laid down, evidently with deliberation, the opinion that "Keats has written nothing greater than the last stanza of his 'Ode on Melancholy'" (*Fortnightly Review*, Sept. 1887, p. 430).

THE ART OF KEATS

But this choice poem, which is in one respect more successful than the *Ode to a Nightingale*, in that it keeps its high level to the very end, while that falls in the closing stanza, is also carefully excluded from the collection in the *English Poets*, while the second-rate *To Autumn* finds a place. Mr. Forman, again, after claiming that "in work later than *Endymion* there are probably more passages wherein the thought or feeling, whatever it may be, is expressed with an almost absolute felicity than will be found in the like bulk of work by any other modern English poet," observes that "the odes *To a Nightingale, On a Grecian Urn*, and *On Indolence, The Eve of St. Mark*, and *La Belle Dame Sans Merci*, may be named among the most sustained examples of this lofty felicity." *La Belle Dame Sans Merci* is certainly a perfect success; but I will affirm that the *Ode on a Grecian Urn* is inferior to that *On Melancholy;* and that the *Ode on Indolence* and *The Eve of St. Mark* are not to be named in comparison.* The two latter pieces will not for a moment

---

* It is discouraging to find Mr. Swinburne thus adjudicating on the Odes:—"Perhaps the two nearest to absolute perfection, to the triumphant achievement and accomplishment of the very utmost beauty possible to human words, may be that to Autumn and that on a Grecian Urn; the most radiant, fervent, and musical is that to a Nightingale; the most pictorial and perhaps the tenderest in its ardour of passionate fancy is that to Psyche; the subtlest in sweetness of thought and feeling is that on Melancholy" (*Miscellanies*, p. 216). These distinctions are assuredly not scientific; indeed they are well-nigh meaningless. The poetry nearest to absolute perfection and to the utmost beauty possible to human words, must be the finest; and few lovers of verse will set the Odes which Mr. Swinburne so describes above that *To a Nightingale*, which he himself on another page ranks as "one of the final masterpieces of human work in all time and for all ages." My proposition is that in the "beauty possible to human words" the *Ode to Melancholy* stands next this, the loveliest; that it is such beauty, rightly considered, that constitutes poetic success; and that to use the terms

support the claim of absolute felicity made for Keats, with their many prose lines,* their entirely earthly architecture, and their almost complete lack of eminent beauties. Mr. Forman, it is to be feared, has suffered that blunting of the critical sense which is apt to overtake laborious editors. In a note he speaks of "What I believe I am not alone in regarding as Keats's masterpiece—*Isabella.*" The avowal is decisive. If *La Belle Dame Sans Merci*, the *Ode to a Nightingale*, and the Chapman sonnet are to rank as masterpieces, *Isabella* is not worthy of the name. Even *The Eve of St. Agnes*, which Leigh Hunt preferred to it, is far from deserving the title; but it is a much less

"radiant," "musical," subtle in sweetness of thought and feeling, and so forth, except in respect of beauty of expression, is merely to darken counsel. Doubtless I shall be blamed for ranking the odes *To Autumn* and *On a Grecian Urn* distinctly below that *On Melancholy;* and I can but solicit a careful comparison of their workmanship. I say that the last has a much higher average of felicitous phrase and cadence and a less percentage of the alloy of commonplace term and prosaic association than the others. In all probability it is the motive and the line of exposition that have hindered the *Ode on Melancholy* of its due appreciation among English readers, who are wont to call such sentiments "morbid," and so to dismiss them. I may here note that in his article on Keats, Mr. Swinburne has been somewhat careless in alleging that the *Ode to a Nightingale* "is immediately preceded in all editions now current by some of the most vulgar and fulsome doggerel ever whimpered by a vapid and effeminate rhymester in the sickly stage of whelphood." In the Aldine edition, edited by Lord Houghton, and important to the student for its chronological arrangement, the *Nightingale* is immediately preceded by *Melancholy*. And when we are discussing the art of expression, it may be observed that such tumid rhetoric as that quoted could in any case be spared by readers of Encyclopædias.

 * Such as these, in the *Ode on Indolence* :

   "For I would not be dieted with praise
   A pet-lamb in a sentimental farce—"

"farce" rhyming with "grass."

crude piece of work than *Isabella,* which, though it contains some stanzas of wonderful pictorial and dramatic power, is simply swarming with desperately bad lines. Take a handful :

> If Isabel's quick eye had not been wed
> To every symbol on his forehead high—

> Though young Lorenzo in warm Indian clove
> Was not embalmed—

> O Isabella! I can half perceive
> That I may speak my grief into thine ear—

> And many once proud-quivered loins did melt
> In blood from stinging whip—

> When 'twas their plan to coax her by degrees
> To some high noble and his olive-trees—

> They dipp'd their swords in the water and did tease
> Their horses homeward with convulsed spur,
> Each richer for his being a murderer.

> To-day thou wilt not see him, nor to-morrow,
> And the next day will be a day of sorrow.

There is little fine work here; no concision; no painstaking; the number of vile and far-fetched rhymes, and further-fetched ideas, is overwhelming; and to quote all the passages vitiated in the process of rhyming would fill pages. Nothing could be worse than the bankrupt line with which the poet crowns the crowning picture :

> At last they felt the kernel of the grave,
> And Isabella did not stamp and rave.

Some of us have since remedied the omission.

Not long ago a writer in a leading London journal spoke of *The Eve of St. Agnes* as one of the most perfect poems in the language; a judgment fitted to make one despair of newspaper criticism. That poem is not nearly so faulty as *The Pot of Basil;* but it has sufficient faults

THE ART OF KEATS

to ruin it. It has one or two great lines—this, for instance:

> The music yearning like a god in pain—

but a deplorable number of commonplace or bad ones, of which let these samples suffice:

> And back returneth, meagre, barefoot, wan,
> *Along the chapel aisle by slow degrees.*
> The sculptured dead on each side *seem to freeze.*

> Whose heart had brooded all that wintry day
> On love, and wing'd St. Agnes' saintly care
> As she had heard old dames full many times declare.

> Supperless to bed they must retire
> And couch supine their beauties lily white.

> The hallow'd hour was near at hand, she sighs:
> Amid the timbrels, and the throng'd resort
> Of *whisperers in anger or in sport;*
> 'Mid looks of love, defiance, hate, and scorn.

> Hot-blooded lords
> Whose very dogs would execration howl
> Against his lineage: not one breast *affords*
> Him *any mercy* in that mansion *foul*
> Save one old beldame weak in body and *soul.*

—all from the first ten stanzas. What constitutes perfection in poetry if such workmanship does not negate it?

Isabella, or *The Pot of Basil, The Eve of St. Agnes,* and *Lamia,* it must be said, are all as distinctly failures as *Endymion. Lamia,* which Lord Houghton calls "quite the perfection of narrative poetry," will perhaps be the last defended. It, too, has its fine passages, such as:

> ever, where she willed, her spirit went
> Whether to faint Elysium, or where
> Down through *tress-lifting waves* the Nereids fair
> Wind into Thetis' bower by many a pearly stair;

and

> Like a young Jove with calm uneager face;

THE ART OF KEATS

but, like *Isabella* and *The Eve of St. Agnes,* besides having many artistic blemishes it has the fatal, all-penetrating fault of entirely subordinating the theme to the execution. In all three cases Keats has made his subject a mere excuse for a long-drawn panorama of word-painting; and when the painting is in large part slovenly what is left to be said? The truth is, Keats was a boy, though truly a marvellous one; and for a boy to do work that is both extensive and elaborate is hardly possible, be he as precocious as he may. Though he have the most excellent critical taste —and Keats was on the whole an excellent critic—he cannot yet have sufficiently co-ordinated his creative and critical faculties. He can rarely produce the most thrilling effects, which are those got by the effortless distillation of much feeling and experience. If he is a born poet his very wealth of images will at first lead him astray. He will "ever let the Fancy roam," and if he attempts large canvases they are sure to be diffusely filled. It is, indeed, an open question whether perfect poetry can ever be got on a large scale—whether Poe was not right in disallowing all long poems. The day of the epic is done; and in severe moods one grows a little dubious even about *The Ring and the Book.* However that be, the weakness of Keats's long poems is all too obvious. We go through *Endymion* looking idly for sweet things, and finding many, but struggling through much marshy ground; the tragedy of Isabella's story never really rises on us; in the *Eve of St. Agnes* we are chiefly impressed by the *bric-à-brac* and the confectionery; the pathos of the Lamia's lot, the weird side of the legend, are never reached. Nor can one well gainsay the verdict of Mr. Arnold that *Hyperion* too comes short of being a success, if by a success we mean a poem to which we often and delightedly recur. The test is a hard one, no doubt, and it will play havoc with some of Mr. Arnold's work, as well as with most epics; but ultimately there is no evading it; and the time has come to apply it here. For one reason or another, a dozen once famous volumes of verse, Thomson's *Seasons*, Akenside's *Pleasures of Imagination*, Young's *Night Thoughts*, Campbell's *Pleasures of Hope*, not to mention other names, have failed to stand the test, and passed to the lumber-room of literature. If *Hyperion* holds its ground better, it must be because of the peculiar sympathy we give to Keats; the work itself, with all its merit, misses the accent of immortality, the intense Dantean vibration of inward life which defies the numbing fingers of oblivion. They do not stay with us, those Titans in reduced circumstances, strong as is much of the poet's versification in comparison with his previous things. One regards the poem involuntarily as a piece of technique, and finds it indeed very remarkable as such; but that is all. It leaves us cold, Shelley's and Byron's admiration notwithstanding. Certainly there was no finer modern blank verse than the opening description of Saturn; and as a single picture that will probably live as long as anything of the kind in literature; but a few admirable passages cannot so vitalise a long and diffuse and unprogressive poem as to make it enduringly attractive to readers beckoned by an increasing multitude of choice performances in all literatures. It was very like Shelley, who could see that *Endymion* was "replenished" with faults and disfigured with false taste, to pronounce *Hyperion* in large part written "in the very highest style of poetry." It was high-toned, it breathed enduring defiance of tyrannous power, and it was done in the grand style; all shining excellences in Shelley's eyes. But the fatal fact remains that it is elaborate to no purpose, a kind of feat of artistic training, which could at best serve to put the artist in "condition." A long mythological poem, to be enjoyable, must have an interesting action; and what action could be got here, save of that kind which, in the language of the horse-mart, means "no go"?

And yet, failures as his elaborate works were, hopeless failure as is the long *Cap and Bells*, there remains ample ground for saying that Keats was a great poet, prematurely cut off. His failures were the inevitable and instructive failures of a boy of genius aiming at great things. To have failed as he did at his years was to show greatness; to succeed to the extent he did was hardly a better proof. It may be set down as an axiom that only a great poet can do a perfect piece of work, however small, of a great kind; and Keats really did this. Though of course it must be kept in view that had he not carried in him the seeds of disease we probably should not have had from him such precocious work, we yet constantly feel that had he lived he would have produced poetry which would have superseded all his early productions, as the mature works of other great poets have done theirs. The very faults of his long poems (setting aside the *Cap and Bells*), and of his early work generally, are the faults of a luxuriant and not of a deficient gift: he riots in utterance as the young Shakspere did, perhaps in part by reason of lacking like him a strict or full schooling, but clearly also by virtue of an intoxicating sense of new power over language. Beside all the great poets of his time, beside Wordsworth and Coleridge and Shelley, he stands at least as original and as self-centred as they, and he sounds as new a note in song. From his first vehement assault, in *Sleep and Poetry*, on the mechanical host who followed the "decrepit standard" of Boileau, to his last nobly tender sonnet, he is a unique and inspired artist, great

THE ART OF KEATS

of heart and sincere in speech. He was no mere sensualist, despite the strong sensuous tendency recognisable in his features. He had a true heart, great sympathies, noble aspirations.* In politics he was as definitely democratic as his friends, Hunt and Shelley; and he could not die in peace amid the despotism of Naples.† He was resolutely determined to get knowledge; he made the keenest appraisement of his contemporaries; he was relentlessly self-critical; and he saw his way to great things. "One of my ambitions," he writes, "is to make as great a revolution in modern dramatic writing as Kean has done in acting." Boyish, no doubt; but though *Otho the Great* is a failure, it is certainly not so very bad as Mr. Lowell would make out; indeed to my mind its opening lines, and still more those of the fragment *King Stephen*, suggest not altogether feebly the thick thunder of Shakspere,‡ whose technique, one can surmise, Keats perceived and assimilated as readily as he did that of Milton. This quick intelligence is powerfully suggestive of great capacities. At an age when most poets and blank verse play-writers are, as it were, but beginning to see that there is such a thing as technique, he had a delighted and

---

* This, written in 1884, was put with much less fulness of recognition than is set up in every reader of Mr. Colvin's *Keats* (1887) and Mr. Sharp's *Life of Severn*.

† Houghton writes (Memoir in Aldine ed., p. xv.) that "there is nothing in his letters or his recorded conversation to show that he took even an ordinary interest in the public discussions of his time." But see the *Vision* version of *Hyperion*, lines 147-181.

‡ Since this was written, I find that Mr. Swinburne had before put forward a similar opinion in his article on Keats in the *Encyclopædia Britannica*, reprinted in his *Miscellanies*, 1886 : " In this boyish and fantastic play of *Otho the Great* there are such verses as Shakspere might not without pride have signed at the age when he wrote and even at the age when he rewrote the tragedy of *Romeo and Juliet*."

THE ART OF KEATS

confident appreciation of it. See with what an expert's ecstasy he dilates on Milton's art :

"Milton has put vales in Heaven and Hell with the very utter affection and yearning of a great Poet. It is a sort of Delphic abstraction, a beautiful thing made more beautiful by being reflected and put in a mist." "The light and shade, the ebon diamonding, the Ethiop immortality, the sorrow, the pain, the sad sweet melody, the phalanges of spirits so depressed as to be 'uplifted beyond hope,' the short mitigation of misery, the thousand melancholies and magnificences of the following lines [he quotes Book I. l. 533–567], leave no room for anything to be said thereon, but 'so it is.'"
"Book VI. line 58. *Reluctant*, with its original and modern meaning combined and woven together, with all its shades of signification, has a powerful effect."

And his criticism of his own work, when once it is fairly out of his hands, is just as certain. There is the ring of perfect sincerity in his avowal of the faulty character of *Endymion*, his admission that it is "slipshod," his final remark to Shelley that he "would willingly take the trouble to unwrite it, if possible."[*] And not the ripest of critics ever passed a more penetrating comment than that in his own preface :

"The imagination of a boy is healthy, and the mature imagination of a man is healthy; but there is a space of life between, in which the soul is in a ferment, the character undecided, the way of life uncertain, the ambition thick-sighted : thence proceeds mawkishness, and all the thousand bitters which those men I speak of must necessarily taste in going over the following pages."

The rapidity of his advance is indisputable. In the first Book of *Endymion* he had originally written a passage of six lines describing Peona's song, in which there were such touches as "the fainting tenors of a thousand shells," "a million whisperings of lily bells," and "the nightingale's complain, caught in its hundredth echo"—characteristic work, and not without charm, as

[*] *Shelley Memorials*, 3rd ed. p. 142.

THE ART OF KEATS

Mr. Forman indicates; but the florid strokes were all struck out, and a marginal alteration left the passage thus:

> 'Twas a lay
> More subtle-cadenced, more forest-wild
> Than *Dryope's lone lulling of her child—*

the finest couplet in *Endymion*.* *Lamia*, Lord Houghton's note tells us, Keats "wrote with great care, after much study of Dryden's composition"; and the poet writes of his work on it: "I have great hopes of success, because I make use of my judgment more deliberately than I have yet done;† but in case of failure with the world I shall find my content." There is as little of Dryden in *Lamia* as of Spenser in the early *Imitation of Spenser*: failure as it is, it attains a much more advanced versification as well as a subtler poetry than Dryden's. And the poet's "I shall find my content" is memorable. His long poems will in course of time be left to the reading of the literary specialists: there will be no time for people of all-round

---

* A partial exception to this rule of improvement is the production of *Hyperion: A Vision*, after the *Hyperion* which begins with the marble massiveness of form we have all admired. It must reluctantly be granted that Mr. Colvin has proved the *Vision* to be a recasting, and not the first version, as Lord Houghton's and later editions taught us all to believe. But though by general consent the clean-cut and quasi-Miltonic piece be the more impressive, the later poem is in its way also a notable performance; and some ardent admirers of Keats find in its far ampler expression of his own way of thought and feeling a greater because a more individual performance. It is clear that he swerved back from the first as "too Miltonic," and lacking in spontaneity. But it has not been noted, I think, that the influence of Cary's Dante, seen at times in the first version, is more abundantly visible in the second.

† A little earlier he had said of the *Ode to Psyche* that it was the "first and only" poem with which he had "taken even moderate pains." This was in February of 1819, after he had written his two finest sonnets, and just before the *Ode to a Nightingale*.

THE ART OF KEATS

culture to go through the inferior work of all the poets: but now that we have them, and think of the poet's grave, we cannot wish they had not been written. Were they nothing else, they are noteworthy documents in the history of literary evolution. All our subsequent poets take something from Keats. Tennyson's debt has long been recognised; * we find pieces of pure Tennyson in *Hyperion*, as—

> Until at length old Saturn lifted up
> His faded eyes, and saw his kingdom gone,
> And all the gloom and sorrow of the place
> And that fair kneeling goddess ; and then spake
> As with a palsied tongue.

Our other great poet, too, is singularly forestalled in the remarkable song, not to be found in the *English Poets*, which Keats wrote to the Spanish air Miss Reynolds used to play him : those lines—

> Lift the latch ! ah gently ! ah tenderly, sweet !
> We are dead if that latchet gives one little clink !

and the "lips pulp'd with bloom," are very Browning. And here in *Hyperion* spoke Mrs. Browning before her time—

> Leave the dinned air vibrating silverly.

Not in water, assuredly, is Keats's name written. "What porridge had John Keats?" asks Mr. Browning, sardonically pointing to the success of subsequent mediocre imitators. Well, one is glad to think of the "I shall find my content."

---

* Tennyson himself declared late in his life that Keats, though a "great master," had not been his model. That is true, but still he learned from him. Cp. Mr. Colvin, *Keats*, p. 219.

THE ART OF BURNS
(1884)

THE spectator of the new Burns statue on the Thames Embankment who considers closely its literary as well as its artistic significance, is apt to be led to some reflections which were not suggested in the course of the unveiling proceedings. His first feeling, of course, is one of pleasure in view of such a proclamation that the realm of literature is universal. Everything which tends to bring the note of culture into the environment of the mass, everything which helps to extend the intellectual life through the region of the ceaseless social struggle, makes for the general well-being, and is to be welcomed by the lovers of light. Considering the straits of orators in these matters, too, it would not be fair to examine narrowly the various reasons laid down for be-statuing a given celebrity—reasons of which, in the case of Burns, the sum-total is something like this: That Burns, in a general way, did not need a statue; that in Scotland, where he is best known, it is natural that he should have many statues; and that in London and other cities where he is not so well known, it is desirable to bring him into universal notice by means of statues. Such peculiarities of reasoning need not disturb those who realise how rarely it is that an act prompted by disinterested emotion can successfully be made to appear a highly utilitarian proceeding.

A priori approbation, however, gives place to scrutiny and reflection, and the process is not altogether tranquillising. Here is a statue in which the sculptor has expressed his idea of the poetic function by seating his poet on a tree-stump, with a pen in his hand and a scroll at his feet, looking into the sky for a word. Did Sir John Steell, one wonders, ever hear of a poet's definition of poetry as "emotion recollected in tranquillity"? It would appear not. His poet is exhibited as a creature in whom emotion and expression are simultaneous, and who carries about his writing materials in order to catch his inspirations ere they go. The circumstance goes to deepen a despondent feeling about the future of British statuary—an opinion reinforced by an examination of the feeble and valueless *Alexander and Bucephalus*, an early work of Sir John Steell's, recently added by subscription to the mob of bad statues in Edinburgh ; and by the recollection that the demand for statues of Burns appears to set blindly in the direction of this sculptor, whose reputation is the result of long practice in fulfilling such commissions, and who is thought to rise perfectly to the occasion when, instead of producing an absolute replica of a previous statue, he somewhat alters the pose of the figure. It may be urged that the sculptor, planning a statue for the public street, is bound to represent in some conventional form the known function of the person he images ; and though this principle cannot be allowed to justify a convention which is demonstrably a violation of artistic principles of a higher scope, it may be allowed that the British statuary is, perhaps, to some extent coerced by his

THE ART OF BURNS

conditions. That granted, however, there remains the question as to the condition of taste and culture among those who are the sculptor's judges—those who are delighted by these representations of Burns in a poetic ecstasy, and who cheer the declaration that he is one of the great poets of the world.

It is the peculiar feature in the fame of Burns that whereas other renowned poets are being for ever freshly laurelled by studious critics, not only do his praises come mainly from the inexpert multitude, but the voices of the few critics who deal with him carefully are ignored. The name of Carlyle is in these days hardly less universally known than that of Burns, but the number of admirers of Burns who have fully reckoned with Carlyle's criticism is probably very small indeed. That essay of fifty-six years ago remains, on the whole, the soundest judgment that has yet been passed on the poet. Despite its labouredness and its lack of unity, it gives on the whole a much fairer estimate of the man than does the able paper of Mr. Robert Louis Stevenson ; while it still presents the most outspoken verdict the public have heard on the literary value of Burns's work. It is a signal proof of Carlyle's critical power and originality that at the time of the publication of Lockhart's *Life* he was already able to see that the current estimate of some of Burns's most popular pieces was wrong ; and that he did not hesitate to pronounce *Tam O'Shanter* a merely brilliant rather than a great production. His remarks on that poem, like the essay as a whole, lack unity, as if they had been penned piecemeal before the whole matter was thought out : first the poet is blamed for not giving poetical life to the story, as Tieck might, and then it is admitted that "for strictly poetical purposes not much *was* to be made of it ; " but the judgment that *Tam O'Shanter* is

THE ART OF BURNS

"not so much a poem as a piece of sparkling rhetoric" may judiciously be set against that of admirers who, with Alexander Smith, pronounce it "immortal, unapproachable," and "the crowning glory and masterpiece of its author." We have in it a farcical narrative treated at best in the spirit of Aristophanic farce; and no amount of force and dexterity of execution can gain for such a poem those associations of subtle delightfulness which references to fine poetry call up for us. It is apt to create confusion, however, to say as Carlyle does that such a production is unpoetical, and that *The Jolly Beggars* is the most poetical of Burns's "poems," as distinguished from his songs. The precise explanation—so far as Carlyle's decision is justifiable—is that while metrical writing, of which the generic term is poetry, may at times be less exalted in its strain of thought than certain samples of the non-metrical writing we term prose, the former as a rule is the outcome of, and tends to communicate, a feeling of mental exaltation, while the latter, more often than not, expresses and induces unemotional states of mind; and we accordingly use the term poetry as connoting exalted feeling, and prose as implying something more ordinary. Now *Tam O'Shanter* is a story such as ministers to rustic fun; and though Burns gives it a certain Aristophanic quality, the story as a whole remains on the rustic level, while *The Jolly Beggars*, despite the nature of the theme, is infused with a "world-humour" that takes it above the merely rustic range; and is, indeed, to this day the less appreciated poem among the populace. Carlyle's verdict on *The Jolly Beggars* is worth quoting:

"The subject truly is among the lowest in Nature, but it only the more shows our poet's gift in raising it into the domain of art. To our minds this piece seems thoroughly compacted—melted together,

THE ART OF BURNS

refined—and poured forth in one flood of true *liquid* harmony. It is light, airy, soft of movement, yet sharp and precise in its details; every face is a portrait; that *raucle carlin*, that *wee Apollo*, that *Son of Mars*, are Scottish, yet ideal; the scene is at once a dream, and the very Ragcastle of 'Poosie-Nansie.' Further, it seems in a considerable degree complete, a real self-supporting whole, which is the highest merit in a poem. . . . Apart from the universal sympathy with man which this again bespeaks in Burns, a genuine inspiration and no inconsiderable technical talent are manifested here. . . . It would be strange, doubtless, to call this the best of Burns's writings; we mean to say only that it seems to us the most perfect of its kind, as a piece of poetical composition strictly so called."

The last sentence brings us to the main critical question in regard to Burns : Was he, after all, one of the world's greatest poets? Carlyle's final judgment is that he was not, and, what is specially to be noted, that he could not be in his circumstances ; and seeing that Carlyle on the whole admired and liked Burns, his judgment, as that of a great Scottish man of letters, must be allowed to deserve close consideration. The critic veers and hesitates a good deal, certainly, on the question whether Burns, living the life he did, could possibly have done great poetic work. On one page he pronounces all Burns's writings "imperfect fragments" "that wanted all things for completeness ; *culture, leisure,* true effort, nay, even length of life ; " on another he insists in opposition to those who prescribe culture for poor poets, that poetry lies in the heart, not in the tongue ; and, again, that Burns, without any more culture, might have found blessedness in poetry. But the distinct purport of the essay is that Burns's verse is valuable mainly on account of the poet's genuineness and practicality, not of his art. " We can look on but few of these pieces," it says, " as in strict critical language deserving the name of poems ; they are rhymed eloquence, rhymed pathos, rhymed sense ; yet seldom essentially melodious, aërial, poetical." And though Carlyle goes on to speak of Burns as by far the best of British song-writers, it is evident that he is regarding the song as something less than a poem. True, he lays it down that the song "requires nothing so much for its perfection as genuine poetic feeling, genuine music of heart," and as yet having "its rules equally with the tragedy;" which leaves us in some perplexity as to the critic's fundamental principles; but seeing that he all along distinguishes between the song and the poem, we must conclude that he does not reckon Burns a great poet on the strength of his lyrics. Now, what the majority of the admirers of Burns do is to feel with Carlyle the spontaneity of Burns's songs; to take vigour of versification for high poetic art, ignoring the critical distinction; and to pronounce Burns accordingly one of the greatest of poets.

As against this popular verdict, and in partial distinction from Carlyle's finding, there has to be formulated the explicit principle that a song is either good poetry or bad, and deserves to rank as literature or not, in respect of the quality of its ideas and the charm with which they are expressed. The judgment which begins by separating songs from the department of poetry amounts practically to a declaration that songs as such fall below the level of literature proper; which even the coolest critic of Burns cannot explicitly allow. What has to be done is to judge his songs, like his longer poems, on their literary merit. In point of fact, however, most Scotchmen of critical taste—and these must be the final judges—will admit to-day that the majority of Burns's songs have no permanent literary value; that very few indeed can rank as quite successful poems; and that, all things considered, this could not well be otherwise.

Perhaps the best way to establish this somewhat

THE ART OF BURNS

dangerous-looking proposition is first to take up one of the few of Burns's lyrics which may be pronounced perfect; the first version of the song, *The Banks of Doon*. I quote it in full, as it is chiefly known in the shape of the later version, which appears to have been produced in order to suit the air to which it is sung.

> Ye banks and braes o' bonie Doon
>   How can ye blume sae fair !
> How can ye chant, ye little birds,
>   And I sae fu' o' care?
>
> Thou'll break my heart, thou bonie bird,
>   That sings upon the bough;
> Thou minds me o' the happy days
>   When my fause love was true.
>
> Thou'll break my heart, thou bonie bird,
>   That sings beside thy mate;
> For sae I sat, and sae I sang,
>   And wist na o' my fate.
>
> Aft hae I rov'd by bonie Doon
>   To see the woodbine twine;
> And ilka bird sang o' its love,
>   And sae did I o' mine.
>
> Wi' lightsome heart I pu'd a rose
>   Frae aff its thorny tree;
> And my fause lover staw' the rose,
>   But left the thorn wi' me.

I have substituted the first line of the second version for the original one, which was "Ye flowery banks o' bonie Doon," the alteration being obviously intended by the poet as an improvement, as it is not required for the music. He felt, there can be no doubt, that "flowery" was not genuine Scots. Perhaps, had he been rigorous, he would have altered the third stanza; to my Scotch ear, at all events, "thy mate" and "my fate" do not ring absolutely true; but they do not amount to a real flaw; and there is no other suggestion

THE ART OF BURNS

of one. Here then is a lyric which will compare with one by Shakspere, by Goethe, by Heine, by De Musset, or by Tennyson. The *motif* is one which is as perfectly poetic in the case of a rustic as of a high-born maiden ; a woman's wounded love demanding a refined treatment, which Burns by no means always gives to expressions of more prosperous attachment, even when the singer is a woman. We find such a song worth reading and remembering for certain distinct reasons. A few other songs of Burns's approach this in sustained serious delicacy and choice expression, as for instance *The Posie*, of which this is the first stanza—

> O love will venture in whar' it daurna weel be seen,
> O love will venture in whar' wisdom ance has been ;
> But I will down yon river rove, amang the wood sae green,
>   And a' to pu' a Posie to my ain dear May.

Scots wha hae wi' Wallace bled, too, is a noble lyric as it now stands. Originally the fourth lines of the stanzas were longer by two syllables than they are in the received version : the terse, fierce " Let him turn and flee ! " for instance, having at first read, " Traitor ! coward ! turn and flee ! " while " Let him follow me ! " has taken the place of " Caledonian ! on wi' me ! "*
In regard to almost all of the other favourite songs of Burns, however, I venture to dispute the popular verdict, which is given with almost no attention to details of workmanship. Thus it is the fashion, in Scotland at least, to praise *Highland Mary* in entire disregard of the fact that every one of its rhymes is vicious, and some atrocious ; and even Carlyle seems to join in the admiration of the lyric *To Mary in Heaven*, of which every line is in the conventional, obsolete

---

* The old readings are retained in Alexander Smith's editions (of which the "Globe" is one); mistakenly, I think, though Burns is said to have made the improvements reluctantly under pressure.

THE ART OF BURNS

English taste of last century. It has hardly one truly felicitous phrase. Take again the early song *Mary Morison*, which Alexander Smith pronounces "exquisite," and which has indeed one fine quatrain—

> Yestreen, when to the trembling string
> The dance gaed thro' the lighted ha',
> To thee my fancy took its wing;
> I sat, but neither heard or saw—

here the effect of the fortunate lines is marred by several conventional English phrases, as "make the miser's treasure poor," "the rich reward secure," and "wreck his peace." So, in *Wandering Willie*, the line "The simmer to nature, my Willie to me"—on which Christopher North, in the *Noctes Ambrosianæ*, makes the Shepherd bestow a eulogy that is rather high-pitched, considering that no rustic Scotch girl would talk of Nature—is followed by these lines of turgid English—

> Rest, ye wild storms, in the cave of your slumbers;
> How your dread howling a lover alarms!

Between incongruity or conventionality of diction on the one hand, and comic quality or lack of delicacy on the other, the great mass of Burns's songs miss fair literary finish or serious value, with the result that they will not bear reading by people of trained taste who are familiar with Scots. This is a judgment verifiable by citation of stanzas and passages innumerable which all persons of literary culture, at least all experts in the study of poetry, will admit to betray thoroughly inferior workmanship. Just as we find a few of Burns's songs exquisite in respect of tenderness of feeling and melody and simple grace of phrase, we find the mass faulty in respect of literary crudity when they are not pitched on the lower range of the comic. If we take his drinking and other humorous songs into account we shall of

THE ART OF BURNS

course find more which are successful in their kind. It is obviously easier for a poet writing in a popular dialect to make a good humorous song than one which shall well express deep feeling, for the reason that most words in his vocabulary have commonplace associations, thus lending themselves for the most part rather to broadly humorous than to refined ideas. It has often been pointed out that when Burns is deeply serious he almost invariably writes in English; see, for instance, *To Mary in Heaven*, the latter part of *The Cotter's Saturday Night*, *Man was made to Mourn*, the greater part of *The Vision*, the prayers, the latter half of *To a Mountain Daisy*—in fine, all his serious verse except a few of the tender love-songs. The reason is plain. For the Scottish peasant the language of serious ideas is that of the Bible and of serious books—all written in English. He may express domestic griefs and universal emotions in the vernacular; but if he rises to the utterance of abstract thoughts which are refined or dignified, he must think them in English. For a hundred years before Burns, the language of Scottish prose writers was that of Englishmen, and the associations of Fergusson's and Ramsay's Doric verse are mainly of an every-day order. It was inevitable that Burns should think of his English models (he knew Pope, Shenstone, and Thomson, it appears, before Fergusson) when he dealt with the themes he had in common with the English poets. Now, it is generally conceded, even by his most devoted admirers, that Burns tends more or less to be stiff and artificial when he writes English, that is to say, that he conformed to the English style then in fashion, instead of expressing his own individuality, as he did when he wrote Scots; though the national clericalism has the effect of blinding the orthodox to the stiltedness of one-half of *The*

THE ART OF BURNS

Cotter's Saturday Night, and the pedestrian quality of the other, and it is assumed that *To Mary in Heaven* must be fine because of the nature of the subject.

If, then, Burns's lot in life was so conditioned that his most ambitious poetry had to be cast in an idiom which was not that of his daily speech, and in which he had no spontaneous felicity; if his happiest verse deals for the most part with ideas which are not subtle; if his culture and leisure were scanty; if his songs are mostly for the singing of the illiterate—to what conclusions are we led in regard to his permanent place in literature? Of necessity to those of Carlyle, that he cannot rank, in respect of poetic achievement, with the great singers of the world; that his song is as a "little Valclusa Fountain" beside the great rivers of poetry. But to see and state the case truly, we must impress upon ourselves that Burns's shortcoming is emphatically the result of unfortunate conditions; that, poetry being an art, its successful pursuit calls for leisure and culture; and that, with the exception of his rural surroundings, all the outside details of Burns's lot made against the best development of his gifts. In denying him the highest rank, we are not making light of these gifts; we are simply asserting the immutable truth that every organism is profoundly influenced by its environment.

To realise this law fully in regard to Burns, we have only to study the cases of those poets whom we may consider him to have rivalled in respect of natural powers—say Tennyson or Heine. Heine is, perhaps, overrated as a mere lyrist; on that head only the closest familiarity with the German language can justify a positive opinion; but there need be no hesitation in saying that Tennyson's songs are almost invariably of a perfect finish, while Burns's are so very seldom; and this is so, in the main, because Tennyson has been able

THE ART OF BURNS

to give his whole life to his art, while Burns could only give the spare hours of a life whose toil began in boyhood and lasted till death. And it will be found that every great poet of whose life we have any knowledge was so because he was able to give his best hours to the cultivation of his genius. If Shakspere stands alone among the great poets in respect of the restrictedness of his early education, he none the less made writing the main business of his life. In short, the idea that a working Scottish farmer, no matter what his gifts, could produce a body of poetry that would entitle him to rank with the greatest poets of the world, can only be sincerely harboured by people who conceive of a poet as a creature of entirely abnormal intelligence, going about habitually with pen and paper, in the open air, and having fits of inspiration, in which his words came to him. And, to put it plainly, it is because of the still primitive condition of the taste of the majority that Burns is still so frequently and fervently praised. Ignorance rarely begets modesty of literary judgment; and every member of a Burns club, however little he knows of the poetry of the world or even of the English-speaking people, is unhesitating in proclaiming that Burns's poetry is unexcelled. In connection with no other poet, perhaps, is there such a body of merely prejudiced admiration, accompanied with so much random publication of eulogy that has no critical value whatever. A rich enthusiast gives the poet a new statue, and some popularly respected amateurs of literature pronounce opinions which the crowd echo, and which have just the value of the crowd's literary judgment.

The importance of Burns in literature and in history is, after all, to be tested rather by those "Poems" which Carlyle finds, on the whole, unpoetical, than by even the

THE ART OF BURNS

best of the songs. The lyrical faculty is rare and precious, but it does not necessarily imply a powerful understanding; and Burns's poetry, as a whole, does imply this. Nay, more: the style of these vernacular poems of "rhymed eloquence, rhymed pathos, rhymed sense," is excellent in its kind, the satirical poems especially possessing a pith and pungency not excelled by Butler, Swift, Pope, or Dryden. To a Scotch reader the force and vividness of their style are perhaps more apparent than to an Englishman, just as an English ear can perhaps hardly appreciate* the full felicity of such lines as—

> We twa hae run aboot the braes,
> And pu'd the gowans fine—

lines which must have been written by Burns, though he said most of *Auld Lang Syne* was old. The songs—the handful of pure gems and the mass of the others with their flaws, their touches of careless beauty, and their spontaneous, homely exuberance—are proofs of a born lyrical power which with culture might have done splendid things: the body of verse which deals with the Scottish life of the time testifies to an intelligence of rare vigour and penetration. In these pieces, indeed, Burns outgoes all other British literature of the kind. Not since Swift has there been written satirical verse of such sinewy terseness and idiomatic energy; and Burns is above Swift exactly as humour is above bitterness. Questions of poetic art aside, then, it is right to recognise the reasons for the exceptional devotion to Burns prevailing in Scotland. It is difficult to over-estimate what he has done to save his countrymen from the

* Arnold has, however, spoken feelingly of the "almost intolerable pathos" of the *Auld Lang Syne* stanzas. See the Introd. to the *English Poets*.

THE ART OF BURNS

extremities of fanaticism, Pharisaism, and Philistinism; and it is certain that his influence among the English-speaking nations has been mighty for democracy. But it is well finally to keep in view that his poetry, as such, belongs to a comparatively early stage of literary development, and that it is popular in the ratio of its primitiveness. The fact that he is the poet of the uninstructed merely proves that he is not, in the main, on a high plane of poetic art. Let him be recognised as the Scottish people's poet, and the poet of popular instincts, by all means; and let him have his statues in virtue of his popularity—statues in a primitive taste, if needs must. But let the student, instead of joining in the acclamations of the people over their poet, point out to the people that their poet, like themselves, misses half the right fruition of life because the world is so evilly ordered.

STEVENSON ON BURNS
(1896)

I

THE platitudes of the Burns centenary in Scotland have been ruffled in a not unwholesome way by a sharp breeze of dispute, unwittingly raised by Lord Rosebery, when after doing finished homage to the memory of Burns he proposed that Scotland should raise a memorial to Stevenson. That proposal evoked from a Scotch member of Parliament, not ill-qualified to speak on Scotch questions of any kind, an emphatic protest. Dr. Robert Wallace, the member in question, sits for a division of Edinburgh, and is in many ways an excellent type of Scotch capacity, though perhaps not of Scottish conduct. He began public life as a minister of the Church of Scotland; ranked high in Edinburgh as an intellectual preacher; was made Professor of Church History in the University; did very well in that capacity also; took to preaching heterodoxically on such matters as prayer; was duly arraigned; was gingerly let off; found a way out of his uncongenial position in the proffer of the editorial chair of the *Scotsman*, vacated by the death of his friend Russel; gave, however, dissatisfaction in that capacity, having only the literary taste without the practical productiveness which constitutes the writing editor; and at length, when well on in middle life, came to London to study for the bar and begin life again as an English barrister. It was after attaining that status that he was triumphantly elected a member for the city of his former career, being indeed a very capable platform performer; and he has kept the seat through several administrations, despite some friction set up by his occasional indocility to the crack of the official whip. He thus possesses the now rare qualification of *doctor utriusque juris;* and in his time has played many educative parts. I mention these matters in advance to show that what the hon. gentleman may say, rightly or wrongly, on the merits of Stevenson's treatment of Burns, is not the mere unqualified prattle of a politician on a literary question quite out of his sphere, but a judgment worth listening to, and probably worth discussing. It represents a good deal of Scottish opinion, not all of the commonest sort.

II

Still, newspaper letters of protest against proposed memorials are not the best ways of handling delicate questions of literary and ethical criticism; and Dr. Wallace's censure of Stevenson's essay on Burns is more effective as a bomb than as an argument. It runs :—

"I admit all that can be said in favour of Stevenson. He was not an original or stupendous genius, but he was undoubtedly a perfect stylist. But he did one thing which no Scotsman, and, for that matter, no true critic, can ever forgive. He published, and republished, a mean, Pharisaical, gratuitous, and utterly inaccurate attack on the memory and character of Burns, a man worth a hundred of him. When I read it I said to myself, this man may have, and does have, ability, but he is essentially a middle-class prig, in my opinion the most contemptible section of existing humanity, but to which some of the loudest admirers of Stevenson belong. Besides, Stevenson sneered at most things Scotch. I object to the proposed memorial, without some qualification."

The conclusion is lame and laming, not to say impotent and paralysing. If Stevenson really sneered at most things Scotch, that alone would be a very sufficient reason against giving him a Scotch monument, whether with or without "some qualification," though it would not quite settle the question of his judicial capacity. The final note of mere patriotism overcrows the note of criticism, though the criticism to start with is extremely loud, not to say uproarious. Hence the whole has been stigmatised, by one of the few Scottish journalists who correct rather than flatter the national foibles, as "the sort of havering which renders Scotland and Scotsmen ridiculous." Dr. Wallace, however, has replied with adroitness and good humour, pointing out that he does not, as he had seemed to do, asperse Stevenson the man as priggish and Pharisaical, but meant these epithets to bear expressly on the offending essay. Thus narrowed down, and when further relieved of the unprofitable issue as to Stevenson's having dared to sneer or smile at things Scotch, the question is perhaps worth looking into as one of pure criticism; though it seems also worth while to take it up, as is here done, on the side of the relation of Burns and Stevenson to Scotch sentiment. Some of us have long felt that the uncritical and not seldom maudlin adoration of Burns in Scotland has come to be a species of national fanaticism, representing no longer to any great extent the sunny influence of Burns's humanity on a frost-bitten and Pharisaical society, but the virtual restriction of popular thought and culture to one round and one stage. As a matter of fact, despite some literary adjuncts, the worship of Burns in Scotland is the one literary occupation of the unliterary, the anniversary sentiment of the classes who do not read. Hence those of us who think as aforesaid have small sympathy with Dr. Wallace when he says :—

> "Burns's influence, not only literary but moral, political, and religious, is a matter of national, perhaps wider, importance, and whatever recklessly and wrongly impairs it should, I think, be duly resented by every true Scotsman. I think Stevenson's attack tends strongly this way .... essentially an improper, disrespectful, wrong-headed performance."

There is really not the least likelihood of Burns's prestige in Scotland being shaken by any criticism, Scottish or other ; and it is not going too far to say that it is much better for the average Scotch mind to be seriously perturbed by Stevenson's essay than to stay in the state of unintelligent worship which is kept up by the bulk of Scotch writing on the subject. Dr. Wallace's style of patriotism says more for his generosity than for his wisdom. It is distinctly more profitable for the conventional entity "Scotland" to wake up to the fact—scantily recognised there till America and England had abundantly proclaimed it—that in Stevenson she has unexpectedly produced a new man of genius, than to be further established in the faith that she once had one in Burns, whom she let die in hugger-mugger for lack of patient contemporary sympathy. If patriots of Dr. Wallace's way of thinking would but think out their creed, they could scarcely miss seeing that, supposing Stevenson's attitude to Burns be really priggish and Pharisaical, the attitude towards Burns in his lifetime of average Scotland, as represented by average Ayrshire and Dumfriesshire, clerical and lay, was incomparably more so. Then to "sneer at Scotch

STEVENSON ON BURNS

history," as Dr. Wallace says Stevenson did, would so far be a fairly justifiable proceeding. If a large part of last century Scotland stoned her prophet, it is not clear why we should respectfully cherish all Scottish memories.

This much said, however, Dr. Wallace's outburst has something left in it for the unbiased, or let us say the less biased critic to muse upon. Stevenson's trial of Burns is not quite a decisive performance. It carries us out of the region of platitude, which is a great matter ; but, to use the safe old phrase, it "does not say the last word." It is a fresh and vivacious ethical effort, but it raises more problems than it takes account of. Perhaps, then, it may help us to a judgment of a more scientific albeit of a much duller character.

III

There are in truth two aspects of Stevenson's essay on *Some Aspects of Robert Burns* which, though not fitly to be attacked in such terms, are not utterly incongruous with the bald epithets of "middle-class," and "priggish," and "Pharisaical." But before applying any epithets at all, we have to realise that the essay was a young man's work. It was written before Stevenson had accumulated that kind of sympathetic knowledge of human nature which later fitted him to give a deep interest of character to motives of romance ; and for lack of that acquirement some of the stories he wrote about the same time were, to the thinking of some of us who already admired him greatly as a writer, perplexingly poor. Already in 1882, when reprinting it with his other critical essays, he prefixed an essay which not only warmly repudiates in particular the crudely hostile view of Burns which some journalist had superimposed on his, but indicates a new critical perception of the truth that criticism in general is very much a matter of a "point of view" that is either arbitrary or empirical, or both. His remarks on this head, made with his own peculiar candour, go far to qualify the whole estimate by implication, if not explicitly. "The writer of short studies," he explains, "having to condense in a few pages the events of a whole lifetime, and the effect on his own mind of many various volumes, is bound, above all things, to make that condensation logical and striking. . . . By the necessity of the case, all the more neutral circumstances are omitted from his narrative; and that of itself, by the negative exaggeration of which I have spoken in the text, lends to the matter in hand a certain false and specious glitter. . . . The proportions of the sitter must be sacrificed to the proportions of the portrait; the lights are heightened, the shadows overcharged; the chosen expression, continually forced, may degenerate at length into a grimace; and we have at best something of a caricature, at worst a calumny." (Preface by way of criticism to *Familiar Studies of Men and Books*, 1882, pp. ix-xii.) This must be pronounced an imperfect excuse for leaving unrectified a given blend of caricature and calumny; but at least it constitutes a partial retractation. And when we come to compare his treatment of Burns with his handling of some phases of character in his later romances, we shall see that these imply a certain new breadth of perception which involves a sweeping revision of the old verdict. This being so, the essay as a whole is to be adjudged immature; the work of a man at "the merciless age," the age before he has, as the Scotch Mr. Campbell-Bannerman has so pleasantly put it,

STEVENSON ON BURNS

"come to the time of life at which he almost begins to believe he has faults of his own." And if those who care mainly about the literary sparkle of the thing will not hear of a criticism so founded, they have only to study the essay as a substantive piece of exposition and argument, in order to see that it was not properly thought out. Like Carlyle, Stevenson was more of an artist than of a thinker; and like Carlyle he has failed to co-ordinate his comments on Burns. It is something of a pity that the two most important essays by Scotsmen on Burns, containing as they do some of the soundest, freshest, and most outspoken criticism of Burns's work, should yet be inconsistent alike in their literary and their ethical argument, and should further be inconsistent with each other on the literary point. On the ethical side, Carlyle vacillated between jeers at the society which set a Burns to gauge beer-barrels and a George the Third upon the throne, and moralisings on the fault of Burns in being so disposable; with a further lurch towards resentment of the pitying and censorious view where entertained by small-brained people. On the literary side he swung still more confusedly between wrath at those who thought culture necessary for a poet, "as if poetry was of the tongue and not of the heart," and the assertion on his part of that very view, that culture might have been an enormous advantage to Burns's performance.

In his concrete estimate, Carlyle, finding the bulk of Burns's work, however admirable, to be Aristophanic rather than strictly poetic, decides that it is in respect of his songs that he is strictly a poet; and finally figures him as a "little Valclusa fountain," as beside the great rivers of poetry. Such an estimate clearly needed technical justification and support, which

STEVENSON ON BURNS

Carlyle did not and probably could not give. Stevenson on the other hand takes the surely sounder critical view that the bulk of the songs are of no great value, but speaks of them with undiscriminating disesteem, even though incidentally calling one "immortal." It is, he says, "melancholy that a man who first attacked literature with a hand that seemed capable of moving mountains, should have spent his later years in whittling cherry-stones." To this hardy criticism we shall return later, in connection with Stevenson's ethical estimate of the singer; and then, too, we shall be better able to weigh his very original judgment that Burns, after his blaze of success and his unsatisfactory marriage, was really grown incapable of great work.

"He had lost his habits of industry, and formed the habits of pleasure .... he was thenceforward incapable, except in rare instances, of that superior effort of concentration which is required for serious literary work. He may be said, indeed, to have worked no more, and only amused himself with letters. The man who had written a volume of masterpieces in six months, during the remainder of his life rarely found courage for any more sustained effort than a song."

Keeping in view the connection of the literary judgment here with the ethical, which last is for the present our main concern, we have to note, before analysing that, the lack of correlation above spoken of. A number of passages in the essay strike such different keys of temper, without any resolving modulation between, that they must be pronounced to need rewriting. For instances:

"He [Burns] had no genteel timidities in the conduct of his life. He loved to force his personality upon the world. He would please himself, and shine. Had he lived in the Paris of 1830, and joined his lot with the Romantics, we can conceive him writing *Jehan* for

STEVENSON ON BURNS

Jean, swaggering in Gautier's red waistcoat, and horrifying bourgeois in a public café with paradox and gasconnade."

". . . . his admirable talk, and his manners, which he had direct from his Maker, except for a brush he gave them at a country dancing school, completed [in Edinburgh society] what his poems had begun. . . ."

" This strong young ploughman, who feared no competitor with the flail, suffered like a fine lady from sleeplessness and vapours ; he would fall into the blackest melancholies, and be filled with remorse for the past and terror for the future. He was still not perhaps devoted to religion, but haunted by it; and at a touch of sickness prostrated himself before God in what I can only call unmanly penitence."

" Country Don Juan as he was, he had none of that blind vanity which values itself on what it is not; he knew his own strength and weakness to a hair: he took himself boldly for what he was, and, except in moments of hypochondria, declared himself content."

"Burns, on his part, bore the elevation [of his Edinburgh success] with perfect dignity; and with perfect dignity returned, when the time had come, into a country privacy of life. His powerful sense never deserted him.'. . . He was always ready to sacrifice an acquaintance to a friend, although the acquaintance were a duke. He would be a bold man who should promise similar conduct in equally exacting circumstances. It was, in short, an admirable appearance on the stage of life—socially successful, intimately self-respecting, and like a gentleman from first to last."

" He had chosen to be Don Juan, he had grasped at temporary pleasures, and substantial happiness and solid industry had passed him by."

These touches are clearly not congruous. The portrait thus painted lacks underlying unity of colour. To make your white very white, and your black very black, is not the way to get a good likeness, or a good picture in words any more than in pigments. Nor does it suffice to paint-in one element as it looks by itself, and then the others as they look by themselves; for the colours of things in company modify each other. There must be correlation ; which is the artistic side of demonstration, of reasoning. Carlyle seems to have written his essay in spurts, as different views of the case came to him, without testing their coherence; such being his habit of mind and of work. Stevenson may or may not have done this; but it will be found that his criticism is put out of tone by the chronic forcing of one of the notes sounded above.

IV

This jarring note is the recurring phrase "village Don Juan," "professional Don Juan." It might be called the key-note of the essay, if the essay were true to any key. And yet, on Stevenson's own showing, the phrase is false. Against all his iterations of it, there stands this decisive admission: "He remained to the last imperfect in his character of Don Juan, and lacked the sinister courage to desert his victim." That is to say, Burns was not a professional Don Juan at all. The name means for us, in literature, not the Don Juan of Byron but the Don Juan of Molière and Mozart; the entirely non-moral male, incapable of real passion or compassion. Burns at his worst is perhaps less near the Don Juan type than was the Duke of Wellington, as we see him in the singular account published a few years ago of his relations with "Miss J——," and in the classic anecdote of his reply to the lady who threatened to publish his letters: "Dear Fanny, Publish away and be damned." Yet nobody would think it accurate to describe the Duke of Wellington as a professional Don Juan. His "victims" seem to have come more than half-way to him; as Stevenson admits was done in several cases by those of Burns. After telling how the poet, vacillating violently between contrary courses, suddenly married Jean Armour, Stevenson writes:

STEVENSON ON BURNS

" He was, as he truly says, 'damned with a choice only of different species of error and misconduct.' To be a professional Don Juan, to accept the provocation of any lively lass upon the village green, may thus lead a man through a series of detestable words and actions, and land him at last in an undesired and most unsuitable union for life."

Then is it the professional Don Juan who lands himself and stays in an undesired and unsuitable union? Is it the professional Don Juan who waits for the "provocation of any lively lass" before laying serious siege to her? And is it the characteristic of the average man, not a milksop, to resist philosophically such provocation? The epithet, it is clear, will not stand: we may indeed surmise that Stevenson, with his faculty of self-criticism, would have admitted as much on pressure in his later life.

But his criticism of Burns's conduct, of course, does not stand or fall with the epithet. There remain the facts dealt with, the passages in Burns's letters. Sooth to say, it is not so much the things Burns did as what he said about them that lays him open to the worst kind of blame. His actions were those of a man of strong passions, woefully apt to be carried away by them, but not a cold-blooded wrong-doer. Esau in the myth sells his birth-right for a mess of pottage; but the traditional censure of him, in the mouth of those who never knew fierce hunger, and who have besides been primed with the moral lesson, such as it is, which he was invented merely to illustrate, is not very impressive to thoughtful people. Unfortunately Burns is in worse ethical case than the hirsute Hebrew, in that he was a letter-writer. There is no denying that his tone in his letters to men about some of his affairs with women is extremely offensive. He was not only ready to kiss and tell (a proceeding which even in his age an old Scotch lady of the anti-Puritan school pronounced to be that of a "dawmed villain" in the case of the heir to the throne), he talks of his seductive tactics in a way which would justify our calling him—not a Don Juan; the tone is far too crude and fatuous to suggest any real mastery of the business—but a very detestable lady-killer indeed; were it not that we can so easily see the letter to be mostly bravado, the fatuity of the impressionable man posing as Lovelace after having in reality half lost his head. It is after quoting the letter in which Burns speaks of being "an old hawk at the sport" that Stevenson writes: "I avow a carnal longing, after this transcription, to buffet the Old Hawk about the ears." And indeed a moral buffet from the recipient of the letter, an expression of quiet contempt, might have done its writer a world of good. But it is just here, curiously enough, where Stevenson's censure is not unjustified, that it in some distant measure justifies Dr. Wallace's epithet of "prig." The previous injustice of calling Burns a professional Don Juan is injustice pure and simple, the use of an unjustifiable epithet. It is the not so unjust but more pretentious denunciation of the poet's real offence that raises a certain suspicion of youthful priggishness.

All of us who choose to criticise Burns have this huge advantage over him, that his Life and Letters have been published with absolute unreserve, while ours have not been, and are not likely to be. Stevenson made a not very generous use of that advantage; as Arnold did of the love-letters of Keats to Fanny Brawne, when he said they were those of a mawkish apothecary's apprentice. No access has been given to the love-letters of Arnold, and rightly so; but one of his biographical poems, in the group entitled "Switzerland"—a poem which has called out some not unwarrantable animadversion—suggests that some of Arnold's youthful follies may have been of a more unamiable kind than those of Keats. Stevenson, again, in one of his youthful essays talks with not a little frankness, though still under safe cover, of the sensations of repeated "sinning;" and his friend Mr. Henley, in a piece of verse understood to be a portrait of him, partly describes him as "lover and sensualist." But I do not at all mean to suggest that Stevenson could ever have incurred such blame as he passes on Burns. In such matters he was sure to be chivalrous, chivalrous in the sense in which Burns was not. What I do suggest is, first, that even he might have come in for somebody's vituperation if his life lay as naked to the light as does that of Burns; and, further, that he made a certain semblance of "pose" of his chivalry on this particular side. He has told how he once flung out of a French theatre exclaiming at the baseness of the "*lâche*" who was hero of the piece; and how the old gentleman to whom he addressed himself assured him that he was "very young." That performance of his was not mere pose, not mere priggishness; but, taken in the light of one other avowal as to one of his youthful doings, it gives a basis for some less crude characterisation. It is in his bright biography of the late Fleeming Jenkin that he has told how he over persuaded that Professor to give him a certificate of attendance at the university class of Engineering when he had not made any proper attendance. Stevenson wanted the certificate to satisfy his father, who had specially desired that he should attend the course. Professor Jenkin was displeased, and at first refused the certificate, but Stevenson was coaxingly importunate, and the Professor gave way. To some of us, the story, frankly as it is told, is not quite pleasant. There are various ways of being unchivalrous; and I think it not unlikely that Burns, if similarly placed, would have refused to take that particular way. And if that estimate be right, it would follow that the very righteous tone taken by the youthful Stevenson in regard to Burns's special derelictions tends just a little towards the Pharisaical.

Let me hasten to explain that this suggestion is not a mere *tu quoque*. The answer to Stevenson's criticism of Burns goes much further than that. It involves a challenge not merely to Stevenson's practice but to his and a great many other people's moral code, to their whole philosophy of conduct: it impeaches, indeed, at some points the moral code normally acted on by all of us. The complete answer, in fine, raises the question whether the ordinary conventions of social ethics are not as often as not scientifically absurd, and, what is more, cowardly.

V

Let us agree, to begin with, that Burns was immoral in his treatment of some women, and offensively unchivalrous in some of his talk about it. The question is, are his deviations from rightness and chivalry really greater than those committed by, let us say, anybody else, in some other direction? And let us push the question, raised as it is by Stevenson's criticism, in the light of others of Stevenson's writings. In his essay on Burns he has been very severe on the physical side of the sex passion. In his stories of *Kidnapped* and *The Black Arrow* he has given us glimpses of another physical passion, the passion of fighting; and in his story of *The Wreckers* he has given us two lurid pictures, first of the same passion as expressing the instinct of self-preservation, and again of the passion of money-making. All alike are ethically interesting. In

STEVENSON ON BURNS

Kidnapped we have the brilliant figure of Alan Breck, perhaps the most original figure in Stevenson's gallery. Alan is very vain, very *rusé*, very boastful, very quarrelsome, very gleeful over a successful bout of killing; yet he is generally found very likeable. Why? Partly because he is spontaneous, warm-blooded, at bottom unselfish and "good-hearted;" partly because a social and a literary convention unite to treat the love of fighting and the act of killing, in a great many circumstances, as rather fine things. Such things a man may do, and yet not only escape our criticism, Stevenson's criticism, but keep our liking, Stevenson's liking. So with his acts of deceit; so with his readiness to shed a friend's blood on a quarrel of punctilio. For all these acts there is boundless indulgence. Why, then, not for the faults of Burns? There can be no question of utilitarian test; for the fighter, the ruffler, works far more unmitigated evil than the uncalculating amorist. There has been no scientific or rational comparison at all. There is a convention, a tradition, which denounces "sins of the flesh," and singles out one sort of act as such; there is a tradition, a convention, which gloses or glorifies certain kinds of bloodshed and the lust therefor; and there an end.

All this comes out quite unconsciously in Stevenson's earlier stories—all, that is, that his sexless romances allow to appear. It has been said of him that he "compounds the sins he is inclined to, by damning those he has no mind to—introduce in his narrative." Though the subtlest and finest of his books, *Prince Otto*, is a masterly study of sex motives, he has been on the whole singularly indifferent to them as a romancer, giving the zest of his imagination to the themes of adventure which thrilled his boyhood. And on these, in his earlier work, he is boyishly unethical; as indeed the romance of adventure had need be. In *The Black Arrow*, certainly, there is a touch of side light, of second thought, as when the heroine in boy's attire cries out on the fierce fashion in which the boy-hero has killed a man, and the hero defends his act : "I ran me in upon his bow." But in the vivid picture of Richard Crookback panting for battle—"his face was pale as linen, but his eyes shone in his head like some strange jewel" —there is the tacit understanding that, barring all "crimes" commonly so-called, the spectacle of the fierce young warrior hewing his way in the press is stirring and superb. All these outbreaks of the beast within us are not merely condoned but paraded. The animal side of hate, of malignity, is all right. It is only the animal side of love, of sympathy, that is wrong. As for unintended wrong-doing, there is a moving passage over the incurableness of the wrong done by Dick to the old shipmaster whose vessel he caused to be lost ; but there is no suggestion that Dick was thus a miserable sinner. It is only in such a case as Burns's that the unintended ill results of thoughtless actions are righteous penalties, and the acts purely detestable.

In *The Wreckers*, however, we seem to feel that Stevenson has awakened to the real complexity of ethics, and the utter futility of the conventional codes. He gives us two very singular problems.* First there is the young American who vainly tries to be an artist in Paris, and goes back to make money as a ship-knacker in San Francisco. He is virginally chaste ; and in Paris he is infuriated by the brutality with which a young Frenchman casts off an elderly mistress. In San Francisco, still sexually exemplary, he trades in con-

* The book is written in collaboration with Mr. Lloyd Osbourne, whose work can at times be confidently distinguished ; but the scheme of the whole—a bad scheme, no doubt—is joint.

STEVENSON ON BURNS

demned ships, buying them cheap, patching them up to pass muster, loading them, insuring them, and sailing them in the full expectation that they will sink with their crews. Stevenson cannot have drawn or assisted in drawing that picture without realising what a comment it was on the very code which he had so confidently applied to the case of Burns. The virginally chaste man is personally loyal to his friends, is kindly, is really self-sacrificing, and yet he sends whole crews to their death without a scruple, for mere gain. The case is perfectly possible, as human nature goes; similar cases have been known; and Stevenson probably knew of one such as he describes. Yet he shows no sign of feeling about Jim Pinkerton as he had felt and written about poor Burns.

Then we have the extraordinary episode of the beastly massacre of a whole crew by Carthew and his companions. Mr. Lang, in reviewing the book, protested a little against that episode, which he found needlessly sanguinary. He was perhaps not as much shocked by it as by Burns's sending of the present of carronades to the French Government; but still he was shocked. Other people might go so far as to say that the episode is abominable. But it is quite clear that Stevenson did not feel there was anything so detestable in it as he had found in Burns's amours and vulgarities. Would he then have written the Burns essay in the same strain in his latter years as he gave to it in his youth? If so, we should be perfectly entitled to say that his ethics were finally farcical, and that his dispraise need matter nothing to anybody. But, all things considered, it seems extremely unlikely that he could have spoken in his thirties as he had done in his twenties. His later work seems to negate the possibility.

In any case, we are entitled to say that not only the

moral implication of his later work but our own moral reason annuls the authority of his sentence of pillory against Burns the amorist. Burns was very far from being a bad man. He was not anti-social. He did not callously cause suffering. He had very little capacity for sustained malignant emotion. He was generally and practically benevolent, from his youth up. He was abnormally sympathetic; which amounts to saying that he was abnormally moral. In spontaneously sympathising as he did alike with the American Revolution and the French Revolution, he showed himself to be morally far above the average of the respectable people of his generation. He was a better and truer man than Burke, revered by that generation and the next as the champion of political righteousness; he was a far truer man than Coleridge, revered by many of his generation and more of the next as the champion of Christian mysteries and Christian morals. And to say these things is not merely to make an *illi quoque* defence: it is to point to the only principle that can rationalise ethical judgment, the principle of comparison. The ordinary criticism of prominent literary men is as a rule on a par with the moral tone of the theatre gallery over a melodrama. There is a preposterous assumption of virtue on all hands, every sinner in the house being free to indemnify himself for his own occasional misdeeds by hissing those of the bold bad man of the play, who is made to figure in the capacity of sinner pure and simple. In biography, save where the contrary licence is taken to make the subject blameless, there is little field for the simple symmetries of the melodramatist; but when the biographer has done his work it is still possible for the critic to supervene, and place the sins of the biographee, or some of them, in duly unjust isolation, trying them by a code which covers only a few sins in particular instead of sinning in general; and appealing for the verdict to a jury which has hardly pondered the first principles of morals.

From such procedure, even when undertaken by a man of genius, himself on the way to an uncommon subtlety of moral insight, and already capable of much discrimination, we turn to the spectacle presented by the lives of the judges and jury—say, the actual lawyers, unblamed of society, who have earned their bread by the sweat of their brow-beating, their prevention of justice and their promotion of injustice; the actual judges, who, after that preparation, sit qualified to sermonise wretches on their unprofitable sins; the traders whose rule of life has been to get the most possible for the least possible; the company-jobbers, who live by exploiting credulity; the clergy, who do that with a difference; the politicians—but stay. It will be answered that the classes of citizen thus in return impeached are as a rule, as men go, despite their deviations from ideal righteousness, good fellows enough. So be it: that is the criterion we want: and it need only be said further that Burns was at least as good in his way, genius apart; and that any arrangement by which he is pilloried for that jury to pelt is not to be endured. And now let us come straight to the prosecuting counsel himself, and put the straight question: Is it any less blameworthy to be unable to resist the temptation to call a dead man unjustly by an evil name than to be unable to "resist the provocation of any lively lass on the village green"? And is it more or is it less chivalrous? At least the poet seems to have faced his risks. Stevenson, with plenty of chivalrous sentiment, did not exactly do as much. After having spoken of Burns's touch of brutality, he himself penned at least one brutal page, concerning which, as it is aimed at an unnamed man, we can do no more than note that it *may* possibly have signified a worse yielding to a low temptation than the open shot at the dead Burns.

But, once more, the purpose of this criticism is not to cast rejoinders at a humanist whom few could read, and still fewer could know, without an ever-growing goodwill. It is to challenge a prevailing moral code which Stevenson in his youth rather echoed than expounded; and to say that some of us at least, having looked into the matter and found the code a chaos of unreasoned convention and mindless tradition, will not be bluffed by either literary or religious solemnities into treating it with respect. The question is not one of the due or undue influence of Burns over Scotch or any other life. It is one of pure ethics and pure criticism, to which the nationality of the critic and the criticised has no relevance. And so far it must be decided against the critic.

VI

The ethical issue, then, being disposed of on ethical principles, there remains the critical, in so far as we have seen that bound up with the other. And here it must be remarked that Stevenson did oddly in combining his criticism of Burns's character with the doctrine that "There is indeed only one merit worth considering in a man of letters—that he should write well; and only one damning fault—that he should write ill." As the classic Don Juan was damned, a man of letters would seem to be somewhat damned in being called a professional Don Juan. But apart from that, there is the æsthetic damnation dealt in the above-quoted estimate of Burns's later work, the songs, as a whittling of cherry-stones. Perhaps there is here again a giving way to the temptation to say a telling thing without anxious regard to justice. A song is scarcely so trivial a thing as Stevenson's sentence would imply; and it is really not clear how he decided on the merits of poetic work when he could thus make light of the lyric as such, while bestowing such high praise on verse of which much is unimpassioned, comic, or didactic. As one of those who maintain that Burns's song-writing is over-estimated by his countrymen, I cannot indeed entirely demur to the judgment on its literary side. But it is excessive and indiscriminate, lumping in the category of cherry-stones one performance elsewhere admitted by the judge to be "immortal," and taking no account of a number of Burns's non-lyrical poems which compare favourably enough even with the accredited "masterpieces" of his first volume. When Stevenson speaks of Burns having at first shown a hand capable of moving mountains, he must refer to such pieces as *The Twa Dogs*, *The Jolly Beggars*, *The Holy Fair*, and *Holy Willie's Prayer*, all of them masterpieces of humanism, humour, and satire, though none of them attains to the quality of pure poetry. But in respect of the qualities which mark these as masterly, the later *Tam O' Shanter*, *Captain Grose's Peregrinations*, the *Second Epistle to Davie*, the lines *To Dr. Blacklock*, and *A Man's a Man for a' That*—all written after Burns's marriage—are masterly also; to say nothing of a number of serious poems in English, not masterpieces, but not at all of the nature of carved cherry-stones. Stevenson's high general praise of the poet's powers is that "There was never a man of letters with more absolute command of his means; and we may say of him without excess, that his style was his slave." This surely had not ceased to be true when Burns wrote his best songs.

Still, there is a certain element of truth in Stevenson's summing-up; and we shall best reach the heart of his criticism by coming to that and letting the other issues go. It is to a certain extent true that Burns, after his marriage, fell away from his poetic stature: it is true that his work towards the end shows less alike of concentration and of energy than before. What then? Stevenson, after describing the poet's appearance in Edinburgh society as "admirable" and "perfectly successful," summarily decides that Burns had been spoiled by his taste of pleasure and idleness, and further that the uncongeniality of his wife's mind completed the upset. It is perhaps this part of Stevenson's criticism which comes nearest giving colour to Dr. Wallace's violent account of it as the work of a middle-class prig. For it gives no sign of a gleam of perception of the vital fact that Burns soon after his marriage became an over-driven man, who could not possibly have written as theretofore had he been ever so indifferent to "pleasure," and ever so congenially mated. Stevenson writes as one who not only had no notion of what it would mean to earn a living as a travelling gauger, with a wife and a family to support, but had not even seen that it was fitting to have a notion on the subject. He wrote, in fact, from the point of view of a rather inconsiderate idler; and while he objects to Professor Shairp's treatment of Burns that it is so unsympathetic, he himself is but unsympathetic with a difference. We have his own avowal that he was the head of a household before he had succeeded in supporting himself by his own work for a single year. To an invalid, and one with a high standard of workmanship, that is not the least bit of a discredit; but it is unfortunate that Stevenson was not able to put himself in imagination in the place of a man who had to earn every penny he spent, and that by hard and preoccupying work; and who could accordingly give at best only his tired evenings to the literary tasks either of moving mountains or of whittling cherry-stones. According to Stevenson, he had "lost the habit of solid industry"—this when he was gauger for the Dumfries district, riding two hundred miles a week. It is true that Burns in his youth had been an extraordinarily hard worker, showing in his very ploughing how a superior nervous and cerebral structure means superior energy; and it is true that his work as an exciseman was more irregular than had been his farm-work, at least in summer. But the fact that after thirty he showed less capacity for the twofold travail of the brain and the muscles might suggest to a critic a better explanation than simple spontaneous and causeless deterioration of character. The truth is that Burns's physique was prematurely worn out, and this not by drinking or "debauchery," as we are sometimes told, but by undue toil. He has himself told how from the age of thirteen he had to undergo "the unceasing moil of the galley-slave" on his poor father's farm, and we further know that from his 'teens onward he was subject to occasional palpitations of the heart. That after such a boyhood he did the work he did in adolescence, is a double proof of his native faculty; but the proof carries with it the presumption that his whole powers were early overstrained, or of a nature to be early exhausted. In any case, no man could long go on doing some of the most concentrated literary work of his time while also doing either farm work or excise work enough to keep a family; and if, instead of seeking in the tavern some of the recreation that such a nature as his needed more than most, Burns had industriously plodded away o' nights at systematic "poetry" with a tired body at his fireside, supposing Clarinda's self to be opposite and all the children always quiet in bed, he would but have produced uninspired common sense and common sentiment—doses of the domestic didactic, more of the English verse in which he always tended to be undistinguished, more *Cottar's Saturday Nights*, more *Prayers*, more monodies on the deaths of public personages, than which perhaps even two or three perfect songs are a more durable monument. Great poetry is verily not to be produced by mere "solid industry;"* and there is not one leading poet of Burns's generation or the next who did not have for his work better chances, better intellectual circumstances, than his. Wordsworth had always an unearned income; so had Cowper; so had even Coleridge during a large part of his life; so had Shelley; so had Keats; so had Byron; even the hard-worked Southey had his time of youthful leisure; and each and all of these, like Goethe and Schiller and Richter and Chénier and Goldsmith and Browning and Tennyson and so many another, had a good culture-preparation, with no burden of premature labour save in the partially exceptional cases of Cowper and Keats. And the most industrious of all, Southey, did but prove by his industry that the delicate flowers of genius are not to be reared by the methods of the kitchen garden. It belongs to the common way of superficial thinking to overlook such conditioning facts in the lives of men of letters; most of us being taught by convention to take genius as something transcending all causation; but it might have been looked for that a man of genius should

---

* It seems just possible that before the end, when composing the more factitious chapters of *Weir of Hermistoun*, Stevenson realised what it was to produce with overtasked and failing powers. Some of his last letters express some such consciousness. Yet family accounts, equally trustworthy, represent him as much pleased with some of his last work which cannot please his critical readers.

STEVENSON ON BURNS

have had some intuition of the conditions that genius needs.

Perhaps it was that Stevenson, with his constant ill-health from youth up, took it that where there was physical strength such as Burns's to begin with, all other disadvantages must be of little account: a pathetic excuse and explanation, disarming censure, but leaving us noting that he was wrong. He has in fact judged Burns throughout with hardly a hint that he realises what Burns's burdens and obstacles were, or how much it signifies that the scantily cultured crofter's son did his life's work without any serious respite from the labour which poverty entails. He does not seem to see how much culture means morally as well as intellectually: how much it helps a man to be a gentleman, to be a good Stoic, to burn his own smoke, to escape ugly stumbles, as well as to choose his work, his media, his ends. Above all, as I have said, he makes not a jot of comparative allowance for the invidious lime-light that an exorbitant nationalism has made to beat on Burns's life; and wherever Burns says a light word or does a blundering action, it is treated by the critic *in vacuo*, as if the surrounding air were not all the while vibrating with such words and such actions. In one of his own essays Stevenson has protested against a naturalism which picks out for illumination certain items of life; declaring that he is glad to have the truth if it be the whole truth, but rejects as mere falsity a truth which tells only a fraction of a fact. That criticism is more valid as against his own handling of Burns than against Zola's handling of life; for Zola does suggest averages, and Stevenson's critique does not. He tries Burns more often than not by the standard of the exemplary abstract man, who has eluded biography; and he so gives to his estimate, despite touches of justice and mercy, a certain patronisingness which, as we have seen, evokes sharp comments. When he has to tell how the marriage-lines which Burns gave Jean Armour were thrown back on his hands, and how Burns then turned to Highland Mary, he does it with the air of impeccability hesitating between pity and contempt :—

". . . . with his head down, this poor, insulted poet ran once more upon his fate. There was an innocent and gentle Highland nursery-maid at service in a neighbouring family: and he had soon battered himself and her into a warm affection and a secret engagement."

The " battered " of this passage has reference to Burns's humorously candid avowal that in his youth he was always battering himself into a tender passion for some girl or other : the light word is none too candidly applied by the critic, at a century's distance, to an episode of an essentially different kind. In the same way the affair of Burns's sending the carronades to the French Government, his official snubbing and his wounded cry, is discussed by Stevenson with some such condescending compassion as might be expressed at the time by a "person of quality," rather than with a thinker's or an artist's sense of the pity of it all, and of the ugliness of a world so out of joint. To the nobility of Burns's sympathy with the French and the American Revolutions, Stevenson does show a passing susceptibility ; but not so much as to make us feel that he is not of the political school of Mr. Lang, who biographically rejoices that Burns came later to write his ditty " Does haughty Gaul invasion threat," and so put himself right with the mess-room.

In fine, save for the before suggested explanation, which leaves us fitly sympathetic with Stevenson, we should be moved to pronounce his treatment of Burns surprisingly unsympathetic, and thus in a way surprisingly unintelligent, despite its intellectuality. And it is only, as aforesaid, the sense of the cathartic virtue of such an essay, in a Scotland where centennial and perennial infatuation does not blench even at the raising of a monument to Highland Mary,* that can withhold us from feeling that with all its brilliance the essay had better not have been written. He has well said of another Scottish critic: "The point of view was imposed by Carlyle on the men he judged of in his writings with an austerity not only cruel, but almost stupid. They are too often broken outright on the Procrustean bed; they are probably always disfigured. The rhetorical artifice of Macaulay is easily spied; it will take longer to appreciate the moral bias of Carlyle."† For many people, unfortunately, it will take still longer to appreciate the moral bias of Stevenson's own essay on Burns, even though they may dislike its drift.

* It is impossible not to feel, now that Highland Mary has been thus commemorated, the better title of Lowland Martha, to wit, Mrs. Burns, who bore the heat and burden of the poet's day as few women would.

† Preface to *Familiar Studies*, pp. xiii.-xiv.

CLOUGH
(1887)

To some readers of the various appreciative criticisms which have been passed upon Arthur Hugh Clough, it must have seemed odd that the friendly writers should have so little to say of the poet's measure of success in a pursuit which bulked largely in his artistic work—the writing, in the verse form, of what is none the less analytic fiction. Setting aside the *Mari Magno: or, Tales on Board*, which are also character studies, about half his verse is made up simply of *The Bothie of Tober-na-Vuolich* and *Amours de Voyage;* and to the critic of fiction the latter production cannot well fail to be at least interesting, while the former is known to have interested a good many readers who would not profess to be specially critical. So silent, however, has criticism been on the subject, that there is probably an air of extravagance about an attempt to show that Clough was a great and original artist in fiction.

When, in 1848-9, Clough wrote his *Bothie* and *Amours*,* the leading English novelists were Lytton,

---

* The latter seems to have been completed in 1849, though not published till 1857-8. It was then a pecuniary success, which the *Bothie* had not been. "In a commercial point of view, the publications of the *Amours* has been a great event to me. This is the first

Thackeray, and Dickens; and of these the last, being at work on *David Copperfield* (1849), had yet to write *Little Dorrit*, *Great Expectations*, the *Tale of Two Cities*, *Bleak House*, and *Our Mutual Friend;* while Thackeray was but beginning to produce his masterpieces, *Vanity Fair* dating from 1846-8, and *Pendennis* from 1849-50. Charlotte Brontë had conquered fame by *Jane Eyre;* but *Shirley* only appeared in 1849, and *Villette* was not to come till 1853. George Eliot, again, had not yet dreamt of fiction; and across the Atlantic Hawthorne had thus far produced only his short tales; so that English fiction, on the whole, might be said to have reached only the beginnings of its greatest development. Such a division is, of course, arbitrary, just as, though in a much greater degree, it is arbitrary to make divisions between Dark Ages, Middle Ages, and Modern Times; but when simply put forward for what it is worth, it may serve usefully to emphasise the fact that before the time in question English novelists had done very little in the direction of what is coming to be recognised as the main work of the modern novel, the serious, analytical presentment of normal types of character. The terms here used must be taken as strictly definitive; or, rather, they had better be themselves defined to prevent misconception; and this can best be done by first noting the limitations of the art of the earlier novelists. It will probably not now be generally disputed that, while Defoe once for all gave English prose fiction a bias to circumstantial verisimilitude; and while Richardson, with all his limitations, gave the lead in the direction of a true analysis of character; Jane Austen was practically the first English novelist to attain real success in the rendering of normal

money I ever received for verse-making, and it is really a very handsome sum." Letter in *Prose Remains*, ed. 1888, p. 245.

life—that is to say, the first who gives us no impression of inadequacy within the limits of her undertaking. Richardson is far too much occupied with his thin-spun psychologising to hit off with any vividness the objective totality of his personages as it might conceivably appear to a keen onlooker; for ever pulling the strings, he never seems to get a view of his own drama; and thus the very freshness of method which gave his letter-writing characters, with their serious conformity to the literary conventions of the time, such a hold on the interest of his contemporaries, is for us to-day the great bar to the assimilation of his work. Fielding, again, is unquestionably at his best where his types are neither serious nor normal—that is, where he is giving us *genre* studies, an Adams, a Squire Western, a woman of the people, a sketch in satire, or an effect in comedy. Tom Jones is only inferentially real, and Sophia never becomes more than a suggestion, like Amelia, of a type of young lady which Fielding adored. As for Goldsmith, the general truth of suggestion, the value of the lighter detail, in *The Vicar of Wakefield* is not more obvious than the conventionality of much of the framework and much of the posing; while Scott, finally, hardly once contrives to give true vitality to a character which does not depend for its effect on novelty. There is none the less genius in his projection of the fresh types, as Davie Deans, Cuddie Headrigg, Monkbarns, the Bailie, Dandie Dinmont, and the rest; or in the skill with which the action of Jeanie Deans is made to enshrine her in our memory; but the fact remains that his normal personages, those hypothetically interesting figures round whom his really observed characters are grouped, are the merest "walking gentlemen" and gentlewomen. As to this there was no real doubt among competent readers in his own time; his fame, in so far as it did not depend on the gratitude of ordinary novel-readers for a fresh kind of excitement, being based on the general sense of the felicity with which he drew what were nominally his minor personages. No reader could, in the nature of things, imagine Captain Brown, or Waverley, or Mr. Francis Osbaldistone, anything like as vividly as he did even Counsellor Pleydell or Saunders Mucklebackit; and while the wizard's young ladies are a little more thinkable than his heroes, Diana being admittedly a substantial success, their society is far indeed from having any such fascination for the reader of to-day as it had for the "male of their species" with whom their chivalrous creator provided them. But Jane Austen, as no one saw better than Scott, achieved just such a success in drawing the people of the English upper-middle and middle-upper classes as he had done with the types he had observed in the Scotch peasantry. Here, in a young woman's novels, were people such as every reader met every day, somehow made as real as Borderers and Highlanders; more persistently real, as it happened, by virtue of the writer's general method; and somewhat inexplicably entertaining by virtue of one's very perception that there was nothing irresistibly entertaining in these same people in actual life. It was the triumph of pure art: the commonplace had been made immortal by sheer felicity of reproduction. Not that the new comer at once attained her due classic authority. While the few good readers—who included, let us remember, not only Scott, but, in the next generation, the much-maligned Macaulay—felt that there was here something quite new in fiction, something not attained to by Miss Burney any more than by Richardson, yet the habit of finding the truer touches of novelists mainly in their grotesques, or ostensible comedy-types, was of such long standing that readers still had a tendency to esteem Jane Austen, even as they did Fielding and Smollett, for her more emphasised studies, which were, by the conditions of her art-world, her fools ; and the very perfection of her fools tended somewhat to strengthen the bias. Hence, when George Eliot much later sought to present people of all grades of mind, she could still be met by a criticism which found her Mrs. Poysers and Aunt Gleggs admirable but thought her less piquant studies little worth having in comparison.

In Jane Austen, then, we might almost say, we have the first of the moderns in fiction. He, or she, who does not delight in her cannot be credited with a true taste ; or, let us say (remembering Charlotte Brontë's inappreciation), is one-sidedly developed. This being duly premised, a devout admirer may with a clear conscience go on to say that Jane Austen left unattempted the application of the naturalist method to normal character in its relation to the deeper issues of life. Her art played on the normal in individual experience as well as on the normal in individuality : she drew not only the people who belong to the ordinary drawing-room, but the drawing-room section of their inner life, so to say ; and some will probably have it, with Mr. Harrison, that these were her fixed limits. As I must not overload a note on Clough with a study of Jane Austen, I will not here discuss the matter, but simply posit the fact that her performance was defined as has been said ; and that when she had done there was still left to be achieved in fiction that adequate study of not only the weightier natures, but the more intellectual sides of these, which later thinking tends to demand from the professed student of character. Not less certain is it, however, that before the middle of the century the further step had not been fully taken.

CLOUGH

Setting aside the Marryats and Levers, who never turned to the intellectual side of things at all, we are bound to decide that Lytton lacks truth, and that Dickens, whatever may be thought of his later work, had certainly not so far mastered the serious side of life in his earlier period as to yield a product which will satisfy a cultured reader to-day. But did even Thackeray fully succeed in his earlier work, or in his later, in giving us such an artistic treatment of the intellectual life as can be said worthily to complement his pictures of the simply social life? I cannot better indicate the precise issue involved than by asking how far, say, *Pendennis* now satisfies us as a sketch of a young man with a deep intellectual experience, and how far Thackeray now impresses us as a man able to describe or transcribe such an experience. It implies no touch of detraction from the praise due to Thackeray's consummate and incomparable talent, to say that at this particular point he falls short; that his scope did not permit him to reach those sides of mental life at which he has ineffectually hinted in *Pendennis* (and this is the conclusion pointed to by the later work in *Philip*); or, alternatively, that on this as on one or two other points he wrote down to the standards of the British parlour of his time.

If, then, British fiction in 1848-9 was on the whole thus imperfectly intellectual, so much the more would be the merit of any man who at one stride attained the higher level; and this achievement it is that I venture to claim for Clough, in respect of these two works of his which are in form hexameter poems, but are in essence works of narrative, analytical, psychological fiction. Little read as they still are in proportion to their merits, I will rather assume them to be known to my readers than recapitulate their contents, as the mere telling of their simple stories would reveal nothing of their charm and power, which can only be gathered from a deliberate perusal. What really needs to be pressed is the relation that such works bear to the contemporary novel, and the faculty for fiction to which they testify. In the criticism of Clough's own generation one finds indeed some tribute to the power of the character-sketching in both the *Bothie* and the *Amours;* but—and this is the special point—no clear perception that just this merit, in the circumstances, took the two works out of the list of poetic successes and placed them high among the fictional, where alone could any analogous art be found, and where, further, it would be hard to find anything equally subtle in the same line. Doubtless it was the simple fact of Clough's having written in hexameters that stood mainly in the way of the proper classification ; and it will be necessary to consider what that fact substantially amounts to.

What seems to me to have been done by those who say that Clough proved we could have good English poetry in hexameters is : having found that a work in hexameters may be entirely successful in its art, to assume that it is therefore first-rate hexameter verse. Now, the literary question raised by Clough's hexameters is rather too complex to be so simply disposed of. It includes, to begin with, the old question as to what the technical "values" of poetry really are ; and on this there is need to guard against obscuring the issue by discussing the kind of impression we get from those classic poets to whom the hexameter was native. Asking rather what are the constituent elements of our own best poetry, we find that they may be resolved into effects of cadence, consonance, and concentrated and charming verbal expression ; that without these the verse form has no value, whatever be its metre; and that no metrical form, as such, gives the least permanent security for their presence. It almost follows from this that true poetic values, unalloyed by effects which are not such as to justify the verse form, can only be had from short poems—that all lengthy works in verse inevitably involve much inferior performance, and that such works must rely for their acceptance on the reader's pleasure in the successful passages inducing him to tolerate the others. For a variety of reasons, I believe that Clough quite felt all this, at least in his younger days; and I accordingly do not believe that in writing the *Bothie* and the *Amours* he was aiming at strictly poetical effects at all.* This opinion has been ere now expressed; Mr. Swinburne having suggested in his essay on Mr. Arnold's poems, that Clough meant his hexameters to be regarded as "graduated prose" and not as poetry; on which Professor Masson rejoins to the effect that such a view is quite out of the question. But if, instead of saying anything about "graduated prose," a phrase which simply raises the further question why Clough did *not* write graduated prose pure and simple, if that were the kind of effect he wanted—if rather we say that he aimed at an effect which was not poetic, I think we should be stating the plain truth. On the face of the matter, very much of the *Bothie* and of the *Amours* is humorous; in fact, humour, buoyant in the first and sombre and subtle in the second, pervades the whole conception of the two works; which is as

* The source of his impulse is noteworthy: "Will you convey to Mr. Longfellow," he writes to Emerson in 1849, "the fact that it was a reading of his 'Evangeline,' aloud to my mother and sister, which, coming after a reperusal of the 'Iliad,' occasioned this outbreak of hexameters?" (*Prose Remains*, p. 140.)

much as to say that they are not to be classed as poetry proper, if indeed they are to be called poetry at all. I am, however, sufficiently conscious of the psychological difficulties of the problem to prefer waiving the last challenge, and simply to say that where verse is humorous its effects, granting them to have certain analogies with those strictly poetic, certain properties which clearly belong to the verse form, are nevertheless of a distinctly different order from those others. This may seem at bottom a truism, but on the acceptance of it there depends such a point of practice as the deciding not to give the same name to horse and ass because both are cattle for riding. Humorous verse has undoubtedly this quality in common with beautiful verse, that when it is quite successful we return to it on the sheer strength of the fascination of the words, in their kind; and such charm over us is assuredly a special credential of the finest verse. It is the words, and the order of the words, that make the poetry; not the idea as it might be paraphrased in any prose form, however accurately. Well, one cannot help being repeatedly charmed with those lines of Peacock's:

> " The mountain sheep are sweeter,
> But the valley sheep are fatter;
> We therefore deemed it meeter
> To carry off the latter "—

for their happy fusion of rhyme and humour, which would be utterly lost in a prose statement; whereas it is just a fusion of rhyme and beauty that perpetually captures us in the lines:

> " Music that gentlier on the spirit lies
> Than tired eyelids upon tired eyes ";

and a charm of pure quintessential beauty of choice expression, absolutely dependent upon phrase and cadence, that conquers memory in those of Arnold's:

CLOUGH

" As the pale waste widens around him,
As the banks fade dimmer away,
As the stars come out, and the night-wind
Brings up the stream
Murmurs and scents of the infinite sea."

But since the "rhythmical creation of beauty," to use Poe's phrase, has thus so inexpressibly different an effect from that of the rhythmical creation of amusement, an effect so much more different from the latter than from that of fairly elevated prose, one hardly cares to give the name of poetry to both. I would finally say, then, that Clough wrote in hexameters because there was a certain artistic effect he was able to get from hexameters, which served his purpose, but which he never regarded as the same in kind with that which he aimed at in his finer rhymed poetry. And this particular artistic effect, accruing to the hexameter as he handled it, was not, as I take it, a strictly metrical or cadencial effect at all, but one of delicately humorous parody—so delicate that while the humour was often effusive it could be refined away at need till it put no check on a perfectly serious intonation and purpose. Clough, in short, wrote in hexameters not because he thought that special metre, *quâ* metre, tractable to serious verse, but because the hexameter was the metre of Homer and Virgil to begin with, and thus afforded endless opportunities for jests of style that would appeal to academic readers; and because further there was no blank measure in which pungency and piquancy could be better maintained at less cost of enforced dignity. He had thus the two resources of parody of classic manner and parody of rhythm in general; a combination, I suppose, the more difficult to analyse and describe truly because it is so unique. For the rest, it is needless to renew the other dispute as to whether Clough's verses were true hexameters after all. Mr. Swinburne says not; and Poe, to judge from his assaults on Longfellow's attempts, would probably extend his ban to Clough's. As to the latter, it may perhaps be agreed that, deliberate quaintness apart, they are " about as good as they make 'em," as the youth of London say; and no more needs to be granted.* Clough's own opinion on the subject is difficult to gather; the only clues being this brief " Note " on the back of the title-page of the first edition of the *Bothie:*

"The reader is warned to expect every kind of irregularity in these modern hexameters; 'spondaic' † lines, so called, are almost the rule; and a word will often require to be transferred by the voice from the end of one line to the beginning of the next;"

and some passages in the first of his *Letters of Parepidemus*, as this:

"Homer's rounded line, and Virgil's smooth verse, were both of them (after more puzzling about it than the matter deserves, I have convinced myself) totally unlike those lengthy, straggling, irregular, uncertain slips of *prose mesurée* which we find it so hard to measure, so easy to read in half a dozen ways, without any assurance of the right one, and which, since the days of Voss, the Gothic nations consider analogous to classic hexameter." ‡

It may be added that his careful translations from Homer in hexameter, though extremely interesting, do

---

* Mr. Arnold considered (Lectures *On Translating Homer*, p. 79) that " Mr. Clough's hexameters are excessively, needlessly rough." The *tu quoque* cannot be foregone. Mr. Arnold's own hexameters are insupportable—neither classic nor English.

† I do not quite understand what Clough here meant by "spondaic." Surely Poe was right in deciding that the ancient hexameter was spondaic, and that English hexameters fail just for lack of spondees. Clough's hexameters are just about as trochaic and dactyllic as other people's.

‡ *Works*, i. 397.

CLOUGH

not make good English verse; while his other *Essays in Classical Metres* are entirely afflictive.

There will still be put by some, perhaps, the further question, Why did Clough write in verse at all if his purpose was to any extent serious fiction? I would say, on that, that he happened at a particular period to be steeped in Greek verse, and at the same time overflowing with "criticism of life" as he saw it around him; and that he found in these works of his the fittest expression possible for him at the moment. It so happened that he could write elastically and spontaneously at the given time in the given manner; the manner being in itself a stimulus peculiarly fit in his case. He seems never to have written prose with any such facility as is shown in the *Bothie*, which would appear to have taken only somewhere about a month in the writing: his prose essays are mostly laboured and ineffectual; heavily packed with culled passages of Latin verse; never seeming to kindle all along the line, or to be written because of a clear sense of something to say. They never write themselves: they are composed; and smack of Carlyle and I know not how many other intellectual fashions of his young days. But in the *Bothie* we seem to have the exuberance of a holiday-making undergraduate with the keen judgments, the wide observation, and the musings, of the ripening man. Hence, an artistic success without parallel in its kind. There is, I venture to say, no piece of fiction in the language, within similar compass, which can compare with this for quantity and quality, in its combination of truth, force, and variety of character-drawing, truth of environment, depth of suggestion, and range of association and sympathy. No English writer has yet appeared who has shown the skill to pack such a picture and commentary as that of the opening banquet-scene into anything like the same space of prose. Told in prose at the same length, indeed, the multifold description and episode would have an air of crowding, of willed terseness, such as we have in Flaubert's *Salammbô;* whereas the verse, with all its load of significance, seems positively to loiter by the way, in the mock-Homeric and Miltonic iterations of epithets and dallyings with phrases and descriptions. It seems to be written for the sheer humour of the thing; and yet Thackeray could not have better have turned the humour to the account of the portraiture. Admiring notice has been taken by Mr. W. M. Rossetti of one line which conveys a whole story :

" Pipers five or six, among them *the young one, the drunkard* "

—a touch even more simply effective now than it was in the first edition, where the epithet "drunken" came again in the line further on, about the small piper nodding to Lindsay; but the section is full of similarly weighty strokes. The tutor, "the grave man, nicknamed Adam," so admirably exhibited by a series of incidental, effortless dramatic touches as the story goes on, is already permanently outlined by that phrase and the lines on his dress; the "shrewd ever-ciphering factor" is as it were henceforth identifiable; the whole cast of character of each of the students seems to be known definitely once for all; even the *attaché* and the Guardsman are individualised by an imperceptible touch; the Marquis of Ayr gesticulates before us; and Sir Hector, in particular, is at once photographed and permanently revealed by a few lines of burlesque comment and the incomparable report of his toast-speech on *The Strangers*, the entire creation being accomplished in a sort of unconscious addendum to the scholar's smiling apostrophe :

CLOUGH

"Bid me not, grammar-defying, repeat from grammar-defiers
Long constructions strange and plusquam-Thucydidean."

—the last epithet a paragraph in itself.* There lacks nothing to indicate the entire Highland environment; and with the all-round allusion there is thrown in one entirely sufficient vignette of the student's living-place and bathing-place:

"Where over a ledge of granite
Into a granite basin the amber torrent descended,
Only a step from the cottage, the road and the larches between them."

So matchlessly vivid is it all that one could almost swear it a faithful transcript from actual fact; but the chances are that the total opening section, like the piece as a whole, is an artistic combination of various recollections and various fancies. In the first edition the "pastoral" is thus dedicated: "My long-vacation pupils will I hope allow me to inscribe this trifle to them, and will not, I trust, be displeased if in a fiction, purely fiction, they are here and there reminded of times we enjoyed together." It could be wished that some of these pupils had put on record, for the enlightenment of future critics, some note as to the element of traceable fact in the artistic whole.

The easily evolving story of the *Bothie* is so steadily pregnant from first to last that to touch on all its good points would be to make a commentary much longer than the book; and it must suffice me here to touch on one or two points only before turning to the *Amours de Voyage*. One is, the success with which Clough has given us, in Hewson, a type of hot-headed young enthusiast, in such a way as to secure abundant sympathy

---

* The general reader will perhaps excuse an elucidatory reference to a choice sample of Anglo-Thucydidese in the footnote on page 300 of Marsh and Smith's *Student's Manual of the English Language*.

and full understanding, without for a moment turning him into a hero and challenging our homage. Where before had anything of the kind been done? I cannot recall a youthful Radical in English fiction who is not either intellectually magnified, or handled with a hostile animus, or thrust down our throats. In Clough there is no such malpractice: the lad is treated with absolute insight and absolute kindliness, yet without a shade of flattery, and becomes for us, enthusiast as he is, as absolutely real as Sir Hector, or as any observed personage in any novel; and how much fictional skill went to doing this can only be indicated by suggesting a comparison of Hewson with any other imagined young democrat the reader can think of, Felix Holt included. Another noteworthy feature is the presentment of the girl Elspie Mackaye, a study which may be suspected of idealism, but which is yet wonderfully true, as those who have known the Highlands at all widely or intimately can testify. Elspie is perhaps specifically the Highland girl of a fine type as one sees her in vacation-time; but, granting that, she is charmingly well drawn; and the proportion of idealisation is, it may be said without hesitation, much below that infused in Dorothea Brooke or Maggie Tulliver, not to speak of Myra and Romola. It may be doubted, indeed, if she is not to the full as true as Ethel Newcome. Now, this again constitutes a great success, when it is considered how lightly, how dramatically, Clough has laid his touches on. Girls of the people we have had in abundance in more recent fiction; but one so estimable and yet so little idealised, or one drawn with such strong simplicity, it will not be easy to call to mind; and I can think of nothing so good of earlier date.

A power to paint women of another type might very safely have been inferred from the sketch of Elspie in the *Bothie;* but the *Amours de Voyage* furnishes the decisive proof. Having the encouragement of the judgment of most of his readers to consider the *Bothie* a success, Clough made his next attempt at fiction an essay in hexameters likewise ; this time, however, so obviously disclaiming a poetic purpose, by throwing his story into the form of letters, that the fact of its not having been generally dealt with as a novel is a little surprising. The power of the character studies in the *Amours*, as in the *Bothie*, has not been overlooked ; but what has been awanting is the distinct recognition that in both works the versifier has surpassed the existing prose fiction on its own ground. For the whole work of these Italian letters is no less fine, if less brilliant in form, than that of the earlier composition ; the quieter tone being in fact the outcome of the greater subtlety of the study. What he attempted in this case was a study of the mind of a cultured and original Englishman in Rome, as acted upon on the one hand by the historic associations of the city and the contemporary problems connected with that history, and on the other by his intercourse with the inevitable person of the other sex, with whom he gradually falls in love, though the affair, so far as the story goes, comes to nothing. Told in its scanty detail, the narrative is about as slight as a fiction could well be ; but it is just the investing of such a plot with permanent interest that makes the work the masterpiece it is. As in the earlier piece, the workmanship is perfect nearly all round. There is no inadequacy. The commentary on Rome and its history ; the sketch of the acquaintances whose appearance on the scene begins the story ; the man's self-criticism and self-satire ; the woman's reticent self-revelation ; the prattle of the sister ; the interludes on the Roman political situation ; the chimes of half-elevated song that seem to lend themselves subtly to the note of passion, at first obscure, afterwards swelling to something of a lyric strain, only to die away finally in the minor—it is all masterly, as perfect as it is original. We shall not see just such another performance. Hexameter stories in imitation of Clough would be by many degrees more unsatisfactory than imitations of Whitman, for the simple reason that his work is so infinitely more difficult to equal; but it seems to me to-day, looking first at Clough's work and then at the developments fiction has taken and is taking in Russia, France, and America, that here in England this merely privately famous man of the schools had curiously anticipated later tendencies and achievements by a whole generation. All that is most characteristic of the best new work—the graded half-tints, the simple drawing, the avoidance of glare and melodrama, the search for the essential interest of the normal—all of it belongs to these experiments in hexameters. There has been no equally good portraiture of feminine character *in minimis* and in whole before or since. But, what is more, Clough had really philosophised his fiction in a style quite beyond the faculty of all but one or two of the moderns; contriving to make an intellectual man both ideally impressive and artistically true; a rare feat in the novel, where the anatomy of the higher grades of mind has hitherto been attempted with so little real success. The forceful simplicity of the unpretentious drawing of Claude can be best appreciated when contrasted with the labour bestowed on Daniel Deronda—and the result. Clough's work has the masculine weight and precision that in Turguénief make a short story live in the reader's mind like a great experience. Much tolerable workmanship will be forgotten before this.

CLOUGH

There is, indeed, an air of paradox in saying that one of the ablest performances in modern fiction, which at its best is above all things naturalistic, is one cast in the artificial form of letters in verse; and certainly the phenomenon is fitted to make us very careful how we theorise about right and wrong in art forms. Say what we will about hexameters, it is clear that these verse-novels of Clough's are "idealised" work as beside prose realism: so far as treatment goes, the method is obviously not that of naturalist fiction. In fact, Clough is at times not careful to preserve verisimilitude even within his artistic limits; as when he makes one of Mary Trevellyn's letters to Miss Roper* begin thus:

> You are at Lucca baths, you tell me, to stay for the summer;
> Florence was quite too hot; you can't move further at present.
> Will you not come, do you think, before the summer is over?

Since the letter could obviously have been made to read in a less impossible manner and yet convey all the facts required, the workmanship here must be pronounced faulty. But, making allowance for such faults of detail, which belong to inexperience in an uncommon method, what could be more essentially naturalistic than the whole presentment of the women's cast of mind and way of taking things? It is singular how perfectly the contents of actual letters are suggested in Clough's hexameters; so scrupulously sunk to the strictly prosaic level, wherever necessary, as to stop just short of the flavour of burlesque. Lines which in themselves are absolutely *banal*, conveying epistolary phrases also *banal* in themselves, yet curiously retain just the needful artistic value for the suggestion of a girl's femininely veiled emotions and hopes and fears; the commonplace letter becomes alive for us by its burden of narrative

* Canto v. 3.

implication, very much as it would in a novel as realistic as sifted prose could make it. Indeed we may search a hundred prose novels in vain for such delicate fidelity of suggestion. The touches in the portrait are as refined as any of Mr. Henry James; and yet how much more real is the lady than some of that artist's presentments!

But no less essentially true, on the other hand, does the painting remain when it rises above the commonplace into sheer poetry, as in these fine lines* in which Claude comments on the failure of the Italian rising:

> Whither depart the souls of the brave that die in the battle,
> Die in the lost, lost fight, for the cause that perishes with them?
> Are they upborne from the field on the slumberous pinions of angels
> Unto a far-off home, where the weary rest from their labour,
> And the deep wounds are healed, and the bitter and burning moisture
> Wiped from the generous eyes? or do they linger unhappy,
> Pining, and haunting the grave of their bygone hope and endeavour?

If there were any danger of this apostrophe lessening our sense of the reality of the sceptical, critical young Englishman, unrestfully musing at Rome, it would be sufficiently averted by the unflinching fall of key and pitch that follows:

> All declamation, alas! though I talk, I care not for home nor Italy; feebly and faintly, and but with the lips can lament the Wreck of the Lombard youth, and the victory of the oppressor. Whither depart the brave?—God knows; I certainly do not.

The snatch of poetry, equally with the half-real half-affected cynicism, and with the general mordant criticism on Rome and humanity and its ways, is part of the presentation of the young man's mind; a true product of the century in its restless analysis of its instincts. Nothing in the story is more dramatically convincing than the hero's passage from the analytical mood to

* Canto v. 6.

that of charmed surrender to the feminine attraction he had just been analysing. Half-way, we have this :—

Allah is great, no doubt, and Juxtaposition his prophet.
Ah, but the women, alas! they don't look at it in that way.
Juxtaposition is great ;—but, my friend, I fear me, the maiden
Hardly would thank or acknowledge the lover that sought to obtain her,
Not as the thing he would wish, but the thing he must even put up with . . . .
Ah, ye feminine souls, so loving, and so exacting,
Since we cannot escape, must we even submit to deceive you?
Since, so cruel is truth, sincerity shocks and revolts you,
Will you have us your slaves to lie to you, flatter and—leave you?

The girl indeed did not "look at it that way;" the one sex being as faithfully reproduced as the other. Her first judgment is perfectly "observed":

I do not like him much, though I do not dislike being with him.
He is what people call, I suppose, a superior man, and
Certainly seems so to me; but I think he is terribly selfish.

Later we learn from the silly sister that

Mary allows she was wrong about Mr. Claude *being selfish;*
He was *most* useful and kind on the terrible thirtieth of April.

And in a postscript :

Mary has seen thus far.—I am really so angry, Louisa—
Quite out of patience, my dearest! What can the man be intending?
I am quite tired ; and Mary, who might bring him to in a moment,
Lets him go on as he likes, and neither will help nor dismiss him.

He indeed did not make rapid progress, for before the doctrine of Juxtaposition we had this :

I am in love, you declare. I think not so; yet I grant you
It is a pleasure indeed to converse with this girl. Oh, rare gift,
Rare felicity, this! she can talk in a rational way, can
Speak upon subjects that really are matters of mind and of thinking
Yet in perfection retain her simplicity . . . .

CLOUGH

No, though she talk, it is music; her fingers desert not the keys; 'tis
Song, though you hear in the song the articulate vocables sounded,
Syllabled singly and sweetly the words of melodious meaning.
I am in love, you say; I do not think so, exactly.

And still the woman is woman, as in this postscript to a letter of the silly sister:

.... All I can say for myself is, alas! that he rather repels me.
There! I think him agreeable, but also a little repulsive.
So be content, dear Louisa; for one satisfactory marriage
Surely will do in one year for the family you would establish;
Neither Susan nor I shall afford you the joy of a second.

To which the silly sister adds a post-postscript:

Mr. Claude, you must know, is behaving a little bit better;
He and Papa are great friends; but he really is too *shilly-shally*,
So unlike George! Yet I hope that the matter is going on fairly.
I shall, however, get George, before he goes, to say something.
Dearest Louise, how delightful to bring young people together!

And yet again the girl, after a "let us say nothing further about it" as to a deviation of Mr. Claude from the agreed-on travelling plan of the party, half opens her heart thus:

Yes, my dear Miss Roper, I certainly called him repulsive;
So I think him, but cannot be sure I have used the expression
Quite as your pupil should; yet he does most truly repel me.
Was it to you I made use of the word? or who was it told you?
Yes, repulsive; observe, it is but when he talks of ideas
That he is quite unaffected, and free, and expansive, and easy;
I could pronounce him simply a cold intellectual being.—
When does he make advances?—He thinks that women should woo him;
Yet, if a girl should do so, would be but alarmed and disgusted.
She that should love him must look for small love in return; like the ivy,
On the stone wall, must expect but a rigid and niggard support, and
E'en to get that must go searching all round with her humble embraces.

And he too had his reasons:

CLOUGH

Is it my fault, as it is my misfortune, my ways are not her ways?
It is my fault that my habits and ways are dissimilar wholly?
'Tis not her fault; 'tis her nature, her virtue, to misapprehend them;
'Tis not her fault; 'tis her beautiful nature not ever to know me.
Hopeless it seems—yet I cannot, though hopeless, determine to leave it:
She goes—therefore I go; she moves—I move, not to lose her.

And then comes the swerving aside, the result of the silly sister's George having said

Something to Mr. Claude about what they call his attentions;

and Mary's postscripts multiply, and Miss Roper explains, and Mr. Claude eagerly decides to follow and propose; and the travellers journey at cross purposes and never meet; and the foiled lover, half content to accept the decision of Fate, decides to winter in Egypt, while the now heart-sore Mary returns with her party to England. There is something peculiarly modern in this ending that is no ending; something indefinitely in advance, technically speaking, of the symmetrical *denoûments* of previous fiction; something artistically in advance of much good fiction of our own time. Alike artistically and philosophically the whole is closed by one of the half-lyric strains which begin and end the cantos:

So go forth to the world, to the good report and the evil!
Go little book! thy tale, is it not evil and good?
Go, and if strangers revile, pass quietly by without answer.
Go, and if curious friends ask of thy rearing and age,
Say 'I am flitting about many years from brain unto brain of
Feeble and restless youths born to inglorious days:
But,' so finish the word, 'I was writ in a Roman chamber,
When from Janiculan heights thundered the cannon of France.'

The end is thus fittingly on the plane of idealist art; and yet who will say that the whole has not been as rigorously true a presentment of the literal life as the most determined naturalist could achieve? It is English naturalism, certainly : Clough, whose "name is handed down in William Arnold's *Rules of Football* as the best goal-keeper on record," was substantially English in his tastes. But all the same he had here succeeded in putting into an unlikely enough and ostensibly idealist art-form a piece of character fiction more essentially naturalistic than anything produced anywhere up to his time; nay, more deeply so than anything done in the forty years since, for he had contrived to handle a man's philosophy and a woman's emotions in a love-story with equal ease and verisimilitude, and to give his tale in hexameters a philosophic ripeness without a tinge of pedantry. The critical lesson is the old one that there are no rules for geniuses; that, as it has been put afresh by a gifted though faulty fictionist of our own day, Mr. Moore, "art is eternal; that it is only the artist that changes; and that the two great divisions—the only possible divisions—are, those who have talent, and those who have no talent."*

For most men verisimilitude in fiction and drama will be best attainable by the most strictly natural media; but Shakspere, again, could put more reality into blank verse dialogue than the Nashes and Lylys could put into prose; and there is no calculating the capacity of an original faculty to innovate in method, or to lead captive the captivity of form. And I do not scruple to risk derision by thus mentioning Clough in the same breath with Shakspere, being satisfied that he had some measure of Shakspere's endowment; though the scanty recognition of it among his countrymen promises small acceptance for such a view.

It may well be that it is the smallness of Clough's product that has hindered the recognition of his real greatness; mere volume counting for so much in the impres-

* *Confessions of a Young Man*, p. 121.

sion made on the world even by fine work; and it may be too that his comparative failure in serious poetry has affected the general attitude toward his whole remains. I say comparative failure; for his poetry well-nigh makes up by its deep intellectual interest for its lack of the true poetic charm. *Dipsychus* and the rest of it is indeed better worth reading than a good deal of verse of much wider vogue.* It has not, however, truly caught either the trained or the untrained ear; and this, with the habit of treating his hexameters as being equally with the rest essays in the poetic art, goes far to account for the limited character of his reputation. Then his *Mari Magno: or, Tales on Board* must have helped to subdue the critical tone in his regard, for here, there can be no doubt, the artistic failure is as complete as the earlier success. To account for it, we must fall back on the accounts we have of Clough's mental constitution—the slowness of his mind to set to work at all times, and the conditions of his health in his later years. He had written his good things under the two strong impulses of physical vigour and Italian travel; and in the absence of similarly happy conditions he produced nothing more that could be ranked beside

* Mr. Lowell has twice spoken very highly of Clough's poetic merit, but with significant differences of expression. One passage runs:—" Clough, whose poetry will one of these days, perhaps, be found to have been the *best utterance in verse* of this generation " (Essay "On a Certain Condescension in Foreigners," *My Study Windows*, 6th ed., p. 56). The other is, " We have a foreboding that Clough, imperfect as he was in many respects, and dying before he had subdued his sensitive temperament to the sterner requirements of his art, will be thought a hundred years hence to have been the *truest expression in verse* of the *moral and intellectual tendencies*, the doubt and struggle towards settled convictions, *of the period in which he lived*" (Essay on "Swinburne's Tragedies," *ibid.* p. 157). The latter verdict will doubtless hold good of Clough's total product, but it in effect gives up the point of his strictly poetic success.

them. In the *Mari Magno* we have an all too decisive test of the fitness of rhymed verse as a vehicle for narrative that aims at being serious without being archaic; and a proof of Clough's wisdom in choosing the hexameter even where his purpose was not tinged with humour. In that, the freedom of the medium allowed him to be serious and impressive when he wanted; in the rhymed pentameter, applied to fictional purpose, verisimilitude was far harder to reach; and even the simple seriousness that was all he now had in his mind is continually turned to absurdity by the pitfalls of the rhyme. When a man gravely writes in the couplet measure of "A beauteous woman at the table d'hôte;" and tells how, on board ship, he

"amid a dream
Of England, knew the letting-off of steam"—

artistic charm is over and done with. The couplet, like the hexameter, might have been used humorously; but for a sober, matter-of-fact tale, as Crabbe had sufficiently shown, it is the fatallest of all metrical conveyances.

And yet in these hopeless verses are contained two tales which, in their structure and detail, still betray the mind of a born fictionist; a mind which sees characters instantaneously as organic wholes, and has no more difficulty in presenting them with all their specific differences than a good portraitist has in giving the lines of different faces. We are told that Clough had a wonderful eye for scenery, remembering the hang and lie of roads and hills, streams and valleys, in a fashion that surprised his friends. He had just such a faculty for discriminating character. The slightly-sketched tale-tellers in the *Mari Magno* are like drawings by Keene; and through the racking couplets the people of the stories, especially of the second, keep their form and colour with the same steadiness that is seen in the hexameter novels. The old curious felicity of indicating a character by a few touches is not gone; and the reader, when he can forget the versification, seems to have gained some new knowledge of life from the few pages he has turned over. The people are "observed:" we feel that we have been reading transcripts from actual private histories. And we can understand how different from ordinary biographical eulogy is Professor Shairp's reminiscence, *à propos* of Clough's unsuccessful try for a Balliol Fellowship in 1842: "I remember one of [the examiners] telling me at the time that a character of Saul which Clough wrote in that examination was, I think he said, the best and most original thing he had ever seen written in any examination." Why, with this genius for a great art, Clough did so little in it, and never seemed even to realise clearly where his genius lay—this is a question the answering of which raises divers points as to his total idiosyncrasy, his training, and his intellectual environment.

Something has to be allowed for a constitutional lack of productive energy, otherwise definable as intellectual fastidiousness, the physical side of which is perhaps to be looked for by the clue of the paralysis which finally struck him down after a fever. Of his character as seen in childhood his sister testifies: "One trait I distinctly remember, that he would always do things from his own choice, and not merely copy what others were doing." And again: "Arthur even then was too fastidious to take off his shoes and stockings and paddle about as we did."* The child was father to the man. Nor was native fastidiousness the only force at work. In his prime he gives, in a letter to a friend, this account of his hard schooling:

* Memoir in *Poems and Prose Remains*, 1869, i. 4, 6

CLOUGH

" I may, perhaps, be idle now; but when I was a boy, between fourteen and twenty-two throughout, I may say, you don't know how much regular drudgery I went through. Holidays after holidays, when I was as school, after a week or so of recreation, which very rarely came in an enjoyable form to me, the whole remaining five or six weeks I used to give to regular work at fixed hours. That wasn't so very easy for a schoolboy spending holidays, not at home, but with uncles, aunts, and cousins. All this and whatever work, less rigorous though pretty regular, that has followed since during the last ten years has been, so far as external results go, perhaps a mere blank and waste; nothing very tangible has come of it; but still it is some justification to me for being less strict with myself now. Certainly, as a boy, I had less of boyish enjoyment of any kind whatever, either at home or at school, than nine-tenths of boys, at any rate of boys who go to school, college, and the like; certainly, even as a man I think I have earned myself some title to live for some little interval, I do not say in enjoyment, but without immediate devotion to particular objects, on matters as it were of business." *

And to that picture of destructive education he adds another touch in the *Passage on Oxford Studies* extracted in the "Prose Remains," describing the sickness of heart that overtook him on going to the university, at the prospect of endless classics: "An infinite lassitude and impatience, which I saw reflected in the faces of others, quickly began to infect me." Such a youthful experience must have told on the adult man, laming the springs of creative energy and dispiriting the abnormal genius.† But it is with a sense of fresh exasperation that one thinks of such a faculty being further weakened for practical performance by the effeminate ecclesiastical atmosphere of the Oxford of the Newman epoch, when currents of febrile mysticism and timorous scepticism drew young men this way and that; not one in a hundred of those affected being able to attain a stable

* *Poems and Prose Remains*, i.

† At Oxford, according to Clough, who was, however, probably exaggerating, the verdict on the *Bothie* was that it was "indecent and profane, immoral and (!) communistic."

and virile philosophy. Clough himself said afterwards that for two years he had been "like a straw drawn up the draught of a chimney" by the Newman movement; and it would not be going too far to say that if he were not one of those "wrecks" declared by Mr. Gladstone to have been "strewn on every shore" by the academic tempest in question, he was at least left less seaworthy for life. It has become a little difficult to think either of the mystics or of the half-hearted sceptics as men of high intellectual power: it seems a trifle strange in these days that one such as Clough, having once realised the force of the rational criticism of the popular creed, should be unable robustly to readjust his life to the sane theory of things. But so it was. The character-student suffered as much from the disintegration of his inherited faith as did any hectic disciple of them all; and when he found he could be neither Catholic nor Protestant he seemed to lapse into a sense of intellectual homelessness. The English universities, in which the nation's best educational endowments are turned mainly to the account of training men to preach to the illiterate or the unquestioning the religious system of the Dark Ages, seem to unfit men systematically for any independent appraisement or application of their natural powers. The reigning theory of things in these venerable halls—at least till just the other day—was that a scholar, having undergone the venerable curriculum, is to be a clergyman or a barrister, or possibly a doctor, or alternatively a private gentleman or politician or ornamental man of business, agreeably conscious, through a gentlemanly middle life, of once having studied the classics. Thackeray only took to literature for sheer need of money; Lytton is almost our only other novelist who had an academic preparation, and as an artist he gained little enough by it, though one can see that the same preparation can be very valuable in many ways, apart from the mere instruction it nominally implies. Spencer, Grote, Mill, and Lewes—not to speak of Gibbon—almost seem to owe their power of working on original lines to the accident of missing the university stamp; Darwin, Huxley, and Tyndall, to judge by results, need never have entered a college door. Even the late Professor Balfour remains a promise of possibilities.

But this by the way. The relevant facts for us here are that Clough, missing what seemed his natural career as a priest, had yet been so permeated by the ecclesiastical and university view of human activity as to be in a measure unfitted to apply his powers in any other way. He could not settle down peacefully in intercourse with men who had definitively turned their backs on an impossible faith: there is evidence that he found such men uncongenial in their decided rationalism, as they doubtless found him in his melancholy retrospectiveness. One feels that just twenty years earlier the same Clough could have quietly found his way into the clerical grooves, like many another man of potential genius, leaving no literary legacy of any importance to his countrymen, and living to face alike Strauss and Newman with the sheathing prejudices of profession and habit. In fine, we may say that he stood in religion and philosophy as he did in his fiction—between two widely-different generations; sundered from the past, but slow to begin to face the future. But whereas his religion had been a profound prepossession, the removal of which taxed his whole moral nature and left him lamed with the struggle, his spontaneous and hardly purposive excursion into the field of intellectual art yielded a remarkable result, suggestive no less of the manifold intellectual forces that lie cramped or latent around us, than of the power of certain institutions and conventions to keep them down.

It is not fitting, however, that the last word on such a personality as Clough's should be a suggestion of frustration. Frustration, after all, is a matter of comparison, and whatever impression he may make on later readers, he was to his own generation, which in that way could best judge him, an impressive and not a weak figure. Let us remember him by the words of one whose name will live with his longer than these comments:

"I mention him because, in so eminent a degree, he possessed these two invaluable qualities—a true sense for his object of study, and a single-hearted care for it. He had both, but he had the second even more eminently than the first. He greatly developed the first through means of the second. In the study of art, poetry, or philosophy, he had the most undivided and disinterested love for his object in itself, the greatest aversion to mixing up with it anything accidental or personal. His interest was in literature itself; and it was this which gave so rare a stamp to his character, which kept him so free from all taint of littleness. In the saturnalia of ignoble personal passions, of which the struggle for literary success, in old and crowded communities, offers so sad a spectacle, he never mingled. He had not yet traduced his friends, nor flattered his enemies, nor disparaged what he admired, nor praised what he despised. Those who knew him well had the conviction that, even with time, those literary arts would never be his. His poem, of which I before spoke, has some admirable Homeric qualities—out-of-door freshness, life, naturalness, buoyant rapidity. . . . But that in him of which I think oftenest, is the Homeric simplicity of his literary life." *

Homeric simplicity is perhaps not the description which would suggest itself to most men; but whatever words can serve the literary memory of the author of *The Bothie of Tober-na-Vuolich* and *Amours de Voyage* will be ungrudgingly allowed by those who can appreciate the singular independence of his work.

* Matthew Arnold, *On Translating Homer; Last Words*, ad fin.

CONCERNING ACCENT, QUANTITY, AND FEET

AN APPENDIX TO "POE"

IT may not be without interest, for some readers, to look into the dispute as to the scansion of classic verse, which one critic (see p. 105) has settled, so far as Poe is concerned, by the easy method of charging with ignorance the challenger of orthodox practice. The dispute, which one would suppose must have tended to arise chronically even in the Dark Ages, is apparently at least as old as the "revival of learning," and seems to have been freshly embroiled when the Byzantine Greeks handed over to Western Europe the enigma, helplessly contemplated by them, of a classic Greek verse marked by accents which were neither those of living and spoken Greek, nor those needed to make the verse scan rhythmically. Already it was hard enough to scan many of the Latin classics; and many earlier grammarians would have answered to the picture drawn by Montaigne of the pedant bent on leaving to posterity the true measure of the verse of Plautus, which was still to seek. But the Greek problem was still more obscure: being in fact unsolved for most students to this day, the mere historical data as to the entrance of the present marks into the manuscripts being awanting. I am not aware that any systematic survey of the whole discussion has yet been made,* and I can only pretend here to glance at the main features, which, indeed, are as much as most readers will care to contemplate.

* See a helpful sketch of one line of the discussion on verse principles in the preface to the late Sydney Lanier's *Science of English Verse*, 1880.

APPENDIX

I

According to Foster,* though Scaliger had objected to certain Greek accents in particular, there was no general dispute about the "faithfulness and propriety of the Greek accentual marks" till the time of Isaac Vossius (1618-1688), the previous wrangles of scholars having been mainly over the sounds of the letters taken singly. Vossius flatly declared that the accentual marks, not being even nearly coëval with the script, deserved no attention; and as nobody could reconcile them with any tolerable scansion, his view was welcomed by "several of the learned, particularly in Holland and Germany."—Henninius for instance, published a book in support of it in 1684, and he in turn was supported by other scholars, at intervals, down till the issue in 1754 of an anonymous " Dissertation against pronouncing the Greek language according to accents," which was known to be the work of the Rev. Dr. Henry Gally, a scholarly cleric, son of a French Protestant refugee. Gally's thesis was that the Greek language, from the time of Alexander, had been gradually corrupted; and that though at first accents may have been placed according to quantity, they gradually followed the corruption of pronunciation, till they finally represented that alone.† "No manuscripts that are one thousand years old and upwards have any accents;"‡ therefore the marks had no authority. This was the main position of Vossius and Henninius, sustained however by an independent argument on grounds of reason and the essentials of rhythm. At the same time, here also following previous opinion, Gally laid it down that originally the accent marks "were musical;"§ without however doing anything to develop the point, or to connect it with his main argument as to the corruption of the spoken tongue. The argument was thus substantially negative; but in this form it made considerable headway in England, as it had already done on the continent. So far did the movement go that Greek editions began to appear without accentual marks; and in a collection of verses presented by the University of Oxford to the king, no accents appeared. It was at this point

---

* *An Essay on the Different Nature of Accent and Quantity*, 2nd ed. Eton, 1763, p. vii.
† *Dissertation* cited, pp. 109, 139, 145.   ‡ *Ibid.* p. 3.   § *Ibid.* p. 2.

APPENDIX

that Foster undertook, *à propos* of Gally's essay, to vindicate them by a theory which, though he put it as antagonistic to the Vossian view, was really in a measure reconcilable with that, his contention being that the Greek accent marks stood for rise and fall of *pitch* or *tone* in utterance.

His attitude towards Gally, however, was specifically hostile, his aim being at once to vindicate the antiquity and genuineness of the accent marks, and on the other hand to show that Gally was wrong in assuming that a raised tone (=acute accent) necessarily involved a stress. Admitting that stress generally accompanied the raised or "acute" pitch in England, Foster pointed out that it did not in Scotland, where the voice is frequently raised on the weak final syllable of a word; and he cited various expressions from ancient authorities to show that the "acuted" syllable was rather quickened than made longer. Gally's position was, broadly, that acute accent meant stress, that stress meant more time, and that time meant quantity. Foster's was that the acute accent meant simply raised pitch, and was essentially different from time and quantity. For the rest, both writers held by the old idea that certain vowels must always have long values, because they are naturally "long," or capable of prolongation; though by thus making, say, *goad* a long syllable and *God* a short, they were shutting out the possibility of a consistent scheme of rhythm. Nor did either draw any light from the datum, accepted by both, that prosody was originally a matter of music. Gally replied with asperity to the asperities of Foster, who replied in turn; and there the matter was left. In practice it was settled by an adoption of both doctrines in so far as they were compatible. Foster, making the accentual marks signs of pitch, left the student free to do what Gally proposed—scan the verse without them. He had further opened up a new hope for rational prosody by proceeding to show that, despite a conventional maxim to the contrary, English verse was as much a matter of quantities as Greek or Latin. Quantity had here the intelligible meaning of syllable-stress. Foster claimed to stand upon reason and common sense, as Vossius and Henninius and Gally had done. But there remained, it appears, an unfailing source of dispute in the simple fact that the universities remained seminaries of tradition, keeping their eyes fixed on the past instead of relating themselves to the present. The manipulation of one dead

APPENDIX

language and literature was occupation enough for even a lively intelligence; but the universities held by two; and Greek and Latin verse alike had thus to be read by one abstract theory, deduced from half-comprehended documents, or merely framed on the tradition set up by these. Thus the accommodation of Greek verse to the supposed Latin accents of Quintilian goes on to this day, despite the fact, insisted on by Foster,* that Quintilian and Servius declared the verse accentuation of the two tongues to be different.

Nor does it seem possible to solve the problem by mere resort to the documents. Every point in the inquiry is open to dispute. The Romans, who did not use accent marks as a rule, had a mark, the *apex*,† a short horizontal line, apparently meant to distinguish long syllables from short, in cases where the same word form had different meanings according to pronunciation; and this mark seems later to have been actually confused with marks of pitch in late Roman inscriptions.‡ But then Quintilian also indicates that in Roman pronunciation "acute" (*acuta*), or "circumflex" (*flexa*), implied a *long* syllable, and "grave" (*gravis*), a *short* one. That is, a short syllable was to be pronounced with a lowered tone, and a long one with a raised or a changing tone. Difficult as it is for moderns to conceive this fastening down of articulation to tones of voice as well as to stresses, there seems no escape from the conclusion that such was the ancient practice as regards the delivery of verse. On the other hand it appears from several authorities among the Greeks that for them "acute" (ὀξύς) pitch meant a quick syllable, and "grave" (βαρύς) a long one.§ There is thus absolute uncertainty in the terms from the moment at which the two prosodies come together.‖ And the difficulty was doubled by the fact that the Greek correlative terms *arsis* and *thesis*, applied to stress and ease of syllables, came each to have the two contrary meanings. Arsis meant the raising of the hand or foot in counting or beating time, and thesis the setting of it down; but as either movement might

---

* *Dissertation* cited, p. 301. † Quintilian, *Inst. Orat.*, i. 7.
‡ Foster, pp. 117-119.
§ Aristotle, *De Anima*, c. 7; *Problemata*, xxix. 37; Plutarch, *Quæstiones Platonicæ* (cited by Foster, p. 278).
‖ Macrobius suggests a further perplexity by noting that an acute *sound* is made by rapid vibration. *In Somn. Scip.* ii. 4.

APPENDIX

serve to mark stress, and people would tend to mark it in different ways, the words came to be absolutely ambiguous.* All the while they continued to signify rise and fall of *tone*; so that a problem in which there was need for very exact discrimination of terms, was rendered desperate by a peculiar confusion of them.

It is thus nearly as hard to guess how the mediæval grammarians read the classic verse as to divine how the ancients spoke it. Aristotle,† analysing speech, speaks of stress and lightness of breathing, length and shortness of sound, and of an acute, a grave, and a medium sound; a classification which seems to provide simply for verse scansion in the modern "accentual" sense. So with Priscian's doctrine ‡ that "*habet quidem litera altitudinem in pronunciatione, latitudinem in spiritu, longitudinem in tempore.*" It would seem to express simply the facts of pitch or tone, openness or closeness of vowel formation, and length or brevity of stress in pronunciation. But the giving of these attributes to *quidem litera* on the one hand, and the giving of equal importance to pitch and vowel form, leave open opportunities of endless dispute; and when Scaliger defined "quantity" as the "triple dimension of length, breadth, height," he left to the schools as elastic a conundrum as heart could wish. What resulted was, for one thing, a fantastic discrimination between a stressed syllable and a long syllable—a distinction fatal to all realisation of rhythm.§ Thus Melanchthon wrote:

> Time and tone are by no means the same qualities of a syllable. Accordingly the terms of one are not applicable to the other. You err if you

---

* *Cf.* Du Méril, *Essai philosophique sur le principe et les formes de la versification*, 1841. Du Méril attributes the confusion to the double connection of poetry with music and dancing. It is to be noted that in our own day the orchestra leader raises his wand to mark a note, where the foot, or the hand in counting, is struck down for the emphasis.

† *Poetics*, xx.

‡ Cited by Foster, p. 19.

§ We shall see later that in our own and other modern verse there is a subtle element of quantity in the sense that among both stressed and unstressed syllables there are differences of shortness or facility of enunciation—that, apart from stress, syllables alter in facility of utterance according to their consonantal content and context. But this is not what the old prosodists were after, or at least not what they brought out. It clearly represents only their element of *doubtful syllables*.

APPENDIX

say that acute and long, or grave and short, are the same. I must dwell upon this because the mob of grammarians speak of it unintelligently. Not all long syllables are acute; in *Virgilius* the *vir* is long, but not acute. Not all acutes are long; in *Virgilius* the *gi* is acuted, although the syllable is short. Many of us in Latin make the *i* in *philosophia* acute; and the same with *theologia, prosodia,* not that we suppose the *i* to be long, but that it is to be acuted and pronounced in the Greek manner, not in the Latin. The words being Greek have not been so adapted to Roman tongues as to lose their native tone.*

Foster apparently supposes this to be an assertion that in *Virgilius* the stress was laid on the first syllable, while the second was merely pronounced in a higher tone. This is surely not the meaning. What is asserted is that though the stress is laid on the second syllable it remains short—the short sound of *i*, as distinguished from the sound (in English *ee*) which can be prolonged—while the *vir*, having the sound of the long Latin *i*, counts as long though it be not emphasised. This is borne out by the rest of the sentence, which shows that "acute" meant "stressed" as regards the Greek words cited. Melanchthon's prosody was a confused convention.†

On such bases, despite the impression made by Foster on many readers, no durable doctrine could be raised; and Foster himself, by acquiescing in Johnson's working rule for English prosody, virtually gave away his cause. Johnson pronounced "acute tone" and "long quantity" in English to be "equivalent by acting together;" and this Foster cited as a "confirmation" of his doctrine.‡ Johnson's rule was of course a mere evasion of difficulty. It must have struck many readers that not only were the Scotch capable, as Foster said, of raising the voice on a short final syllable, but the English were capable of lowering it on a stressed syllable. The word "impossible," for instance, is often begun on a high note, with a drop on the rest of the word; and in verse the phrase "to be or not to be" falls as naturally from a high note on the "to be" to a lower on the "not" as *vice versâ*. It might have been supposed that these considerations would have suggested to Foster's own generation the

* Cited by Foster, pp. 119-120.
† Foster cites Erasmus (*Dialog. de pronunc. ling. Græc. et Lat.*, p. 124), Beza (*Alphabet. Græc.*, p. 72), and Gerard Vossius (*Aristarch.* ii. c. 10), as coinciding with Melanchthon, on the difference between accent and quantity.
‡ As cited, p. 48.

APPENDIX

need for carrying the explanation of the Greek accents further, especially as it was agreed that these accents had originally been musical signs. But no further step was taken in that age. Walker, writing his *Observations on the Greek and Latin Accent** early in the present century, admits that the difficulty about accent and quantity has long been the *opprobrium et crux grammaticorum*, and notes that "Vossius, Henninius, and Dr. Gally produce a great number of quotations which seem to confound accent and quantity, by making the acute accent and long quantity signify the same;" while "White, Michaelis, Melanchthon, Foster, Primat, and many other men of learning, produce clouds of witnesses from the ancients to prove that accent and quantity are essentially different." Walker—who says so many just and forcible things that the final nullity of his treatise is surprising—complains of the lack of careful analysis of the subject matter; but himself leaves it confused for lack of such care. Thus he fixes the meanings of "long" and "short" to what may much better be described as open and close vowels, and leaves the meaning of "accent" in that equivocal state in which it was left by Foster and Gally. These laxities quite preclude the settlement of the dispute. Walker cannot see that "*fat*," with its close or limited vowel sound, is in a very practical sense as "long" as "*far*," with its open or prolongable vowel; since in "*fatness*" the first syllable normally *bulks* more to the ear than the second, whether or not it actually takes longer to sound; and an open-vowelled syllable, as against any other, can do no more.† It may easily happen, and it very often does happen, that a syllable with a so-called short vowel is harder to sound quickly, by reason of an awkward collocation of consonants, than one with a so-called long vowel; and a verse-maker has much more need to look to this circumstance, next to that of stress, than to the alleged quantitative value of vowels.

---

* Published with his *Key to the Pronunciation of Classical Proper Names*.
† The fallacious line of investigation was led up to by Dionysius of Halicarnassus, who laid it down truly enough that longs and shorts differed among themselves, some longs being longer than others. Foster accordingly (p. 33) shows how the same thing occurs in English and Latin. This was a valid plea as against the dogma that a long was exactly the length of two shorts; but it does not take note of the essential fact that variations of length in *accentuated* syllables—variations which, in any case, are not measurable—leave scansion unaffected, and tell only on expression.

APPENDIX

Quantity, in fact, in spoken verse, consists of stress and of the consonantal total of syllables. The presupposition that certain vowel sounds are in themselves "long" is the ruin of a discussion in which the nature or meaning of *syllabic* length is the problem to solve. And it lands Walker in hopeless contradictions. He writes (§ 24): "As to the long quantity arising from the succession of two consonants, which the ancients are uniform in asserting, if it did not mean that the preceding vowel was to lengthen its sound, as we should do by pronouncing the *a* in *scatter* as we do in *skater*, I have no conception of what it meant; for if it meant that only the time of the syllable was prolonged, the vowel retaining the same sound, I must confess as utter an inability of comprehending this source of quantity in the Greek and Latin as in English." It is strange that such a scholar should not see the point. The *a* in *metal* is in every sense short; but it clearly becomes longer in *metallic*, before the doubled consonant—a rule of spelling not indeed always observed, but fairly general. Now, Walker's own nomenclature makes the *a* in *metallic* a "short" vowel; so that the *a* in *metal* must rank as extra-short. The hopelessness of that crux may have been Walker's reason for not seeing the point raised in the rule he cites, which, for the rest, goes far to show that ancient quantity (chanting apart) was just modern quantity; and that as a rule a long syllable was for the later "ancients," as for us, just a stressed syllable. When Walker tells us that the *o* in *Cicero*, in Latin and English, is "long," though unaccented, and the *i* short, though accented, he shows the utter irrelevance of the school terminology to questions of scansion. But worse remains. While thus taking accent as = stress, Walker finally agrees with Foster in making it mean voice pitch or inflexion. He detects the confusions of Foster, "that excellent scholar," who makes "acute accent" = close vowel (as in *man*) and "grave accent" = open vowel (as in *mane*); but he himself (like Foster) finds (§ 27) "the strongest reason to suppose that the Greek and Latin acute accent was the rising inflexion, and the grave accent the falling inflexion, in a lower tone." Yet he had just before (note on § 22) accepted Foster's remark that the old accent marks could not mean sentence inflexions (= "oratorical accent"); since such inflexions constantly vary according to the context. The confusion could have been at once got rid of by recognising that quantity in speaking *must* amount substantially

APPENDIX

to the same thing as stress—the remaining elements of quantity counting for something as regards euphony, but not enough to affect scansion—and by surmising that the Greek accent-marks represented mainly the survival of a knowledge of the old fashion of chanting the verse, in which length would sometimes coincide with stress and sometimes not. But Walker, laying too much weight on his own very acute dictum that singing and speaking differ as leaping and sliding, or motion and rest, rejected the already proffered explanation that the "speech" of the ancients was "a kind of singing;" and while deciding (§ 28) that the Greek and Latin verse must have been extremely monotonous, he would not consider the possibility of a state of transition from the primitive to the subtilised. Finally, having disparaged the rhythm of the ancient verse without accounting for its crudity, and contradicted himself as well as all the other writers on both sides, he leaves the subject in confessed confusion, expressing the hope that "some future philosophical inquirer, with more learning, more leisure, and more credit with the world than I have," will solve the problem, on the basis of his own "entire conviction that the ancients had a notation of speaking sounds."

The hope has not been fulfilled as regards English research. Coleridge glanced at the matter as he glanced at so many matters, seeing into it acutely, but lacking the patience and the grip needed to settle it, or to solve his own contradictions.* The passage in his Table Talk† begins by declaring that "the distinction between accent and quantity is clear;" the third sentence runs : "I do not think it possible to *talk* any language without confounding the quantity of syllables with their high or low tones"—a deliverance deriving from Foster's school, and sounding strangely in the mouth of a man who must have known how to scan verse by his inner ear, without any use of tones whatever. The matter is at bottom not one of tone but of time and stress, since one may talk monotonously if one will. Changes

---

* His surprising claim in the preface (1816) to *Christabel*, that he had introduced a "new principle" in "counting in each line the accents, not the syllables," suggests that with all his assumption of learning on metres, he had made no very close investigation of the subject. The kind of line he claims to have originated abounds in Shakspere and in Milton, to mention no others.

† August 23, 1833.

APPENDIX

of pitch are in a measure coincident with changes of stress; that is all. For the rest, Coleridge's own admission that common conversation must have been accentual carries with it the conclusion that when verse ceased to be customarily chanted it must inevitably gravitate to accentual bases. Yet he thus concludes, after showing well enough that the *old* accentual marks must have had reference to a conventional chant rhythm :

> Besides, can we altogether disregard the practice of the modern Greeks? Their confusion of accent and quantity in verse is of course a barbarism, though a very old one, as the *versus politici* of John Tzetzes in the twelfth century* and the Anacreontics prefixed to Proclus will show; but these very examples prove *à fortiori* what the common pronunciation in prose then was.

There is no "barbarism" in the matter. What the modern Greeks have done, as we shall see, is to lose hold of a certain cherished barbarism of the ancients. They identify accent with quantity because to separate them is to maintain a barbarism that has nothing but its antiquity to recommend it. Whether the significance of the old accent marks be discoverable or not, the modern Greeks have clearly done well to cast in their lot with the tendencies of living speech.

II

Some approach to a solution of the problem begins to be made when the inquiry is turned on the psychological sources of whatever prosodical system the Greeks had—the origins of their poetic art. And this step is completely taken for the first time, so far as I have seen, in the *Essai philosophique sur le principe et les formes de la versification* of M. Edelestand du Méril, published in 1841, one of the most learned books ever written on the subject. At the outset M. Du Méril lays his finger on the evolutionary character of the whole body of classic verse:

> The Greek metric has reached us only in a state of perfection which supposes many changes; and we do not know what causes have successively

---

* As to these see Foster, pp. 202-207. Coleridge probably had his attention called to the whole subject by a reprint of Foster's and Gally's essays, published in 1820.

APPENDIX

produced them; we do not even know whether the need of harmony which so rapidly perfected the language acted independently on the versification, or whether the imitation of any foreign poetry exercised also an influence on its developments. That even its nature is not entirely known to us is proved by the differing explanations of scholars; and it may be added that the insufficiency of the data prevents our fully understanding it. With the Greeks, as with all peoples in the early ages of their history, music was inseparable from poetry; declamation was a chant, which for a long time made the main difference between verse and prose; and when the profession of the poet and that of the musician were separated, they were still called by the same name. A knowledge of the music is thus necessary to the thorough comprehension of the ancient versification; and the documents which time has spared us are too few, and seem too contradictory, to let us draw any conclusions. If, like music, poetry finally had a separate existence and developments peculiar to itself, the power of custom would still be apt to preserve the ancient declamation in its most essential points, and the metric doubtless would not wholly clear itself of the consequences of its origin. It was no less closely connected with dancing. On that it was, perhaps, even more dependent; several of its technical expressions were derived thence, and it was describable by the same name. The rhythm of the dance then was not unconnected with the developments of versification, and we are quite ignorant concerning it.*

Further, he concludes that

When words had not syllables enough to strike the ear strongly, the Greeks and Latins usually lengthened the last. More often, however, quantity seems to go by no principle whatever; we can only explain it by the necessities of the rhythm, or the convenience of the poet.† Causes so diverse led to so many anomalies that writers of the most undoubted erudition have found in prosody no other reason than a usage, which was not

---

* *Essai* cited, pp. 2-6. In support of his statements, M. Du Méril gives an abundance of references. Among others he points to the choruses of Aristophanes and the popular songs in Athenæus, BB. vii. and viii., as perhaps giving some clue to an early popular versification. He suggests also a possibility of Egyptian and Persian influences (Herod. ii. 79; Plato, *Laws*, ii.; Plutarch, *Is. et Os.* 24); and points to the Egyptian representation (Wilkinson, ch. vi.) of a singer who beats his measure, with an instrumentalist accompanying him. Of the poets and singers he notes that both were called *sophistae* (Æschylus *ap.* Athen. l. xiv.); and he points out that among the dances the prosodia, the dithyrambs, and the parthenias exacted dancing (Athen. xiv.; Aristot. *Poet.* iv.). For the view that the term "foot" came from the dance, he refers to Aristotle, *De Anima*, and Suidas, remarking that certain feet—the pyrrhic, the trochee, the chorea, the anapæst, and the iambus—certainly were named from dances. Both dancing and poetry, he notes, were called *emmeleia*.

† P. 78.

341

APPENDIX

even universal, and did not always affect pronunciation. Vainly do we seek any systematic regularity.*

And he acutely reasons that the absolute ambiguity of the words *arsis* and *thesis* came of the double connection of poetry with music and the dance.' But while thus relegating the subject to uncertainty, M. Du Méril here and there attempts constructive solutions, which naturally clash. In one note † he observes that "the Greeks seem even to have sought to put in opposition the accent of the verse and that of the words." Elsewhere,‡ while arguing that originally all Greek rhythms were fixed by music, he claims that "all the syllables had thus a musical value which conformed to the natural tendencies of the pronunciation." And yet again he refers§ to a passage in the 14th Book of Athenæus as proving that "the verses of the Homerids have not come down to us as they composed them." Seeing that he had also noticed the fatal confusion set up by the counter-senses of *arsis* and *thesis*, it might have been supposed that he would have seen the possibility that the accent marks may at times *reverse* the syllable values, an acute standing for short, and a grave for long. But this possibility is not recognised even in the latest and ablest treatise on the subject, the *Essai comparatif sur l'origine et l'histoire des rhythmes* of M. Maximilien Kawczynski (1892). This learned and ingenious work, which goes over the old ground of Vossius and Foster without reference to their theses, and which has probably profited by the earlier research of M. Du Méril, arrives at the old conclusion that the Greek accent marks had really a musical signification. Noting that Bentley, Ritschl, Huemer and others, argue that the ancients sought to make the metrical ictus coincide with the natural accent, and that Lucian Müller argued (as we have seen M. Du Méril did) that they sought on the contrary not to let them coincide, M. Kawczynski asks "How reconcile opinions so contrary? In rejecting both." ‖ Like M. Du Méril ¶ he rejects ** the German *a priori* method of solving the problem, pronouncing that Bentley and Hermann alike resorted to *a priori* sophisms for lack of knowledge of the bases of ancient rhythm. His positive conclusions may be best understood by the line of primitive music to which he sets the first line of the *Iliad*:

* Pp. 98-99.   † P. 38, *n*. 2.   ‡ P. 76.   § P. 43, *n*. 3.
‖ *Essai* cited, p. 57.   ¶ As cited, pp. 38-39, *note*.   ** P. 58.

APPENDIX

Μῆ - νιν ἄ - ει - δε θε - ὰ Πη - ληϊ - ὰ - δε - ω 'Α-χι - λῆ - ος

"It was very much thus," says M. Kawczynski,* "that the *aedes* sang the wrath of Achilles, obliged as they were, willy nilly, by the rhythm, to change the συνεχής (continuous) prosody for a prosody ἐκ διαστημάτων" (determined by intervals). I confess to a difficulty in grasping M. Kawczynski's theory of the process of transition ; and must content myself with citing his important suggestion that a new upset of the system was effected by the development of the lyre :

> As long as the Greek musical system was contained in the limits of a tetrachord, the melody had need accord with the accents ; but when it developed the greater system . . . . the melodies began to pass beyond their original limit, and no longer accorded with the accents, which were finally disregarded.†

It is to be feared that M. Kawczynski's able argumentation on the Greek musical system, by way of settling the problem of prosody, will seem to some readers a case of explaining *obscurus per obscurior;* and it remains finally puzzling how he can be sure, with M. Du Méril, that the musical system of the Greeks "derives from the system of their accentuations."‡ But it seems reasonable to conclude with him § that

> The ancient accents were of an essentially melodic character ; which disposes at once of all the contradictions in which modern philology has lost itself. The ancients sought neither to make the accents coincide with the ictus, as some would have it, nor to avoid that coincidence, as others argue. The accents had no connection with either the ictus or the rhythm.

It is interesting to set beside this the line of mediæval intonations to which Scaliger long ago ‖ set the first line of the Æneid :

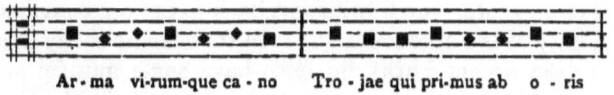

Ar - ma vi-rum-que ca - no   Tro - jae qui pri-mus ab o - ris

* As cited, p. 66.   † P. 71.   ‡ P. 73.   § P. 72.
‖ Cited by Foster, p. 297.

343

APPENDIX

This combination of highs and lows with longs and shorts Foster held to coincide with the directions for scansion given by Bentley in his tract *de metris Terentianis*, where the opening lines of the Æneid are marked

> Árma virúmque cáno Trójae qui prímus ab óris
> Itáliam fáto prófugus, Lavínaque vénit
> Líttora ; múltum ílle et térris jactátus et álto
> Vi súperum sáevae mémorem Junónis ob íram ;

with the comment :

> He that reads those verses properly and tunefully will pronounce them according to those accentual marks; not as schoolboys scanning them, and placing the accents at the beginning of each foot, as,
>
> Italiám fató profugús, La—
>
> but according to the rhythm of the whole verse; in which not one word has the accent on the last syllable except *virúm*, and that properly on account of the enclitic *que*.

Foster points out that *Lavinaque* should be accented on the *a* for the same reason, but is otherwise quite satisfied that Bentley and Scaliger mean the same thing ; though Scaliger evidently makes long the notes which Bentley says the schoolboys accent, and it is hardly to be supposed that Bentley meant that the schoolboys *raised their tone* at the beginning of each foot. Schoolboys, like other people, stress syllables in a special degree to mark scansion, and they are more likely to lower than to raise their tone on the stressed syllables, even though it be their habit to make stress coincide with raised tone in ordinary speaking and reading. As for Bentley's marking, if it merely means a rule for raising and lowering the voice it is a vain device ; and if it is meant as a rule for stressing, I at least cannot scan by it. In M. Kawczynski's musical marking of the first line of the Iliad, again, I find a workable scansion (setting aside the pitch of the notes and taking longs for stresses); but that scansion makes a long syllable of a grave accent and a short of an acute, which brings us back to the old conviction of the futility of the accent marks. All that can be safely inferred is that the accent marks did once have some musical significance.* As M. Kawczynski remarks, they were still in use for

---

* This was partly recognised by Vossius and Henninius, who surmised that the accents were borrowed by the grammarians from the musicians.— Foster, p. 179.

APPENDIX

musical notation in the middle ages. " M. de Caussemaker shows us this as regards mediæval Latin, in which the signs of the acute, grave and circumflex accents were employed as fundamental *neumes*. Of these three signs combined together are composed all the other *neumes*.' " *

III

In fine, on every line of research we are led to admit that Poe was perfectly justified in pronouncing the classic tradition, as given in the universities, a hopeless medley of contradictions and unintelligible dogmas. A dozen discussions before and since his time bear him out. Every now and then a wind of inquiry shakes the conventions of the schools, and reveals nescience, dissidence, chaos, where use and wont had seemed to rest on intelligent agreement. Eminent philologists offer elucidations, and are forthwith denounced for heresy. Niebuhr, dealing with the "*horridus numerus Saturnius,*" falls foul of the ancient grammarians.

Atilius Fortunatianus and others among them, being ignorant of its real nature, confined their remarks to a couple of lines that were extant, especially to the following :

Malum dabunt Metelli Naevio poëtae,

n which according to the opinion of the time a hypercatalectic senarius appears. Terentianus Maurus, who belongs to the end of the third century, speaks of it in treating of the Anacreontic verse, because the first part of the Saturnian resembles it. But the true Saturnian verse is quite different. . . . It is capable of a variety of forms, and is quite independent of Greek metres. The Latin expression for rhythm, which was not applied to Greek metres till a later time, is *numeri*. The Greek metre is based upon music and time, but the Romans actually *counted* syllables and *rarely if at all measured them;* a *certain number of syllables* was necessary to constitute rhythm. Our [German] forefathers, too, had no idea of long or short syllables after the Greek fashion ; in the old hymns of the Latin Church likewise short syllables are used as long, and *vice versa*. Plautus and Terence in their iambic and trochaic verses in reality observe the rhythm only and not the time. The same is the case with all Northern nations.†

---

* Caussemaker, *L'Art Harmonique aux XIIe et XIIIe Siècles*, p. 160, planche 37, cited by Kawczynski, pp. 72, 73.

† *Lectures on the History of Rome*, 3rd Eng. ed., pp. 64-5. Who will may go into the Saturnian controversy in Ramsay (*Manual of Latin Prosody*, 5th ed., App. x.). Niebuhr was right as to the verse not being on a Greek metre.

APPENDIX

It is not surprising to learn from an editorial note that another German scholar, Professor Schneidewin, "severely criticised Niebuhr's expressions respecting the Saturnian verse;" for his remarks on Roman verse in general are ostensibly in flat contradiction of the common scholastic doctrine. To me they are barely intelligible; but it will not do to reject them on the mere ground of common consent. Within the sphere of the (theoretic) common consent there is really as much practical contradiction as between Niebuhr and the schools; and successive discussions among English scholars have left the entire subject in blank uncertainty.

A famous modern instance is the discussion which arose out of Mr. Arnold's *Lectures on Translating Homer*. The lecturer, differing from Heyne and Liddell and Scott as to an accent in Homer, took occasion to remark* that "if we disregard quantity too much in constructing English hexameters, we also disregard accent too much in reading Greek hexameters. We read every Greek dactyl so as to make a pure dactyl of it; but to a Greek the accent must have hindered many dactyls from sounding as pure dactyls." On this Mr. Spedding, moved by Mr. Arnold's arguments and experiments to write a clever paper on *English Hexameters*,† not only pulled to pieces English hexameters in general and Mr. Arnold's in particular, but ventured on certain generalisations concerning the hexameter of antiquity. In logic the reviewer had every way the advantage of the lecturer, with whom that was never a strong point; but the reviewer was in turn challenged on his prosody. He had declared that "verses in which the accent falls on every one of the six long syllables (that is, on the first syllable of every foot) are rare even in Homer;" whereupon Mr. Munro, the Bentley of his generation, announced that "such verses, instead of being rare, are among the very commonest types of Homeric rhythm,"‡ and that he had counted sixteen or seventeen of them between verses 78 and 178 of the *Iliad*. "I suppose," comments Mr. Spedding on this later, "he does not read Homer as I was taught to do;" which seems highly probable.

* *On Translating Homer*, p. 95.
† Reprinted in his *Reviews and Discussions*.
‡ Paper on the Inscription at Cirta, Camb. Philos. Soc., Feb. 13, 1860, cited by Spedding, *Reviews and Discussions*, p. 337.

APPENDIX

But the matter did not end here. Mr. Spedding, making some very classic-sounding hexameters of his own, said something about accent and quantity; whereon, as Mr. Spedding records for us, Mr. Munro further dissented. "'The old Greeks and Romans (he [Munro] tells us, p. 30) had an instinctive feeling for and knowledge of *quantity*, upon which instinct depended the whole force and meaning of their rhythmical measured verse.' But in the course of the third century 'quantity perished'—perished so completely from the earth that 'it does not exist even potentially in any modern language.' No modern ear can recognise it; we know it 'only by the rules of prosody.' Consequently ' our English reading of Homer and Virgil has *in itself* no meaning.'" On the first head Mr. Spedding confesses that he does not know on what evidence Mr. Munro's dictum as to the loss of quantity is founded, and can therefore offer no criticism; a course which I in the present connection may well follow;* but as against the proposition that quantity "does not exist even potentially in any modern language," I am struck by the statement of that excellent linguist the late Viscount Strangford † that " Eastern [*i.e.*, Persian or Turkish], like classical metre, is quantitative, not accentual" at the present moment. I am struck also by the statement of Professor Newman that many scholars have

no vivid *feeling* of the difference between Accent and Quantity; and this is the less wonderful, since so very few persons have ever actually *heard* quantitative verse. I have; by listening to Hungarian poems, read to me by my friend Mr. Francis Pulszky, a native Magyar. He had not finished a single page before I complained gravely of the monotony. He replied : " So do *we* complain of it"; and then showed me, by turning the pages,

---

* See, however, the explanation given by M. Charles Defodon, in his article on *Prosodie* in the *Dictionnaire de Pédagogie*. M. Defodon, embodying in part Foster's view, lays it down that Latin verse had, apart from longs and shorts, an *accent tonique* consisting in a raised pitch on certain syllables independently of their quantity; that there arose thus "a sort of struggle between the accentuated and the metrical (*sic*) syllable;" and that in the ages of decadence the "exclusive predominance of the *accent tonique*" obliterated the old " distinction between longs and shorts which had constituted quantity." I confess I cannot follow M. Defodon's thesis, which seems to me to confuse *accent tonique*, so called, with normal stress. M. Defodon ends by saying, with Munro, that the cadence of the ancient verse cannot be caught by our ears.

† *Selected Writings of Viscount Strangford*, 1869, i. 269.

APPENDIX

that the poet cut the knot which he could not untie, by frequent changes of his metre. Whether it was a change of mere length, as from Iambic senarian to Iambic dimeter, or implied a fundamental change of tune, as in music from *canon* to *minuet* time, I cannot say. But to my ear, nothing but a tune can ever save a quantitative metre from hideous monotony.*

So that there would seem to be modern quantitative verse in the strictest technical sense, in those nations whose literature is least modern. When scholarly authority is thus nonplussed, is it too madly presumptuous an adventure of common sense to suggest that quantitative scansion may after all have been, in classic as in Eastern verse, the only partially determinate natural accentuation succeeding on the primitive practice of chanting;† and that Horace's protest against the leniency of his countrymen to the lax metres of his poetic predecessors gives a clue to this transition? Not every amateur, says Horace, can detect ill-modulated verses; and to Roman poets is given an unworthy licence. Past generations have praised alike the numbers and the point of Plautus—very tolerantly, not to say foolishly, in the poet's opinion. He, protesting, will not take the licence he might, but will beat out his rhythms *digitis et aure*, regardful of the Greeks. Is it extravagant to say that this points to a transitional structure of verse reaching towards that precision of accent which seems to have been attained "in the third century;" and that even Horace's verse would be read in his day with a measure of accent, though with a certain artificiality of syllabification, the result not of any

---

* *Homeric Translation in Theory and Practice*, 1861, p. 14.

† Professor Newman himself points to this solution. "No accentual metre can reproduce the sound, rhythm, 'movement,' of a quantitative metre, made primarily for musical time and for singing."—Preface to his translation of *Iliad*, 2nd ed., p. viii. *Cf.* preface to his translation of *Horace*, p. ix. He there declares that it is absurd to attempt to translate in the original metres, that being impossible. Professor Ellis, on the other hand, claims to have translated Catullus in the original metres. But the very fact that Professor Newman confesses himself unable to reproduce the quantitative scansion after hearing it, leaves his negative verdict somewhat weak. M. Du Méril (as cited, p. 9) offers a simpler explanation than that of M. Defodon, saying merely that the ancients had no difficulty about the value of longs and shorts, which were settled by the recurrence of words in different verses; and that this valuation became impossible when versification came to be based on *real* pronunciation. But this ignores the antecedent influence of chanting, elsewhere admitted by M. Du Méril.

‡ *De Arte Poetica*, 263-4. Note the whole passage, 251-274.

APPENDIX

occult sense of quantity but of primitive usages of chanting declamation?*

On this let us again hear the scholarly opinion of Professor Newman. He declares that Mr. Arnold's way of reading Homer

begins by wilfully pronouncing Greek falsely, according to the laws of *Latin* accent,† and artificially assimilating the Homeric to the Virgilian line. Virgil has compromised between the *ictus metricus* and the prose accent, by exacting that the two coincide in the two last feet and generally forbidding it in the second and third foot. What is called the "feminine cæsura" gives (in the Latin language) coincidence on the third foot. Our extreme familiarity with these laws of compromise enables us to anticipate recurring sounds, and satisfies our ear. But the Greek prose accent, by reason of oxytons and paroxytons, and accent on the antepenultima in spite of a long penultima, totally resists all such compromise; and proves that particular form of melody which our scholars enjoy in Homer, to be an unhistoric imitation of Virgil.‡

Homer apart, then, the versification of Virgil—and why then not that of Horace?—*was* a transitional species, passing from primitive and quantitative to accentual. On such a view, Horace and Virgil (not to speak of Homer) could not well have the subtle continuity which belongs to modern verse as to modern music; and this would doubtless sound blasphemy to the schools, where the musical perfection of classic verse is a dogma held irrespectively of agreement as to how the verse should be read. "Though every classical scholar readily admits the superiority of Latin versification over that of modern languages," wrote Dr. Nuttall sixty years ago,§ "still there is no branch of education less profitably cultivated or less understood. . . . . Unfortunately the *practice* of modern teachers and professors is contrary to their *theory*." Similarly Mr.

---

* Compare Coleridge: " The distinction between accent and quantity is clear, and was, no doubt, observed by the ancients in the recitation of verse. But I believe such recitation to have been always an artificial thing, and that the common conversation was regulated entirely by accent."—*Table Talk*, August 23, 1833. See the whole passage and the editor's note in comment.

† On this obscure point compare Niebuhr, as cited above, with Ramsay, who endorses the general view that the Romans adopted the elaborated Greek system (*Manual*, as cited, p. 309). But see also Foster, as cited, chapters viii. and x.

‡ *Homeric Translation*, p. 15. § Ed. of Juvenal, 1836, p. xxvi.

APPENDIX

Munro alluded to a "wondrous harmony we feel" in the verse whose rhythmic principle we cannot grasp, a suggestion which in Mr. Spedding's quiet analysis gets to look little like nonsense. The acute and versatile Dr. Latham, in his turn, ceases to be clear when he takes up this theme. "Professional grammarians," he writes,* "men who deal with the purely philological questions of metre and syllabification, with few exceptions confound accent and quantity." For himself, he goes on to explain that "in English Latin there is in practice no such thing as quantities, or rather English quantities are not Latin quantities," inasmuch as "in Latin the length of the syllable is determined by the length of the vowels and consonants combined." But there is no physiological or psychological explanation, no attempt to explain the implied statement that in English the quantities are vocalic merely.

Professor Newman, as usual, speaks emphatically:

> Our English pronunciation even of Virgil so often ruins Virgil's own *quantities*, that there is something either of delusion or of pedantry in our scholars' self-complacency in the rhythm which they elicit.†

But Professor Newman speaks even more plainly than that on the subject of ancient metres, in a passage which ought to be brought to common knowledge:

> I have the conviction, though I will not undertake to impart it to another, that if the living Homer could sing his lines to us, they would at first move in us the same pleasing interest as an elegant and simple melody from an African of the Gold Coast; but that, after hearing twenty lines, we should complain of meagreness, sameness, *and loss of moral expression*: and should judge the style to be *as* inferior to our own oratorical metres as the music of Pindar to our third-rate modern music. But if the poet, at our request, instead of singing the verses, read or spoke them, then from the loss of well-marked time and the ascendency reassumed by the prose accent, we should be as helplessly unable to *hear* any metre in them, as are the modern Greeks.‡

This from (*pace* the *manes* of Mr. Arnold) the ablest modern translator of Homer. And finally even Mr. Munro, despite his deliverances as to quantity, and his denial that the ancients had any accent such as ours, confesses that "neither his ear nor his reason recognises any real distinction of quantity, except that which is produced by accentuated and unaccentuated

---

* *Opuscula*, 1860, p. 75. † *Homeric Translation*, p. 16.
‡ *Homeric Translation*, p. 14.

APPENDIX

syllables," so that ear and reason alike leave us with a "meaningless" scansion of the classic hexameter. That was the view tranquilly reposed in at last by Mr. Spedding, who genially confessed to having just discovered that all his life he had been reading three favourite lines of Virgil with five false quantities! He was willing to allow that "we know as little about Virgil's pronunciation" in one "particular as in others—that we know, in fact, nothing whatever about it."* Alike with the "false" quantities and the "true," Mr. Spedding still found his Virgil very delightful. Doubtless; but such phenomena promise ill for any settlement of classic rhythm.

It will be observed that the majority of our scholars thus far have not even taken note of the problem of musical complications, though that had been repeatedly pointed to. Inconsistencies apart, Coleridge had pointed to the solution of the mystery of accent and quantity, as others had done before him, and as Professor Newman and M. Kawczynski have done since; but as the later discussions show, the clue went for nothing with the schools, which went on as before, either hammering out the crude classic rhythms by rule of thumb or reading with no sense of rhythm at all, but all the while asserting that there is no verse-melody like that of the classics. The stiff rhythms of Horace are supposed to exemplify the same laws as the living lilts of Catullus, who proceeded on an original genius for rhythm; and the measure of Virgil is assimilated by brute force, as Professor Newman indicates, to that of Homer. Finally, the superstition of quantity holds its ground like a creed; and those who, like Walker and Munro, admit that they can only conceive of quantity in terms of accent=stress, go on alleging what Foster and Walker scouted—a lost and mysterious power of rhythmic discrimination among the nations which handled verse rhythm in its earliest developments. The general outcome is that classic verse is read with little real enjoyment by the few who do read it, and is made a mere nightmare for most of the youth to whom it is taught.

Everywhere we have the same confession; sometimes from sceptics, sometimes from teachers confident that they can put

---

* *Reviews and Discussions*, p. 338. Compare, on this question generally, the opinion of Clough on the classic hexameter, *Works*, i. 397. (Cited in this volume, p. 311.)

APPENDIX

matters right. M. Manoury, Chanoine of Séez, a good Grecian, writes that

> Les études Grecques ont fait d'heureux progrès en France depuis une soixantaine d'années. La langue Grecque n'a pas été seulement enseignée dans tous les collèges de l'État et du clergé, mais on a vu briller, dans l'Université et dans l'Église, des hellenistes d'un mérite incontestable. Et pourtant, chose singulière, plusieurs de ces savants qui lisaient et admiraient Homère ne savaient pas scander les vers d'Homère ! *

M. Manoury thinks he can put matters right; and so does his Latinist colleague, M. Lejard, who notes as regards Latin that

> Des critiques d'ailleurs estimables avaient enseigné de vive voix et imprimé dans leurs ouvrages que les incorrections de métrique, dans Virgile, se comptaient par centaines. D'autres avaient expliqué, par des raisons que nous ne saurions admettre, ce qu'ils appelaient les irrégularités de sa versification. Cependant il est indubitable, disons-nous, que les vers les plus irréguliers en apparence, chez le grand poète latin, suivent des règles fixes empruntées à Homère. Nous avons donné la clef de ces difficultés, et désormais nos jeunes amis des Muses n'ont plus trouvé un seul vers dans Virgile, Horace, Ovide, Lucain, Juvénal, &c., dont ils ne pussent aisément se rendre compte.†

I will not attempt to discuss the explanations of M. Lejard, beyond saying that on the face of them they only carry back the trouble to Homer, and that in practice they have the effect of reducing verse to "rules" which seem to negate versification as ordinarily conceived. He leaves us diffident, as he found us.

And the best of our own professional prosodists, by their confident affirmation of things unintelligible, only deepen our distrust. The learning and the scholarly judgment of Ramsay are, I believe, alike undisputed; and yet it is impossible to study his Latin Prosody without feeling that it reaches no scientific principle. It sets out, as needs must, with mere rules for practice, resting on no generalisation, syllable-values being treated in detail before we are told anything of verse; and the treatment of "Accent, Quantity, Emphasis, Metre, Rhythm, Metrical Ictus, Arsis, Thesis," is relegated to an appendix, which begins with the confession: "It is not our intention to enter into any lengthened discussion with regard to these

---

* *Prosodie Grecque*, 1883, p. 27.
† *Nouveau traité de prosodie latine*, 1884, préface.

APPENDIX

topics, upon which many volumes have been written to little purpose."*

They cannot well be to less purpose than the doctrines here set forth by Professor Ramsay. Following Foster, without recognising that, despite Foster, English usage has made "accent" in verse mean stress, he bluntly defines it as variation in pitch or note; and goes on to observe that "much confusion has arisen from the circumstance that in English long quantity is always or almost always accompanied by an elevation of pitch." Now, what we all now mean by accent in scansion† is not at all a pitch but *stress*, and it is the coincidence of stress and real quantity that sets up the insoluble problem of the classicists, with their factitious discrimination between vowel sounds of equal stress, as in *fat* and *fate*. Stress, as we have seen, may as well go with lowered or unchanged as with raised pitch. The confusion is twice confounded when Ramsay goes on to declare that "*Emphasis* is perfectly distinct both from *Accent* and *Quantity*, and signifies the comparative energy or fulness of the voice in pronouncing *different syllables*..... Emphasis is *not* confined to single syllables, but may be employed in the enunciation of words, or sentences, or paragraphs." Here we have emphasis first defined in the sense of syllable-stress, which is what quantity resolves itself into in reading; and then defined as general meaning-stress, a totally different thing. Nor is this all. We are further told that "*different* from any of these is the *Metrical Accent* or *Ictus Metricus*, the name given by grammarians to the stress which must be laid upon particular syllables in repeating verse, in order that the rhythm of the measure may be made perceptible to the ear." This is the fourth bogus conception made out of the one fact of syllable-stress, which is all that we can find beneath. A metrical accent there certainly is, but it is not

---

* *Manual of Latin Prosody*, 5th ed. p. 268.

† Ramsay was specially misled by the fact that when we speak of, say, "a Scotch accent" we mean a number of details of intonation and pronunciation, of which voice inflection is one. But this is not the "accent" of verse or of syllables separately. Foster expressly pointed out that the word accent was used by one writer " in four very wide and different senses, expressing sometimes elevation, sometimes prolongation of sound, sometimes a stress of voice compounded of the other two, and sometimes the artificial accentual mark."—Introd. p. xiii.

APPENDIX

"different from" syllable-stress, being simply a selection of the main syllable-stresses in a line when it is not the whole series of these. But confusion becomes chaos when we yet further learn that the ictus falls either on the first or on the second syllable of a *spondee* according as the verse is trochaic or iambic. Who shall utter to us the spondees of this theory? The word has no other meaning than "(a foot of) two syllables of equal stress," as "good God." We are hard pressed to find spondees in English on the quantitative definition; but on the ictus theory we may find plenty. They would merely be awkward trochees or iambs.

It is with something like gratitude that we find the Professor, instead of alleging fresh significances for *arsis* and *thesis*, contenting himself with saying that the syllables on which *ictus* falls are in *arsis*, and the others in *thesis*. Thus at least *ictus* is admittedly *arsis* for us to-day, whatever *arsis* may have meant for the ancients of different periods; though the Professor will not admit that *thesis* is short quantity. He finally bequeaths to English prosody a system of accent marks which combines in placid confusion the two notations of pitch and stress, by marking thus the words

"$\bar{lee}bert\acute{y}\ of\ \bar{cons}c\hat{i}ence$"

to represent them as "uttered by a lowland Scotchman." What he meant was that, as Foster had pointed out,* a lowland Scotchman of the past, while scanning just as an Englishman does, tended to raise his voice on the final syllables of words. But even this tendency is no longer general—if it ever were—among lowland Scotchmen, even in their native land;† so that the values of accentual marks have been confused in a standard Prosody to no better purpose than that of commemorating one varying provincial intonation.

IV

It was in the face of this unending discussion that Poe, convinced of the hopelessness of resort to academic tradition,

* As cited. p. 69.
† The prevailing voice inflection in Glasgow, for instance (a bad result of the blend of the Scots and Gaelic intonations in a busy community), would be the exact reverse of that noted by Ramsay. And Glasgow is the largest Scotch city.

APPENDIX

proposed to construct a metrical system on purely rational grounds. As it happens, he is not the only modern metrist who has ventured to overrule traditional prosody at a pinch altogether. M. Lurin, an *avocat* of Lyons, published in 1854, after but independently of Poe, a scheme of rhythm which seems to have passed out of notice.* Like so many other scholars, M. Lurin confessed the deadlock in practice.

> Tous les faits nécessaires à l'intelligence de cette poésie ont été réunies, et cependant une obscurité profonde reste encore étendue sur elle. Pourquoi, d'ordinaire, ceux qui scandent ces metres n'en comprennent-ils pas le rhythme ? pourquoi ne les sentent-ils pas, même dans les vers composés par eux ? On peut avouer plusieurs raisons de cette singulière anomalie : Les principes des anciens sur le rhythme ne nous sont point parvenues ; des notions pratiques, seules, nous ont été transmises, et, comme telles, elles ne sont ni définies ni classées.

And he resorted to drastic measures, as did Poe.

> Les auteurs venus avant nous, et qui nous ont guidé pas à pas dans cette carrière, out reproduit les divisions données par les grammairiens latins : nous les avons discutées et réformées lorsqu'elles étaient contraire à des principes qui sont de tous les temps parcequ'ils dérivent de l'organisation même de l'homme.

But the method of M. Lurin does not seem to have influenced the text-books ; and neither, of course, has Poe's. It is perhaps only as apart from the question of classic prosody that it is worth while to discuss it now.

To my mind, the *Rationale of Verse* is a brilliant essay towards the simplification and logicalisation of a prosodical method which is essentially incapable of reduction to scientific bases ; and in that sense its failure is its success.† That is to say, we

---

* *Méthode pour restituer à la poésie Latine sa veritable harmonie.*

† The late Sidney Lanier, in his very able *Science of English Verse* (1880), declares that Poe's essay is " permeated by a fundamental mistake, quite fatal to the usefulness of even the shrewd detached glimpses occurring here and there "—the mistake, " namely, that the accent makes every syllable *long*—a conception wholly unaccountable to the musician, and so absurd as to render a large proportion of existent music and verse theoretically impossible." The value of Mr. Lanier's verdict on this one point may be gathered from the fact that (p. 123) he actually scans the triplets of Tennyson's

Half a league, half a league, half a league onward

APPENDIX

have here a close and lucid argument, which, by doing nearly all that can be done to reorganise the analysis of verse into "feet" on the old plan, proves once for all that the primitive expedient of the "foot" is impotent to solve the psychological problem which verse presents. Whether or not we agree with Poe in rejecting the old scansions of Horace, we can all see that "feet" are purely arbitrary divisions of the complex rhythms of modern verse, and leave half of even the rhythmic phenomena uncodified. Poe's bold undertaking to "scan correctly any of the Horatian rhythms, or any true rhythm that human ingenuity can conceive," while "employing from the numerous '*ancient*' feet the spondee, the trochee, the iambus, the anapæst, the dactyl, and the cæsura, alone"—this is but a short cut to the proof that neither these nor the other "feet" can really analyse verse as we read it to-day. That he, reputed a fine reader, should fail to see this, is puzzling to the extent of suggesting that there is extreme presumption in thus dismissing his argument. But, feeling as I do the pellucid clearness and almost flawless unity of the *Rationale* as a composition—qualities which are the special stamp of Poe's literary work—I cannot but think that he has acquired his confidence in his conclusions at the cost of ignoring the deeper issues. He has

as a series of *absolutely equal short syllables*, and that he was capable (p. 174) of scanning thus the great line in Emerson's *Brahma* :

When mē | thĕy fly | Ĭ am | the wīngs—

a crudely bad reading, in a case where his own principle of "sounds and silences" (treated of below) should have led him to the true rhythm, which is:

When mĕ they fly ˇ Ĭ am the wīngs.

In the same way he declares (p. 71) that in the line

Rhythmical roundelays wavering downward

all the syllables are equally long, though four are stressed ; but that if we alter "rhythmical" to "rhythmic," the first syllable at once becomes longer than before. It obviously *does not*. What happens is simply a brief pause in the place of the dropped syllable "al." I can only conclude that Mr. Lanier's devotion to musical practice led him often to hear verse with the musical instead of the inward ear, and so to sacrifice sense to sound. His attack on Poe is a complete fiasco, which connects with the worst error in his own book. Poe's identification of stress with length is perfectly sound ; and it was the vitiation of Mr. Lanier's ear by analogies drawn from music that led him to dispute it.

APPENDIX

assumed that all verse gives, even to an alien, the key to its proper pronunciation; whereas it is quite certain that we may mispronounce foreign verse while making it yield a consistent rhythm.* He has disposed of some of the confusions of his predecessors by overlooking some of the problems which confused them. As he says, and as we have seen, "there is perhaps no topic in polite literature which has been more pertinaciously discussed, and there is certainly not one about which so much inaccuracy, confusion, misconception, misrepresentation, mystification, and downright ignorance on all sides,† can be fairly said to exist;" and, that being so, it is too much to suppose that a mere return to the simpler "feet" will settle everything. In his own critique on Longfellow's ballads we have the pregnant deliverance: "In short, the ancients were content to read *as they scanned*, or nearly so. It may be safely prophesied that we shall never do this: and thus we shall never admit English hexameters." Very true and sound; but how, on that view, can we proceed to chop our verse into old scansions?

We must distinguish between Poe's sound conception of the nature of rhythm, and his view that all rhythm resolves itself into feet of equal values. The two are equally approved of by

---

* See, for instance, Mr. Hamerton's account of the results got by a studious Frenchman from the verse of Tennyson (*Human Intercourse*, p. 89). Many of us have similarly found that our *à priori* reading of French alexandrines would not square with French declamation of them. It is thus difficult to gainsay Mr. Hamerton when he insists (p. 90), that "we are all of us disqualified, by our profound ignorance of the pronunciation of the ancient Romans, for any competent criticism of their verse."

† As one proof that Poe did not exaggerate, take the fact that in such a standard English compilation as Brande and Cox's *Dictionary of Science, Literature and Art*, we have the statement, under the article *Metre*, that "a line is said to be *acatalectic* when the last syllable of the last foot is wanting"; whereas that is the definition of *catalectic*, an *acatalectic* line being one with its full complement of syllables. In an earlier compilation, *Brande's Dictionary*, the same blunder is found, and a line with a superfluous syllable is there said to be "hypercataleptic." *Catalectic* is misapplied, too, by Professor Jenkin, following Mr. Goold Brown. (*Papers*, i. 150.) If Poe had done such things, there would be some excuse for charging him with ignorance of his subject. But indeed the scientific nullity of the terms thus gravely presented as throwing light on the subject of metre, is one of the strongest proofs of the futility of what passes for verse analysis in the schools.

APPENDIX

Dr. Sylvester in his vivacious volume on *The Laws of Verse:*

I am satisfied that .... Edgar Poe is perfectly right in the principles laid down by him in his *Rationale of Versification*, that the substratum of measure is time; that an accented syllable is a long syllable, and that an unaccented syllable is a short one of varying degrees of duration; *and that feet in modern metre are of equal length.* Professor Newman is of an opposite opinion, and goes the length of saying that *accent* is so far from lengthening that it even tends to *shorten* syllables, instancing the first syllable in "female" as shortened by the accent, and of course implying that it is shorter in fémale than it would be in femále; to argue against such an assertion (which, I think, no one who is not time-deaf will be found to concur with) would be like reasoning upon colours with one who is colour-blind.*

We need not stay to discuss the blunder of Professor Newman, who for this once has certainly tripped. But we must pause over the categorical assertion that "feet in modern metre are of equal length." This proposition, which is inconsistent with Dr. Sylvester's own previous remarks on syllable-groupings,† assumes that feet are real segments, organic divisions, of a line; and that there are no feet save those which Poe allows— no bacchius ($\smile - -$), no cretic ($- \smile -$), no amphibrach ($\smile - \smile$), no antibacchius ($- - \smile$), and no molossus ($- - -$) or tribrach ($\smile \smile \smile$), to name no others of the old list. Now, it happens that the asserted equality even of the feet accepted by Poe and Sylvester breaks down at the very outset, seeing that in the terms of the case a spondee is longer than either an iambus or a trochee, while the "cæsura" of Poe is shorter than these. But we may waive this checkmate and still show that Dr. Sylvester is wrong. Unless we merely beg the question as to the length of feet by refusing to recognise any that are longer than the spondee, it will be found impossible to adhere in practice to this canon. If we measure our feet by natural pauses or stresses, we must at times recognise others. Take Tennyson's line

* *The Laws of Verse*, 1870, pp. 64–5.

† "No one seems to have drawn special attention to the distinct character and aspect attaching to every different form of syllable-groupings in a ine. The working out of this theory belongs to the subject of *rests*, there being an incalculably small but still perfectly sensible interruption of breathing between every two *groups of syllables*" (p. 36). These groups of syllables cannot be pretended to be equal feet.

APPENDIX

>Oh art thou | sighing for | Lebanon

The only natural divisions are those I have marked; and the third foot here is not a dactyl like the others, but a cretic. And in the next line :

>In the long breeze that streams to thy delicious East

we may just as fairly make the divisions thus :

>In the | long breeze | that streams | to thy | deli | cious East,

or thus :

>In the long breeze | that streams | to thy delicious East

as in any other way. Poe, I suppose, would divide "Lebanon" into a trochee and a cæsura, and would divide the second line thus :

>In the long | breeze | that streams | to thy | deli | cious East,

calling "breeze" a cæsura. But the cæsura and the iambus "deli" cannot be pretended to be as long as the opening anapæst. I maintain that Dr. Sylvester, if he were to pronounce "deli-" as long a foot as "that streams" or "-cious East" or "In the long," would lay himself open to some such vivacity of denunciation as he has allowed himself towards Professor Newman; and though some of his verdicts as to verbal beauty are startling, I can hardly think he would venture to dispute that the line as a whole is rhythmically beautiful. So with the fine line in Browning's version of the *Agamemnon*:

>Through the delicately pompous curtains that pavilion well :

it may be divided mechanically into trochees which disguise its rhythm, or into syllabically unequal bars which reveal it.

One illustration from Poe's own essay suffices to raise the issue in a decisive form. Analysing the rhythm of the opening lines of Byron's *Bride of Abydos*, and deriding the attempts to formulate it by the mechanical methods of the grammarians, he proceeds to show how the flow is not properly to be measured by single lines, and how, on the contrary, it pulses from verse to verse, only making a structural pause at intervals of several lines. Accordingly he prints the passage continuously, to show that it is a series of dactyls broken only at these points; as thus :

APPENDIX

Know ye the | land where the | cypress and | myrtle Are | emblems of | deeds that are | done in their | clime Where the | rage of the | vulture the | love of the | turtle Now | melt into | softness now | madden to | *crime* | Know ye the | etc.

The word "crime" is here classed as a cæsura, or long syllable constituting a foot of equal length with the dactyls; later on the syllables "fume Wax," "twine, And," and "done, Oh," are similarly italicised as spondees, also equivalent in time to the dactyls; and finally "tell" is another cæsura. Now, in another essay, the criticism of Longfellow's ballads,* Poe treated the first line of this very passage as consisting of "three dactyls and a cæsura," observing that "myrtle" "is a double rhyme, and must be understood as one syllable." He might as well have called it a trochee with the value of a spondee or a dactyl; since the final effect of his analysis is to show that all rhythm is a matter of relative time or stress values, and not of syllables; but in any case his earlier decision showed that the first line of the *Bride of Abydos* might be read as one of dactyls ending with a cæsura, and the second as one of amphibrachs equally ending in a long iambus of the value of a cæsura or amphibrach, as thus:

Knōw yĕ thĕ | lānd whĕrĕ thĕ | cyprĕss ănd | mȳrtle
Ăre ĕmblĕms | ŏf dĕeds thăt | ăre dŏne ĭn | thĕir clīme

Dr. Sylvester, applauding the "exceedingly interesting observation that all these lines run into one another,"† objects that Poe "makes a difficulty, for which there is no occasion, about the words 'twine, And,'‡ which he says 'is false in point of melody,' for that we must force "And" into a length which it will not naturally bear.'" Dr. Sylvester argues, rightly enough so far, that "twine," ending a line, takes after it a slight pause, which with the "and" would make out the value of a dactyl. But he oddly fails to see that the same principle of pause upsets elsewhere the alleged dactyls in which line-ending pauses occur. We pause after "turtle" and "clime" just as we pause with

* *Works*, Ingram's ed., iv. 362.
† It should be noted that Bentley applied the same principle to classic anapæstic verse (Jebb's *Bentley*, p. 14).
‡ In the lines "Where the virgins are soft as the roses they twine, And all, save the spirit of man, is divine"—where the movement may as fairly be called anapæstic as dactylic, with long iambs at the end of the first and the beginning of the second line.

APPENDIX

Dr. Sylvester after "twine," and—with Poe—after "crime." Then "clime" should be for Dr. Sylvester, with its pause, a trochee, and for Poe a cæsura; while for both the next line must begin with an anapæst. And I, in turn, might as fairly call it a cretic. So, after "turtle," which with its pause equals a dactyl, we may resolve the next four words into two amphibrachs.

In fine, even if we could scan all kinds of verse with the few kinds of feet on which Poe proposed to proceed, these feet themselves often indicate no corresponding facts of verse structure, being but variable ways of marking beats in a given rhythm. Rhythmal pleasure being, as he rightly says, a perception of more or less complicated equalities (the pleasure tending to refine with the complication), the process of counting, if it is to give any assistance beyond broadly describing a lilt, should either be complicated with the refinement of the rhythm itself, or be reduced to some underlying psychological principle. There is no time-unit; and if a dactyl in a given line is to have the same time-value as a trochee—which Poe allowed, going on to call an anapæst in an iambic line a bastard iambus, and a pæon primus in a trochaic line (as "Many are the") a quick trochee—it becomes plain that our feet are a pure convention, that the sole rhythmic fact is the fluctuant relativity of long and short, or stress and slur,* in verse movement; and that of such

* The late Professor Shairp has left an interesting account of some counsel given him on the subject of scansion by Clough, which is worth reproducing here :—" He repeated in his melodious way several lines " [of the *Bothie*, then about to be published] " intended to show me how a verse might be read so that one syllable should take up the time of two, or conversely two of one. The line which he instanced (altered, I think, from *Evangeline*) was this :

White | naked | feet on the | gleaming | floor of her | chamber.

This was new to me, as I had not risen beyond the common notion of spondees, dactyls, and the rest. . . . He bade me scan the first line of the *Paradise Lost*. I began: ' " Of man's : " iambus.' 'Yes.' ' " First dis—" '—There I was puzzled. It did not seem an iambus or a spondee it was nearly a trochee, but not quite one. He then explained to me his conception of the rhythm. The two feet 'first disobe—' took up the time of four syllables, two iambic feet: the voice rested awhile on the word 'first'; then passed swiftly over 'diso—', then rested again on 'be—' so as to recover the previous hurry. . . . A clue it was in the fullest sense of the term : it gave me an insight into rhythm which I had not before, and which has constantly been my guide since, both in reading and writing."—

APPENDIX

movement as a whole the final criterion is just its pleasurableness, or agreeableness to a constitutional need for a jerkless continuity in scansion as in motion. Poe would quash the pyrrhic, or foot of two short syllables, on the ground that shortness is only the negation of length, and that two shorts therefore mean nothing; but equally, longness is only the negation of shortness, so that the cæsura and the spondee are disallowed by the same reasoning. If it was worth while to show analytically that the line is an arbitrary measure, much more was it to show the essential arbitrariness of the foot, even for the classic metres, which after all must have allowed a variety of modulations of which the most complex foot scansions can give no account. Not only are long and short correlatives, but scansion like musical tempo admits of *rallentando* and *accelerando*; and if, further, accent is in our own verse so irretrievably bound up with length of syllable, how shall we serve ourselves with the expedients that were inadequate for tongues that are held to have reckoned their verse originally by conventional vowel quantities?

Whatever may have been the case in Greek and Latin verse in their later stages, when reading had taken the place of chanting, it is quite certain that in our own verse a rhythmic effect is often partly dependent on certain variations of pause or time-*space* between syllables *—a factor of which foot-scansion takes no account. For instance, in Tennyson's song, "A spirit haunts the year's last hours," the general iambic movement is always varying into anapæstic and dactylic, and trochaic, and into yet another which might be called (after Poe) cæsural; and that all this variation is never rugged or jarring is due to the fact

(Clough's *Poems and Prose Remains*, Memoir, i. 32.) Clough was evidently reasoning on the same lines as Poe, and laying his finger (as we shall see below) on the rhythmic essentials of verse as against mere syllable-counting. He, too, therefore, was tending to discredit the "foot." The line quoted by Professor Shairp could obviously have been marked thus:

    White | naked | feet | on the gleaming | floor | of her chamber.

* I had written this before meeting with Sidney Lanier's *Science of English Verse* (1880), which clearly and fully lays down the principle that rhythm is a series of "sounds and silences." I believe that his is the first clear statement of the principle, though, as we have seen, Clough and Poe both pointed towards it. It will be seen below that Lanier, in my opinion, sometimes fails to apply his principle aright. It will be seen, too, that the principle as I apply it does not square with the exposition of the late Professor Fleeming Jenkin in his essay of 1883 *On Rhythm in English*

APPENDIX

that the verse as it were insists on variations of time-spacing or tempo, which perfectly unify it. For instance, in the lines:

> My very heart faints and my whole soul grieves
> At the moist rich smell of the rotting leaves,
>   And the breath
> Of the fading edges of box beneath,
>   And the year's last rose—

no pedal marking whatever can tell the total rhythm. The first line, by academic doctrine, may be said to contain an amphibrach, a spondee, a pyrrhic and a molossus. Poe would perhaps have said that it is made up of two iambs, a cæsura, an anapæst and a spondee, making "faints" the cæsura; but this would obscure the facts of the rhythm of "my whole soul grieves." What really happens in that phrase is a very minute pause before the third and fourth words, with the result of giving each so nearly the time-value of "my whole" as to keep the movement fluent; and the same thing happens before "faints," so that the whole movement is essentially iambic, with the slight real variation of the anapæst "and my whole." So, in the last line, the scansion essentially is

> And the yēar's ˘ lāst ˘ rōse,

the blanks being more marked than in the first line.

Doubtless this rhythmic fact is what is pointed to in the principle of the cæsura; but then the idea of the cæsura, which, as Poe protests, is "grossly misrepresented in the classic prosodies," has hardened into a prescription of pause for one form of verse and one length of metre; and though Poe's adoption of it as a principal element in scansion brings us a long way nearer science, and though this partly justifies him in writing as he does of Coleridge's "nonsensical system of what he calls 'scanning by accents'—as if 'scanning by accents' were anything more than a phrase"—he himself does not logically carry out the true principle. He defines the cæsura as a foot of "a single long syllable," *whose length however varies*. In truth the cæsura is neither a long nor a short syllable, but partly a lengthening of a syllable and partly an element of time between

---

Verse (reprinted in his *Papers*, vol. i.). His pauses are often irrelevant to rhythm, and often quite arbitrary in themselves. His essay, however, is an effective refutation of the false metric of Dr. E. Guest's *History of English Rhythms*.

APPENDIX

syllables. It clearly is so in the line which Poe gives as consisting of three cæsuras :

> March ! march ! march !

as again in Tennyson's

> Break ! break ! break ! *

When, however, we come to

> On thy cold gray stones, O sea !

we have long syllables enough ; and on Poe's principle we might scan it as an anapæst followed by either two spondees or four cæsuras ; but there is no such element of pause as arises in the first line, or at least the pauses are much more minute. Again, Poe gives us this scansion :

> Ă breāth | căn māke | thĕm ās | ă breāth | hăs māde,

making five iambs. This is rhythmically false : no good reader would scan so. He would read, pedally speaking :

> Ă breāth căn māke thĕm | ăs ă breāth hăs māde,

and if we are to be logical in pedal notation we should make the line one of two feet of five syllables each, as some of the ancient grammarians would actually have made it. What has really happened is a pause after "them," making the real scansion run

> Ă breāth căn māke thĕm   ăs ă breāth hăs māde,

and *so* keeping up an iambic movement, with the slight variation of one anapæst. And this is the cue to the rhythmical essence of the first line of *Paradise Lost*. The total rhythm is

> Ŏf mān's ˘ fīrst dĭsōbēdĭence ¯ ănd thĕ frūit.

That is to say, the movement is essentially iambic, with the easy variation of two anapæsts. In *Hamlet*, again, the notation of the most famous line is

> Tŏ bē ŏr nōt tŏ bē ; ˘ thăt ĭs thĕ quēstiŏn,†

---

* Lanier, I find, had notated this very line with music-rests (Work cited p. 138).

† To my surprise I find that Lanier measures the line thus, using however music-notes (Work cited. p. 172) !—

> Tŏ bē | ŏr nŏt | tŏ bē | thăt ĭs | thĕ quēstiŏn.

APPENDIX

the pause sparing us the jar of stepping from an iamb straight into a trochee (as in "away, rascal") a much less agreeable shuffle than that from a trochee into an iamb (as in "Or to take arms," or "Heavily hangs").

It may be argued that this method of analysis will serve to certificate the most unrhythmical verse at will as rhythmical; but that is a needless fear.* A bad verse is so because it puts in a

In the same way he scans

and
Whether | 'tis nō | blĕr īn | thĕ mīnd | tŏ sūffer

Thĕ slīngs | aňd ār | rŏws ōf | oŭtrā | gĕŏus fōrtunĕ

He goes on, it is true, to stipulate that the pauses of stage delivery will necessarily interrupt the movement he has marked out; but he gives these scansions as "a scheme of that rhythmic intention upon which the writer projected his work." Now Shakspere cannot have *intended* to stress "is" and "in" and "of." He must have intended a pausation; and it is odd that Lanier did not here see an application of his own principles of "sounds and silences." Lanier again puzzles me by, in his own words, (p. 173) "passing Milton with the single remark that *Paradise Lost* is written in the same typic form of 3-rhythm with Shakspere's plays," that is in the rhythm of

In maiden meditation fancy free.

The very first line of *Paradise Lost* should strike on the sense of any metrist by its new resort to the principle of pauses, in modification of the simple rhythm. As for Tennyson's "Half a league" line, before referred to, it is clear that the rhythm goes thus:

Hālf ă lēague,... Hālf ă lēague,... Hālf ă lēague ōnwărd ;

the movement being made inwardly iambic by the pauses, till the third triplet, fusing with the final trochee, becomes a dactyl, preparing for the dactyllic movement of the next line:

Āll iň thĕ vāllĕy ŏf dēath ⌣ rōde thĕ six hūndrĕd.

* I find, however, that Lanier, after forgetting to apply his principle to cases where it clearly comes into play, overstretches it in defence of Shakspere's oft-discussed line (*Measure for Measure*, ii. 2):

Splitt'st the unwedgeable and gnarled oak
Than the soft myrtle; but man, proud man.

Lanier agrees with Coleridge that the pause needed after "myrtle" keeps the rhythm right, pointing out (p. 193), that if we read—

Than the soft myrtle *tree*; but man, proud man—

it is faultless. Here he forgets, as did Coleridge, that the proposed

APPENDIX

continuous run diversities of step which disconcert us ; and no aid from pauses can cure such jars. We may, by pausation, make a risky line of Milton nearly quite rhythmical, as in

> ˘ Būrns ˘ āftĕr ˘ thĕm to the bōttŏmlĕss pīt ;

where the undue stress on "them" is now the only flaw. But no pausation can cure such lines as Mr. Lowell's

> Forty fā | thĕrs ŏf frēe | dŏm ŏf whŏm | twĕnty brēd . . . .
> Ēach hăs sīx | truĕst pāt | riŏts fŏur dīscōv | ĕrĕrs ŏf ē | thĕr,

where the anapæstic intention stumbles as if in epilepsy.

When we go to the root of the matter we find that already among the ancients there was glimpsed the fundamental truth that metrical divisions are not the constituents of rhythm but artificial derivatives from it. This is implied in the maxim Μέτρου πατὴρ ῥυθμός, "rhythm is the father of metre ; "* and in the saying of the grammarian Charisius, "Nihil est enim inter rhythmon et metron nisi quod *rhythmos est metrum fluens, metrum autem sit rhythmos clausus.*" Gally, last century, also put it well when he said that "Metre differeth from rhythm as the *Species* from the *Genus.*" The right account is given by M. Kawczynski, who, rejecting † "the grave error of German philology, which consists in considering rhythmic as essentially different from metric," sums up (p. 52) that "there exists no difference of principle between metre and rhythm : on the contrary, metre . . . . is only a measure, a certain dividing" (*coupure*). Then feet are arbitrary divisions, not equipollent units constituting a rhythm.

All this may sound like emptying Poe's essay of all importance, but I am fain to repeat that its value lies in carrying

---

rhythmic pause comes in *where there is already a pause necessitated by the sense;* so that the ear is balked anyhow. Either there is a pause of two stresses (= a spondee), which disorders the movement, or the sense-pause (which would have to be made even after *tree*) cancels the rhythm-pause. *The ear cannot solve the double difficulty.* The verse, lacking an essential syllable, is thus really imperfect, though I do not doubt that Shakspere so wrote it, seeing that in the rest of the passage he tries rhythmical experiments.

* Ascribed by M. Kawczynski (p. 52) to Longinus ; and by Dr. Gally (as cited, p. 81) to the Scholiast on Aristophanes, *Nub*, 638.

† P. 139.

APPENDIX

analysis so far that the omitted final step is easy. It struck at the endless series of academic "feet," of most of which not one man in a thousand now knows the names, forcibly enough to make plain the expediency of throwing foot measurement aside. Even while standing for feet, and so leaving foothold to the test of absolute number of syllables, it effectually puts out of countenance the benighted pedantry which would read and print "silv'ry sea" and "th' eternal." It contains many acute and suggestive ideas on the origin of verse* and rhyme, which I do not think have yet been superseded. And it supplied the first † and almost the only reasoned indictment of what commonly pass for English hexameters.

V

The most questionable passage I find in its close packed exposition is the statement that "comparatively the French have *no* accentuation; and there can be nothing worth the name of verse without;" and that the French heroic is "the most wretchedly monotonous verse in existence." But such partially mistaken judgments on French poetry are too common in English literature to permit of Poe's receiving more than qualified blame. He is countenanced by Ramsay ‡ and by the

---

* Poe's theory that verse began with the spondee is well worth investigation in connection with the rhythmic chants of the uncivilised races; and his suggestions on this and other heads are curiously supported by research in other directions. Compare his remarks on primitive variations of verse form with the early notions of Rabbi Azarias on Hebrew poetry, cited in Lowth's *Preliminary Dissertation* on Isaiah, and later conclusions, as set forth, for instance, in G. G. Bradley's *Lectures on the Book of Job*, p. 11. Hennequin remarks (*Ecrivains Francisés*, p. 137), that Poe's views on metre have been "since confirmed by German researches."

† I ought perhaps to except Foster, who (p. 64) pointed to the scarcity of spondees in English, though without explicit reference to the question of hexameters.

‡ Ramsay, affirming that in French "quantity is unknown," proceeds to allege that "the correct pronunciation of that tongue can only be attained by abstaining from dwelling longer upon any one syllable than upon any other; and it is precisely this very peculiarity which renders it so difficult for us to enunciate it with accuracy." This is simply hopeless nonsense, and Ramsay evidently could not have intelligently noticed the pronunciation of a single line of French verse. If there were no other difficulty in French for British tongues than that he imagines, we should all be boulevardiers.

APPENDIX

startling proposition of Mr. Lowell * that Diderot's choice of prose for his dramas was "dictated and justified by the accentual poverty of his mother tongue." Yet Mr. Lowell would surely not have set the verse of Lessing, which he disparages,† above Hugo's; and it is hardly conceivable that he would deny to Hugo's and Musset's and Baudelaire's verse, meaning apart, great rhythmic resource. Mr. Arnold has likewise spoken of the monotony of the French alexandrine; but he is answered by Mr. F. W. H. Myers,‡ who points out that

> There is no normal arrangement of feet to which a French alexandrine tends to recur. All that is necessary is that there should be an accent (and consequently the end of a word) in the sixth place, and again in the twelfth place, at the end of the line. It is therefore a mistake to try to read French alexandrines as if they were to be referred to an iambic type. The number of accented syllables in a French alexandrine varies, and their position varies also. Sometimes the line has no marked accents except in the sixth and twelfth places; sometimes it has a marked iambic character, sometimes an anapæstic character.

Still, the opinion that French verse is accentless is continually heard. It is expressed by a very competent critic of verse, Mr. William Larminie, in a very intelligent recent study on *The*

---

* Essay on Lessing, in *English Poets*, Camelot ed., p. 305, *n*.

† When so much is being made of the supposed monotony of the French alexandrine, it is worth while to cast a glance at the German management of pentameter blank verse, which normally makes that measure as monotonous as any, despite its capacities. Lessing secures pause-variety by losing all fluidity; and Schiller, in preserving fluidity, often becomes unbearably monotonous. The vice of sing-song inheres deeply in his dramatic verse. Coleridge said "it moved like a fly in a glue-pot," but that is inexpressive exaggeration. It moves in a rut, Schiller being bent on imitating Shakspere, but unable to catch the nervous ever-varying pulse of Shakspere's versification; so that he gives us the echo of Shakspere's orotundity without the oceanic diversity of vibration which in Shakspere almost always vitalises the rhetoric. He resorts at times to desperate devices by way of varying his rhythm, such as ending lines alternately with words of one and two syllables; but the effect is only to reveal his failure to seize the higher secrets of blank verse. Perhaps there never will be first-rate German blank verse (for English ears) on the English model. German is, perhaps, too polysyllabic for the finer effects, just as French seems too clean cut for the rolling effects. German tragedies should be in prose (even Heine fails to make nervous blankverse), and German epics in Vossian hexameters.

‡ *Essays: Modern*, p. 123. Compare the remarks of Mr. George Moore, *Confessions of a Young Man*, pp. 308-9, to similar effect.

APPENDIX

Development of English Metres. Mr. Larminie undertakes to show, and does show, what Foster showed long ago, and others have shown since, that, despite endless assertions to the contrary, English verse contains an element of quantity *operating through and conditioning stress.* He makes out his case by noting what Gally and Foster alike noted, that syllables differ in length in respect not merely of vowel-lengths but of the varying difficulty of combining certain consonants quickly. We need not go anew into that point, further than to note that Mr. Larminie does not recognise the complexity of the problem as to ancient quantities, which he unduly simplifies. The specially challengeable part of his doctrine is what follows :

The language, however, has other resources [than quantity]. How do they compare with those of other languages? Latin, which has a much more perfect quantity, has no stress. But English has stress of a very energetic kind, which greatly helps out the quantitative deficiencies. *Italian has no quantity*, but it has stress. *French has neither.**

This is one more proof of what Mr. Larminie himself remarks, that questions of versification in general are still very unsettled. I really do not understand how he can illustrate his doctrine as to either Italian or French verse. To say that Italian verse has no quantity, but only stress, in terms of Mr. Larminie's own definitions, is to imply that its syllables vary only in respect of stress and non-stress. Now it clearly varies also in respect of the varying values of the non-stressed syllables. In the second line of the *Divina Commedia*,

Mi ritrovái per una selva oscura,

we have the *a* in *selva* not merely unstressed but passed over more quickly than the *a* in *una*, the final *a* in *selva* and the *o* in *oscura* being pronounced together in something like the time given to the *a* in *una*. In the fifth line :

Questa selva selvággia ed aspra e forte,

we have a similar shortening twice. Then in Italian verse some syllables, apart from stress, are pronounceable more quickly than others ; which characteristic is exactly what Mr. Larminie has shown quantity to consist-in in English. The fact that the leading quantitative features in the two languages are not

---

* Article cited, *Contemporary Review*, November, 1894, pp. 725-6.

APPENDIX

the same—that in English we often find syllables made harder to enounce by collocation of consonants, while in Italian we only find syllables made specially easy by collocation of vowels—does not alter the essentials of the case. In English we do find the Italian phenomenon, if not *vice versâ*. And it was doubtless perception of the common quantitative element or possibility in the verse of the two languages that led Milton to his boldest innovations in blank verse, as in the opening line of the *Paradise Lost*, which instantaneously upsets the commonplace iambic model and creates an English verse with a Dantean freedom of scansion.

As to the statement that French, again, has neither stress nor quantity, let us take, from a contemporary authority on French prosody, a few samples of scansion of alexandrines of Racine :

> Oui, je *viens* dans son *tem*ple ado*rer* l'Eter*nel*,
> Je *viens* selon l'*u*sage an*ti*que et solen*nel*,
> Cé*lébrer* avec *vous* la fa*meu*se jour*née*
> Où sur le *mont* Si*na* la *loi* nous fut don*née*.

Here we have, with four marked stresses in each line, two distinct rhythms, that of the first and third lines being anapæstic, that of the second and fourth iambic—to use the old terms where they really have a descriptive value. But though the iambic movement, mechanically scanned, gives six feet or beats where the anapæstic movement gives only four, yet the habit of giving four marked metrical stresses brings it about that two of the iambs (*selon* and *et sol*) are relatively short ; so that though quantity is indeed a less noticeable factor in French verse than in either English or Italian, there is here a certain included element of quantity, while the element of stress is salient and all-important. I confess that for me the sudden and sharp transition from the anapæstic to the iambic movement, line by line, is somewhat disconcerting and unenjoyable ; but for Frenchmen it is evidently otherwise.* The truth is that French

---

* M. Castil-Blaze, in his *L'Art des Vers Lyriques* (1858), p. 18, warmly denounces the *vers antipathiques* in which the movement trips up and changes ; but he seems to resent them only on behalf of the singers who have to sing them. For an English reader the objection holds equally good against verse for reading, where iambic lines alternate with anapæstic, and where a single line may alter its stride after the cæsura. It would seem, however, that whereas the greater elasticity of rhythm and range of

APPENDIX

heroic verse, though unfortunately fixed rather closely to a tradition in the limitary period associated with the name of Malherbe, has been gradually suppled like every other, especially where it is handled by masters. Frenchmen go back to-day with pleasure to Racine because he had the gift of varying his rhythm, thus meeting the fundamental craving set up by all marked monotonies. He even deviated from the main rule that the stress in French verse shall fall on the last syllable of all words not ending in *e* mute, as in the lines (thus scanned by M. Defodon):

> Dieu pour*r*a vous mon*trer* par d'impor*tants* bien*faits*
> Que sa pa*role* est *s*/*a*ble et ne trom*pe* ja*mais*;

and again in this, in *Andromaque:*

> Non, non, il les ver*ra* triompher sans obstacle;
> Il se *gar*dera bien de troubler ce spectacle,

where *triompher* can only be stressed on the last syllable by changing abruptly from iambus to anapæst, and where *gardera* can only be read as a dactyl, in complete contravention of the dogma of the final syllable. So too Boileau, disregarding the normal stress in French on the second syllable of "Florence," has written

> Dans *Flor*ence ja*dis* vi*vait* un méde*cin*.

An English taste, indeed, is surprised to find that the French ear does not allow a latitude of another kind. M. Defodon, insisting on the rule of four main stresses or beats, rejects as prosaic the second of these lines of Molière, because of its six stresses:

> Quel avan*tage* a-t-*on* qu'un *homme* vous ca*resse*
> Vous *ju*re ami*tié, foi, zè*le, es*time,* ten*dresse*

—where, there being no jostling change in the rhythm, an English ear would be disposed to find an agreeable variation, somewhat as in that line of Tennyson cited for its newness by Mr. Watson:

> Sucked from the dark heart of the long hills roll
> The torrents.

---

accentuation in English gives us the requisite variety of movement, without resort to abrupt alterations, and so leaves us hostile to them, the old alexandrine, at least, either needed abrupt transitions to relieve it, or only admitted of such when framed by the rules.

APPENDIX

As was pointed out ages ago by commentators on Virgil, variation of *pause* in a given rhythm is one of the secrets of the best versification, at least in blank verse : and it was shown at least as early as last century, by an English critic of somewhat precarious insight,* that in Latin and English alike the great artist, Virgil or Milton, is marked off from the inferior artist, Ovid or Cowley, by this very faculty of pause variation † among other things. Ronsard, a man of genius, felt ‡ the tendency to monotony in the alexandrine, and wrote his *Franciade* in another measure by way of protest. This alone, however, would not have cured the trouble even if the new metre had been generally adopted. Part of the harm lay in the common lack of pause-variation—a lack which is nearly as obvious in the English heroic couplet, in most hands, as in the French alexandrine. Pope's skill partly consisted in varying its stresses. As Foster noted,§ there is an element of special vivacity in his verse, in respect that the iambic line there frequently begins with a trochee, as in

Die of a rose in aromatic pain—

a variation which does not disorder the movement, seeing that the line-pause prevents any shock. And while Englishmen were generally complacent over their rhymed couplet, many critical Frenchmen were complaining of the monotony of their classic alexandrine, the special trouble of which is the median cæsura, or central pause. It is certainly a little difficult to explain how the French have been so long fettered by that when they have secured so much variation of stress in other ways, especially seeing that in this regard also freedom anciently existed. Dr. Nordau is not without justification when he jeers,‖ in his very Teutonic manner, at the young French

---

* *Letters concerning Poetical Translations, and Virgil's and Milton's Art of Verse*, 1713. Attributed to William Benson. This writer avowedly owes much to Erythræus (J. V. Rossi), who anticipated Poe in pointing out the element of rhyme in classic Latin verse, and Mr. Lanier in dwelling on vowel-colour.

† "The sense variously drawn out from one verse to another" (Milton, pref. note to *Par. Lost*).

‡ See the preface to his *Franciade*.

§ As cited, p. 59. It is to be noted that Foster also recognised the rhythmic supremacy of Milton.

‖ *La Dégénérescence*, French trans., i. 243-4.

APPENDIX

poets who exult so much in the discovery of a freedom which other literatures had attained long ago. As a matter of fact it had once belonged to French verse as to others. M. Quicherat cites * from Jean de Meung (1260-1320) the alexandrine :

> Quand l'entrée est mauva*i*se du bien spirital;

and from Clement Marot the decasyllabic line :

> Par sainte eg*l*ise christianissime,

where the cæsural stress falls in the middle of a word, thus prohibiting a pause. As regards verse of ten syllables, where the problem arises in the same way as in that of twelve, he is able to cite † from the anonymous fifteenth-century poem *l'An des sept dames* a whole series of lines in which the bondage of the cæsura is shunned :

> Je te supplie, ô toi plaisante Muse
> Que les *poëtes* nomment Aréthuse . . . .
> Et vous, *naïades*, déesses tres belles . . . .
> Parmi les *roches* et resonnans bois,

and so on. Indeed M. Quicherat declares the disregard of cæsural pause to have been one of the characteristic traits of the French versification of the twelfth and thirteenth centuries. Lost to the alexandrine in the classic period, the early freedom was partly preserved in pentameters even by Voltaire, as in the lines

> Il ne re*p*ose point, car je l'entends . . . .
> Elle vous *tra*ite mal, mais la nature.

Why the liberty should have been held permissible in the shorter verse and not in the longer is not quite easy to guess. It would seem as if the latter, being the nearest analogue to the ancient hexameter, fell specially under the ferule of the pedants ; whose verse-sense had as a rule been racked to atrophy by the traditional classic prosodies, till at length, reducing all the antique range of cadences to one type, they made the alexandrine the very model of monotony. They refused to allow even the device of slurring the cæsura by continuity of syntax and sense, as in the line

> Ce dieu dont le courroux brulant est si terrible,

---

* *Traité de versification française*, 2e édit., 1850, note 2, p. 323.
† *Id. ib.*

APPENDIX

in vetoing which M. Quicherat joins with the Port Royal, though the most magistral of rebukes to their fanaticism lay under their eyes in the very first verse of the Georgics:

> Quid faciat *laetas segetes*, quo sidere terram.

Under such tyranny lay the alexandrine during ages in which all other tyrannies were shaken. Perhaps the latter fact sufficiently explains the former; but whatever be the explanation of the delay, it has at last come about that, whereas Racine gave variety of accent to the alexandrine short of meddling with the middle pause,* and Chénier gave a new variety of stops and clause-pauses, Hugo went far to break down the middle cæsura,† till at length some contemporary poets (notably Verlaine and his school) boldly put the "sixth place" once more in the middle of a word. So that even Mr. Myers is now wrong in saying that the alexandrine must have its middle cæsura on the last syllable of a word: that rule too is going by the board. It is further (we have seen) a mistake to say even as regards verse, as Mr. Myers does, that "in the French tongue the accent always falls on the last syllable of a word except when that syllable has a mute *e* for its only vowel." There is the final *a* to be allowed for, as in the *pourra* of Racine's line above cited. Mounet-Sully in *Zaïre*, too, scans one line thus:

> Et le rest | e du jour | sera tout | à Zaïre,

making *sera tout* an anapæst like the other "feet." I do not see how the line could well be scanned otherwise.

As regards accentuation in prose, again, the old formula is still more exceptionable. It is to be noted, indeed, that Frenchmen themselves have in recent times come to new views as to the nature of their accent. The all-learned Littré attributes to

---

* He may indeed be said to have meddled with it in the sense that he sometimes made it doubly marked, as in these verses of *Mithridate*:

> Je ne le croirai point? Vain espoir qui me flatte!
> Tu ne le crois que trop, malheureux Mithridate.

Either the first of these lines is bad, making "vain espoir" an anapæst, or we must read it with such a pause as to make five stresses,

> Je ne le croirai point? Vain espoir qui me flatte,

which comes pretty near *Arma virumque cano* in total rhythm.

† Ch. Renouvier, *Victor Hugo: le poète*, ch. xiii.

APPENDIX

our own century the discovery or the demonstration of the fact that French verse is accentual:

> C'est un italien, M. Scoppa, et après lui, M. Quichérat, dans son traité de *Versification française*, qui ont fait voir que notre vers est construit, comme la plupart de ceux des langues modernes, sur le principe de l'accent. La langue française est accentuée comme toutes les langues ses sœurs ; seulement l'accent au lieu d'occuper des places variables est toujours sur la dernière syllabe, quand la terminaison est masculine, et sur l'avant-dernière, quand la terminaison est féminine. . . . Objectera-t-on que, l'accentuation se faisant sentir à une place toujours la même, il en résulte uniformité et monotonie ? Cela n'empêcherait pas l'accent d'exister ; mais il n'y a ni monotonie ni uniformité, les mots réunis en phrases fournissent les combinaisons d'accents les plus variées. Voyez ces vers de Racine, où je souligne les syllabes accentuées :
>
>> Ja*mais* vaisse*aux* par*tis* des *ri*ves du Sca*man*dre
>> Aux *champs* Thessal*iens* os*è*rent-*ils* descen*dre ?*
>> Et ja*mais* dans La*ri*sse un *lâ*che ravis*seur*
>> Me vint-*il* enle*ver* ou ma *fem*me ou ma *sœur ?*
>
> Il est impossible de trouver une intonation plus marquée : elle ne l'est plus davantage dans le grec ou l'italien.*

But Littré, if one may presume to say so, has overlooked a very explicit declaration by Turgot, last century, as to the accentual character of French speech. In contravention of some of Rousseau's dicta on French music, he wrote:

> Il n'est point vrai que l'essence de la langue française est d'être sans accent. Point de conversation animée sans beaucoup d'accent ; mais l'accent est libre et déterminé seulement par l'affection de celui qui parle, sans etre fixe par des conventions sur certaines syllabes, quoique nous ayons aussi dans plusieurs mots des syllabes dominantes qui seules peuvent être accentuées.†

This deliverance implies, inasmuch as it outgoes, the proposition that French verse is accentual ; and it gives an alien the courage to point out that in a great many French words of three and more syllables the accent falls neither on the last syllable nor on the penultimate to an *e* mute. In the above passage itself we have *conversation, convention, affection,* where the antepenult either has the main stress, as in the first case, or is at least equally stressed with the last syllable. And this brings us to face with the fact that the French verse of the past

---

* *Histoire de la langue française,* édit. 1863, i. 328-30.
† Letter to Caillard, *Œuvres de Turgot,* ii. 827.

APPENDIX

limited the accentual resources of the language partly by choice of words and partly by limitation of cadence. When Voltaire, explaining the foreign unpopularity of the French music of his day, wrote that "la prosodie française est différente de toutes celles de l'Europe. Nous appuyons toujours sur la dernière syllabe ; et toutes les autres nations pèsent sur la pénultième ou sur l'antepénultième, ainsi que les Italiens," he wrote quite inaccurately of foreign prosodies, as he did when he further went on to say, "notre langue est la seule qui ait des mots terminés par des *e* muets."* But he was further misleading even as to his own verse (over and above the omission to except words ending in *e* mute) inasmuch as he does not note that in words of over three syllables there is often an earlier as heavily stressed as the final. For instance, in his own lines in *Zaïre*:

>D'effacer Orosmane en *générosité*. . . .
>Je la plains : mais pardonne à la *nécessité*
>Rappeler des chrétiens le culte *incorruptible*. . . .
>Au héros dont tu viens d'*assassiner* la fille. . . .

Again, no theory of final stress could be fully applied to lines ending in *tion* and *ment*, as in these of the *Philosophe Marié* of Destouches :

>Plus je vous considère, avec attention,
>Plus je vois que je cause ici d'émotion. . . .
>Finette sous ses doigts sourit malignement.

So zealously, however, have the rule-makers set their faces against the least relief to the classic cadence that we have M. Du Méril condemning Roucher's line

>Les biches attendaient silencieusement.

"Dans les langues véritablement accentuées," he declares, "la voix varie plusieurs fois ses intonations dans les mots qui ont plus de trois syllabes, et cela *ne peut avoir lieu en français :* c'est la cause du peu d'harmonie des vers ou se trouvent de trop longs mots."† It is difficult not to feel that this is a merely fanatical or pedantic denial to French verse of facilities which are freely taken in ordinary speech, and that the line above condemned is really more and not less "harmonious" than the average alexandrine. And when we turn to one of the later

---

* *Siècle de Louis XIV. Artistes Célèbres*, ad init.
† Work before cited, p. 57.

APPENDIX

poets who have given a new canorousness to French verse while keeping all that is best in the classic spirit, we find these limitary principles once for all set aside. M. Leconte de Lisle, for instance, gives us :

> Et de sa propre gloire un pur rayonnement
> Environnait son front majestueusement.
> *Poëmes Antiques. Bhagavat.*

On the first page of the *Poëmes Antiques*, again, we have the verse

> L'abime primitif ruisselle lentement,

where the last word must bear at least as much stress on the first as on the last syllable, with an effect that for an English ear, at least, is admirable. French poets and French thinkers, in fine, overthrow the tabus of French pedants and regulators,* and warn us afresh that there is no mortmain in art.

Clearly, then, the problems of metres are intricate and full of traps ; and no man is to be put out of court for even a real stumble. But between normal fallibility and entire incompetence there are all stages ; and the latter seems to have been the state of many of the scholars with whose tradition Dr. Browne would silence Poe. "As a proof of the total want of ear in a great Greek scholar," Walker cites this from Lord Monboddo :

> Our accents differ from the Greek in two material respects. First, they are not appropriated to particular syllables of the word, but are laid upon different syllables, according to the fancy of the speaker, or rather as it

---

* As a matter of fact, no foreign critics have more sharply attacked the rhythmical faults of average French verse than Frenchmen themselves have done. M. Castil-Blaze speaks of " cette prose rimée des Français, objet d'une incessante dérision, cette prose bafouée, vilipendée, à bon droit, par des autres nations et même par la nôtre !" and describes the French ear as " perverti, corrompu dès l'enfance par la doctrine de l'Université, par la doctrine de l'Académie " (*L'Art des vers lyriques*, pp. 20, 27). And he could cite from Regnier, Saint-Amant, and Marmontel, as mottoes to his treatise, similar attacks on past practice, winding up with a citation from the *Essai de rhythmique française* of M. Ducondut (1856), who declared that

> Sans rivale notre scène
> Fait envie aux nations ;
> Mais sa lyre méprisée,
> De l'Europe la risée,
> N'a qu'un son d'aigre fausset. . . .

APPENDIX

happens: for I believe no man speaking English does, by choice, give an accent to one syllable of a word different from that which he gives to another.

It is not clear here, indeed, whether by "accent" Monboddo meant voice-pitch or stress. If the former—which was Walker's own definition, and Foster's—Monboddo was quite right, since there is no invariable pitch in any man's utterance of any words. Indeed it is difficult to believe that he meant anything else. But a clear proof of a learned Frenchman's difficulty in realising the freedom of scansion arising out of the element of *pause* in English verse, take these scansions of three English lines by M. Du Méril:

> The treach'rous colours thē fair art betray . . . .
> In words as fashions thē same rule will hold.
> Pope (*Essay on Criticism*).

> Still to the last it rankles, ā disease.
> Byron (*Childe Harold*).

M. Du Méril, scanning purely by equal feet, misses the time-value of the clause-pauses. Into this error, however, he was led by an English authority, Dr. Guest, who marks these very lines in this way,* condemning them for misplacing stresses instead of noting that they are to be read with special pauses which save the rhythm. After that view of English verse-stress from a scholarly Frenchman, misled by an English scholar and specialist, no account of French accent from an Englishman can well be surprising. And when it is so easy for instructed men to err as to the verse of their living neighbours, it behoves us all to eschew confidence in a confused tradition as to the nature of the verse of dead languages.

* *History of English Rhythms*, Skeat's ed., pp. 82, 83.

APPENDIX

NOTE

THE foregoing discussion, tedious as it may be found, deals but cursorily with many important questions of verse technique. Those interested in carrying the investigation further will find much instructive matter in the above-cited works of MM. Du Méril and Kawczynski (of whom the latter often coincides with the former), and in that of Sidney Lanier, on the subject of the sources of rhythm. As to French verse in particular, the student should consult the recent and noteworthy work of M. Robert de Souza, *Le Rhythme Poétique* (Perrin et Cie., 1892), and the treatise of the late E. O. Lubarsch, *Ueber Deklamation und Rhythmus der französischen Verse* (Oppeln and Leipzig, 1888)—a rejoinder to R. Sonnenburg's *Wie sind die französischen Verse zu lesen?* (Berlin, 1885.) Dr. Lubarsch had previously written a *Französische Verslehre* (Berlin, 1879), and an *Abriss* of that.

In the essay of Mr. Larminie, above cited, it is suggested that English verse should seek new resources in assonance. Mr. Larminie has not noted that the experiment has actually been made more than once by Mr. Wilfrid Scawen Blunt. It has also been made by some of the younger French poets. Mr. Larminie's suggestion that the alternative to assonance, as a widening of the field of verse, is the resort to prose, has been emphatically anticipated by Walt Whitman. But, as M. Du Méril notes (p. 21), it was anticipated by several critics of last century, and in a manner by Goethe and Schiller.

www.ingramcontent.com/pod-product-compliance
Lightning Source LLC
Chambersburg PA
CBHW032033220426
43664CB00006B/456